Rosa Kim

FINDING THE LAW
Twelfth Edition

By

Robert C. Berring
Librarian and Professor of Law
School of Law (Boalt Hall)
University of California, Berkeley

Elizabeth A. Edinger
Reference Librarian
School of Law (Boalt Hall)
University of California, Berkeley

AMERICAN CASEBOOK SERIES®

THOMSON
WEST

Mat #40132988

COPYRIGHT © 1931, 1940, 1949, 1957, 1965, 1976, 1984, 1989, 1995 WEST PUBLISHING CO.
© West, a Thomson business, 1999
© 2005 Thomson/West
      610 Opperman Drive
      P.O. Box 64526
      St. Paul, MN 55164–0526
      1–800–328–9352
Printed in the United States of America

ISBN 0–314–14579–6

 *TEXT IS PRINTED ON 10% POST CONSUMER RECYCLED PAPER*

Acknowledgements

We would like to thank Zac and Jake Klein for allowing their mother, Keri Klein, the time to read and re-read this text. We couldn't have pulled it together without her.

Bob Berring would like to thank Kathleen Vanden Heuvel and Michael Levy, my collaborators in Advanced Legal Research for more lessons and inspiration than they will ever know. Special thanks to Leslie Berring for listening to a great deal more about legal research than any human needed to hear.

Beth Edinger would like to thank her colleagues at Boalt Hall, who have proved over and over again that they are a wonderful bunch of people with whom to work. I am grateful to Lee Neugebauer and Michelle Wu for keeping me laughing with some very funny e-mail messages during a rainy winter. I would especially like to express my love and appreciation for my husband, Jeff Abramson, who learned how to grocery shop so I could finish this text.

Summary of Contents

Table of Contents

_____

FINDING THE LAW
Twelfth Edition

*

A Few Words at the Start

Writing a book about legal research in 2005 calls for either a good deal of courage or a serious dose of craziness. This is because legal research training has become a bit of a dilemma. What follows are the yin and the yang.

The yin is represented by the first year law student of this era. She arrives at law school experienced in using databases and search engines. She can use *Google* to find almost anything and she may go long stretches between looking at books when she is researching. At law school she will find WESTLAW and LEXIS, the Ferraris of databases, waiting for her. Both will have powerful, easy-to-use search engines and she will be offered a tasty menu of training and support (not to mention free t-shirts and other prizes for using the systems). WESTLAW and LEXIS will be available 24 hours a day on her laptop for no apparent cost. Life will be good.

The yang is represented by legal information. Cases, statutes, administrative materials and secondary sources and the finding tools that accompany them are deeply rooted in the world of books. Even as WESTLAW and LEXIS have prospered and grown, the heavy hand of the world of books has continues to influence legal research. The law student of today needs to understand and show some respect for the world of books if she is to understand how the databases are built and how to use legal information. Just as important, older lawyers, who happen to be the folks who control the courts, law firms and government agencies, have not escaped their roots in the books. Nor is it likely that they ever will. They will expect the new law school graduate to understand the old system. Therefore our modern law student must grapple with books, indexes and the full panoply of paper resources. Life will be hard. So we wrote this book to try to help.

This book is premised on the fact that the reader will primarily use WESTLAW, LEXIS and other Internet sources. But it recognizes that she will have to understand the world of books as well. We try to accommodate both views. Keep in mind that our goal is to tell you what information you can find, and a few good ways to find it. We recognize that someday someone will write an edition of this book that is not printed on paper and which discusses only digital information, but that day has not yet arrived.

The editing of this text ended in April, 2005. We welcome your suggestions, comments, corrections and criticisms. Feel free to e-mail us as berringr@law.berkeley.edu or eedinger@law.berkeley.edu. Do not be surprised when we answer. We both enjoy the research process and love to talk about it. We hope that we communicate some of that enthusiasm in the pages that follow.

Chapter 1

THE CONTEXT OF LEGAL RESEARCH

A.   Introduction.
     1.   Research in Two Worlds.
     2.   The Economics of Research.
     3.   Learning About Legal Research.
B.   The Big Picture.
     1.   The United States as a Federal System.
     2.   The United States as a Common Law System.
          a.   Judicial Decisions and Precedent.
          b.   Is the Precedent Still Good Law?
     3.   The Obsessive/Compulsive Nature of Legal Research.
     4.   Legal Jargon.
     5.   Legal Authority.
C.   Conclusion.
D.   Additional Reading.

A. INTRODUCTION

Legal research is a puzzle. A typical first year student entering law school might expect that the study of how to use legal materials, how to find particular cases, statutes and regulations, and how to successfully answer the question posed by a teacher or a boss would be central to legal education. In fact, most of the first year of law school is spent reading and analyzing excerpts of cases[1] as presented in casebooks. Casebooks are collections of severely edited judicial opinions that have been chosen by the casebook authors. These books are invariably the work of law professors who teach in the field and are usually done as team efforts. Unlike the original versions of casebooks that first appeared in the 19th Century and which consisted of nothing *but* cases, the modern casebook contains additional materials and commentary. The edited cases remain the core of the casebook and the staple of the law school diet.

The modern casebook is usually a rather desiccated collection of the salient parts of a number of judicial opinions. It is by its nature a hothouse text -- the material is all there, preassembled and arranged. Rarely does a casebook require the student to read external materials, and when the students in a first year law school class are assigned "outside" reading, it is usually put on reserve in the law library. Thus it is possible for a first year law student to navigate through the common law courses that make up the first year of law school without doing any real research at all.

Of course, most law schools have a moot court experience at some point in the first year of law school. The moot court exercise will require students to argue an appellate case or a motion by first preparing a written brief and then carrying through an oral argument. Research may be involved here, but once again, the materials may be pre-assembled. There are frequently large numbers of students working on the same problem making the research process into more of a scavenger hunt than a real research experience. Moot court students may be directed to the materials that they need, and certain materials may even be designated as out of bounds. This hothouse variety research could hardly be deemed a "real" research situation, to say nothing of the fact that most lawyers do not do the specialized style of research that is typical of appellate practice.

---

1   Here, the word "case" describes the written opinion of a court.

Every law school has a course designed to teach legal research skills to first year students. These courses try to instill basic research proficiency but they face enormous challenges. They must bridge the gap between the use of computer systems and paper, they must teach the use of a whole new set of materials, but, hardest of all, they must teach legal research in isolation. Since the rest of the first year consists of traditional courses taught out of casebooks and readers, the research course lacks any context in the first year. How can a student master legal research skills if they have no place outside the course to practice them? Learning research skills in such splendid isolation is rather like learning to ride a bicycle by reading a book. It is boring, nothing makes much sense and you experience none of the fun. Without context research skills are dry as dust and blow away just as easily.

One of the ideas that this book will build upon is that of **context**. To master research you must understand the context of a research problem, you must see it in a real world setting. This seldom happens in the first year of law school but it is the key to success in the real world.

Before we discuss legal research skills we will provide a bit of context for the enterprise itself. Before you begin to understand the sources of the law and the process of legal research, it is good to know some background information. There are some special challenges that you will face and we believe that you should know about them from the beginning.

1. Research in Two Worlds

First, the legal researcher of today lives in two worlds: paper and digital. Over the past one hundred years legal publishers developed an intricate set of printed materials which controlled the flow of legal information. Most of this apparatus was built around cases. Elaborate systems of reporting, digesting, tracing and evaluating cases developed. Mastering these systems was the core of legal research courses until very recently. The lawyer graduating from law school in 1970 had to know how to use the traditional paper-based, case-centered tools. The research system was so fixed and stable that no one really thought about it very much. It was just there, it seemed like it always had been there and everyone assumed that it always would be. It was a world of case digests, printed citators, looseleaf services and fugitive government documents. Times were different. Dinosaurs did not roam the earth, but there was no e-mail.

Today's student cannot safely ignore this paper world. Much of the WESTLAW and LEXIS systems, as well as Internet sources, are built upon it. To understand the heart and soul of legal research you must comprehend how the tools work, how they are assembled, and much of that knowledge still lies in the paper sets. In addition, there is a human component here. Old style, traditional research is the only kind of research that some senior lawyers, judges and law professors accept as legitimate. That will change in the course of the next generation, but it has not completely changed yet. Many of those in decision-making roles are part of the world of paper information.

The new world of legal research floats in an ocean of electronic information. In the past twenty years the variety of digital databases has grown, and the information which they store and the search methods for using them have improved enormously. Two of the systems, WESTLAW and LEXIS, now play the central role in the research process, and will be an important part of today's law school experience. The vendors of these systems invest considerable sums in providing training, materials and low cost usage of their systems to law students.

The Internet plays host to a dizzying array of websites, some free to the public, some on a pay-as-you-go basis, which have expanded the horizons of research. Law, which had once been the most book-centered of disciplines, is morphing before our eyes. Some law firms are totally networked and are led by true cyberspace cowboys who are on the cutting edge of the information revolution. Some courts are similarly advanced. Right now the only constant is change because new formats, new search engines and new ideas bloom constantly.

For now, law students must learn to use both the digital and print sources. This will appear irrational at times since, for all but the true computer-phobic, law student life will be so much easier online. But real research skills depend on understanding both sources. It is important to keep in mind that a law student's use of WESTLAW and LEXIS is premised on the willingness of the vendors of online databases to supply their products to law schools at a deep discount. There is no cost to most law students who use LEXIS or WESTLAW. The vendors of the systems are willing to underwrite the law students' initial forays into electronic research in hope of gaining future users.[2] The pay-off for the vendors comes after law school. Once out

---

2   Remember, though, that LEXIS and WESTLAW are not free. Your law

of the cocoon of legal education, your world will change and online usage will be billed to your employer. Some employers may not have all the online systems or may severely restrict the use of such systems. You may have to rely heavily on a combination of paper and electronic sources, or on paper alone. Those who work in small practices or public interest organizations will face even more challenging budgetary constraints. Intelligent choices about format and resource allocation will have to be made. These are questions that no one had to consider in 1980. Today's intelligent researcher must know how to use both kinds of material.

2. The Economics of Research

When legal information consisted of the traditional sets of books that reported cases and statutes, the idea of thinking of legal research in economic terms seemed bizarre. Although the sets did cost money, it was easy to think of them as costs that were part of the inevitable overhead expenses entailed in practicing law. After all, every law library had to have them. A lawyer's time had an easily ascertainable value, but the books that she was using were thought of like the payment of the utility bill. Because of this the use of these books was more informal; sloppy research was likely to be tolerated as a young lawyer learned the ropes.

That world is gone. Legal information, like other forms of information, is now a commodity. It is priced by the unit, in different pricing schemes and different combinations. A law firm or other legal entity may pay for use of WESTLAW or LEXIS in any of a variety of ways, but all of them will eventually translate into dollars. Today's legal researcher must factor in how much the research will cost. It may be that a faster or more complete way of gathering data or solving a problem exists, but that cost will force a slower or less complete method to be used. As one senior partner put it, "It is just as foolish to do $2,000 worth of research on a $300 problem as it is to do $300 worth of research on a $2,000 problem." Cost benefit analysis is now part of the research process.

The time of the researcher is also a cost factor. As attorneys in private practice and in some public sectors as well are forced to account for their time in six minute increments, the pressure to accomplish tasks quickly grows apace. A premium will be put on efficiency, and sloppiness or

---

school's library is still paying a considerable sum to the companies so that you can access the databases any time you like.

wastefulness will be disastrous. Learning to be an effective legal researcher is one way to enhance your value to your employer.

To operate in this new world, you must know what information costs, and what levels of performance the particular problem requires. This reinforces the need to understand all forms of information from the oldest to the newest, and it introduces a new level of calculation to the research process.

3. Learning about Legal Research

The great challenge for any research text is to balance the need to communicate the excitement of legal research with the tedium of detail inherent in discussing individual research tools. No book can hope to describe it all, and no book can hope to accurately detail the latest advances in technology. If we try to grow too detailed we will lose the reader to a fog of daydreams. Even if we could describe everything perfectly, everything that we said would be outdated the day that we wrote it. Technology will not hold still. This book strives towards two goals. It will attempt to provide the student with a firm grounding in how the tools of legal research *function*. This should prepare you to handle legal information in any form. It should prepare you to use traditional tools or the newest that technology offers. We will attempt to provide a comprehensive discussion of each of the tools that one might encounter. By using both a macro and micro approach, this book should become a resource. At some point in the future when the student is asked to prepare a legislative history, this text should be of help. No one, not even the authors, aged and wise as they might be, knows all of this material by heart. Learn the patterns, the way things work, and then look up specific information when it's needed. If you understand the functioning of the tools, you will always be able to fall back on the text for details.

B. THE BIG PICTURE

Understanding a few basic ideas about the American legal system will greatly assist you in becoming an effective legal researcher. These ideas provide a template for all that follows. Some of them touch on quite fundamental issues where this text can not offer much detail, but it will still help you to understand the lay of the land. If you get a handle on these ideas, you are ahead of the game.

1. The United States as a Federal System

The United States is a federal system. When the Constitution was adopted, it represented the agreement of thirteen colonies, each of which wished to retain as much independence as possible. Though the balance of federal and state power has shifted dramatically over the years, each state retains law making power in some areas. In other areas, the federal government holds sway. Inevitably, some areas are ambiguous. There will be entire courses, and parts of other courses, in the law school curriculum devoted to various aspects of the balance of these powers. For purposes of legal research, however, the salient point is that there will be a profusion of materials to deal with in doing research. Every state and the federal government have its own court system, its own legislature and its own group of administrative agencies. Each of these bodies will publish its own materials. Each is important. On many subjects the law in Colorado may be very different than the law in Ohio. During the drafting of this edition of this book the states are working through different approaches to same-sex marriage and the use of medicinal marijuana. The federal government has positions on each issue as well. No one can master the idiosyncrasies of the legal system of every state; it is hard enough to keep up with your own state let alone to worry about others.

This book will attempt to introduce patterns of publication that aid in understanding the common features among all of these materials. Most of them do follow fairly predictable lines, but the great river of materials is an intimidating distraction. The need to provide bibliographic detail is unavoidable, and this book will try to be a resource to the user. In addition, Appendix B lists guides that have been prepared for the researcher working in one specific state jurisdiction. These sources treat state publications in the depth of detail that a practitioner will need in order to work in that particular jurisdiction.

2. The United States as a Common Law System

The United States is a common law country. The roots of the common law lie in English history. The rationale for what we do may be lost in the mists of time. Worse, the way in which the United States has evolved its own version of the common law has been full of twists and turns. For the purposes of legal research several facts are clear.

a. Judicial Decisions and Precedent

Judicial decisions and the doctrine of precedent play an especially important role in American legal research. The common law was based on the belief that there was a set of customs, a way of doing things, which was common to the English people. This set of customs was unwritten, but it was very real. When judges rendered opinions they were to draw on the "common law" for legal principles. Judges did not "make" the law, a judge instead was to draw upon the common law for the relevant principle. Once a judge enunciated a common law legal principle, especially once the opinions of such judges were written down, then that principle was frozen. After it was published others could refer to it. Even if the facts in a subsequent case differed, the same legal principle could be applied. This is the concept of *precedent* and the use of *analogy*. Once a judicial opinion on an issue of law was settled, then it was settled for all time and could be referred to by other courts and judges. This process of referring to fixed precedent was called *stare decisis*. Thus it became important to find earlier cases that might be relevant to the legal questions raised in any legal research problem.

Someone unfamiliar with this system might ask about the role of legislation. Shouldn't the elected legislators of the relevant jurisdiction be making the law? That seems obvious today, but in the development of the English common law the legislature had almost no role. A very small amount of legislation was passed, and it was seen as filling in the missing spots of the common law. Great legal writers like William Blackstone, who wrote his *Commentaries* at the end of the 18th Century, mistrusted the actions of the legislature and preferred the perceived elegance of the common law.

American legislatures today pass thousands of laws each year touching on any subject they please, and the myth of a perfect overarching common law has been abandoned for decades. But the holdover of the common law heritage is that American judges can "make" law when necessary. In fact, although most judicial opinions today interpret statutes or administrative rules, American judges still have great power. Reconciling this power in a democratic society, when judges who are often not elected can be given such power, is the frequent subject of scholarly analysis. Here it is only necessary to note that appellate court decisions still have precedential value, and finding a case on point is a major goal of research. Jurisdiction is crucial here. Only the court in your jurisdiction has legal authority. A court in another jurisdiction does not hold power outside its jurisdictional boundaries. Such a decision can be used as persuasive authority, but it does not bind the court.

b. Is the Precedent Still Good Law?

There is a judicial hierarchy within each jurisdiction. A court higher on the ladder can always reverse or revise a court that is lower down if a case is appealed and considered. There is also a time factor here. A court may change its mind and reverse itself on an issue later in time when a subsequent case raises the same issue. A flat-out reversal is a rather rare occurrence, however, since it puts incredible strain on the common law tradition. The court is contradicting itself, and that can quickly create problems. The ultimate expression of the cynicism that this can produce was the late Justice William O. Douglas's statement that constitutional law is whatever five Justices on the United States Supreme Court think it is. This cynical statement has been much criticized but it points to a real problem. Reversals do occur and it will be vital to the researcher to unearth them.

If you find a case you wish to rely on, it will be important to find out not just if it has been overruled, but how it has been treated. Courts sometimes criticize or limit past opinions rather than overturning them. You will need to know if that has happened. Cases are organic, they grow or wither. There is a universe of tools that you will need to master in order to succeed at this. Such mastery is an essential part of the research process. Chapter 3 is devoted to exploring this process.

3. The Obsessive/Compulsive Nature of Legal Research

One of the most distinctive and difficult features of American legal research is the obsession that many American legal researchers have with finding *every* relevant case. To an American law student immersed in the system this seems only natural, but research need not be done in this manner. The English, from whom we inherit the common law system, have never believed in publishing every possible case. The drive to publish and to retrieve every case is a peculiarly American phenomenon. It can be traced back to some decisions made in the 19th Century by American lawyers and by the legal information market.

English legal publishers and court reporters selected cases for their value, focusing on those which made new or useful points or were otherwise likely to be important to lawyers and judges. From the earliest of American publications, however, most of the reporters sought comprehensive rather than selective coverage. Although not always achieved, this was a goal through the 19th Century. But efforts at reporting remained unsystematic, the system grew chaotic as the 19th Century progressed. American law was growing, the number of jurisdictions was increasing and the volume of case law was becoming unmanageable. Lawyers were crying out for even more cases. Into this breach stepped John B. West.

Mr. West was not a judge, lawyer or librarian, he was a salesman. He saw that lawyers wanted cases and wanted them quickly. To meet that need he founded the West Publishing Company[3] and decided that the best approach would be to publish every appellate decision from every jurisdiction in a standard format. Rather than having editors choose what cases were useful, West published them all, and published them quickly and cheaply and let the researcher decide which cases were useful. The result was the *National Reporter System*, a set of case reporters which will be discussed in the chapters immediately following this one. The *National Reporter System* drove almost all competitors out of the market. Coupled with the *American Digest System*, a method West developed to classify all of the cases by subject, the West system came to dominate American law.

Publishing all of the cases and allowing the lawyer to sort out what was important allowed obsessive research to flourish. The reporter volumes on the shelf are filled with many trivial, repetitive cases, but because there might be a gem hidden in the compost heap the researcher felt compelled to check them all.

This obsessiveness was capped by the development of the *Shepard's* citation system. Frank Shepard designed a system of tables that allows you to take the citation to a case in which you are interested and find every subsequent mention of that case by later courts. Once again, the mention might be trivial or repetitive, but if a subsequent opinion mentions that citation, it will be listed in *Shepard's*.[4] *Shepard's* performs other functions,

---

3   The company is now owned by Thomson Corporation, and is referred to as Thomson-West in this text when we're talking about its modern incarnation. See footnote #4 for a discussion of LexisNexis.

4   This company is now owned by LexisNexis, the other large publisher of legal information, which, in turn, is owned by Reed Elsevier. To avoid confusion,

of course. It tells the researcher if the case has been overruled or modified, for example. But at its heart is the listing of every subsequent mention of the case. Looking up a case like *Roe v. Wade* in *Shepard's* is an awe inspiring act. There are thousands of listings. This text will devote a chapter to using citators, and will describe how online systems are affecting this use. For the purposes of traditional legal research, however, we can note that by 1910 the perfect paper tools for obsessive research were in place. West was reporting virtually every appellate decision, and then classifying it into its digest system, and the Shepard's Company was listing every subsequent citation of the case.

This obsessive/compulsive research style has carried over into other sources as well. The standard operating procedure for American legal publishers has been to provide everything and more. Legal information consumers are thus presented with a myriad of tools that contain staggering amounts of information. It has lead to database overload. One of the most basic principles of information theory is that the larger a database is, the more difficult it is to work with. Law is a collection of mega-databases. This may be the biggest challenge facing the researcher.

4. Legal Jargon

Studying law involves learning a new language. Every field has its own set of terms and special usage, but law not only creates but is also shaped by its language to a very high degree. The traditional adage that law school teaches one to "think like a lawyer" refers in part to your ability to use legal terminology effectively. There is no simple way to accomplish this. Much of it will come via osmosis during law school.

There are three common problems caused by jargon. The first concerns **words that have a common meaning in everyday usage but that have a special meaning in the law**. A word like "consideration" has meaning for the typical person but it carries a very special meaning when discussing Contracts. Words like "negligence" may have a meaning in normal conversation that is not nearly as precise or difficult as their meaning in the field of Torts.

---

when we're talking about the online database, we'll call it LEXIS, and when we're discussing a print publication from this company, we'll use LexisNexis.

A second problem centers on **words that are used almost exclusively in law**. Words like "remittitur" and "joinder" in Civil Procedure are examples. These are terms of art, developed to serve special needs in legal parlance.

A third problem involves the use of **Latin phrases**. One of your authors is old enough to have learned Torts from a professor who thought that law students should be able to read and understand Latin. Law is peppered with Latin phrases and maxims like "*de minimus non curat lex*" and "*nudum pactum.*" As you are reading an opinion you may stumble across such a phrase. While it is always possible to hazard a decent guess about a phrase's meaning, to do so can be dangerous.

The point here is to read very carefully and, whenever you are in doubt, use a legal dictionary. There are a wide variety of legal dictionaries available but the current king of the hill is Brian Garner's revision of *Black's Legal Dictionary*. In *Black's Legal Dictionary* you will find definitions of all of the above kinds of words and phrases and citations on where to see them in use. Since every law library worth its salt has a copy of *Black's* available and since it can be found on WESTLAW as well, there is no excuse for not checking whenever in doubt. Learning to read very carefully, understanding each word is essential for a lawyer.

In Chapter 4 we will discuss keyword searching and we will find that legal jargon is a key element in database searching as well. The more things change, the more they stay the same.

5. Legal Authority

Traditionally, legal research texts divided all legal sources into primary and secondary authority. ***Primary authority is a statement of the law itself.*** It is not commentary on the law or a description of the law, it *is* the law. Finding primary authority has long been the focus of most legal research.

In a common law jurisdiction like the United States, there are two basic sources of primary authority: appellate judicial decisions and statutes. The role of cases and precedent has already been discussed. It is important to note as well that **not all parts of a judicial opinion are primary source material.** Only when a judge is resolving an issue of law is the opinion primary source material. Judges often write quite discursive opinions. A judge may lament the decline of Western civilization, discuss the cinema or ramble as he or she pleases, but that part is nothing but *dicta*. ***Dicta is a term that means any words in the appellate opinion that do not relate to resolving an issue of law.*** Only when the judge resolves an issue of law does primary authority appear. Additionally, the written resolution of an issue of law that appears in a concurring opinion or in a dissenting opinion does not count as primary authority. If you are reading an opinion written by a court that has more than one judge and there are several opinions, the primary source lies only in the majority opinion of the court.

Statutes and administrative materials are primary sources, but sorting them out can be tricky. Enactments of the legislative body in a jurisdiction are clearly primary sources of law. Constitutions and treaties also fall under this rubric as statutory in nature. The delicate part arises in the matter of administrative law. Technically administrative agencies are created by legislative enactment, and their law-making power is delegated to them by their authorizing statute. Therefore, all administrative rules and regulations are subject to legislation. The enormously complex entities that federal and state agencies become are often systems unto themselves and you are sometimes hard pressed to think of them as simple creatures of a legislative act, but they are. Because of the pervasiveness of administrative law in today's legal system, and the complexity of materials that comprise administrative publications, most commentators now list administrative materials as a distinct and separate source of primary authority.

In the end, it is probably only of importance in textbooks like this one how we classify the materials. The import... point is that administrative materials are vital to legal research in the real ...
school curricula will never call on the student ...
make the treatment of them in Chapter 8 eve...

Complicating the notion of primar...
three types of materials intersect at many poi...
statutes or regulations, statutes or regulation...
particular decision or a line of cases or a par...
administrative rules may implement cases o...
must be adept at navigating between these ...

Quite simply, secondary sources c...
information that looks official, like the hea...

Mandatory law:
· Supreme court opinions.
· majority opinions
Holding/rationale part of case is mandatory. All else is dicta (words that don't relate to resolving issue in appellate opinion)

the annotations to a statute, is secondary. They are written by editors who work with the publishers, not by the lawmaker. Someone has intervened between the researcher and the primary source. In research you have to rely on such interpretive aids, and in some cases they will take on decisive importance, but they are not primary. Several chapters will be devoted to types of finding aids and advising on when and how to best use them.

C. CONCLUSION

Legal research calls for a body of skills which require an appreciation of traditional sources and an understanding of digital legal information. If approached functionally, concentrating on how tools work and why they work in a particular way, the great body of information will yield it secrets. Memorizing the names of all the sets of materials in this book is less important than understanding how they work. If you can accomplish that, you can have a bit of the old book world and the newest in computer technology and make them work together.

D. ADDITIONAL READING

Grant Gilmore, *The Ages of American Law*, (The Storrs Lecture Series), Yale University Press (1977). Professor Gilmore was one of the giants of 20th Century legal thinking. This short book explains a great deal about the legal system and how it works. The book is thirty years old, but still useful and still in print in paperback.

Laurence Friedman, *A History of American Law*, 2nd ed., Simon & Schuster (1985). This award winning book provides terrific background on the underpinnings of the legal system. It is in your library and also available as a paperback.

Chapter 2

COURT REPORTS

A. INTRODUCTION

American law, both in its popular manifestations and in the minds of many of its practitioners, focuses upon case law. Law students study using the case method, lawyers portrayed in the media are almost always litigators, and the American legal system -- along with the common law system generally -- is most easily distinguished from other legal systems by its heavy reliance on the precedential value of judicial opinions.

Traditionally, legal research courses and texts have given considerable attention to cases, their forms of publication, and their finding tools. This emphasis was justified by the complicated modern systems of case publication and digesting, but it was also a result of the commonly shared assumption that mastering case law research was the most important and the most necessary first step in legal research.

We will approach the subject of judicial opinions from several angles. First we will discuss just what a judicial opinion is. This is not a metaphysical exercise. We believe that you have to understand the true nature of a judicial opinion to be able to work with it successfully. Second, we will look at the component parts of a case. Understanding each part of an opinion is important for grasping its meaning and the parts can be great hooks to use when doing free-text searching online. Third, we will look at the skeleton of judicial reporting by taking a close look at the manner in which cases have been published for the last century. At first this will take us into the world of books, but the template of the printed sets has migrated to WESTLAW and LEXIS.

B. WHAT ARE CASES?

What is a case? In approaching this question we are going to assume that you are just as uninformed as we were when we went to law school. When we arrived at law school it felt as if we were walking in on Act II of a three-act play. Everyone else seemed to know what was going on. Of course, most folks are lost. But no matter, we will start at the beginning and talk about where cases come from.

To understand what a case, or judicial decision actually is, it helps to think first of the court systems that produce it. We will give you a model to begin. Think of courts in a pattern like that this three-part court diagram below.

```
+--------------------------------------------------+
|                                                  |
|           The Court of Last Resort               |
|                                                  |
|                        ↑                         |
|                                                  |
|             The Appellate Court                  |
|                                                  |
|                        ↑                         |
|                                                  |
|               The Trial Court                    |
|         May have subject specific subdivisions,  |
|                e.g., a Family Court              |
|                                                  |
+--------------------------------------------------+
```

At the first level (where a case begins) you will see the trial court. At the second level there is an appellate court. Perched at the third level is a court of last resort. We use generic names for the three levels because of the challenges posed by our federal system as set out in Chapter 1. Each state has its own court system with its own local variations. Floating above that is the federal system. Throw in the various territories and the problem is apparent. Each of these jurisdictions has its own court system, just as it has its own legislative bodies and its own administrative agencies with their own administrative rules and regulations. All of these different courts, bodies, or agencies use their own nomenclature -- you can't remember all of them by heart, and you can't tell just by looking at the name of a court in a particular jurisdiction what it means. Only someone with memory powers like those of the Dustin Hoffman character in *Rain Man* could hope to memorize them all. Our solution is to use this generic functional model, and the functional model *does* apply in every jurisdiction. Wherever you go there will be some functional equivalent of the levels shown in this diagram.

1. The Trial Court

Each jurisdiction is going to have some form of a trial court. The trial court level might be divided into segments. It may be divided according to the amount in dispute, like a superior court or a municipal court. (That's what we call them in California. It might have a different name in your jurisdiction.)[1] There may be subject specialty trial courts, like family courts, juvenile courts or drug courts. Don't try to memorize them because they change from jurisdiction to jurisdiction. What matters is that the trial court level is the first step in the judicial process. It is the part of the process that is fixed in our popular consciousness, complete with witnesses, a jury and courtroom drama. But what happens at this stage is not the stuff of cases, though this is where it all begins.

At the trial level, there are two kinds of questions that might be presented: issues of law and issues of fact. Issues of fact are determined by the finder of fact, and that can be a judge or a jury. Different jurisdictions will have different rules as to when a trial is done before a jury, or only before a judge, but in either case, factual determinations are made. Issues of law are always decided by the judge.

It is time for us to invoke that most venerable law school gambit, the hypothetical situation. Hypothetical situations are something that first year law professors just love to use in class. When we create a hypothetical situation, we create our own world. So here is ours:

Let's say that one of your authors – Bob – is preparing to give a lecture on legal research. He is thinking about how he wants to do a really great job. He wants to make his students able to walk into the library or sit down at a computer terminal, and know what they are doing and – even better – why they are doing it. Engrossed in thought, (and if you ever saw Bob thinking you would know just how apt the term "engrossed" really is), he is crossing the street carrying a double latte when he is suddenly struck by a Lamborghini Diablo driven by Britney Spears. Bob is injured. His leg is broken. As a result of the injury, he can't make it to the school to do his lecture. He loses his self-esteem. He loses sleep, weight, friends and hair.

---

1   In New York the trial level court is generally called, oddly enough, the Supreme Court. This is also Family Court, Surrogate's Court, the Court of Claims, etc., at the trial level. This is what we meant when we said each jurisdiction has its own vocabulary.

There might be any number of damages. (This is what your Torts course will cover.)

Bob claims that Britney was driving at an excessive rate of speed, that she hit him while he was in the crosswalk and, instead of keeping her eyes on the road, she was checking her makeup in the rearview mirror. He says that after the accident, she jumped from her car and shouted, "Oops, I did it again!" Britney, however, claims she was driving at a legal rate of speed and that a clearly drunken Bob leapt in front of her Lamborghini while screaming, "More money for education!" Now, given these two conflicting stories, what would happen in the real world? In the real world, this matter would probably be settled by the relevant insurance companies. But, in our hypothetical world, let's assume the parties can't work it out. We are in one of those rare situations where the conflict can't be resolved any other way, and everyone ends up in court.

The court we will end up in is a *trial court*. The trial court resolves issues of law and issues of fact. When most of us think "court," we think of trial courts and we think of the resolution of issues of fact. (Think *Ally McBeal*, *The Practice* and the Law half of *Law & Order*.) Remember Bob's claims about the crosswalk and Britney's driving, and her contentions about his actions? Was she speeding? Was he inebriated? These are all issues of fact, and they will be determined by the *trier of fact*. In popular culture we tend to think of the jury as the trier of fact, but judges can also make factual determinations. The casting for this role depends on the jurisdiction and the nature of the matter at hand. Sometimes the parties get a choice. The real point here is that the issues of fact are determined at the trial court level and they get frozen there. Please note that at anytime we make a generalization there will be exceptions, and that is true here too, but, *in general*, you cannot appeal issues of fact: they remain frozen. If the trier of fact, be it jury or judge, says Britney was driving within the speed limit, then she was driving within the speed limit. Trial lawyers win or lose the factual battles and the results are locked in place. None of these factual determinations produce our written judicial opinion, but it is coming.

There is another kind of question that comes up at the trial court level, that is., questions that concern issues of law. For example, if Bob wanted to introduce a witness who would say that he heard Britney Spears bragging afterwards that she had "knocked down another librarian," Miss Spears' attorney might jump up and say "I object! That's hearsay, you can't admit that." The judge would have to rule on this issue of (evidentiary) law

– is the statement hearsay or not? Legal questions come in many forms. There might be a question of statutory interpretation or a common law problem. The exact nature of the legal issue doesn't really matter. What does matter is that we have an issue of law, and the judge makes the ruling on an issue of law. Issues of law can be appealed to a higher court, but the issues of fact cannot. The facts remain frozen and it is only the issues of law that travel up to higher courts. We are repeating ourselves, but this is important. Issues of law will be the subject of the cases that you will read. This is why so many of the cases that you read are so boring. They're boring because while at the trial court you might have all sorts of drama, with Britney (or Bob) crying on the stand and the lawyers engaging in spectacular pyrotechnics. Those fireworks disappear on appeal. At the appellate level and above the facts are often leached out. The judges are focusing only on issues of law.

2. The Appellate Court

Where do you appeal these issues of law decided at trial? You move to the next level of the court diagram: the *appellate court*. At the appellate level a court might have to take a case, or the court may have some discretion. As ever, it varies. Because the appellate level focuses on issues of law, everything changes. You don't have witnesses, you don't have juries. What you have are lawyers on each side. Those lawyers prepare written briefs which set out their point of law trying to convince the court to rule their way. The lawyers probably will get a chance to make an oral argument in front of the court. At most law schools this kind of appellate argument is exactly what you are going to learn and practice in Moot Court.

The appellate level may have one judge or there may be three judges. The judge (or judges) then considers the briefs and the oral arguments in order to reach a decision. In many matters the appellate court will not produce a written decision. They may just affirm or deny the ruling of the trial court. But in some matters the appellate court might decide to write an opinion. If the appellate court does decide to write an opinion and decides to publish it, *then* we have a judicial opinion. *A judicial opinion is the written resolution of issues of law from an appellate court or higher.* There will be exceptions to this generalization, too, because in the federal system the trial courts (Federal District Courts) serve a variety of functions, and oftentimes Federal District Courts will produce written opinions, but for now, let's stick with the general definition of a written resolution of an issue of law by the appellate court or higher.

Do all appellate opinions get published? No. Every jurisdiction, every state, every one of the Federal Courts of Appeal has its own rules as to what gets published. The resolution of our hypothetical matter will be important to Britney and Bob. They certainly want to know who won, but the judge may decide that this particular decision does not make any new law and does not merit entry into the stream of precedent. By not publishing an opinion, the Court can limit the application of its decision to only Bob and Britney.

The question of what gets published is actually quite a hot topic these days. All you need to know for now is that most decisions at the appellate level don't get published. The ones that do make it through the hoop of publication are part of what you will find on WESTLAW, LEXIS and in the case reporter volumes.

3. The Court of Last Resort

What if the parties still want to fight after the appellate court has rendered its decision? In almost every jurisdiction there is another level of appeal: the *court of last resort*.

In most jurisdictions the court of last resort is called the Supreme Court.[2] At this level, the court of last resort almost always has discretionary jurisdiction. That means they don't have to take every case. You have to ask them to consider your question of law, and it is up to them whether they will or not. There may be legislation or constitutional provisions that require the court of last resort in a particular jurisdiction to take a particular case, but in general it is up to them. The Supreme Court of the United States has thousands upon thousands of requests every year, importuning them to take cases, but they take only a few. (It is called "granting *certiorari*" or "granting *cert.*" to the cognoscenti.) This form of discretion is going to be the case in almost every jurisdiction.

Let's assume that the Supreme Court of California, where Bob lives, does take the case of *Berring v. Spears*. At the court of last resort lawyers will once again write briefs. These briefs again focus on the issues of law that are in play. A court of last resort may accept only one of the issues of

---

2   However, this is not invariably true. For example, New York calls its court of last resort the Court of Appeals. You know New Yorkers, always trying to keep you on your toes.

law you'd like to appeal, or they may accept several for argument. Once the written briefs are submitted, oral argument may be scheduled. Lawyers who are specialists in appellate advocacy will present ideas to the court and answer questions. There is variation among jurisdictions, but courts of last resort tend to have five, seven or nine judges. This group of justices will then mull over the matter and decide it. Once again we ask the question, does everything that such a court writes get published?

For a court of last resort the general rule is yes. In every jurisdiction the court of last resort is so important that it does publish everything. But not every matter that they take under advisement is going to result in a written opinion. All they have to do is affirm the decision from below or overrule the decision from below, and that does not necessarily require a written opinion. A single word, "affirmed" for instance, disposes of the matter between Britney and Bob, and it makes the appellate court's opinion the last word on the subject. But in many situations, when they have taken the matter and have heard the arguments, the court of last resort will issue an opinion. That's what this thing called a case, or a judicial opinion, is: the written resolution of issues of law, usually from the appellate level and above. While many matters will not result in a judicial opinion, when a decision is produced and designated for publication you will find it on WESTLAW, LEXIS and in the printed judicial reports as well as in a variety of other places.[3]

Because the judicial panels at the appellate level and above are composed of groups of people, there can be disagreement among the judges. Our tradition is for one judge to write the opinion of the court for the whole panel. There is a name at the beginning of the opinion, as in "Berring, J." The "J" stands for Judge or Justice. (When Bob was a law student he thought that all judges must be named Jim, John and Jane until someone explained that to him.) The judge writing an opinion will not just name a

---

[3]   There is some weirdness here. An opinion is officially published only if the issuing Court deems it so. Often a Court will write an opinion addressed to the parties, but will not designate the opinion for publication. But information vendors like LEXIS and WESTLAW can gain access to such opinions and may load them into their database. Thus you may read an opinion which is not published. There is even a new printed Thomson-West set called the *Federal Appendix* which contains printed unpublished opinions. *Printed unpublished opinions?!* You just cannot tell us that legal research is not hilarious.

winner. If an opinion is written, it is done because the court wants to explain why the winner won. Judicial reasoning is important for the doctrine of precedent. Remember the discussion of precedent and analogy from Chapter 1. Much of your time as a law student will be spent trying to parse out what judges mean in these opinions. It is no simple task. Opinions can run for many pages, and they can be strewn with speculation on everything under the sun. But the only thing that represents the law is that part where the judge resolves an issue of law. The rest is *dicta*.

Sometimes within a multi-judge panel there is disagreement. If so, then the opinion discussed in the paragraph above is dubbed the ***majority opinion***. If one of the judges agrees with the result -- she thinks that Britney should win -- but does not agree with the reasoning used in the opinion, she can decide to write a separate opinion. This is called a ***concurring opinion***. In it the judge will say why she agrees that Britney should win, but that she has an entirely different rationale for doing so. This weakens the power of the majority opinion of the court.

Sometimes there will be judges who disagree with the result entirely. Such a judge thinks Bob should have won. He might write an opinion explaining why the majority of the court (or, even the concurring judge) is wrong and why. This is a ***dissenting opinion***. There used to be a tradition of trying to avoid dissents, but in recent years they have been very prevalent. The Supreme Court of the United States decisions often feature a majority opinion, a concurring opinion or two and a dissent or two. Some of the dissents can be quite harsh. Justice Scalia is renowned for his colorful dissents. You will even find judges or justices who concur in part and dissent in part. Our all-time favorite case for this purpose is *Regents of the Univ. of Cal. v. Bakke*.[4] This was a case about affirmative action in the 1970s. It made it to the Supreme Court of the United States and each of the nine Justices wrote an opinion. Making sense out of circumstances like that – who agrees with what and why – is a true art form. It is an art form that you are going to be studying this year. Our chart below sums up the types of opinions.

One of the most important things to keep in mind when you are reading judicial decisions is that they are not mystery stories. This is not like

---

4   *Regents of the Univ. of Cal. v. Bakke*, 43 U.S. 265, 98 S.Ct. 2733, 57 L. Ed. 2d 750 (1978). Frequently you will find the full citation to a reference in the footnotes.

a Sara Paretsky or Elmore Leonard novel where there is a surprise ending. The judges have ruminated and argued about the case. Various drafts of opinions may have passed back and forth. It can be a very political process. The case that you are reading is not a balanced account of the arguments made in the lawyers' briefs, it is the strongest statement of the winning position. This is why if you read a dissent in a case, it often sounds like a different matter entirely. The author of the opinion handcrafts it. Keep that in mind.

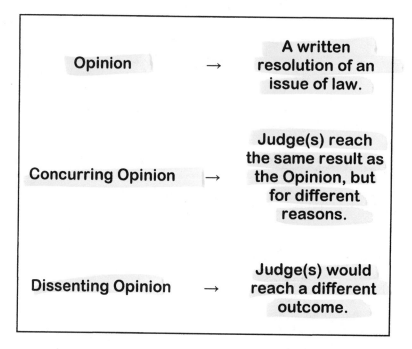

Opinion	→	A written resolution of an issue of law.
Concurring Opinion	→	Judge(s) reach the same result as the Opinion, but for different reasons.
Dissenting Opinion	→	Judge(s) would reach a different outcome.

There is one more variation worth noting. Sometimes the court does not want to have an individual write the opinion. In that case they can issue a *per curiam* opinion.[5] In a per curiam opinion the whole court is writing. It might be something really simple, it might be something really complex, but in either case a *per curiam* decision is not as strong in precedential value.

---

5   *Per curiam* is Latin. The law is still strewn with Latin phrases and outmoded expressions. When you encounter these you must look them up. Honest. Learning these things is important and may save you from getting gutted in class. Just this once we'll translate for you: *per curiam* means, "by the court."

Now that we've looked at what a case is, we want to look at why cases are important. That means looking at the doctrine of precedent.

C. THE COMPONENTS OF A DECSION

We now get mechanical and look at the parts of the judicial decision that you are going to encounter. While there is inevitable variation, the parts are pretty generic. You will find them whether you use WESTLAW, LEXIS, case reporter volumes or an Internet website. First we will describe the various parts of a case then we will show you what they look like using the case of *In re Marriage of Bonds* as an example. We've printed out screen shots of that case from both WESTLAW and LEXIS and put them at the end of this section and marked them up for you, pointing out the parts of the case we're about to describe (and a few others besides, added by the editors at WESTLAW and LEXIS) (Illustrations A & B).

1. The Caption

The caption is the name of the case. In our example that is *In re Marriage of Bonds*. You will note when you look at the example that the names of the parties are actually longer than *In re Marriage of Bonds*. There are special rules for how one correctly abbreviates the caption. There may be a group of people suing a different group of people, or perhaps a corporation is suing someone. So we need a standard way to abbreviate case captions. *A Uniform System of Citation*, published by the law reviews of Harvard, Yale, Columbia and Pennsylvania Law Schools and popularly called *The Bluebook*, has long been the bible of citation. It is not easy to use and it has not adapted very easily to digital information. Still you may have to learn how to use it. Several other citation systems now challenge it. Your school may use the *ALWD Citation Manual* and some states have their own rules of citation required by the courts.

Typically, you call the first party the plaintiff and the second party the defendant -- that's one we all learned from watching television shows. Law students use the pi (π) sign for plaintiff and the delta (Δ) for defendant. No one knows why, so feel free to make up your own rationale. A reported decision is most likely one that is on appeal so that the party who was the plaintiff at the trial court level may be the defending party in this action.

Nomenclature might reflect that fact. Depending on the jurisdiction, you might find the first party called the appellant and the second the appellee. In some jurisdictions, the first party is the petitioner and the second is the respondent.

You should be careful about the order of the parties' names. Remember that we are reading cases from appellate level courts or above. Sometimes as the case works its way through the system, the parties reverse their position. If Bob sued Britney at the trial court level and won, she would be the party who was appealing. (Feel free to make your own joke here.) In some jurisdictions they switch the order of the party names when this happens. In some cases they might actually change parties' names. If Beth sues the U.S. Attorney General we would have *Edinger v. Ashcroft*. But when John Ashcroft stops being Attorney General and is replaced by Alberto Gonzalez, the case becomes *Edinger v. Gonzalez*.

2. The Docket Number

Each case has a docket number. That number is an alphanumeric assigned by the court for internal filing purposes. If you want to go look at an actual case file, you might need the docket number. Docket numbers are also excellent hooks to use when doing a keyword search. You have to be careful when you use them as you have to get it right, but they are unique so they yield good results. Docket numbers may grow even more important as new format-neutral citation systems are built.

3. The Headnotes

Almost every case that you find will have headnotes. What is a headnote? Headnotes are written by an editor who reads the case for you and attempts to extract each point of law that is resolved in the case. The editor may work for the court or for WESTLAW or LEXIS. If there is an editor at the court, you might get her headnotes and also those done by the commercial publisher. The editor will summarize in the headnote what the court has decided. Commercial headnote writers strain to find as many headnotes as possible. You may find dozens in front of an opinion. Compare the United States Supreme Court Reporter version of a case with the same case on WESTLAW and LEXIS. You will see wholly different headnotes. Writing these things is an art form, not a science.

The headnote will carry a number, or it will be hyperlinked online, so that you can go the section of the text that the editor was reading when she wrote the headnote. This helps you focus your research and it also lets you check on whether you agree with her or not.

Some research instructors advise folks never to rely on headnotes. After all, headnotes are the work of someone who stands between you and the words of the court. Except in Ohio (no joke) headnotes are not statements of the law. So you should not rely on them. But trust us, if some night you have to read three hundred cases in two hours, it is okay to look at a headnote or two.

4. The Syllabus

The next thing you're going to find with every case is a syllabus. A syllabus is a summary of the case. Someone has read the case for you, and then prepared an abstract of it. The syllabus is usually very direct. It says this case came from here, it's about this, and here's how the decision came out. The syllabus is prepared by the clerk of the court or perhaps by an editor at a commercial publishing house. In our examples at the end of this chapter, you'll note that the editors at LEXIS and WESTLAW have written a summary of the case *and* there is a syllabus from the Reporter of Decisions at the Supreme Court of the United States. These good folks are trying to tell you what happened. This is not primary source material, it is not the law itself, but it is a summary of it. For a first year student reading the syllabus of a case is like reading Cliff Notes. Sometimes even the syllabus will be hard to read because it might be very technical, but it's there to help and guide you. The syllabus is also important because in WESTLAW or LEXIS, the syllabus provides a kind of normalized language that can help you if you're keyword searching, and make you more productive.

5. Names of Counsel

The names of the lawyers who carried the appeal forward are listed. If you are really puzzled about why a case came out the way it did, try e-mailing the winning side. Remember that the opinion is often resolving issues raised in the briefs. To understand an opinion it really can help to know what the questions were. Remember, the winners are usually more happy to chat than the losers.[6]

6. The Opinion

We discussed the forms of opinions in the previous section. When you are looking at our example of *In re Marriage of Bonds* at the end of this chapter, note that the opinion was unanimous.

7. Citation Form for Cases

In the world of paper, case citations followed a standard format. Here it is for the *Bonds* case:

In re the Marriage of SUSANN MARGRETH BONDS and BARRY LAMAR BONDS. SUSANN MARGRETH BONDS, Appellant, v. BARRY LAMAR BONDS, Respondent, 24 Cal.4th 1, 99 Cal.Rptr.2d 252 (2000).

Let's break it down a little, and see what things mean:

SUSANN MARGRETH BONDS	↔	Plaintiff, Petitioner or Appellant
v.		
BARRY LAMAR BONDS	↔	Defendant, Respondent or Appellee

---

6   Some who reviewed the manuscript of this book thought that this advice was deranged. It may well be deranged but we have done it. In the 2001-2002 academic year Bob called the lawyers who appeared in two cases in the Contracts casebook that he was using. The cases appeared nonsensical. The lawyers were happy to explain why. So, it may be deranged, but it can be effective.

24	↔	Volume
Cal.	↔	Reporter, *California Reports*
4th	↔	Series
1	↔	Page

99	↔	Volume
Cal. Rptr	↔	Reporter, *California Reporter*
2d	↔	Series
252	↔	Page

(2000)	↔	Year of Decision

If there is an official citation, it goes first (24 Cal. 4th 1). If there is a citation to the *National Reporter System*, it goes second (99 Cal. Rptr. 2d). If there is a third relevant cite it can be added as well. The second citation (and any that follow it) is called a parallel citation. The volume number, set, page number formula is very reliable.

Illustration A
Screen captures from LEXIS showing *In re Marriage of Bonds*

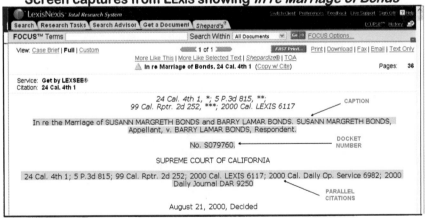

***

Illustration A, con't.

CASE SUMMARY ←——— SUMMARY WRITTEN BY
LEXIS EDITORS

PROCEDURAL POSTURE: Respondent husband petitioned for review of California Court of Appeal order, reversing the trial court's judgment, holding premarital agreement was involuntary because appellant wife lacked independent counsel, determining she had not waived counsel effectively, and concluding evidence needed to be subjected to strict judicial scrutiny to determine voluntariness of agreement.

OVERVIEW: The day before the parties married, they entered into a written premarital agreement in which each party waived any interest in the earnings and acquisitions of the other party during marriage. The court concluded the court of appeal erred in determining that because appellant wife was not represented by independent counsel when she entered into the agreement, the voluntariness of the agreement needed to be subjected to strict scrutiny. The circumstance that one of the parties was not represented by independent counsel was only one of several factors that needed to be considered in determining whether a premarital agreement was entered into voluntarily. Substantial evidence supported the determination of the trial court that the agreement was entered into voluntarily. Appellant did not forgo separate legal advice out of ignorance. Instead, she declined to invoke her interests under the community property law because she agreed, for her own reasons, that respondent's and her earnings and acquisitions after marriage should be separate property.

OUTCOME: Judgment reversed and remanded. Appellant wife failed to meet burden of showing premarital agreement was involuntary, even though she was not represented by independent counsel, absent the presence of other factors including evidence indicating coercion or lack of knowledge. Lack of independent counsel alone was not reason to subject voluntariness determination to strict scrutiny.

CORE TERMS: premarital agreement, independent counsel, marriage, Uniform Act, voluntariness, premarital, earnings, wedding, undue influence, spouse, substantial evidence, challenging, acquisitions, enforceability, coercion, signing, separate property, waived, community property law, burden of proof, disclosure, recalled, community property, married, confidential relationship, enforceable, marry, dissolution of marriage, dissolution, unconscionable

***

Illustration A, con't.

LexisNexis(R) Headnotes • Hide Headnotes ←——— HEADNOTES
WRITTEN BY
THE LEXIS
EDITORS BEGIN
HERE

Family Law > Divorce, Dissolution & Spousal Support > Property Distribution > Community Property 📑
HN1 Property acquired by spouses during marriage, including earnings, is community property. Cal. Fam. Code § 760. More Like This Headnote

Family Law > Divorce, Dissolution & Spousal Support > Property Distribution > Marital Property 📑
Family Law > Marital Duties & Rights > Premarital Agreements 📑
HN2 Parties contemplating marriage may validly contract as to their property rights, both as to property then owned by them and as to property, including earnings, which may be acquired by them after marriage, and Cal. Civ. Code §§ 177-181 and Cal. Fam. Code § 1500 provide for such agreements. More Like This Headnote

Family Law > Marital Duties & Rights > Premarital Agreements 📑
HN3 In California, a premarital agreement generally has been considered to be enforceable as a contract, although when there is proof of fraud, constructive fraud, duress, or undue influence, the contract is not enforceable. More Like This Headnote

Contracts Law > Contract Interpretation > Interpretation Generally 📑
Family Law > Marital Duties & Rights > Premarital Agreements 📑
HN4 The rules applicable to the interpretation of contracts have been applied generally to premarital agreements. More Like This Headnote

Family Law > Marital Duties & Rights > Premarital Agreements 📑
HN5 The validity of a premarital agreement does not turn on whether the parties contemplated a lifelong marriage. More Like This Headnote

Family Law > Marital Duties & Rights > Premarital Agreements 📑
HN6 Cal. Unif. Premarital Agreement Act, Cal. Fam. Code, § 1600 et seq., sets out the law of premarital agreements, including such matters as the nature of property subject to such agreements, the requirement of a writing, and provision for amendments. Cal. Fam. Code, §§ 1611-1614. More Like This Headnote

***

Illustration A, con't.

SUMMARY:

CALIFORNIA OFFICIAL REPORTS SUMMARY ◄——————

OFFICAL
SUMMARY
WRITTEN BY THE
COURT
REPORTER

In a dissolution of marriage action, the trial court entered a judgment upholding the validity of a premarital agreement, finding that the wife did not meet her burden of showing that the agreement, in which the wife waived her community property rights, was involuntary (Fam. Code, § 1615), even though she had not been represented by an attorney and her husband had been. (Superior Court of San Mateo County, No. F-19162, Judith W. Kozloski, Judge.) The Court of Appeal, First Dist., Div. Two, Nos. A075328 and A076586 reversed and remanded after determining that the agreement was subject to strict scrutiny because the wife had not been represented by counsel.

The Supreme Court reversed the judgment of the Court of Appeal to the extent that it reversed the judgment of the trial court on the issue of the voluntariness of the premarital agreement, and remanded to the Court of Appeal with directions. The court held that the Court of Appeal erred in holding that premarital agreements are subject to strict scrutiny where the less sophisticated party does not have independent counsel and has not waived counsel according to exacting waiver requirements. Such a holding is inconsistent with Fam. Code, § 1615, which governs the enforceability of premarital agreements. That statute provides that a premarital agreement will be enforced unless the party resisting enforcement can demonstrate either (1) that he or she did not enter into the contract voluntarily, or (2) that the contract was unconscionable when entered into and that he or she did not have actual or constructive knowledge of the assets and obligations of the other party and did not voluntarily waive knowledge of such assets and obligations. The court also held that substantial evidence supported the trial court's finding that the wife voluntarily entered into the agreement. The court further held that considerations applicable to commercial contracts do not necessarily govern the determination whether a premarital agreement was entered into voluntarily, and that a premarital agreement is not to be interpreted and enforced under the same standards applicable to marital settlement agreements, or in pursuit of the policy favoring equal division of assets on dissolution. (Opinion by George, C. J., expressing the unanimous view of the court.)

***

Illustration A, con't.

HEADNOTES:

CALIFORNIA OFFICIAL REPORTS HEADNOTES ◄——————

HEADNOTES FROM
THE OFFICIAL
CALIFORNIA DIGEST
BEGIN HERE

Classified to California Digest of Official Reports

CA(1a)⚖(1a) CA(1b)⚖(1b) **Dissolution of Marriage; Separation § 78--Property Rights of Parties--Premarital Agreements--Enforcement--Voluntariness-- Wife Unrepresented by Counsel--Standard.** --On appeal from a judgment upholding the validity of a premarital agreement, the Court of Appeal erred in holding that trial courts should subject premarital agreements to strict scrutiny where the less sophisticated party does not have independent counsel and has not waived counsel according to exacting waiver requirements. Such a holding is inconsistent with Fam. Code, § 1615, which governs the enforceability of premarital agreements. That statute provides a premarital agreement will be enforced unless the party resisting enforcement can demonstrate either (1) that he or she did not enter into the contract voluntarily, or (2) that the contract was unconscionable when entered into and that he or she did not have actual or constructive knowledge of the assets and obligations of the other party and did not voluntarily waive knowledge of such assets and obligations. The rule created by the Court of Appeal would have the effect of shifting the burden of proof on the question of voluntariness to the party seeking enforcement of the premarital agreement, even though the statute expressly places the burden upon the party challenging the voluntariness of the agreement.

CA(2)⚖(2) **Statutes § 31--Construction--Language--Words.** --In construing a statute a court should ascertain the intent of the Legislature so as to effectuate the purpose of the law. In determining such intent the court turns first to the words themselves for the answer. Words used in a statute should be given the meaning they bear in ordinary use. If the language reasonably may be interpreted in more than one way, the court may consult extrinsic aids to determine the intent of the Legislature. Courts frequently consult dictionaries to determine the usual meaning of words.

CA(3)⚖(3) **Words, Phrases, and Maxims--Voluntarily.** --"Voluntarily" has been defined as "done by design, intentionally and without coercion." "Voluntary" is defined as "proceeding from the free and unrestrained will of the person; produced in or by an act of choice; resulting from free choice, without compulsion or solicitation." The word, especially in statutes, often implies knowledge of essential facts. "Voluntarily" has also been defined as "of one's own free will or accord; without compulsion, constraint, or undue influence by others; freely, willingly."

***

Illustration A, con't.

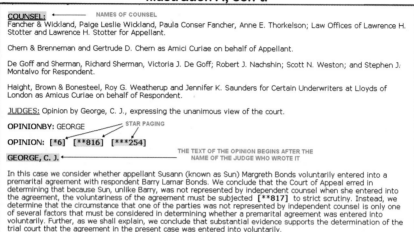

COUNSEL: ←   NAMES OF COUNSEL
Fancher & Wickland, Paige Leslie Wickland, Paula Conser Fancher, Anne E. Thorkelson; Law Offices of Lawrence H. Stotter and Lawrence H. Stotter for Appellant.

Chern & Brenneman and Gertrude D. Chern as Amici Curiae on behalf of Appellant.

De Goff and Sherman, Richard Sherman, Victoria J. De Goff; Robert J. Nachshin; Scott N. Weston; and Stephen J. Montalvo for Respondent.

Haight, Brown & Bonesteel, Roy G. Weatherup and Jennifer K. Saunders for Certain Underwriters at Lloyds of London as Amicus Curiae on behalf of Respondent.

JUDGES: Opinion by George, C. J., expressing the unanimous view of the court.

OPINIONBY: GEORGE   STAR PAGING

OPINION: [*6]   [**816]   [***254]

                    THE TEXT OF THE OPINION BEGINS AFTER THE
GEORGE, C. J. ←   NAME OF THE JUDGE WHO WROTE IT

In this case we consider whether appellant Susann (known as Sun) Margreth Bonds voluntarily entered into a premarital agreement with respondent Barry Lamar Bonds. We conclude that the Court of Appeal erred in determining that because Sun, unlike Barry, was not represented by independent counsel when she entered into the agreement, the voluntariness of the agreement must be subjected [**817] to strict scrutiny. Instead, we determine that the circumstance that one of the parties was not represented by independent counsel is only one of several factors that must be considered in determining whether a premarital agreement was entered into voluntarily. Further, as we shall explain, we conclude that substantial evidence supports the determination of the trial court that the agreement in the present case was entered into voluntarily.

Illustration B
Screen Captures from WESTLAW Showing *In Re Marriage of Bonds*

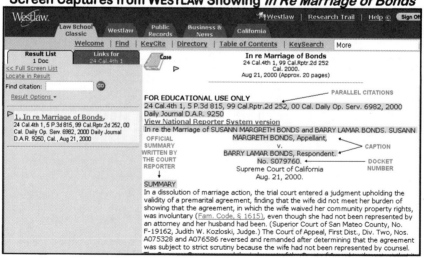

***

Illustration B, con't.

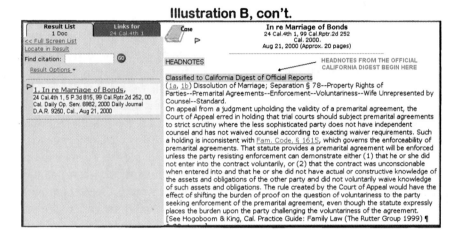

Illustration B, con't.

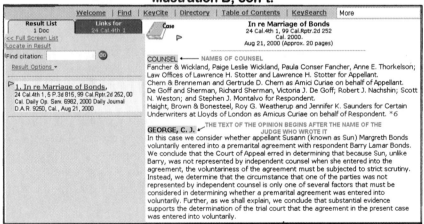

8. Thoughts on Reading Cases

a. The Case as an Information Source

A judicial decision is *not* a balanced discussion of the issues involved in a case, it is the powerful articulation of a certain position. The judge or judges decided the outcome of the issue before the opinion was written. The judge who wrote the opinion marshals the strongest possible arrangement of authorities and arguments to buttress the decided points. Remember – there was another side to the case. If there is a dissent, the opposing position will be outlined in it, but if there is no dissent you will have to look to the briefs of the lawyers who represented the losing side to find counter-arguments and authorities cited. Sometimes looking at the briefs can help you to understand what the judge is saying. WESTLAW and LEXIS are offering links to the briefs in more and more cases so that checking them will become easier. If there is no brief linked to your case you can still find them using paper sources. Locating the paper copies of briefs can be a complex task, so you may need to consult a reference librarian for help in finding these documents.

Beyond understanding that a judicial opinion is the statement of an argument, it is important to realize that a judicial opinion is a tremendous source of possible research paths. The judge authoring the opinion will have collected all relevant authority for the argument and cited to it. Cases, statutes, rules and all manner of secondary sources will be gathered together and carefully cited. In Chapter 4 we will discuss how finding "one good case" can be the key to successful research. Even if the case that you are reading is not exactly on point for you, it can lead you to a case that is. A judicial opinion is constructed from a foundation of sources that you can trace. Each one represents a research opportunity. The opinion is a statement of the law, articulating a certain position, frozen in a moment of time.

Just as you can trace the sources used to frame the arguments in the decision that you are reading, you can follow your case into the future to see what materials have cited to it. Chapter 3 will show you how to perform this function. You can verify the validity of your case but more than that, you can see who has cited it. Maybe your one good case is one that has cited the case that you have found. So you can move forward or backward on the time-space continuum from any case.

The links available in WESTLAW and LEXIS make this task simple but it can be done in paper as well. When doing this be sure that you are careful about the authority of the sources that you use.

Illustration C
Tracing some of the Cases Used by *In re Marriage of Bonds*, and some of the Cases, Articles and Statutes that Used *In re Marriage of Bonds*

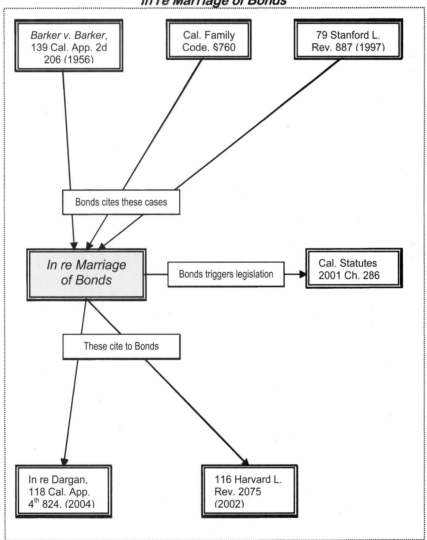

b. The Case and Legal Authority

There is also an art to the manner in which a judge uses authority when she writes an opinion. Sometimes cases are relied on as direct authority, sometimes cases are cited for persuasive power. Very old cases that have never been overruled can be employed or recent developments can be followed. The judge may use cases from other jurisdictions. And the citation of cases is only the beginning. The judge may cite statutes, administrative materials, law review articles, the *Restatements*, treatises or any of a host of other possible sources. You must evaluate the strength of such citations. You may wish to use them or you may wish to follow down the path that they indicate.

To help you understand how to pull apart a case in this way we have prepared Appendix A. Appendix A reprints the decision of the Wisconsin Supreme Court in the case of *Flambeau v. Honeywell*. It is a contracts case that is included in some casebooks. We reprint it in its entirety on one half of a series of pages. On the other half of the page we point out both features of the case and the way that legal authority is used in it. Justice Abrahamson, the author of the decision, was a law professor before joining the Wisconsin Supreme Court and she is a marvelous draftswoman. The case is long, but it is a treasure trove of authority and argument. We recommend that you read it and see a master craftsperson at work.

D. PUBLICATION OF CASES

1. Background

Now that we have discussed what cases really are and the components that go in to a judicial report we turn to the structure of the court reporting system. Because WESTLAW and LEXIS contain all reported judicial decisions you might forget that there is a deep structure to judicial reporting. This structure is still the organizing principle used online and in paper. It is vital that you understand how this system, forged in the days before digital information, works. A bit of history is in order.

The decisions of American courts were not published at all during the colonial period and the early years of independence. American lawyers and judges relied on the decisions of the English courts for guidance, even though only a limited number of those volumes were available here. The first volumes of American court decisions were not published until 1789, thirteen years after independence. Publication of domestic reports developed slowly, and the courts of some states operated for decades without published decisions.

The movement for publication grew, however, spurred by several concerns. There was the patriotic feeling that it was important to construct an American system of jurisprudence. Now that the country had freed itself from English rule, it should no longer be subject to English case law.[7] Yet the doctrine of precedent created a need for the publication of decisions. If American judges rendered decisions which created new rights and responsibilities and changed the common law, those decisions should be recorded and made available to the public. Moreover, the revolutionary times produced a general distrust of judges. Wary of unrepresentative authority, the citizens of the new republic felt that judges should be accountable for the decisions they made. Written decisions and their publication would facilitate that accountability.

Ephraim Kirby's *Reports of Cases Adjudged in the Superior Court of the State of Connecticut from the Year 1785 to May 1788* (Collier & Adam, 1789) is generally regarded as the first American reporter volume.[8] In a preface Kirby discusses the concerns which led to the publication of his reports, including the inapplicability of English law in the new country and the need to create a permanent body of American common law.

The early volumes of privately published court decisions differ markedly from the sophisticated case reporters of today. The individual

---

[7] This is apparent from the "reception" statutes passed by many state legislatures, which accepted English common law but limited the "reception" to those cases which were not repugnant to the law of the newly independent state, and often further limited those to cases decided before the date of independence. *See, e.g.,* Act of January 28, 1777, §§ 2 to 3, 1 *Smith's Pa.Laws* 429 (current version at 1 Pa.Cons.Stat. §1503).

[8] Francis Hopkinson's *Judgements in the Admiralty of Pennsylvania* was also published in 1789, in Philadelphia by Dobson & Lang. Although some later reports include cases decided earlier than those in Kirby and Hopkinson, they were the first to be published.

reporter compiled the decisions (often from his own observation and notes, rather than from texts submitted by the judges), summarized the oral arguments, and often added his own analysis. Many of the early reports were quite unsystematic -- they sometimes contained decisions from several courts, and sometimes even from several jurisdictions. Alexander Dallas' first volume of the *United States Reports* contains only Pennsylvania decisions, and none from the U.S. Supreme Court. His second and third volumes contain cases from both Pennsylvania and the U.S. Supreme Court, and his fourth volume adds decisions from Delaware and New Hampshire.

Systematic official publication of judicial decisions was needed to bring order to reporting, but state appointment of reporters and officially sanctioned publication of decisions developed slowly. The first statute for this purpose was passed in Massachusetts in 1804,[9] and some other states soon followed. The Supreme Court of the United States had no official reporter until 1817,[10] and Pennsylvania had none until 1845.[11] Gradually the nominative reporters gave way to officially published sets of sequentially numbered reports. Some states subsequently renumbered their reports, incorporating the volumes of the nominative reporters as the first numbered volumes in the official set. Other states, particularly those which were among the early colonies, have many nominative volumes without an overall numbering sequence. To determine where particular citations can be found, researchers need to use tables of reports or dictionaries of legal abbreviations.[12]

2. Official Reports

It seems logical that a jurisdiction, be it a state or the federal government, would publish an official version of its cases. The opinions of

---

9   Act of March 8, 1804, ch. 133, 1803 Mass. Acts 449.

10   Act of March 3, 1817, ch. 63, 3 Stat. 376.

11   Act of April 11, 1845, ch. 250, 1845 Pa. Laws 374.

12   For example, the *Bluebook*'s T.1, "United States Jurisdictions," lists nominative reporters and the dates those volumes cover.

the courts represent a statement of the law. As noted in the preceding section official reports were created in many jurisdictions. The United States Supreme Court has an official report of its decisions and so do just over half of the states. To make a report "official" a state legislature can so designate it or the court of last resort in the jurisdiction can require that it be cited if a case is to be referenced.

These official reports are often high quality products, but they suffer from the same maladies that afflict most forms of information produced by a governmental entity. Since lawyers who wish to cite to them must purchase them the profit incentive does not push the publisher to perform. Thus they often appear very slowly. The official version of the decisions of the United States Supreme Court appear in a set called *United States Reports*. This is a fine set but it appears years after the case appears. While some states have timely official reports, others have very slow ones and none of these were originally part of research systems. Lawyers needed quicker access to the decisions in a systematic version that they could safely cite. Thus a privately produced version of decisions, the *Regional Reporter System* appeared.

But where there is an official version of your jurisdiction's reports it remains the required citation. Increasingly state courts are posting judicial decisions on web sites and some are moving towards accepting these as official citations. You should check your jurisdiction carefully and watch developments.

3. *The National Reporter System*: *The Regional Reporter System* - State Decisions

The problems of official reports are set out above. In the 19th Century, as the population grew, the country expanded and became industrialized. The volume of litigation increased rapidly and the official reporting system became overburdened with the proliferation of judicial decisions. Furthermore, the job of Reporter of Decisions in many states became a political position and the publication of cases was subject to the uncertainties of legislative appropriation, so the reports were often inaccurate and frequently slow in appearing. Official reporting suffered from maladies that frequently plague publishing efforts undertaken by the government. Without the market to police them they can become unreliable. Still, more than half of the states still publish an official report of judicial decisions and if you live in such a state, you are required to cite to it. But a commercial set holds center stage.

In 1876, in response to the need for improved and more rapid publication, an entrepreneur in Minnesota, John B. West, started a private reporting system, beginning with selected decisions of the Minnesota Supreme Court in an eight-page weekly leaflet called the *Syllabi*.[13] Coverage gradually expanded, adding decisions from Minnesota federal and lower state courts, and abstracts of decisions from other states. The venture proved so successful that in 1879, West incorporated full decisions from five surrounding states in a new publication, the *North Western Reporter*.

By grouping states, the West Publishing Company was able to publish cases far more frequently than official reports. The decisions could be published every other week in a paperback format called an advance sheet. When a sufficient number advance sheets had been published, West would issue a bound volume of judicial opinions, being careful to maintain the same pagination as the advance sheet so that one could safely cite to either form of the case. Since John West was neither a lawyer nor a scholar he specialized in printing all of the cases in a standard format with no commentary beyond abstracts of the cases themselves.

---

13   When West began his first publications, another commercial approach to reporting was already underway. This was the selective publication of a limited number of important decisions of general interest from the courts in many states, annotated with notes to reflect the state of the law throughout the country. Begun in 1871 by the Bancroft-Whitney Company, the first three of these reporters became known as the "Trinity Series": *American Decisions* (covering from the colonial period to 1868), *American Reports* (covering 1871 to 1887), and *American State Reports* (covering 1887 to 1911). In 1906 the Edward Thompson Company began the rival *American and English Annotated Cases,* which merged with Bancroft-Whitney's series to form *American Annotated Cases* in 1912. Meanwhile the Lawyers' Co-operative Publishing Company had since 1888 been publishing *Lawyers' Reports Annotated,* which entered its third series in 1914. All three publishers joined forces in 1918 to begin a new series, *American Law Reports Annotated.* This set, known as *ALR,* continues to this day as the modern successor to the annotated reports, but its annotations are far more important than the cases it still reprints. *ALR* and its federal counterpart, *ALR Federal,* will be discussed more fully in Chapter 4.

The *North Western Reporter* was a success and West made a brave leap and cut the entire country up into seven regions each operating on the principle of the *North Western Reporter, i.e.* each publishing all of the cases from the states within it. One look at the map of the *Regional Reporter System* in Illustration D and you can see that John West may have been a publishing prodigy but he was no geographic genius. Few sources other than the *Regional Reporter System* classify Oklahoma as a Pacific state. To be fair, in 1880 the western part of the country could well have appeared to a young entrepreneur in St. Paul as one big blob, but the fact that Oklahoma still lies within the *Pacific Reporter* says something about the snail's pace at which the law changes. The only real changes made to the state component of the system was the addition of the *New York Supplement* and the *California Reporter*. These two sets came into being because New York and California were producing so much case law that they were sinking their respective regional reporters. Therefore West added the *New York Supplement*, a set which carried all of the cases from New York courts. Only the cases from the New York Court of Appeals, New York's court of last resort, went into the *North Eastern Reporter*. The same process was repeated in California in 1961 when the *California Reporter* began. It published all appellate decisions from California courts, but only California Supreme Court cases went into the *Pacific Reporter*.

The regional reporters soon drove most other publishers of judicial reports out of business. Within a decade West's *Regional Reporter System* was the standard set for finding American cases. In many ways it still is. Law libraries of any size still carry the regional reporters and WESTLAW and LEXIS still cite to them. As noted above, if you live in a state that has an official report it is the required citation but even then you will use a parallel citation that tells the reader where to find both the official and the West version of your case.

Illustration D
Map of the National Reporter System, State Cases

Regional Reporters (State Cases)

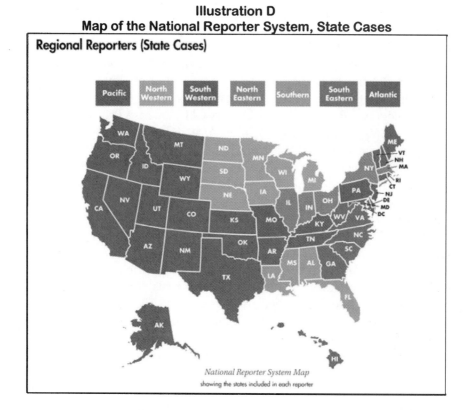

National Reporter System Map
showing the states included in each reporter

The *Regional Reporter System*, along with its federal component which will be discussed below, comprise the *National Reporter System*. The *National Reporter Systerm* is important not just as a reporter of decisions. When John West set it up he used a geographical and jurisdictional basis for organizing decisions. Cases were not grouped by subject, they just appeared chronologically. It could have been done quite differently. West could have served as gatekeeper of decisions and hired experts to sort through the opinions to choose only the important or valuable ones. But the company chose instead to publish every case that the courts designated for publication without any filtering. The cases could have been grouped the by subjects either within a jurisdiction or across jurisdictions. But instead the cases were printed as they were received. There was not even a separation of civil and criminal cases. Lawyers came to accept this arrangement as inherently natural, but it actually reflects decisions made by the West Publishing Company. Thus the *National Reporter System* became an undifferentiated reservoir of cases which could only be searched by the digesting system developed by the West Publishing Company (described in Chapter 4). The cases are the base of the system but you need other tools to find where your case may be.

Not including administrative decisions in the system was also an important decision made early on. Though administrative law played only a tiny role in 1880 throughout the 20th Century its importance grew to be immense. West never took on the publication of administrative decisions. Thus many of them were very difficult to locate until the development of LEXIS and WESTLAW.

West also developed a template for publishing judicial opinions. The West model of what a judicial opinion looked like was so powerful that everyone still follows it today. Earlier reports sometimes reprinted oral arguments, summarized briefs or included essays interpreting the reported decision. The form, shown in this chapter, became the norm. Official reports follow the pattern. It has even migrated to WESTLAW and LEXIS. Time may change this because digital information offers the opportunity for much more flexible forms of reproducing cases but for now you should become familiar with the standard format.

4. *The National Reporter System* - **Federal Decisions**

West Publishing Company also accepted the challenge of publishing federal cases. If West was to have a *National Reporter System* that could promise to print every case, the federal cases had to be included. The *Supreme Court Reporter* began in 1886 and since that date has published every decision of the highest court in the land. The coverage of lower Federal Courts has evolved over the years.

From 1880 until 1931 all lower federal court decisions appeared in the *Federal Reporter*. Since 1932 decisions from the Federal District Courts have appeared in the *Federal Supplement* and the decisions of the Courts of Appeal have appeared in the *Federal Reporter*. A third component, *Federal Rules Decisions* was added after the passage of the Federal Rules of Civil Procedure in 1948.

There has never been a systematic official reporter of lower federal court decision. Until LEXIS burst on the scene, the West volumes were the only way to find such opinions. Indeed some claimed that West had *de facto* become an official reporter -- though cooler heads prevailed. Today the Federal Courts of Appeal and some District Courts are experimenting with using the Internet to officially publish decisions, but no systematic replacement has yet emerged. For now, the Thomson-West reporters hold sway.

In reaction to the fact that the online databases WESTLAW and LEXIS now include decisions that were not designated for publication by the federal courts, Thomson-West has added another component to its system of federal reporters. The set, called the *Federal Appendix*, prints those cases from the lower federal courts that appear in WESTLAW or LEXIS but that do not appear in the *Federal Reporter* or the *Federal Supplement*. The concept of a published set of unpublished opinions may seem a bit surreal but it reflects the fluid state of legal information.

Table 1 is a diagram of the federal components of the Thomson-West reporter system. It also shows what other courts have been covered by these sets. Over the years a variety of special courts have been created by the Congress and when that has happened, they have been included in the *Federal Reporter* or *Federal Supplement*. A set called *Federal Cases* was produced at one time that picked up those lower court decisions that had been published before the *Federal Reporter* was initiated. This makes the coverage complete.

Table 1
The *National Reporter System*

Title of Publication	Cases reported from...
Federal Supplement	Federal District Courts
Federal Reporter	Federal Courts of Appeal (the Circuit Courts)
Supreme Court Reporter	U.S. Supreme Court
Atlantic	Connecticut, Delaware, the District of Columbia, Maine, Maryland, New Hampshire, New Jersey, Pennsylvania, Rhode Island, and Vermont
Southern	Alabama, Florida, Louisiana, and Mississippi

Table 1, con't.

Title of Publication	Cases reported from...
South Eastern	Georgia, North Carolina, South Carolina, Virginia, and West Virginia
South Western	Arkansas, Kentucky, Missouri, Tennessee, and Texas
North Eastern	Illinois, Indiana, Massachusetts, New York, Ohio
North Western	Iowa, Michigan, Minnesota, Nebraska, North Dakota, South Dakota, and Wisconsin
Pacific	Alaska, Arizona, Colorado, Hawaii, Idaho, Kansas, Montana, Nevada, New Mexico, Oklahoma, Oregon, Utah, Washington, and Wyoming
California Reporter	California Supreme Court and appellate courts
New York Supplement	New York Court of Appeals, Appellate Division of the State Supreme Court, and additional state courts

5. WESTLAW and LEXIS

The next stage in American case reporting was the development of full-text online computer systems that put every word of every case into electronic form. WESTLAW, owned by the Thomson Company (a Canadian information conglomerate), and LEXIS, owned by Reed Elsevier (an English/Dutch information conglomerate), provide access to the full text of all federal and state cases. This electronic information is not constrained by the limits of being in paper form. Printing cases in paper requires them to be arranged in a certain way with its indexing keyed to that one specific arrangement. The online searcher can create her own database of cases by using various available tags or "fields" (*e.g.*, date, court, judge). It is as if each time you run a search on LEXIS or WESTLAW a special custom-made case reporter is created. The digital form also allows the searcher to use either keyword search strategies or new associative retrieval systems; this benefit will be discussed when questions of case finding are addressed in Chapter 4. LEXIS and WESTLAW have become accepted in the legal community. Law is the first profession or discipline to have truly moved to online full-text research. It was the availability of cases on WESTLAW and LEXIS that led the way.

Note that where WESTLAW or LEXIS prints a case they retain the citation to the underlying system where possible. If there is an official citation and a *National Reporter System* citation they will be included. There has been great argument about the idea of developing a citation system that is completely divorced from the old universe of paper. It is not hard to imagine a system that would allow citation to materials based on their appearance online. The most popular idea, tagging the case with a unique identifying alphanumeric phrase and then numbering the paragraphs in the text has been experimented with in some states and even adopted in a few jurisdictions. The bottom line though is that for now you must refer to the paper sets. As of 2005 that is still the way that the system works.

LEXIS and WESTLAW include many cases that are never printed as a part of the *National Reporter System* or any official state reporter. This is because before the arrival of the digital databases commentators and judges perceived that too many cases were being published. We discussed this a bit when working through the example of Bob and Britney at the beginning of this Chapter. Each of the Federal Courts of Appeal has experimented with creating rules to govern what cases should be published and which should only matter to the parties in that matter. Some states have taken on the same enterprise. Thomson-West worked closely with the courts and only published those cases that the courts designated. LEXIS saw an opportunity and began to publish cases which to that point had only lived on in court files. The cases were part of the public record and were freely available. The courts did not view them as published into the stream of precedent, but the cases were still on file at the courts. WESTLAW matched LEXIS and began to include these cases in its databases. Some courts reacted by saying that decisions which were not designated for publication could not be cited. So now there are cases that you can read on LEXIS or WESTLAW but you can not cite to them.

There is a rule in information theory that if information exists, it will be used, and increasingly, unpublished decisions are being used. There is a serious battle going on about this issue right now. We will provide citations to some additional readings at the end of the Chapter if you want to learn more about it. What is important for you now is to be sure that your case is not tagged "not to be cited" or "unpublished" in WESTLAW or LEXIS. Over the next few years this will have to be straightened out but for now it is a bit of a mess.

6. The Internet and the Future

The Internet, an amorphous information entity that links computer networks from around the world, contains an increasing amount of legal information, including cases. Many courts, including the Supreme Court of the United States and other federal courts, now post copies of new decisions on the Internet; anyone with the correct equipment and the requisite technical skills can access them and download them to her computer. Illustration E shows the homepage of the Supreme Court, and you can see a link there for decisions from the court.

One of the reasons that the *National Reporter System* remained unchallenged as a systematic reporter of judicial decisions was the substantial cost and effort it would have taken to mount competition. The task of publishing such a set in the world of paper was substantial. In the digital world anyone can upload cases. Nor does one have to worry about being systematic since the *National Reporter System*, WESTLAW and LEXIS are there as a backstop. This means that many publishers, courts and interested groups like law libraries are now making cases available. It is an open question whether these Internet sources will survive in their current form, and it is impossible to predict the permanence of what they are doing. The best current guides to legal resources on the Internet are Internet sources themselves. For now though, you must learn about the official reports, the *National Reporter System*, WESTLAW and LEXIS and you must keep an eye on the future. It is always in play.

Illustration E
The Official Homepage of the Supreme Court of the United States

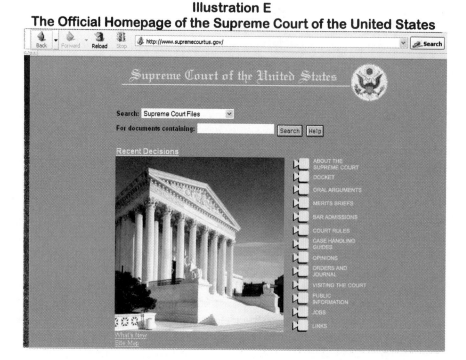

E. SUPREME COURT OF THE UNITED STATES

Though we have talked about federal cases, including the United States Supreme Court, in general, we are going to devote this section to a discussion of the United States Supreme Court in detail. No matter where you live the decisions of the Supreme Court will be important and this discussion will help illustrate how cases are published by the government and private publishing companies.

Each Supreme Court opinion appears in LEXIS and WESTLAW. We have already briefly discussed the official version of printed reports, the *United States Reports*. The historical significance of the Supreme Court argues for a more careful treatment of the printed forms in which its opinions appear. This section centers on those printed forms that you will encounter.

1. History

Today the decisions of the Supreme Court are available in a variety of formats, including three permanent, bound reporters, two looseleaf services, two electronic databases and many websites on the Internet. Its early cases were not so widely reported. The history of their publication corresponds to the brief history of American law reporting already described. The first reports were compiled by individuals and were known as "nominative" reporters. Even after the federal government began to officially sanction the reports, they were still private ventures of the individual reporters. Later sets, including current reprints, have incorporated the nominatives into the general numbering scheme of the *United States Reports* but retained the reporters' names. Thus the first ninety volumes of *United States Reports* are still cited by the name of the individual reporter.[14] The early reporters, their nominative and U.S. Reports citations, and dates of coverage are as follows:

Reporter	Nominative Citation	U.S. Reports Citation	Terms
A.J. Dallas	1-4 Dall.	1-4 U.S.	1890-1800
William Cranch	1-9 Cranch	5-13 U.S.	1801-1815
Henry Wheaton	1-2 Wheat.	14-25 U.S.	1816-1827
Richard Peters	1-16 Pet.	26-41 U.S.	1828-1842
Benjamin C. Howard	1-24 How.	42-65 U.S.	1843-1860
J.S. Black	1-2 Black	66-67 U.S.	1863-1874
John William Wallace	1-23 Wall.	68-90 U.S.	1863-1874

The case in which the Supreme Court held that the reporter had no copyright in the text of the decisions is cited as *Wheaton v. Peters*, 33 U.S. (8 Pet.) 591 (1834), meaning that the case originally appeared in volume eight of *Peters' Reports* and is now in volume 33 of the renumbered set.

---

14   Those working with older collections may find mixed into their sets some of the various recompilations that attempted to reprint earlier cases in smaller and less expensive editions. Perhaps the best known are those of Richard Peters (*Peters' Condensed Reports,* covering 1 to 25 U.S., 1790-1827, in four volumes) and Benjamin Curtis (*Curtis' Reports of Decisions,* covering 2 to 58 U.S., 1790-1854, in 22 volumes). These reprints are no longer used much, but are still found on the shelves of many law libraries and are occasionally needed to trace citations to them in older works.

The financial impact of that decision led ultimately to the demise of official reporting by private individuals and to the beginning of the modern series of officially published *United States Reports*.[15]

2. *United States Reports*

The official reporter for the Supreme Court of the United States is the *United States Reports* (abbreviated in citations as U.S.). Although there are still individual reporters preparing the current volumes, they are now employees of the Court and their names are no longer used to designate their volumes.

The Supreme Court's annual term runs from October to July, and several volumes of *United States Reports* are added every year. Frequently controversial decisions are issued at the end of the term, sometimes is a great flurry. Following the general pattern of publication, the decisions appear first in slip opinion form, followed by an official advance sheet (called the "preliminary print"), and finally appear in the bound *United States Reports* volume. Illustration F-1 & F-2 present the beginning pages of a case in the United States Reports. Note that the official court reporter has prefaced the text of the decision with a syllabus, preliminary paragraphs summarizing the case and indicating what the Court has held.

The *United States Reports* is an accurate, well-indexed compilation of the full official text of all decisions of the Supreme Court of the United States. At first glance it might seem that it should provide quite adequately for the needs of researchers. Unfortunately, as with many official publications, the advance sheets and volumes of the *United States Reports* tend to appear quite slowly. Currently, almost three years pass between the announcement of a decision and its appearance in the advance sheet, and another year before its inclusion in a bound volume. Because of the importance of Supreme Court opinions, this glacial pace of reporting is inadequate for practicing attorneys. In the days before LEXIS and WESTLAW there was a need for quicker access to a printed form of the decisions. In response to the need for more timely publication, commercial publishers

---

15   A history of the case and its impact on Supreme Court reporting can be found in Craig Joyce, "Wheaton v. Peters: The Untold Story of the Early Reporters," 1985 *Sup. Ct. Hist. Soc'y Y.B.* 35.

produce a variety of unofficial reporters which are distributed much more quickly than the official set.

Illustration F-1
The First Page of a Case from *United States Reports*, 468 U.S. 288.

288   OCTOBER TERM, 1983

Syllabus   468 U. S.

CLARK, SECRETARY OF THE INTERIOR, ET AL. *v.* COMMUNITY FOR CREATIVE NON-VIOLENCE ET AL.

CERTIORARI TO THE UNITED STATES COURT OF APPEALS FOR THE DISTRICT OF COLUMBIA CIRCUIT

No. 82–1998. Argued March 21, 1984—Decided June 29, 1984

In 1982, the National Park Service issued a permit to respondent Community for Creative Non-Violence (CCNV) to conduct a demonstration in Lafayette Park and the Mall, which are National Parks in the heart of Washington, D. C. The purpose of the demonstration was to call attention to the plight of the homeless, and the permit authorized the erection of two symbolic tent cities. However, the Park Service, relying on its regulations—particularly one that permits "camping" (defined as including sleeping activities) only in designated campgrounds, no campgrounds having ever been designated in Lafayette Park or the Mall—denied CCNV's request that demonstrators be permitted to sleep in the symbolic tents. CCNV and the individual respondents then filed an action in Federal District Court, alleging, *inter alia*, that application of the regulations to prevent sleeping in the tents violated the First Amendment. The District Court granted summary judgment for the Park Service, but the Court of Appeals reversed.

Held: The challenged application of the Park Service regulations does not violate the First Amendment. Pp. 293–299.

(a) Assuming that overnight sleeping in connection with the demonstration is expressive conduct protected to some extent by the First Amendment, the regulation forbidding sleeping meets the requirements for a reasonable time, place, or manner restriction of expression, whether oral, written, or symbolized by conduct. The regulation is neutral with regard to the message presented, and leaves open ample alternative methods of communicating the intended message concerning the plight of the homeless. Moreover, the regulation narrowly focuses on the Government's substantial interest in maintaining the parks in the heart of the Capital in an attractive and intact condition, readily available to the millions of people who wish to see and enjoy them by their presence. To permit camping would be totally inimical to these purposes. The validity of the regulation need not be judged solely by reference to the demonstration at hand, and none of its provisions are unrelated to the ends that it was designed to serve. Pp. 293–298.

(b) Similarly, the challenged regulation is also sustainable as meeting the standards for a valid regulation of expressive conduct. Aside from

Illustration F-2
The Second Page of a Case from *United States Reports*, 468 U.S. 288.

CLARK *v.* COMMUNITY FOR CREATIVE NON-VIOLENCE 289

288   · Opinion of the Court

its impact on speech, a rule against camping or overnight sleeping in public parks is not beyond the constitutional power of the Government to enforce. And as noted above, there is a substantial Government interest, unrelated to suppression of expression, in conserving park property that is served by the proscription of sleeping. Pp. 298–299.

227 U. S. App. D. C. 19, 703 F. 2d 586, reversed.

WHITE, J., delivered the opinion of the Court, in which BURGER, C. J., and BLACKMUN, POWELL, REHNQUIST, STEVENS, and O'CONNOR, JJ., joined. BURGER, C. J., filed a concurring opinion, *post*, p. 300. MARSHALL, J., filed a dissenting opinion, in which BRENNAN, J., joined, *post*, p. 301.

Deputy Solicitor General Bator argued the cause for petitioners. With him on the briefs were *Solicitor General Lee, Assistant Attorney General McGrath, Alan I. Horowitz, Leonard Schaitman,* and *Katherine S. Gruenheck.*

Burt Neuborne argued the cause for respondents. With him on the brief were *Charles S. Sims, Laura Macklin, Arthur B. Spitzer,* and *Elizabeth Symonds.**

JUSTICE WHITE delivered the opinion of the Court.

The issue in this case is whether a National Park Service regulation prohibiting camping in certain parks violates the First Amendment when applied to prohibit demonstrators from sleeping in Lafayette Park and the Mall in connection with a demonstration intended to call attention to the plight of the homeless. We hold that it does not and reverse the contrary judgment of the Court of Appeals.

I

The Interior Department, through the National Park Service, is charged with responsibility for the management and maintenance of the National Parks and is authorized to promulgate rules and regulations for the use of the parks in accordance with the purposes for which they were established.

*Ogden Northrop Lewis filed a brief for the National Coalition for the Homeless as *amicus curiae* urging affirmance.

3. *United States Supreme Court Reports, Lawyers' Edition*

There are two commercial sets of Supreme Court decisions which not only publish cases sooner than the official reports but also provide special editorial features for the legal researcher. Both sets are useful even after the appearance of a case in *United States Reports* and therefore are published in both advance sheets and permanent bound volumes. Both have been in existence since 1882.

United States Supreme Court Reports, Lawyers' Edition is now published by LexisNexis. Popularly known as *Lawyers' Edition* (and cited as L. Ed.), the set began by reprinting all the earlier Supreme Court decisions in smaller type and fewer volumes than the official reports. Upon the completion of retrospective coverage, Lawyers Co-op, the company that originally started the set, continued publishing the Court's decisions as they were issued. After reaching one hundred volumes in 1956 (covering through volume 351 of *United States Reports*), it began a second series, known as *Lawyers' Edition 2d* (L. Ed.2d), which continues today.

Unlike the official set, *Lawyers' Edition* issues advance sheets which put decisions in researchers' hands in a matter of weeks rather than months. In addition to printing the official reporter's syllabus and the opinion, the editors at LexisNexis prepare both a "summary" of each case and their own headnotes. They also provide cross-references to treatments of the case's subject in other LexisNexis publications. These features are shown in Illustrations G-1 and G-2, the opening pages of the *Lawyers' Edition* version of *Clark v. Community for Creative Non-Violence*, the same case shown in its United States Reports version in Illustrations F-1 & F-2.

Each headnote in Lawyers' Edition is assigned a topic and section number by the editors. These headnotes are then reprinted, arranged by topic, in the companion set to the reports, *United States Supreme Court Digest*, Lawyers' Edition. The digest allows retrieval of other cases in the same subject area, and will be more fully described in Chapter 4, Case Finding. A table in each advance sheet and volume of *Lawyers' Edition* lists the digest topics and numbers appearing in that volume.

By the time a bound volume of *Lawyers' Edition* is ready for publication, the editors have added other useful features. First, they provide short summaries of the briefs of counsel. This is one of the few variations on

Illustration G-1
The first page of a decision in *Lawyers' Edition*, showing publisher's summary and references to annotations and briefs

[468 US 288]

WILLIAM P. CLARK, Secretary of the Interior, et al., Petitioners

v

COMMUNITY FOR CREATIVE NON-VIOLENCE et al.

468 US 288, 82 L Ed 2d 221, 104 S Ct 3065

[No. 82-1998]

Argued March 21, 1984. Decided June 29, 1984.

Decision: National Park Service anti-camping regulation held constitutionally applied to Washington, D.C., demonstrators.

SUMMARY

The Community for Creative Non-Violence and several individuals brought suit in the United States District Court for the District of Columbia to prevent the application of a National Park Service regulation, prohibiting camping in national parks except in designated campgrounds, to a proposed demonstration in Lafayette Park and the Mall, in the heart of Washington, D.C., in which demonstrators would sleep in symbolic tents to demonstrate the plight of the homeless. The District Court granted summary judgment in favor of the Park Service. The United States Court of Appeals for the District of Columbia Circuit reversed on the ground that the application of the regulation so as to prevent sleeping in the tents would infringe the demonstrators' First Amendment right of free expression (703 F2d 586).

On certiorari, the United States Supreme Court reversed. In an opinion by WHITE, J., expressing the views of BURGER, Ch. J., and BLACKMUN, POWELL, REHNQUIST, STEVENS, and O'CONNOR, JJ., it was held that the Park Service regulation did not violate the First Amendment when applied to the demonstrators because the regulation was justified without reference to the content of the regulated speech, was narrowly tailored to serve a significant governmental interest, and left open ample alternative channels for communication of the information.

BURGER, Ch. J., while concurring fully in the court's opinion, filed a concurring opinion stating that the camping was conduct and not speech.

MARSHALL, J., joined by BRENNAN, J., dissented on the ground that the

---

SUBJECT OF ANNOTATION

Beginning on page 958, infra

Restriction of use of public parks as violating freedom of speech or press under First Amendment of Federal Constitution

---

Briefs of Counsel, p 956, infra.

221

Illustration G-2
The second page of a *Lawyers' Edition* decision, showing headnotes and cross-references

U.S. SUPREME COURT REPORTS   82 L Ed 2d

demonstrators' sleep was symbolic speech and that the regulation of it was not reasonable.

HEADNOTES

Classified to U.S. Supreme Court Digest, Lawyers' Edition

Constitutional Law § 960 — demonstration — camping

1a–1c. A National Park Service regulation prohibiting camping in national parks except in campgrounds designated for that purpose does not violate the First Amendment when applied to prohibit demonstrators from sleeping in Lafayette Park and the Mall, in the heart of Washington, D. C., in connection with a demonstration intended to call attention to the plight of the homeless. (Marshall and Brennan, JJ, dissented from this holding.)
[See annotation p 958, infra]

Parks, Squares, and Commons § 2 — camping

2a, 2b. Sleeping in tents for the purpose of expressing the plight of the homeless falls within the definition of "camping" in a National Park Service regulation defining camping as the use of park land for living accommodation purposes such as sleeping activities, or making

preparations to sleep (including the laying down of bedding for the purpose of sleeping), or storing personal belongings, or making any fire, or using any tents or other structure for sleeping or doing any digging or earth breaking or carrying on cooking activities when it appears, in light of all the circumstances, that the participants, in conducting these activities, are in fact using the area as a living accommodation regardless of the intent of the participants or the nature of any other activities in which they may also be engaging.

Evidence § 102 — First Amendment — application

3a, 3b. Although it is common to place the burden on the government to justify impingements on First Amendment interests, it is the obligation of the person desiring to engage in assertedly expressive conduct to demonstrate that the First Amendment even applies.

Constitutional Law § 934 — expression — restriction

TOTAL CLIENT-SERVICE LIBRARY® REFERENCES

59 Am Jur 2d, Parks, Squares, and Playgrounds § 33

USCS, Constitution, 1st Amendment

US L Ed Digest, Constitutional Law §§ 934, 960

L Ed Index to Annos, Parks

ALR Quick Index, Parks and Playgrounds

Federal Quick Index, National Parks; Parks

Auto-Cite®: Any case citation herein can be checked for form, parallel references, later history and annotation references through the Auto-Cite computer research system.

ANNOTATION REFERENCE

Restriction of use of public parks as violating freedom of speech or press under First Amendment of Federal Constitution. 82 L Ed 2d 958.

222

the West model of case reporting that survived, but the summaries are very short. For real research you should look at the briefs available on WESTLAW and LEXIS. Second, the editors prepare annotations on a few of the more important cases in each volume. These annotations analyze in considerable detail one or more of the points of law covered in the case and present other primary authorities on the same topic. Since 1957 these annotations have been regularly supplemented. References to briefs and annotations, both printed elsewhere in the volume, appear at the bottom of the page in Illustration G-1. Each volume also includes a table of cases reported, an index, a table of cross-references from official *United States Reports citations*, and a table of federal laws cited or construed in the volume.

Lawyers' Edition is part of the research system developed by the publisher to link its various publications. This includes a wide range of primary and secondary sources such as statutory codes, annotations, and legal encyclopedias. Each LexisNexis publication refers the researcher to other LexisNexis products that deal with the same issue.

4. *West's Supreme Court Reporter*

As part of its burgeoning *National Reporter System*, the West Publishing Company began coverage of the Supreme Court in the October 1882 term. Unlike Lawyers Co-op, it did not attempt a retrospective recompilation, and the first volume of the *Supreme Court Reporter* contains cases reported in volumes 106 and 107 of the *United States Reports*. West has published one numbered volume of the *Supreme Court Reporter* (cited as S. Ct.) each year. The volumes grew larger with time, until two physical volumes were needed for the 1959 term's decisions; by 1989, three physical volumes were required for each term's decisions. Now Thomson-West has published each year the numbered volume and two supplements designated "A" and "B" (*e.g.*, volumes 110, 110A, and 110B cover the October 1989 term).

Like *Lawyers' Edition*, the *Supreme Court Reporter* appears much more quickly than the official reports, reaching researchers in advance sheet form within weeks of decisions. It also includes tables of cases reported and of statutes construed in each advance sheet and volume, as well as a table of words and phrases judicially defined. Like LexisNexis, Thomson-West prepares its own summary, which it calls a synopsis, and headnotes for each case. These features are shown in Illustration H, the first page of the

Court Reporter edition of *Clark v. Community for Creative Non-*

Illustration H

st page of a decision in *West's Supreme Court Reporter*,
showing the synopsis and headnotes

Star symbol ↓

Synopsis: Summary of case prepared by editor →

Headnotes, topic, key number ←

CLARK v. COMMUNITY FOR CREATIVE NON–VIOLENCE **3065**
Cite as 104 S.Ct. 3065 (1984)

468 U.S. 288

468 U.S. 288, 82 L.Ed.2d 221

₁₂₈₈William P. CLARK, Secretary of the Interior, et al., Petitioners

v.

COMMUNITY FOR CREATIVE NON–VIOLENCE et al.

No. 82–1998.

Argued March 21, 1984.

Decided June 29, 1984.

Demonstrators permitted to participate in round-the-clock demonstration on the Mall and in Lafayette Park in Washington, D.C., brought action challenging the United States Park Service's denial of permission to sleep in temporary structures permitted to be erected as part of the demonstration. The United States District Court for the District of Columbia granted the government's motion for summary judgment, but the Court of Appeals, District of Columbia Circuit, reversed, 703 F.2d 586. Motion to vacate the order staying the mandate of the United States Court of Appeals for the District of Columbia Circuit was denied, 104 S.Ct. 478. Certiorari was granted, and the Supreme Court, Justice White, held that a National Park Service regulation prohibiting camping in certain parks did not violate the First Amendment though applied to prohibit demonstrators from sleeping in Lafayette Park and the Mall in connection with the demonstration, which was intended to call attention to the plight of the homeless.

Judgment of the Court of Appeals reversed.

Chief Justice Burger filed concurring opinion.

Justice Marshall dissented and filed opinion in which Justice Brennan joined.

1. United States ⬅57

Sleeping in tents for purpose of expressing plight of homeless falls within definition of "camping" in National Park Service regulation. U.S.C.A. Const.Amend. 1; 16 U.S.C.A. §§ 1, 1a–1, 3.

See publication Words and Phrases for other judicial constructions and definitions.

2. Constitutional Law ⬅90(1)

Although it is common to place burden upon government to justify impingement on First Amendment interests, it is obligation of person desiring to engage in assertedly expressive conduct to demonstrate that First Amendment even applies. U.S.C.A. Const.Amend. 1.

3. Constitutional Law ⬅90(3)

Expression, whether oral or written or symbolized by conduct, is subject to reasonable time, place and manner restrictions. U.S.C.A. Const.Amend. 1.

4. Constitutional Law ⬅90(3)

Message may be delivered by conduct that is intended to be communicative and that, in context, would reasonably be understood by viewer to be communicative, and symbolic expression of this kind may be forbidden or regulated if conduct itself may constitutionally be regulated, providing regulation is narrowly drawn to further substantial governmental interest and providing the interest is unrelated to suppression of free speech. U.S.C.A. Const.Amend. 1; 16 U.S.C.A. §§ 1, 1a–1, 3.

5. United States ⬅57

National Park Service regulation forbidding sleeping in certain areas was defensible either as time, place or manner restriction or as regulation of symbolic conduct. U.S.C.A. Const.Amend. 1; 16 U.S.C.A. §§ 1, 1a–1, 3.

6. United States ⬅57

Fact that sleeping, arguendo, may be expressive conduct, rather than oral or written expression, did not render prohibition against sleeping in certain areas of national parks any less an acceptable time, place or manner regulation. U.S.C.A. Const.Amend. 1; 16 U.S.C.A. §§ 1, 1a–1, 3.

It is Thomson-West's headnotes that make the *Supreme Court Reporter* an invaluable research tool. As in *Lawyers' Edition*, each headnote is assigned to a general topic and to a numbered subdivision within the topic. Subject access to the headnotes is provided in the *United States Supreme Court Digest*, a companion set to the reporter. Unlike the *Lawyers' Edition* classifications, however, the "key number" classification system is used not only for Supreme Court decisions but for court decisions throughout the *National Reporter System*. Thus the same point of law discussed in a Supreme Court case can be researched in all reported federal and state court cases through West's comprehensive subject digest system, which will be discussed at length in Chapter 4, Case Finding.

In comparing the editorial treatments in Illustrations G-1 and H-1 and H-2, note that the publishers have assigned different topics to the same judicial text. The fact that the editors of the two commercial publications formulate different statements of the points of law in a case demonstrates the subjectivity of legal research. It also underscores the fact that headnotes are merely finding aids, guiding the reader to the actual words of the decision. In each reporter the numbers of the headnotes are inserted in brackets into the text of the majority opinion, so that the researcher can go directly to a particular point in the opinion.

Another useful feature of both commercial editions is the inclusion in the final, bound volumes of cross-references to the location of the same decision in the competing reporter and in the *United States Reports*. Moreover, each includes within the text of opinions a device known as ***star paging***, indicating where pages begin in the official edition. This enables the researcher to read the more useful commercial version but have available the precise official citations to the case and to any page within the case.

Star pagination is not available until the final bound volumes of *Lawyers' Edition* and the *Supreme Court Reporter*, since the commercial publishers must wait for the government to issue the "preliminary print" pamphlets for the *United States Reports*. The long delay in publication means that the commercial advance sheets are heavily used, and in 1986 West began publishing an "interim edition" of the *Supreme Court Reporter*. The "interim edition" consists of two or three bound volumes, like the permanent edition, so that it can withstand wear and tear better than unbound pamphlets. It lacks parallel references to *United States Reports* and the official reports' final text corrections, however, and is printed on less expensive paper.

5. **Looseleaf Services**

The three standard print versions of United States Supreme Court decisions just described are well-established forms of legal publication, but they are not the only print product that publish the full text of each case. The *United States Law Week,* from the Bureau of National Affairs, meets the need of lawyers, and others interested in national policy or current affairs, to have access to Supreme Court decisions much sooner than the fastest advance sheet of *Lawyers' Edition* or the *Supreme Court Reporter* is available. Because *United States Law Week* reproduces the full text of each slip opinion in a looseleaf binder format, releases containing all of the new cases can be mailed out several times a week, and can be added directly into the binder sets. During the Supreme Court's term, from October to July, the set stays just about as up to date as a print tool possibly can.

USLW has simple indexing and cumulates into large binders at the end of the year. It has added features, like summaries of pending cases and information about the Court's docket. When the term of the Court is over in the summer, it publishes subject summaries of the cases that came down. It also has a section that notes interesting state cases. For those who cannot imagine using a paper tool, there is an online version of it as well.

Since it publishes the cases before other citations are available, *USLW* has its own citation system, which is acceptable to use in research work until one of the three traditional print tools is available.[16]

USLW was once a widely used set, but the role that it plays has diminished in recent years. Before the advent of electronic systems, getting access to the full text of a new Supreme Court case within a few days was quite impressive. Now, online research tools like WESTLAW and LEXIS are supplanting looseleaf services.

16　　A citation to *USLW* is recognized as the standard means of identifying Supreme Court opinions until they appear in the standard reporters. A citation to the *Supreme Court Reporter* is preferred once a case is published in its advance sheets, and then after a long delay a case finally receives its official *U.S. Reports* citation.

F. SUMMARY

This chapter has described the publication of judicial decisions, one of the central sources of American law and one of the most important and interesting forms of legal publication. Although often criticized as an overused and outdated method of learning, the analysis of cases continues to play an essential role in legal education. Case law also has a key role in legal research, not as a pedagogical device but as a vital resource. The central role of court reports in legal research may become increasingly apparent as the discussion returns to them again and again throughout this book.

The variety and overwhelming detail of the published reports should not obscure the literary quality and the multifaceted significance of the decisions they contain. The style of judicial opinions ranges from mundane prose and legalese to the clear, sharp texts of masters like Learned Hand and Oliver Wendell Holmes and the sometimes poetic humanism of Benjamin Nathan Cardozo. One can be moved by the human drama reflected in opinions which struggle to resolve the disputes arising between ordinary people, which reveal the tensions and conflicts besetting groups in society, or which judge the individual who has broken the law. The published cases also reflect the social, economic and political changes which have affected our world. We usually confront these movements as impersonal, abstract forces, but in the microcosm of the law reports they can be seen more vividly. One can trace in decisions on the law of property, for example, the evolution from feudalism to mercantilism to capitalism, and then through the industrial revolution, the welfare state, and the modern post-industrial society. There are more than headnotes, citations, and holdings in these volumes.

G. ADDITIONAL READING

To get a feel for the history and role of judicial opinions in the United States, we suggest that you read the opinion by Judge Kozinski in Hart v. Massanari, 266 F. 3d 1199 (9th Cir. 2001). Judge Kozinski deals with the issue of precedent, the meaning of judicial authority and many other things as well in this wide-ranging opinion. Many think that Judge Kozinski is among the brightest and most idiosyncratic of Federal Judges.

Martha Dragish Pearson, *Citation of Unpublished Opinions as Precedent*,
55 HASTINGS L.J. 1235 (2004).   Pearson's article is a
comprehensive treatment of the current state of judicial opinions
and precedent. Her voluminous footnotes are a treasure trove of
sources on this still-hot topic.

Chapter 3

CITATORS: CASE VERIFICTION AND UPDATING

A. INTRODUCTION

The court is unable to discern whether sloppy research or warped advocacy tactics are responsible for these errors of omission, but the Corporation Counsel is admonished that diligent research, which includes Shepardizing cases, is a professional responsibility ....[1]

The law is constantly changing. As you read this, lawyers and judges are fashioning arguments and writing opinions. Even if you find the perfect case, one that directly answers your question or one that precisely buttresses your argument, you cannot feel at ease. You must immediately ask two questions:

- *Is this case still good law?* That is, as the case moved through the court system did a higher court overrule it? As time passed has the same court reversed itself?

- *Has this case been influential?* Has it gained adherents for its view? Or have a series of subsequent decisions, while not overruling or reversing it, criticized it so sharply that it would be a liability if cited? And, did the legislature act to supersede the ruling with new statutes?

Lawyers need tools to monitor the life of cases, to keep track of a case as it moves through time. Such a source must be as timely as possible and it must be reliable.

For 120 years, this function was performed almost exclusively by an ingenious series of research tools called ***Shepard's Citations***. In 1873, Frank Shepard began printing lists of citations to Illinois Supreme Court cases on gummed paper for attorneys to stick in the margins of their bound reporters.[2] Before long he began publishing his citation lists in book form,

---

1   *Cimino v. Yale University*, 638 F.Supp. 952, 959 n. 7 (D.Conn. 1986).

2   If he had patented this sticky-note idea, he would have been the inventor of Post-It Notes®.

and coverage expanded to include every state and federal court.[3] The idea of using one of the *Shepard's* citators to check up on one's case became so much a part of the fabric of the practice of law that Frank Shepard's name became a verb. Each day thousands of lawyers are asked "to shepardize" a case.[4] Indeed, learning to use the maroon volumes of *Shepard's* became one of the great hazing experiences of American law school. However, it is quite possible that the law student of today will only use *Shepard's* in its online form, and never touch a bound volume of *Shepard's Citations*.

In 1997 **KeyCite** was introduced, and *Shepard's* was no longer an attorney's only option for monitoring cases. *KeyCite* is an online citing system that performs the verification functions of *Shepard's* as well as integrating the user into a series of research pathways. The two systems are owned by rival companies (*KeyCite* by Thompson-West, and *Shepard's* by LexisNexis) and there has been keen competition between them. *KeyCite* will sometimes pick up annotations that *Shepard's* does not (and vice-versa) or editors may assign a different importance to the same cases. This illustrates one of the most important things to keep in mind about legal research: *you must assess the current tools frequently, and be able to make intelligent decisions about what the tools are telling you and when to use some or all of the resources available to you.*

In this Chapter we will describe each of the systems, but we will concentrate on the functions the citators perform. It is our belief that if

---

3   For a history of the company, see, Frank Shepard Company, *A Record of Fifty Years of Specializing in a Field That Is of First Importance to the Bench and Bar of the United States: An Insight Into an Establishment That Has Grown From Small Beginnings to the First Rank in the Law Publishing Field* (Frank Shepard Co. 1923). It will be of interest only to bibliographic types, but it is full of laudatory prose and early photographs of Shepard's staffers at work.

4   This terminology hasn't disappeared from the profession even though new tools have been introduced. Be aware that "shepardizing" is an uncertain term because of these new and different tools. Develop a clear understanding of what is required by the firm, the judge, or the occasion before someone depends upon your research.

you understand what the citator is doing, then the media will not matter.[5] Your task will be to understand what the information is, and how it is being presented. When citators went online the mechanical task of checking a case's standing became relatively simple, however, the weighty professional responsibility for you to personally judge the authority of your case did not change at all. Before you can rely upon a case in court as authoritative, its continuing validity must be determined. *A lawyer who neglects this step may base arguments on cases subsequently reversed or limited in scope, thereby practicing law incompetently and risking embarrassment or worse.*

It is also important to note that the citator methodology, the careful gathering of subsequent citations for research purposes, has been applied to sources other than cases. The citators can be used for statutes, administrative regulations and a variety of other sources.

B. GENERAL FEATURES OF CITATORS

1. Function

Citators perform three basic functions:

1. *Citators verify the authority of your case.*
2. *Citators show you how your case has been treated/used by other courts.*
3. *Citators point you to potential research sources.*

First, let's consider *verification of authority*. The citator alerts you to whether or not your case is still good law – that is, it will tell you whether it has been overruled or reversed. The answer to this crucial question is central to this step in your research.

---

5   For a description of how to use the paper versions of *Shepard's*, see the manual, *How to Shepardize: Your Guide to Legal Research Using Shepard's Citations in Print*, located at:
<http://www.lexisnexis.com/shepards/printsupport/shepardize_print.pdf>

The second function is to alert you to *how the case has been treated*. Have subsequent courts cited it favorably, criticized or ignored it? Judicial opinions are alive. They can grow stronger or weaker.

The functional underpinning of the *Shepard's* and *KeyCite* is very straightforward. Using the same form of comprehensive obsessiveness that John West employed in creating the *National Reporter System*, Frank Shepard determined that his books would allow the researcher to see every subsequent mention of a case that interested him. If a researcher found a case that was on point, *Shepard's* citators would show him *every* subsequent mention of that case. The creators of *KeyCite* have followed the same logic, supplying the researcher with a tool that finds each and *every* mention of a case in the WESTLAW databases of cases and secondary materials. Indeed, *KeyCite* even took this a step further by including unpublished cases that appear on WESTLAW in the retrieval set. *Shepard's* followed suit and now includes unpublished cases found on LEXIS.[6] As this chapter will show, citators can perform many other functions for a researcher, but the heart is the total retrieval of relevant information. This approach will catch any important comments on a case, but it will also catch every trivial mention as well. The point is that it catches everything. It is up to you to sift it out.[7]

Citators can also alert you to subsequent citations of your case which are particularly important. An important mention might include all of those places where the Federal Court of Appeals in your state has used your case. A citator can be programmed to cull this out of hundreds of citations and highlight it. This is an enormous aid for researchers. *Shepard's* and *KeyCite* will take different approaches to pointing you towards which subsequent citations are important and should be examined, but the two systems seek the same end. They are designed to help you find subsequent cases that have a particular impact on the case at hand.

---

6   This also illustrates the competition between the two systems – when one introduces a new feature, the other is very likely to follow.

7   Ponder this for a moment. EVERY SUBSEQUENT MENTION OF A CASE. How many times do you think courts have cited *Roe v. Wade*? If you'd like to know, *Shepard's* or *KeyCite* can tell you.

Citators play *a third function by pointing you to sources for further research*. The theory runs like this: if a subsequent case cites your case, even if it does not affect the validity or strength of your case, it must be discussing some of the same issues. As someone interested in those topics, you may want to check the subsequent case. "Citation chasing" is a popular research strategy. Citators point to more than just cases -- a wide variety of other materials that mention one's case may be included. One can follow a research thread from a case citation into other secondary sources, as described below.

2. Coverage

Shepard's and *KeyCite's* coverage of cases is fully retrospective, back to the first American cases in the 1700's. Non-case materials in both systems include the *American Law Reports*, selected law reviews, and various legal treatises as citing references.

The online versions of these citators are updated on a daily basis, which means that approximately 24-48 hours after LEXIS and WESTLAW receive a case, it has been incorporated as a cited (and a citing) reference. It takes a little longer, however, for the analysis comments to appear in the systems. This means, for example, that your case may be overruled by a citing case, but that notation might not appear for a week or ten days.

3. Online Advantages

Once you've typed your citation into the system of your choice, the electronic versions of *Shepard's* and *KeyCite* show you *all* citing entries cumulated in one listing. Both employ hypertext links which allow the researcher to go directly to a *Shepard's* or *KeyCite* display for any case being viewed, and then from *Shepard's* or *KeyCite* to the text of a citing case. This allows the use of citators as a more integral part of the process of finding and reading cases. Citators have become far more than verification systems.

An important advantage offered by electronic retrieval, (in contrast to the point made in the paragraph above), is that the computer allows you to limit a display to particular request. This is very easily done with the online citator programs. A researcher interested only in a particular point of law, as indicated by a certain headnote number, need not read carefully through several screens of irrelevant cases but can set limits and automatically retrieve only those citing cases on point. The display can also be limited to those cases with particular history or treatment signals, or only those from a specific jurisdiction, so that one can retrieve, for example, only those cases that distinguish or limit the holding of the cited decision.

A final, important advantage of online citators is the fact that they employ familiar interfaces for those new to legal research. *Shepard's* and *KeyCite* are continually being modified to make them more user friendly and intuitive. Rather than learning the print protocols based on a centuries old system, the electronic versions can take advantage of the best new innovations.

C. SPECIFIC FEATURES OF CITATORS

Although their underlying purpose is to indicate the current status and treatment of primary sources, entries in *Shepard's* and *KeyCite* provide a variety of other important information. The various features are indicated in Illustrations A & B, and copies of the full *Shepard's* and *KeyCite* treatments of a case can be found in Appendix A.

1. Parallel Citations

Many cases are published in more than one reporter series. For example, decisions of the Supreme Court of the United States appear in the *United States Reports, Lawyers' Edition* and the *Supreme Court Reporter,* and most state cases are printed in both official reports and one of the regional reporters of the *National Reporter System.* Often researchers have a citation to one version of a case but need to find a different report of that case. A lawyer who has read the unofficial edition of a case may need its official citation to cite in a brief, or a researcher may know only the official citation but wish to use the editorial headnotes available in a commercial version. ***Different citations to the same judicial decision are referred to as parallel citations.***[8]

Citators provide one of the easiest ways to find parallel citations. No matter what citation is typed in, the information retrieved will include a list that has the official and any other unofficial citations to the cited case. Other resources to be discussed later in this chapter can also be used to find parallel citations, but they are neither as convenient, nor as efficient to use.

Illustration A-1
First Screen, *Shepard's* on LEXIS, *In re Marriage of Bonds*, Showing the Summary. Note the Parallel Citations and Shepard's Signal

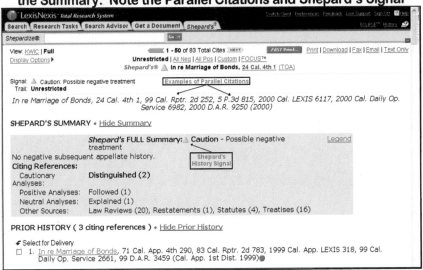

---

8   The concept of parallel citations is currently premised on existing paper sets of case reporters. The revolution in electronic information may bring about major changes, at least prospectively.

Illustration A-2
Shepard's on LEXIS, *In re Marriage of Bonds*, Showing Case History, and the First Citing Decisions

---

PRIOR HISTORY (3 citing references) • Hide Prior History

✔ Select for Delivery
☐ 1. In re Marriage of Bonds, 71 Cal. App. 4th 290, 83 Cal. Rptr. 2d 783, 1999 Cal. App. LEXIS 318, 99 Cal. Daily Op. Service 2661, 99 D.A.R. 3459 (Cal. App. 1st Dist. 1999)●

☐ 2. **Modified by, Rehearing denied by:**
      In re Marriage of Bonds, 72 Cal. App. 4th 94d, 1999 Cal. App. LEXIS 469, 99 Cal. Daily Op. Service 3510, 99 D.A.R. 4455 (Cal. App. 1st Dist. 1999)◐

☐ 3. **Review granted, Depublished by:**
      In re Marriage of Bonds, Supreme Court Minute 07-21-1999, 87 Cal. Rptr. 2d 410, 981 P.2d 40, 1999 Cal. LEXIS 4859, 99 Cal. Daily Op. Service 5823, 99 D.A.R. 7426 (Cal. 1999)◐

   ▸ **Reversed by, Remanded by, Superseded by (CITATION YOU ENTERED):**
      In re Marriage of Bonds, 24 Cal. 4th 1, 99 Cal. Rptr. 2d 252, 5 P.3d 815, 2000 Cal. LEXIS 6117, 2000 Cal. Daily Op. Service 6982, 2000 D.A.R. 9250 (2000)△

SUBSEQUENT APPELLATE HISTORY (1 citing reference) • Hide Subsequent Appellate History

☐ 4. **Rehearing denied by:**
      In re Marriage of Bonds, Supreme Court Minute 10-18-2000, 2000 Cal. LEXIS 8073, 2000 D.A.R. 11290 (Cal. Oct. 18, 2000)◐

CITING DECISIONS (39 citing decisions)

CALIFORNIA SUPREME COURT

☐ 5. **Cited by:**
      People v. Leal, 33 Cal. 4th 999, 16 Cal. Rptr. 3d 869, 94 P.3d 1071, 2004 Cal. LEXIS 7080, 2004 Cal. Daily Op. Service 7097, 2004 D.A.R. 9582 (2004)◐

      33 Cal. 4th 999 p.1009 ◀
      16 Cal. Rptr. 3d 869 p.877 ◀ ⟵ ⟶ | Examples of Pin Cites |
      94 P.3d 1071 p.1077 ◀

☐ 6. **Cited by:**
      Hoechst Celanese Corp. v. Franchise Tax Bd., 25 Cal. 4th 508, 106 Cal. Rptr. 2d 548, 22 P.3d 324, 2001 Cal. LEXIS 3088, 2001 Cal. Daily Op. Service 3851, 2001 D.A.R. 4703 (2001)△

      25 Cal. 4th 508 p.519
      106 Cal. Rptr. 2d 548 p.558
      22 P.3d 324 p.332

☐ 7. **Cited by:**
      In re Marriage of Pendleton & Fireman, 24 Cal. 4th 39, 99 Cal. Rptr. 2d 278, 5 P.3d 839, 2000 Cal. LEXIS 6116, 2000 Cal. Daily Op. Service 6993, 2000 D.A.R. 9275 (2000)△

CALIFORNIA COURTS OF APPEAL

☐ 8. **Followed by:**
      In re Marriage of Mehren & Dargan, 118 Cal. App. 4th 1167, 13 Cal. Rptr. 3d 522, 2004 Cal. App. LEXIS 782, 2004 Cal. Daily Op. Service 4389, 2004 D.A.R. 6076 (Cal. App. 4th Dist. 2004)◆

      118 Cal. App. 4th 1167 p.1170, Headnote: Cal. 4th - 5 ◀ ⟵ | Examples of Headnote References |
      13 Cal. Rptr. 3d 522 p.523, Headnote: Cal. 4th - 5 ◀
      13 Cal. Rptr. 3d 522 p.524

Illustration B
KeyCite on WESTLAW, *In re Marriage of Bonds*, Showing Direct History, Negative Indirect History and the First Citing Cases

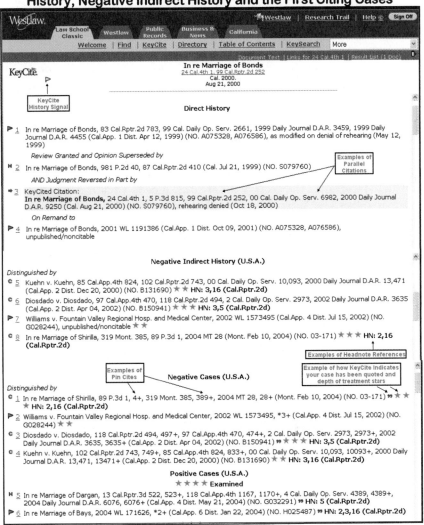

2. Case History or Direct History

Case History (in *Shepard's*) or Direct History (in *KeyCite*) citations, *i.e.*, those indicating prior or subsequent proceedings in the same case, are the first items listed in either citator. The most significant history citations for determining a case's validity are subsequent decisions by a higher appellate court. The citation for the higher court's decision always indicates if the cited case is affirmed, modified, or reversed on appeal.

The history notations are the first step in determining whether or not the case being checked is still good authority. If a case was reversed on appeal, it cannot be cited as authority. Even a reversed case, of course, may contain passages worth reading or reasoning worth considering.[9] It is even possible that a higher court decision is listed as "reversed" even if it did not reverse the judgment on the specific issue being researched. Only by reading and analyzing the citing decision can you determine its precise effect. The notations in a citator assist in case analysis but are not a substitute for reading the decisions. The first clue to what has happened to a case in either system is a red or yellow signal -- red meaning there has been some definite negative history, yellow meaning there may be. Remember, these are just clues, and should alert you to look carefully, not to use them in place of your own critical analysis of the citing references.

Illustration C
***Shepard's* History Signals, as defined on LEXIS**

● -	Warning: Negative treatment is indicated
Q -	Questioned: Validity questioned by citing refs
△ -	Caution: Possible negative treatment
✦ -	Positive treatment is indicated
A -	Citing Refs. With Analysis Available
i -	Citation information available

---

9   Such a case *can* be cited in a brief, as long as it is clearly noted that it is not binding precedent.

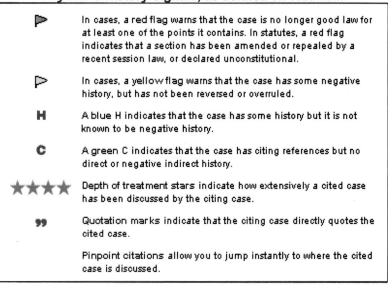

Illustration D
***KeyCite*'s History Signals, as defined on WESTLAW**

In cases, a red flag warns that the case is no longer good law for at least one of the points it contains. In statutes, a red flag indicates that a section has been amended or repealed by a recent session law, or declared unconstitutional.

In cases, a yellow flag warns that the case has some negative history, but has not been reversed or overruled.

H   A blue H indicates that the case has some history but it is not known to be negative history.

C   A green C indicates that the case has citing references but no direct or negative indirect history.

★★★★   Depth of treatment stars indicate how extensively a cited case has been discussed by the citing case.

99   Quotation marks indicate that the citing case directly quotes the cited case.

Pinpoint citations allow you to jump instantly to where the cited case is discussed.

Only decisions which directly affect the result in the case being checked are considered part of its case or direct history. A decision need not be reversed or modified by a higher court, however, to have its status as authority diminished or erased. Subsequent unrelated decisions, by overruling the case or limiting its holding, may yet have an important impact on its status as precedent.

3. Treatment and Related Cases

A case often yields a list of subsequent citing references. In a *Shepard's* display, these citing references immediately follow any parallel citations and case history citations.[10] Both citators provide several ways of

---

10   Note that, for the *Bonds* case, *Shepard's* lists **81** citing references, and *KeyCite* lists **281**. There is an explanation for this discrepancy. The coverage of secondary materials (law reviews, bar journals, treatises, etc.) is different in *Shepard's* and *KeyCite – KeyCite* simply lists every instance of a citing reference in its database while *Shepard's* limits the titles in which it finds citing references.

indicating the attitudes toward the case expressed by later courts or what aspects of the cited case are discussed. The treatment of a case by later decisions may have just as important an effect on its precedential value as a direct reversal or affirmance. Courts do not like to reverse themselves for a variety of reasons, so they may seek other means to weaken a precedent by limiting its application to very restricted circumstances. A lower court that is faced with a distasteful decision from a higher court may seek to maneuver around it, distinguishing it from the case at hand by one fact or another. Such treatment can kill the power of a precedent with a thousand small cuts. You need to know about such treatment.

The different manner in which *Shepard's* and *KeyCite* handle the issue of the treatment of a case is one of the main theoretical differences between the two systems. Over the decades *Shepard's* print citators developed a system for indicating if the citing reference had a specific effect upon the cited case. If the case that was citing yours met *Shepard's* internally developed and rigorous standards indicating a particular style of treatment, a letter would be assigned to it – e.g. an "o" for overruled. The judgment of whether the citing case should have such a letter appended was made by editors at *Shepard's*. These editors were known for being conservative. Oddly, many lawyers did not know the specific meaning of each letter abbreviation,[11] but every researcher knew that a case that cited his **and** had a letter assigned to it was worth reading. It was like tagging the citing case as important. This conservative approach remains in place, but online you are no longer faced with cryptic letters – the treatments are spelled out.

If you only check the number of citing cases, you'll find the numbers are much closer – 38 for *Shepard's* and 37 for *KeyCite*.

11   A table explaining the abbreviations appears in the beginning pages of every printed *Shepard's*, as in Illustration E. Still, many lawyers never bothered to understand the letter designations.

Illustration E
A Chart of the *Shepard's* Editorial Analysis Codes for Cases, as
defined by *Shepard's*.

PRINT	ONLINE	DEFINITION
a	Affirmed	On appeal, reconsideration or rehearing, the citing case affirms or adheres to the case you are Shepardizing.
c	Criticized	The citing opinion disagrees with the reasoning/result of the case you are Shepardizing, although the citing court may not have the authority to materially affect its precedential value.
d	Distinguished	The citing case differs from the case you are Shepardizing, either involving dissimilar facts or requiring a different application of law.
e	Explained	The citing opinion interprets or clarifies the case you are Shepardizing in a significant way
f	Followed	The citing opinion relies on the case you are Shepardizing as controlling or persuasive authority.
l	Limited	The citing opinion restricts the application of the case you are Shepardizing, finding that its reasoning applies only in specific, limited circumstances.
m	Modified	On appeal, reconsideration or rehearing, the citing case modifies or changes in some way, including affirmance in part and reversal in part, the case you are Shepardizing.
o	Overruled	The citing case expressly overrules or disapproves all or part of the case you are Shepardizing.
q	Questioned	The citing opinion questions the continuing validity or precedential value of the case you are Shepardizing because of intervenening circumstances, including judicial or legislative overruling.
r	Reversed	On appeal, reconsideration or rehearing, the citing case reverses the case you are Shepardizing.

KeyCite uses a different method for alerting you to the treatment of her case. The designers of *KeyCite* reasoned that once you have found our if the subsequent citing case has overruled or reversed your case, what you really want to know is which cases treat yours at length. *KeyCite* was designed to point to how much discussion of a case is contained in the citing reference. A system of stars tells you how extensive the treatment of your case is – a paragraph, a few sentences, only a mention -- and whether language from your case is actually quoted by the citing court. Rather than using the letters that indicate certain events, *KeyCite* uses depth of treatment. These systems will be set out in more detail below.

In the case or direct history sections of a citator listing, the references are to the beginning page (or citation) of the relevant case. In the treatment section, on the other hand, a reference to the exact page within a decision on which the case is cited is given in addition to the beginning page. These "pin-point" page references allow the researcher to use a hypertext link that brings them to the exact place in the opinion where the case is being discussed. Both *KeyCite* and *Shepard's* assign words or phrases to some citations in the treatment section to indicate the attitude or effect of the citing court. It is important to note that in assigning these notations, the specific language of the citing court is largely relied upon. *Shepard's* editors have, in particular, developed a reputation for being conservative, and hence they will not indicate that a case has been overruled if such effect is not expressly stated in the later decision, no matter how contrary the holding.[12] This is one reason why this particular citator had such universal acceptance for so long. Other indicators, such as "distinguished" or "questioned" may be just as

---

12   For over thirty years, *Shepard's United States Citations* indicated that the separate-but-equal doctrine of *Plessy v. Ferguson*, 163 U.S. 537 (1896), was questioned in *Brown v. Board of Education*, 347 U.S. 483 (1954), rather than overruled by *Brown*. Only when Judge John R. Brown noted this fact in a recent opinion, *United States v. Holmes*, 822 F.2d 481, 503 n.2 (5th Cir. 1987) (Brown, J., concurring and dissenting), did Shepard's add a belated "overruled" notation into its *Plessy* entry. Although *Shepard's* follows the express words of opinions, it can occasionally be swayed by later criticism.

important as an "overruled" in determining the precedential value of a decision.[13]

The citations in the treatment section of a *Shepard's* listing are arranged by court. Decisions from the same jurisdiction as the cited case are listed first. If cases from the court of last resort and from an intermediate appellate court are published in separate reports, the high court's decisions precede those of the appellate court. Within the listing for each reporter, however, citations are listed chronologically. There is no ranking by importance or effect on the cited case. A citation to an overruling case may appear towards the end of a long list of other cases. Depending on the jurisdiction of the case you are researching, citing references in federal cases and decisions from other jurisdictions follow the list of citations from the cited source's jurisdiction.

KeyCite arranges the citing reference by first dividing them between "Negative Cases" (repeating those listed on the initial screen

---

13   In *Glassalum Engineering Corp. v. 392208 Ontario Ltd.*, 487 So.2d 87 (Fla.App. 1986), the appellee relied on a case, *Gonzalez v. Ryder Systems, Inc.*, 327 So.2d 826 (Fla.App. 1976), the holding of which had been abrogated by an amendment to the Florida Rules of Civil Procedure. As the court noted:

> By Shepardizing the *Gonzalez* case, one would have been alerted that its soundness or reasoning had been questioned in a later case; and by reading that later case, *Rivera v. A.M.I.F., Inc.*, 417 So.2d 304, one would have discovered that *Gonzalez* is no longer the law.

> If counsel did not observe Shepard's "questioned" signal (designated by a "q") and read *Rivera*, then they, at the least, performed inadequately: appellant's counsel (now the beneficiary of this court's own research) lost the opportunity to argue the controlling *Rivera* case; appellee's counsel, the opportunity to attempt to convince this court why we should not, as we do, find *Rivera* dispositive. Without belaboring the point, we remind the bar that, as this case so dramatically shows, cases must be Shepardized and that when Shepardizing, counsel must mind the "p's" and "q's." 487 So.2d at 88 (footnotes omitted).

under "Negative Indirect History") and "Positive Cases." Under the "positive" label, the citing references are then separated by the depth of treatment a court gives to the cited case. A court that "examined" the cited case will have a discussion of a page or more, where the cited case is "discussed" there will be a paragraph or more, and where "cited" the discussion will be less than a paragraph, but more than a sentence. As a visual clue, *KeyCite* assigns stars to reflect the amount of discussion within the citing references, i.e., an "examined" case gets four stars, a "discussed" case gets three, and so on. Within each of these divisions, cases are arranged by jurisdiction and chronology. Unpublished cases will appear last, at the bottom of each section, no matter what the jurisdiction. This is due to their markedly limited value as precedent. Additionally, *KeyCite* indicates if the citing reference directly quotes the case being researched by placing quotation marks next to the citing reference. A direct quotation of a decision can be powerful. All of this extra information is extremely useful to a researcher who must evaluate the state of the law efficiently and expeditiously.

The citators employ another notation system to aid researchers interested in particular points of law in the cited case. Citing references indicate the headnote number of the cited case corresponding to the specific issue being discussed. If a case addresses several issues but only one aspect is relevant to a particular research problem, one simply determines which headnote or syllabus paragraph addresses the issue and scans the listing for that number.

There is an important difference between *Shepard's* and *KeyCite* regarding the treatment of headnotes. *Shepard's* distinguishes between official and unofficial citations in a critical way. That is, *Shepard's* tracks both official and unofficial headnotes when a case appears in more than one publication. You control which headnotes are being tracked by the citation you type into the system. If you use the (official) citation to the *Wisconsin Reporter* the headnotes tracked will be keyed to that publication's editorial treatment. If you type in the *North Western Reporter* citation, then the headnote numbers will be those for the West (unofficial) reporter. A frequent mistake researchers make is to look for the headnote numbers from one edition while scanning the *Shepard's* listing under a parallel citation. At this time, *KeyCite* tracks *only* the Thomson-West headnotes, which are part of the West Key Number System.

Since the citing references found presumably touch upon some or all of the legal issues involved in the original case, a citator can function as a tool for finding related cases. However, any of the later cases listed may make only passing reference to the cited case, particularly if the citation does not include a raised headnote number indicating a specific point under discussion. *KeyCite* has attempted to address this issue with its depth of treatment indicators. Later cases that deal with similar issues but do not expressly cite the original case will not be found through the citators. For these reasons citators are just one possible tool used for finding cases on a particular topic.

For some cases there are few or no citing references in *Shepard's* or *KeyCite*. In such situations a citator is of little help in a search for related cases. The fact that no citations can be found, however, may itself have some meaning. Several court decisions have mentioned the lack of citations as an indication that earlier decisions are of limited merit or scope.[14]

4. Secondary Material and Annotations

Finally, after the references to citing cases, *Shepard's* and *KeyCite* listings include citations indicating when a decision has been mentioned in secondary sources and annotations. These may include bar journals, law reviews, Attorney General opinions or references in *American Law Reports* (*ALR*). Finding an *ALR* annotation which cites one's case may open a door into an entirely new area of research. An article in a law review or bar journal may provide useful background or may place one's case in context. Again, citators can be a crucial center of the research process.

---

14 In *Meadow Brook National Bank v. Recile*, 302 F.Supp. 62, 82 (E.D. La. 1969), the federal district court in applying Louisiana law noted that an 1865 Louisiana Supreme Court case relied upon by the plaintiff was "clearly a maverick decision ... totally ignored by every subsequent decision on the subject."

The courts in *Jeffres v. Countryside Homes of Lincoln, Inc.*, 333 N.W.2d 754, 764 (Neb. 1983), and *Amalgamated Casualty Insurance Co. v. Helms*, 212 A.2d 311, 319 (Md. 1965), used the absence of citations to denigrate decisions from other states which they did not care to follow.

Finally, the listing may also include reference to one or more of the many legal treatises. These are included not only for their scholarly or practical value, but also because they are issued by the same publisher.

D. OTHER CITATORS

1. Looseleaf Services

Some specialized looseleaf services publish sets of citator volumes for cases in their subject area, such as the *American Law of Products Liability Citator*, the *Standard Federal Tax Reporter Citator*, and the *Federal Taxes Citator*. For general research, these are materials which serve some of the same purposes as a *Shepard's* or *KeyCite* citator. Each such set stands on its own and it must be evaluated along the lines set out in Chapter 10.

2. Parallel Citation Tables

The *National Reporter Blue Book*, published by Thomson-West and supplemented annually, consists of lists of case citations for every volume of official reports, with cross-references to National Reporter System citations. For example, using our *Flambeau* citation from Appendix A, the listing for volume 116 of *Callaghan's Wisconsin Reports, Second Series* at page 95 shown in Illustration F, gives a parallel citation to volume 341, page 655 of *West's North Western Reporter, Second Series*.

For approximately half of the states, Thomson-West publishes a *Blue and White Book*, which also has parallel citation tables from regional reporter locations to official reports. The blue pages in one of these volumes duplicates the information provided in the *National Reporter Blue Book*, with parallel citations from the official reports to the regional reporter; the white pages provide the opposite references, from the regional reporter to the official reports. A state's *Blue and White Book* is usually only available in that state.

Parallel citations, of course, can often be found without the use of either a citator or a book of conversion tables. If an official citation is available at the time the regional reporter goes to press, it is provided at the beginning of the decision. Most of the official reports indicate the *National Reporter System* locations of their cases, although several follow the lead of the *United States Reports* and do not supply this useful piece of information.

Illustration F
Partial Page From the *National Reporter Blue Book*
Showing *Flambeau* parallel citation

116 CALLAGHAN'S WISCONSIN REPORTS, SECOND SERIES

Wis.2d Pg.	Vol.	N.W.2d Pg.	Wis.2d Pg.	Vol.	N.W.2d Pg.	Wis.2d Pg.	Vol.	N.W.2d Pg.	Wis.2d Pg.	Vol.	N.W.2d Pg.
1	342	27	289	342	750	493	342	426	693	343	826
23	341	389	298	341	721	510	343	108	694	343	826
35	341	395	305	342	451	537	342	693	694	343	827
40	341	397	322	342	56	550	342	435	695	343	827
61	341	639	331	342	60	559	342	699	696	343	827
95	341	655	339	342	64	580	342	709	696	343	828
122	341	668	347	341	725	605	342	721	697	345	62
150	341	682	352	342	68	629	342	734	698	345	62
166	342	37	360	342	258	645	342	741	698	345	63
206	341	689	371	342	243	650	342	744	699	345	63
217	341	693	374	342	244	657	344	190	700	345	63
227	341	716	380	342	406	664	342	755	700	345	64
239	342	747	388	342	682	672	343	122	701	345	64
246	342	440	410	342	415	679	343	126	702	345	64
254	342	247	432	342	410	683	342	759	702	345	65
268	342	444	443	343	391	687	343	814	703	345	65
281	342	254	477	343	100						

E. SUMMARY

Citators will appear throughout this volume, not only as a means of checking the status of cases but as a basic tool for finding and analyzing case law. It may appear a strange and uninviting system of seemingly endless lists at first. As with many new things, experience will show not only the value of the systems, but their simplicity in use.

The current status of primary sources other than cases also needs to be verified. Statutes may be repealed or amended by the legislature, or declared unconstitutional by a court; regulations may be superseded and treaties abrogated. As these primary sources are introduced in later chapters, means for determining their status, including *Shepard's* citations, will be explained.

F. ADDITIONAL READING

Michael J. Lynch, "Citators in the Early Twentieth Century—Not Just Shepard's," 16 *Legal Reference Serv. Quarterly* 5 (1998).

Patti Ogden, " 'Mastering the Lawless Science of Our Law': A Story of Legal Citation Indexes," 85 *Law Libr. J.* 1 (1993). A discussion of citation services from before Frank Shepard's time to the present.

Mary Rumsey, "Runaway Train: Problems of Permanence, Accessibility, and Stability in the Use of Web Sources in Law Review Citations," 94 *Law Libr. J.* 27 (2002).

Fred R. Shapiro, *Collected Papers on Legal Citation Analysis* (Fred B. Rothman 2001).

Frank Shepard Company, *A Record of Fifty Years of Specializing in a Field that is of First Importance to the Bench and Bar of the United States: An Insight into an Establishment that has Grown from Small Beginnings to the First Rank in the Law Publishing Field* (Frank Shepard Co. 1923). Of interest only to bibliographic types, but full of laudatory prose and early photographs of *Shepard's* staffers at work.

How to Use Shepard's Citations: A Presentation of the Scope and Functions of Shepard's Citation Books and Services with Methods and Techniques to Enhance their Value in Legal Research (Shepard's/McGraw-Hill 1986). A helpful manual, and proof that the publisher still can wield an imposing book title.

Chapter 4

FINDING CASES

A. INTRODUCTION

A "cold" search for case law by subject is never a good idea. Ideally, you will search for cases with some information already in hand. You will know the name of one good case, or have a specific statute reference. Sadly, life is not always ideal. You may have to launch your search with very little more than a question in your mind. If this is the situation, what can you do? While the process is not always easy, it turns out that there is a great deal you can do.

Millions of cases have been decided by the state and federal courts of the United States. Finding the one case that you need is a neat trick, indeed. In the classic movie, *Anatomy of a Murder*, Jimmy Stewart plays a lawyer who is trying to construct a defense for his client. He is shown standing in a law library. He whirls, grabs a volume of case reports off the shelf, opens it and – voila! – he finds the case he needs. This method of case finding, (which we call the Zen Archery method), has the advantage of being both quick and easy. Sadly, your odds of success are akin to buying a lottery ticket as a means of paying your law school tuition. Therefore, this Chapter is devoted to how to find the case that meets your research needs.

It is crucial to keep in mind that when you find a relevant case, you are finding more than just a single opinion. If the case, or part of it, speaks to the issue that you care about, you will have a variety of research leads. The case itself will cite other relevant cases and statutes and thus provide an entry into the history of the topic. You will be able to follow the case and see where it has been cited over time so that you can get a feel for the developments in the law. You can take parts of the case tagged by one of the two great research systems operated by Thomson-West and LexisNexis to find other sources. The case that you find is not an end in itself; finding one good case is often the gateway to a whole world of research.

This chapter will be divided into the following sections:

- **Finding Your Case by Using WESTLAW or LEXIS**
- **Finding Your Case Using Paper Based Methods**
- **The Best Method for Finding Cases**

We emphasize that cold searching for a case by subject should be done only as a last resort. You need to understand the context of your search if you are to have any chance at all. If you come to the research problem with some context you may have the names of relevant cases in hand already. You will also likely have the very jargon words that will make online searching easier. Looking for a case without context, whether you use databases, the Internet, digests or an Ouija board will always be a tough go.

We are unable to discuss subject searching in the abstract, so we will use the following hypothetical search situation as an example:

> *Assume that you are concerned with the question of whether a prenuptial contract that is signed without the advice of a lawyer is valid. How would you find cases that might help you?*

First, context. A few moments with a hornbook, nutshell or something like the *Martindale Hubble Law Digest* to get a working knowledge of the basic concepts and vocabulary will greatly improve your chances of finding a relevant case.

We begin the discussion with finding cases using WESTLAW and LEXIS. As realists we recognize that those are the tools that most researchers, certainly most who read this book, will be using. We will then discuss the traditional digest systems. We discuss the digest systems in some detail because you should understand the structure upon which the new systems are built. If you understand the foundations of an information system, then you will understand it in whatever manner it evolves.

B. FINDING YOUR CASE USING WESTLAW AND LEXIS

WESTLAW and LEXIS are each full-text databases that contain every word of every decision[1] of the state and federal courts. Each also contains a universe of other documents as well. But each is much more than a repository of documents because each contains a powerful set of

---

1   Including all published and many unpublished decisions.

search tools that allow you to locate that "one good case." While you are in law school you will have access to both systems and we encourage you to experiment using each one. All the of the studies show that people settle into using one or the other very early on, and are sometimes heavily influenced by the one that they learned first in law school. You may find that the first one you are trained on works just fine, so you may not want to bother with the other. This would be an error. The systems have significant differences, strengths and weaknesses. One may fit you, or your situation, much better than the other. Experiment! Use your law school years, when both systems are readily available, to become proficient in both.

We will discuss the basic methods used for searching WESTLAW and LEXIS. It is important that you understand them, but understanding them will not be enough to make you a good researcher. WESTLAW and LEXIS are filled with features and new ones are added every day.

The only effective way to master either one is to take the training that they offer and read the materials that they have prepared. Everyone knows that no one ever reads the training manuals, so if you are the one person who takes the time to do so, you will sound like a research guru.

1. Boolean or Free-Text Keyword Searching

The original search engine featured in both LEXIS and WESTLAW was Boolean[2] or free-text keyword searching. (We will use the term Boolean from here on out.) Boolean operators allow you to search a database and ask to see any documents that contain whatever term or terms you specify. Major search engines like *Google* and web directories like *Yahoo!* use Boolean connectors. Unless you are a computer 'phobe you have already practiced the Boolean dance of adding and subtracting terms until you get what you think is a good result.

The power of Boolean searching is that it uses the brute strength of computer power to search every document for the word or words that you specify. The computer does not err, tire or need breaks. The weakness of Boolean searching is two-fold. First, computers are dumb; they only do what they are told. They do not intuit, analogize or make

---

2   "Boolean" refers to a system of logical thought developed by the English mathematician and computer pioneer, George Boole (1815-64).

cognitive leaps. Maybe some day they will, but that day is not yet upon us. Thus, the computer will only retrieve the documents specified in a Boolean search.

Second, most people are not very good at Boolean searching. Even worse, most people think that they are very good at it and this overconfidence makes things far more dire. Because most searches return results, the researcher may believe she has found the desired results. That is not the case. The computer system is just spitting out the cases that fit the search. They might be the perfect cases or they might be a list of losers that are nowhere near what you want. Over-confidence can lead to serious embarrassment or worse.

The core problem with Boolean searching is the dilemma of precision and recall. If you have the skill to create a search that is broad enough to pull in every document that might be relevant, you will end up with a search that returns a great deal of junk. So much junk, in fact, that you will not want to sort through it all. If you are skilled enough to design a search that retrieves only documents that are useful you will be excluding some documents that you would like to see. This dilemma was beautifully described by Dan Dabney in his brilliant article, "The Curse of Thamus," written in 1986.[3] Dabney, who has been a law librarian, a lawyer, a professor and is also one of the creators of *KeyCite*, set out the concepts of human indexing and Boolean searching in this article. He concluded that in a large database there will be an inevitable precision/recall problem. We require students who take Advanced Legal Research at Boalt Hall Law School to read his article. We advise you to read it as well. Boolean searching can accomplish great things, but you must view your results with a very large grain of salt.

What we intend to do is discuss the variations on Boolean searching that WESTLAW and LEXIS make available to you. We will preach a bit about grabbing every advantage that you can in the search process. Then we will offer some tips. We emphasize again that the only way to improve your skills is by taking the training that WESTLAW and LEXIS offer to you. Only hands-on training will work. WESTLAW and LEXIS change constantly. What we write in the Spring of 2005 will

---

3 Daniel Dabney, "The Curse of Thamus: An Analysis of Full-Text Legal Document Retrieval," 78 *Law Library J.* 5 (1986).

be outdated the moment that we write it. Each company invests serious
money to provide trainers and support material. Use them.

a. Approaches to Boolean Searching

(1) Terms and Connectors

(a) "And" and "Or"

At its most basic, Boolean searching allows you to search for a
unique word. Remember our question. Let's say you decided that you
want to see every case in California that uses the word "prenuptial." Just
plug the word "prenuptial" into WESTLAW or LEXIS and you will find all
such cases. But you are not limited to searching for one term. Perhaps
you would like to see all cases that use the word "prenuptial" and the
word "lawyer." You can enter more than one term. This is done by
using connectors. There are two basis connectors: "or" and "and."

- "or" expands the cases you retrieve. Using "or" tells the
  computer to find cases which have either the term before the
  "or" or after the "or." If you ask for:

prenuptial or lawyer

  you will be given the citation to all cases containing either the
  word "prenuptial" or the word "lawyer."

- "and" restricts the cases that you retrieve. Using "and" tells the
  computer to find cases which have both the terms before and
  after the "and." If you ask for:

prenuptial and lawyer

  you will be given citations to cases that contain both prenuptial
  and lawyer.

Terms and connectors are very good at certain types of searches.
If you are searching for an uncommon word like "porcupine" or
"elderberry" it is fast and effective. The same will hold true if you are
searching for a statute by its unique number or the alphanumeric phrase

that makes up a docket number. But the more common your search term is, the harder it will be to catch what you want. Some of the problems are inherent in the English language.

Synonyms. The computer can only search for the words that you specify. In our example, it will turn out that judges sometimes use the terms "premarital" or "ante-nuptial" instead of "prenuptial." The computer will not know this and will miss the cases that use those alternative words. You can fight this by including more and more synonyms, but the longer the search grows, the more problems of precision it will have. WESTLAW and LEXIS work to help you here by retrieving plurals automatically, but that does not help solve the synonym problem.

Ambiguous Terms. Some words have more than one meaning in common usage; some words acquire an extra meaning because of the way that they are used in the law. Think of the word "consideration." In daily use, "consideration" has a set of meanings. In the world of contract law, the terms take on a whole new meaning. The computer system cannot tell the difference.

Stop Words. Both systems will exclude a list of words that are too common to search. Worlds like "the" or "a" occur too frequently to be effective search terms. The systems automatically drop them. Other words are common in legal usage. The word "lawyer" in our search here is just too common and occurs in too many contexts to be useful.

Misspellings. Sometimes the Court misspells a word. The computer will not recognize this and may miss a case that you need. When there was a rash of cases concerning the drug diethylstilbestrol (DES) almost no one spelled it correctly. But the word does not have to be such a mind bender to present the same problem.

Concepts. Boolean searching works best when searching for a specific thing, like a porcupine, but it is very bad if you are searching for a legal concept, like duty of care in Torts. No combination of words will pull up the cases conceptually. Unfortunately, this applies to much of what you will look for in legal research. You are far more likely to be searching for cases on duty of care than for cases about porcupines.

(b) Proximity Connectors

Proximity connectors allow you to tell the systems to search for cases where your terms occur in a certain relationship to one another. WESTLAW and LEXIS allow you to ask the system to find your terms when they are within a specified number of words of each other. Hence you could type in:

(prenuptial or premarital) w/10 contract

With this instruction the system will find cases that use either the word "premarital" or the word "prenuptial" within ten words of the word contract.

In addition to allowing you to ask the system to retrieve only those cases in which the words exist within a specified number of words of one another, they allow you to search using grammatical structures. You can ask that your words be used in the same sentence or paragraph. If you type in:

(premarital or prenuptial) w/s contract

The systems will retrieve cases where the word "premarital" or the word "prenuptial" are used in the same sentence as the word "contract."

Proximity connectors are powerful aids in focusing your research, but they are not always easy to use. It can be hard to predict just how a judge will use words. Nor do the proximity connectors obviate the vagaries of Boolean searching that we discussed in the preceding section. Each system also allows you to specify what order your words are to be used in the system. While the ideal of requiring that the words be used in the same sentence or paragraph seems eminently reasonable, even this can be tricky. You will have to worry about such issues as, "exactly what is a paragraph?" given the use of quotations and indenting in some decisions. You may not have considered such issues since high school, and judges are allowed to make up their own rules.

Here is a chart of some of the terms and connectors used in WESTLAW and LEXIS. Note the small differences.

Table 1
Commonly Used Terms and Connectors in LEXIS

Definition	LEXIS Connector
and	and
or	or
phrase	(defaults to phrase searching)
within n words	w/n
precedes by n words	pre/n
in same paragraph	w/p
in same segment	w/seg
in same sentence	w/s
and not	and not
root expander	!
universal character	*

Table 2
Commonly Used Terms and Connectors in WESTLAW

Definition	WESTLAW Connector
and	&
or	(space)
phrase	" "
within n words	/n
in same paragraph	/p
in same sentence	/s
precedes in same sentence	+s
and not	%
root expander	!
universal character	*

(c) Using Segment Searching

When judicial decisions are put into the WESTLAW or LEXIS database as the parts of each case are tagged. This tagging allows you to search only that particular part of the decision. The component parts of a decision like *In re Marriage of Bonds* from Chapter 2 can be searched as segments. The caption of the case becomes a quick way to locate a case by name. You may want to find all the decisions of a particular judge. Searching only the text of the headnotes in WESTLAW or LEXIS allows you to search the case summaries prepared by editors who try to use what is called "normalized language." Using normalized language means that the editors try to be consistent in how they use terms and in how they express concepts. This helps to control the problems of synonyms, ambiguity and imprecision discussed above. Searching only a segment can be a big help.

(d) Locate and Focus

While there is no way that we can hope to describe all of the special features of WESTLAW and LEXIS as part of this Chapter, we do want to highlight two of our favorite ones. These would be Locate on WESTLAW and Focus on LEXIS. Once you have run a search and have your initial results, these features allow you to run a second search, this time using only your initial results or part of your results, as a database. You can Focus and Locate as many times as you wish to keep narrowing your list of results.

Each time you run a search in WESTLAW or LEXIS you are creating your own custom database. Using segments can make the set of cases that you search smaller and hence help you with the precision/recall dilemma, but Focus and Locate are even more efficient for narrowing the body of information that must be searched. These are powerful aids to Boolean searching and we urge you to use them.

2. Natural Language Searching

Both WESTLAW and LEXIS offer you the chance to eschew Boolean searching and instead to input your search as a normal sentence. Using an algorithm that the systems keep proprietary (they will not disclose how they work),[4] your search will be parsed and your results will be ranked by what the system feels is important. Each system uses a default system for returning these cases. WESTLAW will list the "best" 20 cases; LEXIS will list the "best" 100 cases. Some of these may be of very little use, but you will get that many every time unless you change the default. This can fool the neophyte searcher into thinking that they have found the good cases. All you are finding are the cases that best meet your search as WESTLAW or LEXIS determines – you will never get

---

[4]   While we don't know how the algorithms work exactly, we can make some educated guesses by looking at the results. For instance, cases which use more of the words in your natural language search will be closer to the top of the results list; cases that use the words in your search more often will be closer to the top of your results list; and cases where the words in your search are found more closely grouped together will be nearer to the top of your results list.

zero results with a natural language search, you will always get the default number.

With the caveat of the above paragraph in mind, natural language searching can be a great tool. It does not offer you the control of Boolean searching so it may make you uneasy, but the computer can often make links that you would not have seen. The key here is to put as much into your natural language search as possible. Unlike Boolean searching, where we advise you to be lean, in a natural language search we advise you to be as expansive as possible.

Echoing earlier advice, law school is a great place to try natural language searching. Run some problems in both Boolean and natural language searching. See how your results differ. Find a comfort zone while you aren't being charged for every search.

Here are some natural language searches that we ran in WESTLAW and LEXIS on March 1, 2005 in search of cases on the need for representation when signing a prenuptial contract. Results will be similar in both databases when searching the same cases.

Table 3
Examples of Searches Run in the LEXIS, CA State Cases Database

Search Terms	# of Results	Comments
Prenuptial or attorney	>3000	Precision was very poor. Too many cases contain the term "attorney" for this search to be of any use.
Prenuptial and attorney	73	*In re Bonds* is the first case, but then poor precision because of many "attorney fee" cases.

TABLE 3, continued

Search Terms	# of Results	Comments
Prenuptial and lawyer	16	Better precision because the attorney fee cases were not necessarily included. This search captured *In re Bonds* and other relevant cases.
Premarital agreement and attorney	55	Some relevant cases.
(premarital or prenuptial) and (attorney or lawyer)	170	Poor precision. The first case mentioned premarital adolescent sexual relations.
Premarital or prenuptial) w/25 (independent council)	0	Typo!
(premarital or prenuptial) w/25 (independent counsel)	11	Many relevant cases.

Table 4
Natural Language Search in WESTLAW, CA-CS Database

Search	Results
"Is it necessary to have independent counsel for a premarital agreement to be valid"	*In re Marriage of Bonds* was the first case listed. Several other relevant cases.

3. Subject Searching

a. *KeySearch* and *Search Advisor*

The section that follows will explore the great subject systems of the past, but it is worth noting that WESTLAW and LEXIS have devised new subject systems to help you locate cases. WESTLAW calls its system *KeySearch*, LEXIS calls its system *Search Advisor*. Each work the same way. Cases are grouped by subject, with large initial classifications such as "Family Law" leading to smaller, more precise categories such as "Premarital Contracts." If you use one of these searching systems you gain two advantages.

First, an intervening intelligence has created a subject structure for you. "Family Law" as a subject has been organized into a system that tracks the legal developments in the area. If you are unfamiliar with Family Law, it will allow you to click through and see the accepted existing categories. As you become a more sophisticated researcher, you may reject these categories as not fitting your needs, but as someone new to a subject area it can be a convenient method for organizing your thoughts. It is also a great introduction to the jargon words in an area.

Second, if you search in one of these subject databases you will be searching a much smaller body of cases. All research shows that the smaller the body of information you search, the better your results will be. You can use either Boolean or natural language searching with *Search Advisor* or *KeySearch*.

These systems are being refined daily. Using them well takes a bit of extra effort but it can pay big rewards. Below are screen shots to show the "breadcrumb" trail to a case on our issue of premarital contracts using each system:

Illustration A-1
LEXIS Screen Shot Showing the "Breadcrumb" Trail to Prenuptial Agreement Cases in *Search Advisor*

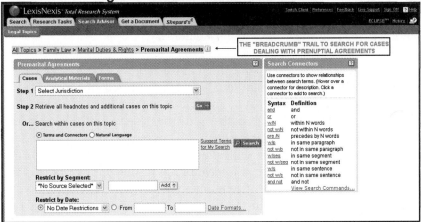

Illustration A-2
WESTLAW Screen Shot Showing the "Breadcrumb" Trail to
Prenuptial Agreement Cases in *KeySearch*

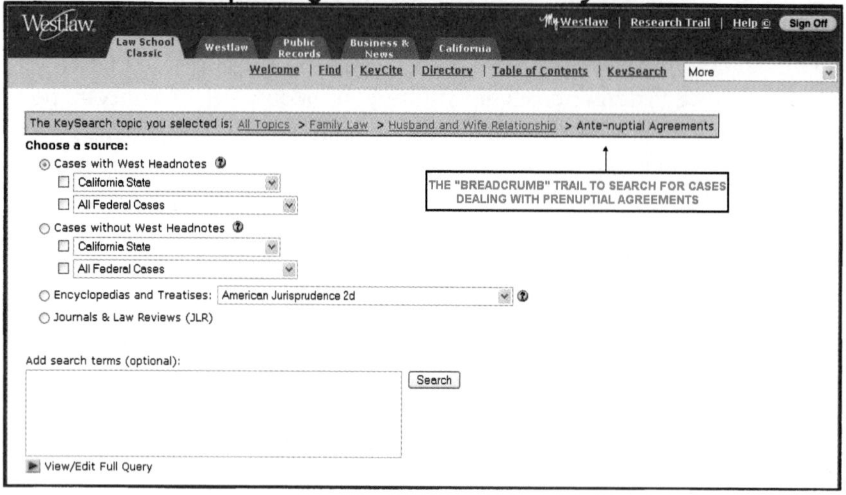

4. Headnotes

In Chapter 2 we discussed headnotes. Each headnote is an abstract of a point of law decided in the judicial opinion. If you click to the number at the beginning of a headnote, you are linked to the discussion that it summarizes so that you can see the language that the editor was reading when she wrote her summary.

Each headnote is also classified into a subject system. The editor attempts to summarize the point of law that is discussed and to put it into a subject system. In WESTLAW, this classification leads you into the Digest system that will be discussed in the next section of this Chapter. In LEXIS, you will be lead into the LEXIS system of organizing cases. Linking from the headnotes will allow you to move into a world of indexed information. Editors will have set up a structure for you so that you can find other cases that discuss the point of law that interests you. It can be quite powerful. Illustrations B-1 & B-2 and C-1 & C-2 show you a headnote and the template the systems provide to help you find more cases assigned the same headnote.

Illustration B-1
The First Headnote of In re Bonds, as seen on WESTLAW

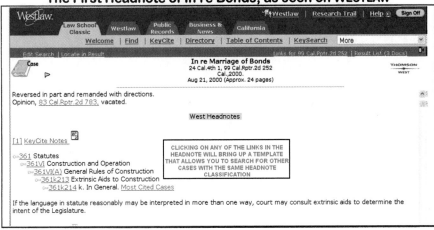

Illustration B-2
The Template that Allows You to Search for Other Cases with the Same Headnote

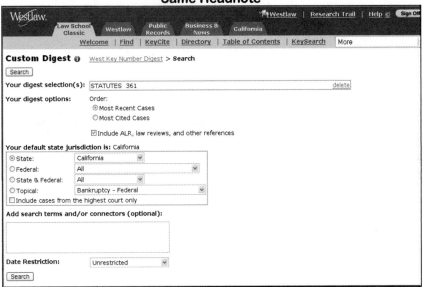

Illustration C-1
The First Headnote from In Re Bonds, as seen on LEXIS

LexisNexis Total Research System

Switch Client | Preferences | Feedback | Live Support | Sign Off | Help

Search | Research Tasks | Search Advisor | Get a Document | Shepard's®

ECLIPSE™ | History

FOCUS™ Terms | Search Within All Documents | Go | FOCUS Options...

View: Case Brief | Full | Custom 1 of 1 FAST Print... Print | Download | Fax | Email | Text Only

More Like This | More Like Selected Text | Shepardize® | TOA

In re Marriage of Bonds, 24 Cal. 4th 1 (Copy w/ Cite) Pages: 41

Service: Get by LEXSEE®
Citation: 24 Cal. 4th 1

24 Cal. 4th 1, *; 5 P.3d 815, **;
99 Cal. Rptr. 2d 252, ***; 2000 Cal. LEXIS 6117

In re the Marriage of SUSANN MARGRETH BONDS and BARRY LAMAR BONDS. SUSANN MARGRETH BONDS, Appellant, v. BARRY LAMAR BONDS, Respondent.

No. S079760.

SUPREME COURT OF CALIFORNIA

24 Cal. 4th 1; 5 P.3d 815; 99 Cal. Rptr. 2d 252; 2000 Cal. LEXIS 6117; 2000 Cal. Daily Op. Service 6982; 2000 Daily Journal DAR 9250

August 21, 2000, Decided

SUBSEQUENT HISTORY: Rehearing Denied October 18, 2000, Reported at: 2000 Cal. LEXIS 8073.

PRIOR HISTORY: Superior Court of San Mateo County. Super. Ct. No. F-19162. Judith W. Kozloski, Judge.

Court of Appeal of California, First Appellate District, Division Two. Nos. A075328 and A076586.

DISPOSITION: The judgment of the Court of Appeal is reversed to the extent that it reversed the judgment of the trial court on the issue of the voluntariness of the premarital agreement. The matter is remanded to the Court of Appeal to determine whether, consistent with this opinion, its remand to the trial court for reevaluation of the termination of spousal support remains necessary, and to consider other issues it declared moot in light of its determination that the agreement was not enforceable: namely, (1) whether the trial court denied Sun due process by excluding evidence supporting her claim that Barry should be estopped from enforcing the agreement, and (2) whether the trial court erred in various respects in interpreting and enforcing the agreement.

LexisNexis(R) Headnotes ◆ Hide Headnotes

Family Law > Divorce, Dissolution & Spousal Support > Property Distribution > Community Property

HN1 Property acquired by spouses during marriage, including earnings, is community property. Cal. Fam. Code § 760. More Like This Headnote ← THIS LINK TAKES YOU TO A TEMPLATE FOR MORE CASES WITH THIS HEADNOTE

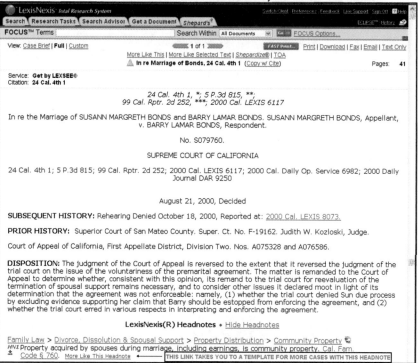

Illustration C-2
The Template that Allows you to Search for Other Cases with the Same Headnote

LexisNexis Total Research System

Switch Client | Preferences | Feedback | Live Support | Sign Off | Help

Search | Research Tasks | Search Advisor | Get a Document | Shepard's®

ECLIPSE™ | History

More Like This Headnote

HN1 - Property acquired by spouses during marriage, including earnings, is community property. Cal. Fam. Code § 760.

Jurisdiction: Coverage Dates

Federal and State Courts:	All Federal & State Courts, Combined
Combined Federal Courts:	All Federal Courts
US Supreme Court	
US Courts of Appeals:	All US Courts of Appeals
US District Courts:	All District Courts
US Special Courts:	US Court of Federal Claims
State Courts:	All State Courts, Combined

Optional: Restrict by Date

No Date Restrictions | From ____ To ____

In the future, run search automatically and skip this page

Search | Cancel

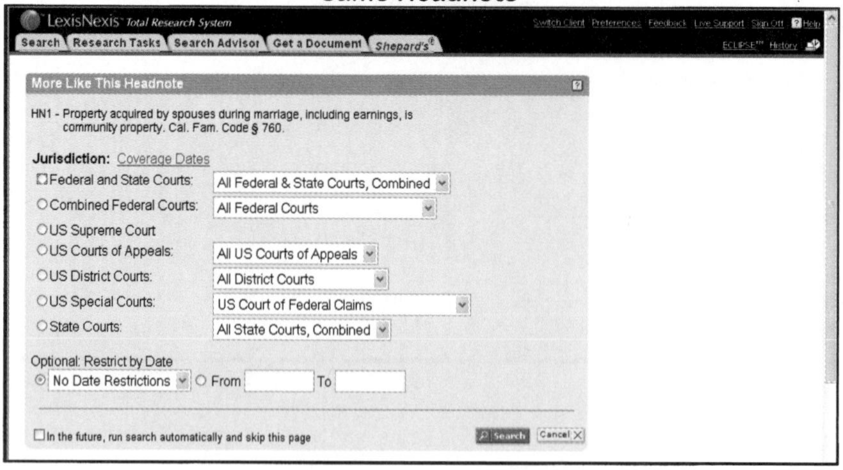

C. FINDING YOUR CASE USING PAPER-BASED METHODS

Until the arrival of WESTLAW and LEXIS with their enormous databases of judicial opinions and their search engines, case digests were the principal means of finding judicial decisions by subject. The challenge of offering subject access to millions of decisions was enormous and the tools that rose up to meet the need are impressive. The West Digest System was not just a way of classifying cases for the researcher to find, it became the definition of the way in which lawyers could think about the law. Lawyers thought of the law in the Digest categories, indeed the Digest categories and the courses taught in the law school curriculum line up quite nicely.

For the law student coming to law school now, much of the following section may seem irrelevant. She may choose to work only online and she may think that *Google* has taught her to search effectively. This is a mistake. There are three reasons that understanding digests is still of great importance.

First, WESTLAW still incorporates the power of the Digest and Key Number System in its search capabilities. You can sit at your laptop and tap into all of the power that we are about to describe. Someone has done an enormous amount of work for you in laying out this system.

Second, in smaller firms, public agencies and in smaller jurisdictions, lawyers still use the paper digests. They are on the shelves of every law library. There is no transaction fee charged for using a book. You may need these skills for your job.

Third, the structure of the digests is deeply embedded in legal culture. Lawyers and judges who graduated from law school before the great personal computer revolution still live in that world. You may work for them. If you do not understand what a digest is, and how it works, you may not work for them for long.

1. West's Topic and Key Number Digests

a. Overview

To build an information system, you need two elements. There must be a database of information and there must be a way of organizing it. The first half of the legal information system built by the West Publishing Company, the *National Reporter System*, was described in Chapter 2. West printed every decision from every court. As part of that process editors at West were preparing headnotes for each decision. The headnotes summarized each point of law in each decision. Thus, West had a database of headnotes covering the points of law decided in every published opinion. Now West needed a subject system in which to organize the headnotes.

The organizing tool would have to provide a subject location for every possible legal point that might be covered in a judicial opinion. Classifications could not be made up as the editors went along, there had to be an existing subject system that provided a listing for every possible legal topic. To meet this need they produced the Topic and Key Number System.

The West Topic and Key Number System divided all foreseeable legal situations into seven major categories:

- **Persons**
- **Property**
- **Contracts**
- **Torts**
- **Crimes**
- **Remedies**
- **Government**

These seven areas are subdivided into more than 450 individual topics, which are then arranged in one alphabetical sequence. Each of the topics is further subdivided in an increasingly narrow refinement, and each of the resulting subtopics is then assigned a classification number, which West calls a "key number." Each topic receives just as many key number subdivisions as it needs. Some of the larger and more complex topics have thousands of key numbers, while smaller topics have only a few. This subject framework seeks to cover every conceivable legal situation that could come up in a case. This effort may represent an oversimplification and potential distortion of the legal universe, but it remains an impressive achievement which has had an enormous intellectual impact on American jurisprudence.[5]

Illustration D shows the beginning of the current list of 450 topics now in use; the full list is printed in the front of most digest volumes. The topics vary widely in scope (*e.g.*, from the very broad "Criminal Law" to the relatively narrow "Bounties") and in current importance (from "Blasphemy" to "Civil Rights"). The subject structure, which was created by West at the end of the 19th Century not only survives, but is still relatively effective and widely used today. New subdivisions within a topic are added periodically, and new topics are occasionally needed, but for the most part West's original divisions have been maintained.[6]

The Digest System is most easily understood by examining how it is constructed. Every decision Thomson-West publishes is read by its editorial staff. Each of the legal issues treated by a decision is identified and abstracted as a headnote. Each headnote is assigned a topic and subtopic key number from the Thomson-West classification scheme. Some headnotes which cannot be so neatly pigeonholed are assigned more than one key number. But every headnote has at least one assigned location. These summaries or abstracts, with their topic names and key numbers, are then placed in separate headnotes at the beginning of the published opinions. A short decision may have just one headnote, while some long opinions have several dozen or more. Illustration E shows a headnote from the *Bonds* decision.

---

5   For a discussion of the impact of West's Digest System on legal thinking, see, Robert C. Berring, "Legal Research and Legal Concepts: Where Form Molds Substance," 75 *Cal. L. Rev.* 15, 24-5 (1987).

6   West continues to adapt its scheme to the changing law, although its changes are slow and cautions. Obviously, changes cannot be made casually or too frequently in a system so large and complex. Nonetheless, in the past decade West has added new topics, such as "Double Jeopardy" and "Racketeer Influenced and Corrupt Organizations," and eliminated others through new combinations and reorganizations.

Illustration D
Partial List of Digest Topics in the *Eleventh Decennial Digest, Part I*

DIGEST TOPICS

See, also, Outline of the Law by Seven Main Divisions of Law preceding this section.

The topic numbers shown below may be used in WESTLAW searches for cases within the topic and within specified key numbers.

1	Abandoned and Lost Property	42	Assumpsit, Action of	77	Citizens
2	Abatement and Revival	43	Asylums	78	Civil Rights
		44	Attachment	79	Clerks of Courts
4	Abortion and Birth Control	45	Attorney and Client	80	Clubs
		46	Attorney General	81	Colleges and Universities
5	Absentees	47	Auctions and Auctioneers	82	Collision
6	Abstracts of Title	48	Audita Querela	83	Commerce
7	Accession	48A	Automobiles	83H	Commodity Futures Trading Regulation
8	Accord and Satisfaction	48B	Aviation		
9	Account	49	Bail		
10	Account, Action on	50	Bailment	84	Common Lands
11	Account Stated	51	Bankruptcy	85	Common Law
11A	Accountants	52	Banks and Banking	88	Compounding Offenses
12	Acknowledgment	54	Beneficial Associations	89	Compromise and Settlement
13	Action	55	Bigamy		
14	Action on the Case	56	Bills and Notes	89A	Condominium
15	Adjoining Landowners	58	Bonds	90	Confusion of Goods
15A	Administrative Law and Procedure	59	Boundaries	91	Conspiracy
		60	Bounties	92	Constitutional Law
16	Admiralty	61	Breach of Marriage Promise	92B	Consumer Credit
17	Adoption			92H	Consumer Protection
18	Adulteration	62	Breach of the Peace		
19	Adultery	63	Bribery	93	Contempt
20	Adverse Possession	64	Bridges	95	Contracts
21	Affidavits	65	Brokers	96	Contribution
23	Agriculture	66	Building and Loan Associations	96H	Controlled Substances
24	Aliens	67	Burglary	97	Conversion
25	Alteration of Instruments	68	Canals	98	Convicts
		69	Cancellation of Instruments	99	Copyrights and Intellectual Property
26	Ambassadors and Consuls	70	Carriers		
27	Amicus Curiae	71	Cemeteries	100	Coroners
28	Animals	72	Census	101	Corporations
29	Annuities	73	Certiorari	102	Costs
30	Appeal and Error	74	Champerty and Maintenance	103	Counterfeiting
31	Appearance			104	Counties
33	Arbitration	75	Charities	105	Court Commissioners
34	Armed Services	76	Chattel Mortgages		
35	Arrest	76A	Chemical Dependents	106	Courts
36	Arson			107	Covenant, Action of
37	Assault and Battery	76D	Child Custody	108	Covenants
38	Assignments	76E	Child Support	108A	Credit Reporting Agencies
40	Assistance, Writ of	76H	Children Out-of-Wedlock		
41	Associations			110	Criminal Law

IV

Illustration E
Headnote #3 from *In re Marriage of Bonds*, as printed in Thomson-West's *California Reporter*

> **3. Husband and Wife ⇐29(9)**
>
> Although the ability of a party challenging a premarital agreement to obtain independent counsel is an important factor in determining whether that party entered into the agreement voluntarily, premarital agreements are not subject to strict scrutiny in those cases in which the less sophisticated party does not have independent counsel and has not waived counsel. West's Ann.Cal. Fam.Code § 1615.

How does West make this subject information available? Each advance sheet and bound volume of the *National Reporter System* has a compilation of all the headnotes in the cases it contains arranged in topic and key number order. Lawyers used to read advance sheets looking for new cases (some still do). If you knew the topics and key numbers that covered your research, skimming the digest would focus the search. This feature has limited utility today.

Much more importantly, Thomson-West takes the same headnotes and publishes them in separate sets covering many volumes of reporters. There are digest sets covering individual states, sets covering separate multi-state units of the *National Reporter System*, a digest for the Supreme Court of the United States and a series of sets covering the lower federal courts.

The printed set is brought up to date by pocket parts in each volume and by supplementary pamphlets published between annual pocket parts. Whenever using a printed set check the back of the volume to see if there is a pocket part that updates it. Also check to see if paper supplements, or volumes, exist. Check with your reference librarian to be sure.

The editorial staff at Thomson-West strives to guarantee uniform treatment of issues of law. The goal is to ensure that points of law are always treated in the same manner. Each headnote touching on a particular point will be sent to the same topic and key number location. Providing uniform editorial treatment for each jurisdiction's opinions and having the points of law in each published decision classified into the same scheme creates a highly effective case finding mechanism. When a researcher locates a case in which a relevant point of law is discussed, the Thomson-West headnotes can be scanned to identify the topic and key numbers assigned to that point of law. These topics and key numbers can then be used as locators in the Thomson-West digests to find other decisions from all Thomson-West reporters on the same issues. The system theoretically allows a researcher to find decisions from any time period in any American jurisdiction on any specific topic.

In these days of computer databases and automatic indexing, it is almost incredible to think that all of this abstracting and indexing is done by human beings. Editors at West are reading and headnoting every case that is published in print. They then place each headnote into the topic and key number structure. Mind boggling!

It should be emphasized that these digests do not constitute legal authority and contain no substantive narrative text. They are effective for identifying and locating relevant decisions, but those decisions must be read and evaluated (and then run through a citator and evaluated again) before being cited in a brief, argument, or memorandum. Each case is decided on its own facts. Its listing under a particular digest topic and key number may be appropriate and helpful, but its relevance and authority for the researcher's purpose must be determined from the opinion itself.

Table 5
Thomson-West's Digest of Federal and State Court Opinions

DIGEST	COVERAGE
Decennial Digests	Covers every case, state and federal, which was decided for the designated ten year period. The *Eleventh Decennial Digest* began in 1997. It is supplemented by the *General Digest*, instead of pocket parts.
United States Supreme Court Digest	Covers all decisions of the Supreme Court of the United States.

Table 5
Thomson-West's Digest of Federal and State Court Opinions, *con't.*

DIGEST	COVERAGE
Federal Practice Digest	Covers all U.S. Supreme Court decisions (duplicating coverage of the *United States Supreme Court Digest*), the U.S. Courts of Appeals, the U.S. District Courts, and various specialized federal courts. The latest edition is the *Federal Practice Digest 4th*, which covers cases from 1987 to date.
Bankruptcy Digest	Covers all cases reported in *West's Bankruptcy Reporter*
Military Justice Digest	Covers the decisions in *West's Military Justice Reporter*
United States Court of Claims Digest	Covers all cases reported in the *United States Claims Court Reporter*, and decisions of the former United States Court of Claims (published in the *Federal Reporter* or *Federal Supplement*).
Regional Digests	There are five regional digests: *Atlantic, North Western, Pacific, South Eastern* and *Southern*. There is no current regional digest for the cases appearing in the *North Eastern* or *South Western* Reporter, although coverage of the ten states in those reporters is provided by state digests.
State Digests	Forty-six state digests are published by West, including one for the District of Columbia. All but two of the digests cover a single jurisdiction, while the *Dakota Digest* and *Virginia and West Virginia Digest* each cover two states. Only Delaware, Nevada and Utah do not have individual West digests; Delaware decisions, however, are covered in the *Atlantic Digest*, and Nevada and Utah in the *Pacific Digest*.

b. Finding Cases in West's Digests

Having described the structure and forms of publication of the various West digests, we turn now to the actual search procedures employed in their use. How do you find cases in the digests? There are three basic approaches: working from a case, by subject searching in the indexes or by analyzing the classification outline of a particular topic.

(1) Starting with a Case

The simplest and often the most successful means of approaching a digest is with a case already in hand. Half the battle of legal research is won by having "one good case" to serve as a basis for finding other cases and resources. As seen in the last Chapter, for example, the *Shepard's* listing for one case can serve as a springboard to numerous later decisions on the same issues. The next section will discuss ways to find that one good case.

When using a digest, starting with a case means that there is no need to search through indexes or figure out the digest's classification system. The appropriate topics and key numbers are already available in the headnotes of the decision in hand. If a headnote has been written for that part of the opinion addressing the issue being researched, the topic and key number assigned to the headnote can be searched in the digests for other relevant cases. Occasionally, the key number assigned covers a very broad area, so that the digest includes abstracts of many irrelevant cases, but more often it's an ideal lead and a shortcut through the indexes and finding aids.

If you have the name of a case and seek its citation, the Digests can help, though WESTLAW, LEXIS and even free systems like Findlaw.com are probably an easier way for all but the computer 'phobe.

Occasionally, a judicial decision is referred to by a "popular name," or a term other than the names of its parties. For example, *Youngstown Sheet & Tube Co. V. Sawyer*, 343 U.S. 579 (1952), is often referred to as the "Steel Seizure Case." The closing pages of *Shepard's Acts and Cases by Popular Names: Federal and State* lists many of these names, and provide reporter citations (but not dates or parties' names). A few of the designations included are very well-known, but many are quite obscure, "popular" only in the broadest sense of the term. In recent years the use of "popular names" has declined precipitously, and very few new cases are being added to the list.[7]

---

7   Similar popular name tables were published in some older Thomson-West digests, including the first *Federal Digest* and the *Second* through the *Sixth Decennial Digest*. These tables have long since been discontinued, but may occasionally be useful for older cases, since the *Shepard's* and Thomson-West tables do not duplicate coverage entirely. *Shepard's Acts and Cases by Popular*

(2) Descriptive-Word Indexes

Each Thomson-West digest includes a minutely constructed index referring to the specific topics and key numbers under which decisions on that subject have been abstracted in the digest. These "Descriptive-Word Indexes" are simply detailed subject indexes to the contents of the digests. The indexes are usually quite large, occupying three or more volumes in most jurisdictional digests.

There are generally two types of entries in a Descriptive-Word Index. Each Thomson-West key number is represented in every jurisdiction and regional digest's index, even if no cases are represented, so the Descriptive-Word Index functions in part as a subject index to the key number classification. Descriptive-Word Indexes for different jurisdictions or regions are quite similar, in that a particular entry will refer in any digest to the same key number. In addition, however, there are entries for specific fact situations represented by individual cases covered in the digest. The Descriptive-Word Index for each jurisdiction therefore contains some entries unique to its jurisprudence.

The *Decennial Digest* and its supplement, the *General Digest*, also contain Descriptive-Word Indexes, but these lists no longer attempt to be comprehensive finding tools. The indexes in the *General Digest* volumes are usually only seven or eight pages long. (If they did index every case digested, of course, the Descriptive-Word Indexes would be nearly as massive as the digests themselves.) If a jurisdictional or regional digest is available, its comprehensive Descriptive-Word Index is usually a better first place to look for general coverage of a subject. The indexes in recent *Decennial* or *General Digest* volumes, however, can be useful resources for searches covering currently developing areas of legal doctrine.

Thomson-West suggests that before consulting a Descriptive-Word Index, you analyze the problem to be searched, and determine very

---

Names serves a far more important function as a finding tool for legislative acts, as will be discussed in Chapter 5.

specific words or phrases to be used by breaking the problem down into the following elements common to every case:

- **the parties involved;**
- **the places where the facts arose, and the objects or things involved;**
- **the acts or omissions which form the basis of the action or issue;**
- **the defense to the action or issue; and**
- **the relief sought**

In practice, one seldom finds a case in which an identical fact situation raises the exact legal issues with which one is confronted. What one realistically hopes to find is a precedent that involves similar facts and the same legal issues. You must usually draw analogies from similar situations. Descriptive-Word Indexes can be quite effective in finding precedential cases, if used with an understanding that they may not always contain the precise factual terms one would wish to find.

c. Summary

The comprehensive scope of the Thomson-West digest system makes it an important case-finding tool. The key number system spans all federal and states jurisdictions, and every point of law treated in a published case fits somewhere and somehow into the classification scheme.

The universal nature of the key number system allows it to be used in all jurisdictions, but sometimes at the expense of recognizing significant differences between states in approaches to jurisprudential issues. Digest classifications are choices made at Thomson-West, not in the courts, and may be misleading or have an unwarranted impact on subsequent interpretation of a holding.[8] Of course the emergence of WESTLAW and LEXIS has significantly reduced this problem.

The greatest strength of the digests, the editorial expertise of its editors, is also one of its weaknesses. Human editors can sort

---

8 " 'If they do a headnote wrong,' says Robert Hursh of Lawyers Co-op, 'it's as though as case has been overruled. Anything they omit is not the law.' " Martin Mayer, *The Lawyers* 431 (Harper & Row, 1967).

information and help the researcher. At the same time, human editors are subject to errors and inherently conservative about change.

Several other case finding methods will be described in this chapter, but the Thomson-West Topic and Key Number Digests remains an ingenious and essential part of the research apparatus. While a digest may not always be the best place to begin a search for relevant decisions, it is often a very effective tool for enlarging a search from the topics and key numbers of a known relevant decision

2. *American Law Reports*

a. Overview of Annotating Reporting Systems

American Law Reports (*ALR*) is a great resource that is sadly under-utilized. It started as a system for printing judicial decisions, but has morphed into a system for printing research annotations. These annotations summarize the law, provide a bevy of citations and are festooned with helpful tools. *ALR* is available in all if its glory on WESTLAW and, in a slightly less grandiose version, on LEXIS. If you find an *ALR* annotation that is on your research topic, you have found someone (an *ALR* editor) who has done a great deal of work for you.

Understanding how an *ALR* annotation is put together aids in understanding the tool. Thomson-West, the publisher of *ALR*, has editors who monitor new court decisions, looking for cases that may resolve a long-standing argument, set out a new question or explore issues in an interesting way. Once a case is selected for annotation, it is assigned to an author who produces a thoroughly researched survey of the particular legal issue, tracing its development and its judicial treatment in all jurisdictions. The editor starts by following the research trail provided by the headnotes accompanying the Thomson-West publication of the case. After finding related cases, the editor traces them through *Shepard's* citators to complete the picture. A WESTLAW search and other research tools are used to find even more cases. The goal is to work through every possible twist of the issue at hand. If successful, the resulting *ALR* annotation will provide a thoroughly researched explanation of the issue raised in the case.

In a sense, this is an upside down version of the Topic and Key Number System methodology. Where the digests have a list of topics prepared in advance and fits every case into its appropriate spot, *ALR* picks only a few cases, and then produces an in-depth exploration of the issues presented. The annotations range in length, depending on the complexity of the issues covered and the frequency with which they arise in published cases, from short articles of a few pages to extensive treatments of several hundred pages. *ALR* is far from comprehensive – it is just a collection of interesting, well-annotated cases – but an annotation on a point of interest can be very helpful.

The text of an *ALR* annotation is very spare and telegraphic in style. The holdings of all the published cases on the particular issue are abstracted, and the discussion is organized so that the cases are arranged to form a cohesive picture of the law. While it is rarely possible to reconcile all conflicting decisions, an annotation presents the decisions in a manner that permits a lawyer to compare their fact situations with his or her own. Do not use the text as persuasive authority. This of the *ALR* annotation as a memo prepared by a research assistant. A great deal of drudgery has already been suffered by others so that you do not have to redo it.

One reason that many people are intimidated by *ALR* is the fact that it has appeared in a variety of series. If you are using the set on WESTLAW or LEXIS this does not matter, although you should be careful to watch for the date of the annotation. If you are using the paper the variety of the sets can be intimidating. The series are:

Table 6
Coverage of *American Law Reports*

SERIES	COVERAGE
ALR (First Series)	1919 - 1948
*ALR*2d	1948 -1965
*ALR*3d	1965 -1980
*ALR*4th	1980 -1992
*ALR*5th	1992 - 2004
*ALR*6th	2005 - present
ALR Federal	1969 - 2004
ALR Federal 2d	2005 - present

The first two series are so dated as to be of little use. They are from a time when the annotations were shorter and less helpful, and the methods used to keep them current are primitive. Beginning with

*ALR*3d, the publisher began to use pocket parts to keep the information up to date. *ALR* Federal represents a decision to put all federal cases in one set, and to treat only state court cases in the regular set. *ALR*4th was introduced without making significant changes or improvements to the set, but *ALR*5th represented a change.

Until *ALR*5th, the publisher represented *ALR* as a case reporter with attached annotations. The reporting of cases was so spotty, however, it could not be taken seriously as a case reporter. Recognizing this, *ALR*5th puts the cases in the back of the book and annotations up front. Further, the editors now do a more thorough job of listing the sources consulted, including the online search that was most successful. These changes enhance *ALR*'s value as a research tool. The publisher has even gone back and compiled a separate volume of the best online searches for all the annotations in *ALR*4th.

b. Using *ALR*

ALR is part of both WESTLAW and LEXIS so it can be searched using the full range of techniques described in Section 1 of this Chapter. Links to *ALR* annotations appear whenever it is cited.

For those using the paper version, *ALR* has gone through its various series and has produced a variety of finding aids. Among these are digests keyed to each series. However, the modern researcher only needs to know that the simplest way to find a relevant annotation by subject is to use the *ALR Index to Annotations*. This index covers the entire series, except *ALR* (First Series), which has a separate index. The general index, is kept up to date by pocket parts. A single volume, soft cover *Quick Index* includes all major annotation reference from *ALR*3d to the present series.

The indexing style of *ALR* is quite different from the analytical set up of the Topic and Key Number System. Some researchers find it to be quite accessible and easy to use, but others think it is obscure. Page through the index to get a feel for it, then try it for yourself.

The citatory systems discussed in Chapter 3 indicate any time a case is either printed in *ALR* or mentioned in an *ALR* annotation. If the case is printed in full, the *ALR* citation is listed as one of its parallel citations.

Online, through LEXIS or WESTLAW, the full-text can be searched for particular terms or phrases, although in many instances it is more effective to look for keywords only in the titles of the annotations. The titles of *ALR* annotations are generally lengthy and descriptive, a title keyword search usually retrieves annotations on point. A full-text search, on the other hand, may turn up several annotations which focus on unrelated issues but include the keywords in describing the facts and holdings of the cases discussed. *ALR* can also be accessed via the online index.

American Law Reports is part of almost every law library, but it is often underutilized. If the researcher can focus on what can and cannot be expected from an *ALR* annotation, the set has considerable value. When you find an annotation on point, you have access to a tremendous amount of prepared research, full of useful cites and helpful leads. Do not neglect *ALR*'s power.

D. THE BEST METHOD OF CASE FINDING

The best method of finding relevant cases is to use the tools designed to help lawyers who are in practice. Such tools place the question into context by describing the parameters of the problem and how it is handled. Research tools designed for practicing lawyers have to provide explanation, updating and the citation to relevant sources. Thus, they will lay out the citations to relevant cases (as well as statutes and other sources that are on point). By reading them you will gain an understanding of the problem and a ready roadmap to the materials that you need. Since much of the pedagogy of law school counsels you to always read primary sources and to avoid reliance on secondary sources, you may not encounter many of these tools in your early years of law school.

1. Practice Books

Practice books are designed for use by lawyers. They are often issued in looseleaf form in paper, and increasingly are available online. They feature indexes done in normal language so that you can look up a term like "prenuptial contracts" and be cited to relevant discussion. These are sometimes sources that you would not cite to a court, but they are great starting places for your research. You will have some background in hand so that you understand where the case fits into the discussion and, of course, you will be given the citation to relevant cases. You can go read the cases yourself but you will find them much easier and you will know why what you are reading is important.   One of our rules for good research is to know what you are doing.

Where can you find practice books? There are separate sets for each jurisdiction. In California, where we both work, the Witkin family of practice sets have long been viewed as the most authoritative. Other sets, like those done by the Rutter Group, are also of great value. No matter where you live, there will be books designed for lawyers in your state. The bigger your state, the wider the range of practice tools that will be available. Your research instructor can fill you in on those used by local attorneys, or you can ask a reference librarian at your law library.   These resources can increasingly be found on LEXIS and WESTLAW.

2. Hornbooks

Hornbooks grew up as tools to help law students understand the subjects that they study. Since the method used in teaching most law school courses, especially those in the first year, put a premium on discussing problem cases and the gray areas of law, a need arose for tools that simply stated what the law was. This is popularly called "black letter law." Hornbooks proved very popular so there will be a hornbook covering almost every law school topic. Thomson-West, Foundation Press, LexisNexis and Aspen all have hornbook series, so for many subjects, there will be several alternatives to try. The hornbook will not focus on the ins and outs of practice in any particular jurisdiction but will, instead, provide an overview of the law.

Thus, the hornbook will provide context, learned discussion and citations to important cases. It is another way to garner both context and citations. Some hornbooks are pretty thick, both in size and style, but they can often get the job done. Some have evolved into serious scholarly efforts which have been cited by the Courts, some are fairly straightforward. Each will have an index, a detailed table of contents and an alphabetical list of all the cases which they discuss or cite.

3. Law Reviews

We will discuss law reviews at greater length in a later chapter but if you can find a law review article that discusses the problem that interests you, then you will have unearthed a great steaming pot of relevant information. The text of the article may help you by describing the law, though law reviews are often written in a spectacularly boring and impenetrable style. But no matter how impenetrable the text of a law review article may be, they are heavily footnoted. The footnotes will contain citations to every case, (and every other possible source) that is possibly relevant. Later on you will see that there are relatively easy methods using computer based systems to find relevant law review articles.

4. Humans

In the real world the best place to get the name of that one good case will often be from a human being. The lawyer or supervisor who asks you to undertake a research problem can often give you the name of a relevant case. There is no better source from which to work. Since this book is designed to acquaint you with the research process we will want you to learn how to find the case on your own, but when you are out in the real world, always ask a human when you can.

E. SUMMARY

The legal researcher of today has an incredible range of tools that can be used for finding cases. The traditional digests, developed in paper, provide a highly articulated method for classifying case law. Developed to take advantage of the power of the intellectual nuance of classification done by human beings it has all the strengths and weaknesses that paper indexing offers. WESTLAW and LEXIS, incredibly rich systems with ever changing and improving databases offer a new world of possibility for one who is searching for decisions by subject. These are parallel universes of case finding. You would be well advised to master both. But the real lesson lies in gaining context and finding the one good case in a secondary source. With that citation in hand, you can use the digests, LEXIS, WESTLAW, *ALR* or any other source with much greater efficiency. Avoid cold searches whenever you can.

F. ADDITIONAL READING

Delgado and Stefancik, "Why Do We Tell the Same Stories?: Law Reform, Critical Librarianship and the Triple Helix Dilemma," 42 Stan. L. Rev. 207 (1989) explores the power of the West Digest System to constrain changes in the law.

Robert Berring, "Chaos, Cyberspace and Tradition: Legal Information Transmogrified," 12 BTLJ 189 (1997) summarized much of one of your author's thinking on the topic of legal information in traditional categories.

Geoffrey C.Bowker and Susan Leigh Starr, *Sorting Things Out: Classification and Its Consequences*, (MIT Press 1999) is a serious study of how we think in categories and how these categories affect us. It uses the field of medicine as a model but its lessons are universal. This is a good read but it is only for the truly interested.

Chapter 5

STATUTES

A. INTRODUCTION

Statutes and other legislative forms are the second category of primary legal sources. American legal education tends to focus on appellate decisions and on cases, and the role of the statue is often underemphasized. In practice, however, statutory law is central to many legal issues. Checking to see if there is a relevant statute is often the first step in approaching a research problem. Indeed, the vast majority of appellate decisions today involve the application or interpretation of statutes, rather than merely consideration of common law principles.

The term *legislation* can be broadly construed to include constitutions, statutes, treaties, municipal charters and ordinances, interstate compacts, and reorganization plans. In this chapter, we focus on federal and state statutes. Briefer discussions of the other types of legislation are included. Administrative regulations and court rules are considered "delegated legislation," but are treated separately in Chapters 8 and 9, respectively.

The federal nature of our government and legal system is important in understanding legislation. The U.S. Congress and the legislature of each of the fifty states has its own structure and procedure for the initiation and passage of legislation. Similarly, the ways in which statutes are first made available may vary from jurisdiction to jurisdiction. The text of a statute may be found on the legislature's official web site, or in an online research system long before the text is available in paper, but its usefulness will be limited until it is integrated into the editorially enhanced research tools.

B. STATUTORY PATTERNS

Each of the jurisdictions in the United States issues its legislative publications according to a pattern. The names of the specific publications differ among the jurisdictions, but the generic equivalent always exists. The pattern of statutory publication is as follows:

Slip or Chaptered Laws
↓
Session Laws
↓
Code
↓
Annotated Code

Although statutory research usually begins in an annotated code, either in paper or online, an understanding of the earlier forms of the statute provides an essential background.

1. Slip or Chaptered Laws

After a bill is passed by the legislature and signed by the President or governor it is said to be "chaptered."[1] The first official publication of a chapter law might be online at an official legislative web site[2] or it might be published in paper as a "slip law."[3] At this stage, you will find the text of the law and the chapter or law number.[4] You may find other helpful information included with the text, such as a legislative digest summarizing the law or the names of the legislative members who sponsored the law. Chaptered laws are the first place you will find the text of the laws, but they are not published in context. That is, each law is published on its own,

---

[1]   A bill that has been passed by only one side of the legislature, *e.g.* the House of Representatives or the Senate, is an "enrolled" bill.

[2]   California, for instance, began this practice in 1993 and stopped publishing bills that had been chaptered in paper altogether.

[3]   Slip laws are separately issued pamphlets, each of which contains the text of a single legislative act. Most states do not distribute slip laws widely. Only larger research law libraries receive them.

[4]   Chapter numbers are usually assigned beginning with the number 1 for each session of the legislature. For example, 2003 N.Y. Laws 123 refers to the 123rd law passed in the 2003 session of the New York State Legislature.

separated from the other laws that relate to it.[5] For this reason, later methods of publication will probably be more useful to you.

2. Session Laws

The term "session laws" refers to the permanent (paper) publication, in chronological sequence, of the slip laws enacted during a legislative session. In other words, session laws are all the laws chaptered in each legislative session compiled in one place in the order in which the law were passed. The federal government and each of the fifty states publish some form of session laws following the end of each legislative session.[6] The official session laws often come out quite slowly. Most jurisdictions also have commercial legislative publication services which provide more prompt access to new laws as they are enacted. These services, providing the texts of new laws in paperback or pamphlet form, are known as "advance session law services."

In most states, the session laws constitute the ***positive law*** form of legislation, *i.e.*, the authoritative, binding text of the laws, and the determinative version if questions arise from textual variations in subsequent printed versions. Other forms (such as codes) are only ***prima facie*** evidence of the statutory language, unless they have been designated as positive law by the legislature. *Prima facie* evidence means that the wording as found is presumptively valid, but can be disproven by reference to the positive law version if there is a discrepancy.

Session law publications have several common characteristics, including subject indexes for each volume and tables indicating which existing laws were modified or repealed by newly enacted legislation. These indexes and tables cover only that year's worth of new legislation and do not

---

5   The relationship between statutes is very important to understanding how they apply because statutes are written hierarchically. A single section of your state's code may tell you that the killing of another human being is murder. Without reading the other sections around this one in the code, you'd fail to find out about manslaughter, or self-defense.

6   To go back to the California example, while slip laws are no longer published in paper, the session laws are the positive law of California and still appear as volumes in the set, *Statutes of California and Amendments to the Codes: Passed at the ... Session of the Legislature.*

cumulate from year to year. Session law volumes are important as archives of the positive law, but they are impractical as tools for most real research for two reasons. First, the volumes come out so slowly they cannot be used for current research, and, second, subject searching is severely limited because they lack indexing beyond each individual year.

3. Statutory Compilations or Codes

As used in this chapter, the term "code" refers to a publication of the public, general and permanent statutes of a jurisdiction in a fixed subject or topical arrangement. Statutory codes preserve the original language of the session laws more or less intact, but rearrange and group them under broad subject categories. You can, for example, find all the statutes relating to adoption in one place, in an order that makes logical sense, rather than having the text of those laws scattered through many different volumes of session laws. In this process of rearranging the individual statutes, amendments are incorporated, repealed laws are deleted, and minor technical adjustments are sometimes made in the text of the laws to fit them into a functional and coherent compilation.

There is no universal subject arrangement into which statutes are organized. Jurisdictions vary considerably in the approach used. Some jurisdictions use a small number of very broad topics, others use a large number of very specific ones. It is a matter of judgment. Since the law, and the areas that it covers, changes so rapidly, one might assume that jurisdictions would rearrange the topical breakdown of codes fairly frequently. This is not the case. Recodifying is laborious and fraught with pitfalls. In the course of rearranging the laws there is the potential for much political wrangling as well as substantial intellectual challenges. It is more likely for a jurisdiction to issue or approve a code and then leave it untouched for years. Newly enacted statutes are just dropped into the code. Often it is left to commercial publishers to keep the code up to date. Sometimes such publishers even update the subject arrangements.

Statutory codes may appear in either official or unofficial editions. Official statutory codes are published or sanctioned by the government. They normally include the text of the law and brief editorial notes as to the authority and historical development of the law. Law students often encounter unofficial statutory codes, perhaps in the form of one title of a state or federal code, printed and sold as a study aid.

Despite their convenience in providing subject access, official codes have certain shortcomings. Like other official publications such as judicial reports, they are often issued very slowly. More important, their limited editorial notes are simply not adequate for most statutory research. They do not provide citations to judicial interpretations of a statute, which are important extrinsic aids in determining its meaning or legislative intent. The researcher must turn to the unofficial, annotated codes for access to this type of material.

4. Annotated Codes

An annotated code reproduces the text and arrangement of the official code. It also incorporates new legislation, revisions and amendments within that structure, and deletes repealed laws just like the code mentioned in the previous section. Its unique contribution to legal research is the inclusion of *annotations* after each statutory section. Annotations are references to relevant judicial or administrative decisions, administrative code sections, encyclopedias, attorney general opinions, legislative history materials, law reviews, and treatises.

The annotated code provides more than just case citations. A brief abstract of each cited opinion is provided. These brief editorial descriptions allow you to browse the annotations to find relevant cases. Since some statutory sections have been construed in thousands of court cases, this can be an enormous time saver.

Annotated codes play other important roles in research. They provide citations to relevant administrative rules, form books, law review articles and other sources. Even smaller publishers will provide cross-references. These features make the annotated code a truly integrated research tool, pulling together a variety of primary and secondary source material.

Another advantage of annotated codes is more frequent updating. Updates to the annotated codes online will appear when the change in the law takes affect, and in paper pocket parts and pamphlet supplements are issued for bound volumes. These features of the commercial annotated codes make them the most effective source for updating most statutory material.

A final feature of annotated codes published in paper is good indexing. Most annotated codes feature good general indexes at the end of the set.[7] These indexes feature entries that consist of words and phrases drawn from common usage. They are often more intuitive and easy to use than the jargon driven indexes and digests built around cases. Since annotated codes do supply citations to cases, this feature can make them a good place to start a search for relevant cases.

C. FEDERAL STATUTES

The U.S. Congress passes several forms of legislation. This section will concentrate on acts and joint resolutions, which are the basic forms of legislation.

Each new act is designated either as a "public law" or a "private law." Usually, private laws are passed for the specific benefit of an individual or a small group of individuals,[8] whereas public laws are intended to be of general application. The two categories are numbered, as enacted, in separate series. Although private laws are issued in a slip law form and appear in the federal session law publication (the *Statutes at Large*), most of the other publications discussed in this chapter contain only public laws.

1. Slip Laws

The first official form of publication of a federal law is the *slip law,* a separately paginated pamphlet text of each law, with no internal indexing. Each new act is designated by a public law number, *e.g.*, Public Law 93-318. The first part of the number represents the number of the Congress which

---

7   It may be hard to believe, but using these paper indexes to the codes is often easier than logging on to a commercial online service and doing a keyword search for your statute. This is because an editor has already given some thought to the use of synonyms.

8   In this century most private laws concern special relief for individuals under the immigration laws, *e.g.* granting citizenship to a specific person outside of the usual application process. For more on this distinction, see Note, "Private Bills in Congress," 79 *Harv.L.Rev.* 1684 (1966).

enacted the law (in this case, the 93rd Congress) and the second part of the number indicates the chronological sequence of its enactment (the 318th public law enacted by that Congress).

The form of the printing is almost identical to that which appears in the *Statutes at Large*[9] and in recent years both the slip law and *Statutes at Large* publication include a brief summary of each law's legislative history following the text. Illustration A shows the first part of PL 93-318, as it appears in its *Statutes at Large* form.

Illustration A
The first part of a law in the *U.S. Statutes at Large*, in a format similar to the slip law, 88 Stat. 244. Note the gloss in the margin that tells you where the section will be codified.

Public Law 93-318

June 22, 1974
[S.1585]

AN ACT
To prevent the unauthorized manufacture and use of the character "Woodsy Owl", and for other purposes.

"Woodsy Owl"
and "Smokey
Bear."
Unauthorized
use, prevention.
Definitions.
31 USC 488b-3.

Be it enacted by the Senate and House of Representatives of the United States of America in Congress assembled,

SECTION 1. As used in this Act—

(1) the term "Woodsy Owl" means the name and representation of a fanciful owl, who wears slacks (forest green when colored), a belt (brown when colored), and a Robin Hood style hat (forest green when colored) with a feather (red when colored), and who furthers the slogan, "Give a Hoot, Don't Pollute", originated by the Forest Service of the United States Department of Agriculture;

(2) the term "Smokey Bear" means the name and character "Smokey Bear" originated by the Forest Service of the United States Department of Agriculture in cooperation with the Association of State Foresters and the Advertising Council.

The slip law is the first authoritative official text of the statute and is rebuttable as evidence of the law only by reference to the enrolled Act. When the *Statutes at Large* are published, they supersede the slip law as authority.

Slip laws in paper are distributed rather slowly. On the Internet, however, they are available the same day they are passed by the U.S.

---

9   *Statutes at Large* is the session law service for legislation of the U.S. Congress.

Congress on *Thomas*,[10] a web site from the Library of Congress. The text will also be available in a number of other places, but *Thomas* is the government's own site.

2. Advance Session Law Services

The two commercial general advance session law services for federal statutes are Thomson-West's *United States Code Congressional and Administrative News* (*USCCAN*) and LexisNexis' *Advance* pamphlets to the *United States Code Service* (*USCS*).[11]   Both services issue monthly pamphlets, generally publishing new federal statutes within a month or two of enactment. In both *USCCAN* and *USCS Advance,* each page of statutory text indicates the location at which it will eventually appear upon publication in the official *Statutes at Large.*

In addition to the text of newly enacted public laws, each service publishes Presidential proclamations, executive orders, amendments to court rules, and selected administrative regulations. Both services include in their pamphlets a cumulative index and various tables that aid in locating the sections of the code which have been affected by recent legislative, executive, or administrative action.

Advance pamphlets are designed only for temporary use, until the new material has been incorporated into *USCS,* while *USCCAN* pamphlets are cumulated at the end of each year into bound volumes. Chapter 6 will discuss how *USCCAN* can aid in legislative history.

Much more timely ways to gain access to information on newly enacted federal statutes will be addressed below in Section 5's discussion of electronic sources.

3. *United States Statutes at Large*

The official, permanent session law publication for federal laws is

---

10   <http://loc.thomas.gov> Links from *Thomas* make the text available in both HTML and PDF format.

11   The *United States Code Service* is discussed below in Section C.4.b.

the *United States Statutes at Large* (cited as *Stat.*). At the end of each annual session of Congress, the enacted public and private laws are cumulated and published in chronological order as the *Statutes at Large* for that session, along with concurrent resolutions, Presidential proclamations, and reorganization plans. In recent years, each session's compilation has comprised up to six volumes (referred to as parts); the several parts for each session bear one volume number.

A federal session law is properly cited by its Public Law number and the volume and page in which it appears in *Statutes at Large.*[12] But variations may occur. A newly enacted law may be referred to only by its Public Law number. On other occasions the name by which the Act was titled in *Statutes at Large* will be used. This can range from very well known statutes like Title IX to rather obscure ones like the Wild Burros Act.[13] To help find a statute when one has only a name, one can consult the popular name tables that will be part of the sets discussed in subsequent sections.

The first eight volumes of the *Statutes at Large* cover legislation from 1779 to 1845. From that point the set moves forward in smaller time increments. The period of time covered in each volume varied until Volume 50 (1938) when the current pattern of one set of *Statutes at Large* volumes for each session of Congress began. Through volume 64 (1950-51), the full texts of newly approved treaties were also included in each volume, but that practice was discontinued when a separate series, *U.S. Treaties and Other International Agreements,* was begun in 1950.

Although the publication of current volumes of the *Statutes at Large* is slow, lagging one to two years behind the end of the session covered, they

---

12   Session laws before 1957 are designated by chapter numbers, not Public Law numbers. Public Law numbers have been assigned to Acts of Congress since 1901, but chapter numbers remained the traditional and primary means of identification until they were discontinued at the end of the 1956 session.

13   The authors sometimes refer to this as the beginning of a severe case of alphanumeric confusion. "Title IX" is the section number where the text of this law appears in the larger act, the Education Amendments of 1972 (P.L. 92-318), as printed in the *Statutes at Large* (86 *Stat.* 373). It does **not** refer to Title 9 of the USC (which happens to be Arbitration), or in any way to where it appears in the *USC*. In the *USC*, Title IX appears at 20 U.S.C. §1681-8 (2000).

are the authoritative text of federal statutes, superseding the slip laws. The *Statutes at Large* is the positive law form of statutes, and "legal evidence of laws ... in all the Courts of the United States."[14] The *United States Code* is only *prima facie* evidence of the laws, except for those of its titles which have been reenacted by Congress as positive law.[15]

Indexes by subject and individuals' names appear at the back of each part of a *Statutes at Large* volume.[16] These indexes facilitate access to each volume, but access to individual volumes is inadequate for most research. You cannot effectively search each session laws volume for statutes on a specific issue, and then analyze successive amendments and repeals in order to determine what laws are currently in force. Effective statutory research depends on the use of the codified versions of federal laws.

4. Codification of Federal Statutes

The most useful publications of federal laws are not those published chronologically, but those that are arranged by subject. The most important of these is the current *United States Code* in its various editions, but one earlier codification which remains a source of positive law must first be discussed.

a. *Revised Statutes*

There are two sets, largely of historical interest, but still valid, which are the foundation of modern federal statute law. The *Revised Statutes of the United States, Passed at the First Session of the Forty-Third Congress, 1873-'74; Embracing the Statutes of the United States, General and Permanent in Their Nature, in Force on [December 1, 1873] ...* and the *Revised Statutes* of 1876. The first represents an attempt to pass a codification of all federal statute law in the form of one statement of positive

---

14   1 U.S.C. §112 (2000)

15   1 U.S.C. §204 (2000)

16   Volumes 71 (1957) to 90 (1976) also included tables indicating which existing laws had been modified or repealed by laws published in each volume. This feature, useful for current awareness but of limited historical value, was discontinued in 1977.

law. The whole thing was enacted as one bill. It was to be the definitive statement of all general statutes that were in force. Because of errors and disputes in the 1873 version, the *Revised Statutes* of 1876 was passed. It redid the job, but this time it was passed as a *prima facie* codification. This experience was so traumatic it took fifty years for another codification effort to be undertaken.

b. *United States Code*

After much legislative travail, a new codification effort was approved on June 30, 1926, and published as 44 Stat. Part 1 under the title: *The Code of the Laws of the United States of America of a General and Permanent Nature, in Force December 7, 1925 ....* It has since been known as the *United States Code* (*USC*).

Unlike the *Revised Statutes,* the new *USC* was not a positive law reenactment and did not repeal the prior *Statutes at Large.* It was *prima facie* evidence of the law, rebuttable by reference to the *Statutes at Large.* However, Congress subsequently began revising the titles of the *USC* and reenacting each into positive law as the revision was completed.[17] For the titles not reenacted into positive law, the *Statutes at Large* remains legal evidence and the *USC* is *prima facie* evidence. A list of titles at the beginning of each *USC* volume indicates which have been reenacted as positive law.[18]

The *USC* is arranged in fifty subjects, each known as a Title, and generally in alphabetical order. The breakdown of fifty subjects for organizing federal law was created in 1926 and has not been changed since,

---

17   The following titles of the Code have been enacted into positive law: 1, 3, 4, 5, 9, 10, 11, 13, 14, 17, 18, 23, 28, 31, 32, 35, 36, 37, 38, 39, 44, 46, and 49.

18   The distinction between titles which are positive law and titles which are *prima facie* evidence is only rarely a matter of concern, since the code text is taken from the original language of enactment. Certain changes in form or numbering may occur in order to fit the text into the existing code framework, but these variations are not substantive. Occasional errors have been made, however, so the distinction is of potential legal effect. *See, e.g., United States Nat'l Bank v. Independent Ins. Agents, Inc.* 508 U.S. 439 (1993); *Stephan v. United States,* 319 U.S. 423 (1943); *Five Flags Pipeline Co. v. Dep't of Transp.,* 854 F.2d 1438 (D.C. Cir 1988); *Royer's, Inc. v. United States,* 265 F.2d 615 (3d Cir. 1959).

even though some topics, like Title 34 (Navy), are now empty. This illustrates both how rare a rearrangement of topics is and how innately conservative legal publishing tends to be.

Titles are divided into chapters and then into sections, with a continuous sequence of section numbers for each title. Citations to the *USC* indicate the title and section numbers, and the year of publication of the volume, *e.g.*, 16 U.S.C. §580p-4 (2000).

Following each statutory section in the *USC,* there is a parenthetical reference to its source in the *Statutes at Large,* including sources for any amendments. This reference enables one to locate the original text, which may be the positive law form, and from there to find legislative history documents relating to the law's enactment. The *USC* also includes historical notes and cross-references to related sections. Illustration B shows the *USC* page on which part of the codified form of PL 93-318, an "*Act to Prevent the Unauthorized Manufacture and Use of the Characters of Woodsy Owl and Smokey Bear*", shown in Illustration A begins.

The *USC* is reissued in a new edition every six years, and updated between editions by annual bound supplements. Each year's supplement incorporates material in preceding supplements, so that only the latest one need be consulted for changes since the last revision. Both the *USC* and its supplement are multivolume works.

The *USC* features a number of useful research aids. These include an extensive general index, filling six large, hardbound volumes in the 2000 *USC* edition, and several tables, such as a popular name table and various parallel reference tables. These features are discussed in greater detail in Section D.1, below.

The *USC* is a well-prepared and effective research tool, accompanied by thorough indexing and helpful tables. Its publication is not as tardy as some other government publications, but its latest volumes still are generally eight months to two years out of date. It also lacks citations to relevant cases. Cases can explain the meaning of a statute, or even invalidate it. For more current coverage as well as for citation to relevant cases it is necessary to use one of the commercial annotated editions of the *USC*.

c. *United States Code Annotated*

In 1927, Thomson-West began publication of an unofficial, annotated edition of the *USC*, entitled *United States Code Annotated* (*USCA*). The *USCA* retains the text and organization of the *USC*, employing identical title and section numbers. In addition to providing the same research aids found in the official *USC,* such as authority references, historical notes, cross references, tables, and indexes, *USCA* offers the three major advantages of an annotated code for researchers: it includes abstracts of judicial decisions, it provides references to secondary sources that aid in the interpretation of code sections, and it is updated on a more frequent basis.

After each section of the text of the law, the *USCA* cites the *Statutes at Large* origin of the text, and includes several editorial features. Where relevant, it provides references to such sources as the *Code of Federal Regulations* and legislative history materials in *U.S. Code Congressional and Administrative News* (*USCCAN*). An annotation section labeled "Library References" contains citations to Thompson-West's American Digest System Topics and Key Numbers, to the legal encyclopedias, *Corpus Juris Secundum* (*CJS*) and *American Jurisprudence* (*Am.Jur.*), and to Thomson-West treatises on the statutory subject.

Following each section of the code which has been interpreted or applied judicially, *USCA* provides "Notes of Decisions," consisting of abstracts of judicial decisions that have considered the particular section. These annotations are usually preceded by an alphabetical subject index, which assists in locating decisions on particular aspects of the statutory section. Because judicial interpretations are a vital part of reading and understanding statutes, these case abstracts are the most important aspect of an annotated code. They also take a great deal of space, causing the *USCA* version of the code to occupy well over 200 volumes. Illustrations C-1 and C-2 show a code section as printed in *USCA,* followed by various research aids and notes of decisions. Note in Illustration C-2 the U.S. District Court decision allowing the use of a chainsaw-wielding caricature of Smokey Bear.

USCA provides extensive annotations of judicial decisions not only for the fifty titles of the *USC*, but also for the provisions of the U.S. Constitution and for several major sets of court rules, such as the Federal Rules of Civil Procedure (in several volumes following Title 28) and the Federal Rules of Criminal Procedure (in several volumes following Title 18).

Access to *USCA* is provided by a multivolume general index for the entire set and individual indexes for each title. Indexes to individual titles are not updated until a volume is revised and replaced, but a new edition of the general index is issued each year in paperback volumes. The set also contains many of the same tables published in the *USC,* which are discussed below in Section D.1.b.

USCA is far more current than the official *USC,* and is kept up to date by several forms of supplementation. The most basic of these is the annual cumulative pocket part, which is inserted in the back of each volume and indicates any changes in the statutory text, additional annotations to judicial decisions, and later notes and references to other sources. For some volumes, a separate, cumulative paperback pamphlet, also issued annually, takes the place of the pocket part. A list in the front of each pocket part or pamphlet indicates the cut-off point for coverage of decisions from the various reporter series.

Unlike official *USC* volumes, which are replaced every six years, *USCA* volumes are generally replaced when the supplementation becomes unwieldy. Several new volumes are published each year, but parts of the set are several decades old. Every volume is up to date, though, since new statutes, amendments, and annotations are printed in its current pocket part or supplementary pamphlet. Every time a *USCA* volume is used, its supplementation *must* be checked for more recent developments.

Between annual pocket parts, other forms of supplementation are used. Legislative and judicial developments are noted in quarterly pamphlets that update the whole set. Each pamphlet is arranged by code section, and contains both the text of new laws and notes of recent decisions. The public laws printed in each pamphlet are listed on the front cover and spine, and the reporter volumes covered are listed in a table at the front of the pamphlet. Because they are not cumulative, it is important to remember to check all available interim pamphlets.

Thomson-West further updates these quarterly pamphlets. During each legislative session, the monthly advance pamphlets of *USCCAN* contain the text of newly enacted statutes in chronological order, and provide parallel tables indicating the code sections affected by the new laws. The table entitled, "U.S. Code and U.S. Code Annotated, Sections Amended,

Repealed, New, Etc.," should be checked to determine whether a statute's status has changed since the last *USCA* pamphlet.[19]

d. *United States Code Service*

The second unofficial annotated federal code publication is the *United States Code Service* (cited as *USCS*), published by LexisNexis. Like all annotated codes, it has notes on judicial decisions and secondary sources, and is frequently updated. The *USCS* has a couple of features which distinguish it from the *USCA*. First, the *USCS* maintains the original title and section numbering of the *USC,* but there is some variation in the text. *USCS* preserves more closely the context and language of the original *Statutes at Large* text and uses parentheticals and notes for clarification.

Why would the language of the *Statutes at Large* differ from the language in the *USC*? Newly enacted laws appear in *Statutes at Large* in the form in which they passed the Congress. They are then put into the proper place in the *USC*. When a provision is moved, its language may have to be changed to conform to the part of the *USC* in which it is being placed. This means that the actual language may differ between the two versions. There should be no substantive difference, only issues of grammar and form. In a wonderful example of how the competitive marketplace functions, each annotated code chooses to follow one of the versions.

Second, like *USCA, USCS* expands on many of the research aids published in the *USC* (authority references, historical notes, cross-references, etc.), in a section titled "History; Ancillary Laws and Directives." It also provides references to the *Code of Federal Regulations* (*CFR*), and under the heading "Research Guide," references to *American Jurisprudence* (*Am.Jur.*), other LexisNexis practice publications, and law review articles.

The case annotations following code sections are located under the title, "Interpretive Notes and Decisions." They usually are preceded by a detailed topical outline and include both judicial and administrative decisions. Illustration D shows some of these features following 16 U.S.C.S. §580p-4. A major difference between *USCA* and *USCS* lies in the manner in

---

19   The information printed in *USCCAN* about *USC* amendments comes from the Office of the Law Revision Council (the arm of the House of Representatives that compiles the *USC*). <http://uscode.house.gov/lawrevisioncounsel.php>

which cases are chosen to appear in the annotations. *USCA* follows the general Thomson-West policy of comprehensive coverage. It provides abstracts of every case that even remotely touches upon the statute. *USCS* is more selective. It prints only those cases that its editors feel are truly relevant. The researcher is presented with the classic trade-off of comprehensive retrieval versus editorial assistance to separate the important from the repetitive.

USCS has a multivolume, paperback general index, issued annually and periodically updated in pamphlet form, and individual title indexes. *USCS* also includes several volumes of tables providing parallel references and citations from popular names.

USCS is updated in much the same way as *USCA*. Cumulative annual pocket parts show changes in statutory text and provide additional annotations. Quarterly supplements entitled *Cumulative Later Case and Statutory Service* function as interim supplementation between the annual pocket parts. *USCS*'s monthly *Advance* pamphlets contain the text of newly enacted statutes, executive documents, court rules, and selected regulations, with tables for determining which code sections have been affected by recent legislative or administrative action.

Also like *USCA, USCS* devotes several heavily annotated volumes to the U.S. Constitution and to major sets of court rules. The rules volumes, however, are all shelved at the end of the set, rather than after the particular titles to which they relate.

There are other differences between these two commercial versions of federal statutes. *USCS,* for example, publishes the frequently amended Internal Revenue Code in several soft-cover volumes that are reissued annually. It also includes a volume of annotations on *uncodified* laws, arranged by *Statutes at Large* citation. Generally, *USCA* tends to be more comprehensive, including notes of decisions that *USCS* editors exclude as obsolete or repetitive. In another respect *USCS* is more comprehensive, because it provides notes of administrative decisions, which are not found in *USCA*. For many provisions, each edition will note some cases the other omits. At any given time, one of the competitors may also be a bit more up to date than the other.

Many researchers work in libraries that subscribe to only one annotated edition of the U.S. Code. For them there is no dilemma choosing which to use. A person with access to both *USCA* and *USCS* should become familiar with each, and will probably develop a personal preference for one or the other. One edition can be used on a regular basis for most research needs, but the other may occasionally be needed for its editorial features or to ensure comprehensive coverage.

Illustration B
Statute Printed in the *United States Code*, 16 USC §580p-4

§ 580p-1   TITLE 16—CONSERVATION   Page 994

§ 580p-1. Property of the United States

The following are hereby declared the property of the United States:

(1) The name and character "Smokey Bear".

(2) The name and character "Woodsy Owl" and the associated slogan, "Give a Hoot, Don't Pollute".

(Pub. L. 93-318, § 2, June 22, 1974, 88 Stat. 245.)

CODIFICATION

Section was formerly classified to section 488b-4 of Title 31 prior to the general revision and enactment of Title 31, Money and Finance, by Pub. L. 97-258, § 1, Sept. 13, 1982, 96 Stat. 877.

SECTION REFERRED TO IN OTHER SECTIONS

This section is referred to in sections 580p, 580p-3 of this title.

§ 580p-2. Deposit of fees collected under regulations relating to "Smokey Bear"; availability

The Secretary of Agriculture shall deposit into a special account to be available for furthering the nationwide forest-fire prevention campaign all fees collected under regulations promulgated by him relating to "Smokey Bear".

(May 23, 1952, ch. 327, § 3, 66 Stat. 92; Pub. L. 93-318, § 7, June 22, 1974, 88 Stat. 245.)

CODIFICATION

Section was formerly classified to section 488a of Title 31 prior to the general revision and enactment of Title 31, Money and Finance, by Pub. L. 97-258, § 1, Sept. 13, 1982, 96 Stat. 877.

AMENDMENTS

1974—Pub. L. 93-318 struck out "under the provisions of section 711 of title 18" after "relating to 'Smokey Bear'."

SECTION REFERRED TO IN OTHER SECTIONS

This section is referred to in sections 580p, 580p-3 of this title.

§ 580p-3. Use of royalty fees; special account

(a) The Secretary may establish and collect use or royalty fees for the manufacture, reproduction, or use of the name or character "Woodsy Owl" and the associated slogan, "Give a Hoot, Don't Pollute", as a symbol for a public service campaign to promote wise use of the environment and programs which foster maintenance and improvement of environmental quality.

(b) The Secretary shall deposit into a special account all fees collected pursuant to this Act. Such fees are hereby made available for obligation and expenditure for the purpose of furthering the "Woodsy Owl" campaign.

(Pub. L. 93-318, § 3, June 22, 1974, 88 Stat. 245.)

REFERENCES IN TEXT

This Act, referred to in subsec. (b), is Pub. L. 93-318, June 22, 1974, 88 Stat. 244, which enacted sections 580p, 580p-1, 580p-3, and 580p-4 of this title and section 711a of Title 18, Crimes and Criminal Procedure, and amended section 580p-2 of this title and section 711 of Title 18. For complete classification of this Act to the Code, see Tables.

CODIFICATION

Section was formerly classified to section 488b-5 of Title 31 prior to the general revision and enactment of

Title 31, Money and Finance, by Pub. L. 97-258, § 1, Sept. 13, 1982, 96 Stat. 877.

SECTION REFERRED TO IN OTHER SECTIONS

This section is referred to in section 580p of this title.

§ 580p-4. Injunction against unauthorized manufacture, use, or reproduction

(a) Whoever, except as provided by rules and regulations issued by the Secretary, manufactures, uses, or reproduces the character "Smokey Bear", or the name "Smokey Bear", or a facsimile or simulation of such character or name in such a manner as suggests "Smokey Bear" may be enjoined from such manufacture, use, or reproduction at the suit of the Attorney General upon complaint by the Secretary.

(b) Whoever, except as provided by rules and regulations issued by the Secretary, manufactures, uses, or reproduces the character "Woodsy Owl", the name "Woodsy Owl", or the slogan "Give a Hoot, Don't Pollute", or a facsimile or simulation of such character, name, or slogan in such a manner as suggests "Woodsy Owl" may be enjoined from such manufacture, use, or reproduction at the suit of the Attorney General upon complaint by the Secretary.

(Pub. L. 93-318, § 4, June 22, 1974, 88 Stat. 245.)

CODIFICATION

Section was formerly classified to section 488b-6 of Title 31 prior to the general revision and enactment of Title 31, Money and Finance, by Pub. L. 97-258, § 1, Sept. 13, 1982, 96 Stat. 877.

SECTION REFERRED TO IN OTHER SECTIONS

This section is referred to in sections 580p, 580p-3 of this title.

§ 580q. National Tree Seed Laboratory; disposition of fees

Notwithstanding any other provision of law, fees received by the National Tree Seed Laboratory, administered by the Forest Service, United States Department of Agriculture, for the provision of a tree seed testing service, shall be retained and deposited as a reimbursement to current appropriations used to cover the costs of providing such service.

(Pub. L. 99-198, title XVII, § 1772, Dec. 23, 1985, 99 Stat. 1658.)

SUBCHAPTER II—INVESTIGATIONS, EXPERIMENTS, AND TESTS AFFECTING REFORESTATION AND FOREST PRODUCTS

§§ 581, 581a. Repealed. Pub. L. 95-307, § 8(a), June 30, 1978, 92 Stat. 356

Section 581, acts May 22, 1928, ch. 678, § 1, 45 Stat. 699; Apr. 24, 1950, ch. 97, § 17(a), 64 Stat. 87, authorized investigations, experiments, and tests affecting reforestation and forest products through cooperation with State and other agencies.

Section 581a, acts May 22, 1928, ch. 678, § 2, 45 Stat. 700; June 15, 1936, ch. 553, 49 Stat. 1515, set forth provisions establishing and authorizing appropriations for specific forest experiment stations.

EFFECTIVE DATE OF REPEAL

Repeal effective Oct. 1, 1978, see section 9 of Pub. L. 95-307, set out as an Effective Date note under section 1641 of this title.

Illustration C-1
Statute Printed in the *United States Code Annotated*,
16 USCA §580p-4

16 § 580p–4   CONSERVATION   Ch. 3

§ 580p–4. Injunction against unauthorized manufacture, use, or reproduction

(a) Whoever, except as provided by rules and regulations issued by the Secretary, manufactures, uses, or reproduces the character "Smokey Bear" or the name "Smokey Bear", or a facsimile or simulation of such character or name in such a manner as suggests "Smokey Bear" may be enjoined from such manufacture, use, or reproduction at the suit of the Attorney General upon complaint by the Secretary.

(b) Whoever, except as provided by rules and regulations issued by the Secretary, manufactures, uses, or reproduces the character "Woodsy Owl", the name "Woodsy Owl", or the slogan "Give a Hoot, Don't Pollute", or a facsimile or simulation of such character, name, or slogan in such a manner as suggests "Woodsy Owl" may be enjoined from such manufacture, use, or reproduction at the suit of the Attorney General upon complaint by the Secretary.

(Pub.L. 93–318, § 4, June 22, 1974, 88 Stat. 245.)

HISTORICAL AND STATUTORY NOTES

Revision Notes and Legislative Reports
  1974 Acts. House Report No. 93–948, see 1974 U.S. Code Cong. and Adm. News, p. 3279.

Codifications
  This section was formerly classified to section 488b–6 of Title 31 prior to the general revision and enactment of Title 31, Money and Finance, by Pub.L. 97–258, § 1, Sept. 13, 1982, 96 Stat. 877.

LIBRARY REFERENCES

American Digest System
  United States ☞3, 40.
  Key Number System Topic No. 393.
  Woods and Forests ☞5.
  Key Number System Topic No. 411.

Encyclopedias
  United States, see C.J.S. §§ 7, 38 to 40.
  Woods and Forests, see C.J.S. § 5.

Forms
  Preliminary injunctions and temporary restraining orders, matters pertaining to, see West's Federal Practice Forms § 5271 et seq.

WESTLAW ELECTRONIC RESEARCH

See WESTLAW guide following the Explanation pages of this volume.

436

Illustration C-2
Statute Printed in the *United States Code Annotated*,
16 USCA §580p-4, *con't.*

Ch. 3   FORESTS & FOREST SERVICE   16 §§ 581, 581a
                                                              Repealed

Notes of Decisions

Constitutionality 1

1. Constitutionality

Statute and regulation relied upon by the United States Forest Service to prohibit environmental organization's use of caricature of Smokey Bear in advertisement criticizing Forest Service's forest management policies violated organization's First Amendment rights; organization's use of chainsaw-wielding caricature of Smokey Bear was unlikely to cause confusion or to dilute the value of Smokey Bear to help prevent forest fires. LightHawk, the Environmental Air Force v. Robertson, W.D.Wash.1993, 812 F.Supp. 1095, 25 U.S.P.Q.2d 2014.

§ 580q.   National Tree Seed Laboratory; disposition of fees

Notwithstanding any other provision of law, fees received by the National Tree Seed Laboratory, administered by the Forest Service, United States Department of Agriculture, for the provision of a tree seed testing service, shall be retained and deposited as a reimbursement to current appropriations used to cover the costs of providing such service.

(Dec. 23, 1985, Pub.L. 99–198, Title XVII, § 1772, 99 Stat. 1658.)

HISTORICAL AND STATUTORY NOTES

Revision Notes and Legislative Reports
1985 Acts. House Report No. 99–271(Parts I and II), Senate Report No. 99–145, and House Conference Report No. 99–447, see 1985 U.S. Code Cong. and Adm. News, p. 1103.

LIBRARY REFERENCES

American Digest System
United States ⇐81, 82(1).
Key Number System Topic No. 393.

Encyclopedias
United States, see C.J.S. §§ 121 to 122.

WESTLAW ELECTRONIC RESEARCH

See WESTLAW guide following the Explanation pages of this volume.

SUBCHAPTER II—INVESTIGATIONS, EXPERIMENTS, AND TESTS AFFECTING REFORESTATION AND FOREST PRODUCTS

§§ 581, 581a.   Repealed.   Pub.L. 95–307, § 8(a), June 30, 1978, 92 Stat. 356

HISTORICAL AND STATUTORY NOTES

Section 581, Acts May 22, 1928, c. 678, § 1, 45 Stat. 699; Apr. 24, 1950, c. 97, § 17(a), 64 Stat. 87, authorized investigations, experiments, and tests affecting reforestation and forest products through cooperation with State and other agencies.

Section 581a, Acts May 22, 1928, c. 678, § 2, 45 Stat. 700; June 15, 1936, c. 553, 49 Stat. 1515, set forth provisions

437

Illustration D
Statute Printed in the *United States Code Service*,
16 USCS §580p-4

FOREST PROTECTION & MANAGEMENT   16 USCS § 580p-4

318, 88 Stat. 244, which appears generally as 16 USCS §§ 580p–580p-4. For full classification of this Act, consult USCS Tables volumes.

Explanatory notes:
This section formerly appeared as 31 USCS § 488b-5, prior to the enactment of Title 31 into positive law by Act Sept. 13, 1982, P. L. 97-258, § 1, 96 Stat. 877.

CROSS REFERENCES
This section is referred to in 16 USCS § 580p.

§ 580p-4. Injunction against unauthorized manufacture, use, or reproduction

(a) Whoever, except as provided by rules and regulations issued by the Secretary, manufactures, uses, or reproduces the character "Smokey Bear" or the name "Smokey Bear", or a facsimile or simulation of such character or name in such a manner as suggests "Smokey Bear" may be enjoined from such manufacture, use, or reproduction at the suit of the Attorney General upon complaint by the Secretary.

(b) Whoever, except as provided by rules and regulations issued by the Secretary, manufactures, uses, or reproduces the character "Woodsy Owl", the name "Woodsy Owl", or the slogan "Give a Hoot, Don't Pollute", or a facsimile or simulation of such character, name, or slogan in such a manner as suggest "Woodsy Owl" may be enjoined from such manufacture, use, or reproduction at the suit of the Attorney General upon complaint by the Secretary.
(June 22, 1974, P. L. 93-318, § 4, 88 Stat. 245.)

HISTORY; ANCILLARY LAWS AND DIRECTIVES

Explanatory notes:
This section formerly appeared as 31 USCS § 488b-6, prior to the enactment of Title 31 into positive law by Act Sept. 13, 1982, P. L. 97-258, § 1, 96 Stat. 877.

CROSS REFERENCES
This section is referred to in 16 USCS §§ 580p, 580p-3.

INTERPRETIVE NOTES AND DECISIONS

U.S. Forest Service cannot prevent small environmental organization from publishing political advertisement featuring depiction of chainsaw-wielding Smokey Bear, where 16 USCS § 580p-4(a) and implementing regulation 36 CFR § 271.3 purport to regulate all uses of Smokey, specifically prohibiting noncommercial uses not furthering message of forest fire prevention, because proposed application of statute and regulation to enjoin "Say it ain't so, Smokey" caricature abridges organization's First Amendment rights. Lighthawk, Environmental Air Force v Robertson (1993, WD Wash) 812 F Supp 1095, 25 USPQ2d 2014.

415

5. Electronic Sources

All of the forms of federal statutory publication discussed above are available for computerized research in either WESTLAW or LEXIS. The online code databases are generally up to date within a few weeks or days; the United States Public Laws databases are often up to date within a day or two. The currency of these databases is indicated on the screens, and should be checked before relying on an online search for current information.

Recently enacted public laws can be found online in both WESTLAW and LEXIS. WESTLAW's database features the full text of public laws from the 93rd Congress, 1st Session (1973) to present. Star paging to the *Statutes at Large* is available for public laws from 1988 forward. *Statutes at Large* references can be retrieved for the years 1789-1972.

In LEXIS, the public laws can be retrieved from the 100th Congress, 2nd Session (1988) to present. *Statutes at Large* is available from 1789 to present in a PDF format, so you can get the benefit of the gloss[20] in the page margins.

WESTLAW and LEXIS also offer the full text of pending federal bills, and bill tracking databases that provide the status of legislation introduced in the current Congress. The bill tracking databases are archived back to the 101st Congress (1989) in LEXIS and the 102nd Congress (1991) in WESTLAW. These archival databases will help you research bills that did not become law. Bill texts are archived on LEXIS back to the 101st Congress (1989) and to the 104th Congress (1995) on WESTLAW.

The current text of the *USC* in both of its commercial annotated versions is also available online, and past versions are archived. The *USC* database in WESTLAW contains the statutory text, *Statutes at Large* references, and legislative history references as they appear in the *United States Code Annotated,* but does not include any of *USCA*'s annotations or other research aids. All of *USCA*'s editorial features (*CFR* references, notes of decisions, etc.) are available, however, in WESTLAW's *USCA* database. Yearly, archived editions of the *USCA* are available from 1990, so that you can find out what a law looked like before amendments were made. LEXIS provides access to the *USC* as published in the *United States Code Service,*

---

20   In more recent years of the *Statutes at Large*, the comments in the margins include where the text will be inserted into the *USC*.

Illustration E
The Statute on LEXIS, *USCA* database

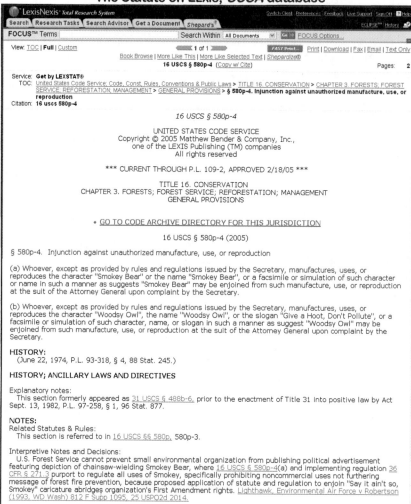

Illustration F
The Statute on WESTLAW, *USCA* database

including the history notes and references to other LEXIS publications, as well as the notes of decisions and *USCS*'s other editorial enhancements. Yearly, archived editions of the *USCS* are available from 1998.

Both WESTLAW and LEXIS have separate databases for the Federal Rules, and LEXIS offers a separate file for the United States Constitution.

The online researcher can retrieve a known statutory provision by searching for a particular citation, or can find statutes on a particular subject by searching for a combination of descriptive words. Because the annotations in *USCA* and *USCS* are usually more descriptive than the formal statutory language, their availability online enhances the researcher's ability to search for sections relevant to particular legal problems.

The WESTLAW and LEXIS U.S. Code databases are often most useful in situations where an issue is not adequately covered in indexes or where a combination of particular terms is important. If the interpretation of a statutory word or phrase is in issue, an online search can be used to quickly and efficiently retrieve all code provisions using that word or phrase. It should be noted that even professional researchers consider finding an unknown statute in an online database a difficult task. Statutory language is often of a tortured construction and difficult to predict.

A search of the code online retrieves only those *sections* which match the particular query. The systems treat each code section as a separate document, so that there are over 40,000 sections or documents in a code database. The online display of a section includes a heading indicating the title and chapter in which it belongs, but otherwise there is little immediate perspective on its place in the subject scheme. To better understand relationships between various code provisions, a searcher can view the table of contents for a particular chapter or title. Both services also allow the searcher to enter commands to display other sections classified before or after a section which matches the search query, thus providing some sense of its context.

D. FEDERAL STATUTORY RESEARCH

Because of the different forms of publication, research in statutory law varies considerably from that in case law. The emphasis is on regularly updated, heavily annotated, primary sources. The need for extrinsic aids to statutory interpretation, such as judicial decisions and legislative history, gives an added dimension to statutory research.

1. Finding Statutes

Statutory research typically begins with a search to determine whether there are statutes applicable to the particular problem or topic under consideration, and then locating the relevant statutory provisions. Sometimes, however, one has a reference to a particular law by number or popular name, and merely needs a table to locate that statute in its code form. There are various indexes and tables for these purposes.

a. Indexes

When confronted with a research problem involving legislation, the best course is to break the relevant issue down into the smallest possible components. Catchphrases and related terms from the issue can then be distilled and taken to a relevant index. The index is likely to send one directly to the relevant legislation. The searching is much more direct than case research.

The general index to the *USC* is quite thorough and extensive, and is updated in the cumulative annual supplements. The official index forms the basis, in fact, for the indexes in both *USCA* and *USCS*, which make only slight modifications in its entries. The major advantage offered by the indexes in the annotated codes is that they are more frequently updated. Both the *USCA* and *USCS* general index volumes are revised and reissued annually. Material in the quarterly pamphlets updating both annotated codes also is indexed. Illustration E shows a page from the general index in the *USC*.

Most of these indexes include plenty of cross-references, which are of two basic types. Cross-references between subject headings provide notice of related statutes covered elsewhere in the index. Entries for terms which are *not* used as subject headings indicate the synonymous or related terms which are used instead. A researcher who looks in the index under "Cattle" finds references to "Animals," "Beef Research and Information," and "Dairies," rather than no entry at all. Since indexers cannot foresee all possible terms a researcher might use, of course, it may sometimes be necessary to reformulate a query before finding any information. If an issue

Illustration E
A typical page from the General Index to the *United States Code*, with an entry for "Smokey Bear"

GENERAL INDEX   Page 442

SMOKELESS TOBACCO—Continued
Comprehensive—Continued
 Grants to States, program development, 15 §4401
 Ingredients, report to Congress respecting, contents, 15 §4403
 Violations, injunctions, 15 §4405
 Label format, 15 §4402
 Liability law unaffected, 15 §4406
 Manufacture, package, for sale or distribution, required warning, applicability, 15 §4402
 Misdemeanor, violation, warning provisions, 15 §4404
 Package, definitions, 15 §4408
 Plan, rotation, display, required statements, submission to FTC, 15 §4402
 Preemption, 15 §4406
 Public education, program development, 15 §4401
 Regulations, promulgation by FTC, 15 §4402 et seq.
 Reports,
  Ingredients, 15 §4403
  Violations, injunctions, 15 §4405
  Submission by FTC, Secretary, contents, 15 §4407
 Sales,
  Definitions, 15 §4408
  Outside U.S., inapplicability of provisions, 15 §4402
 Sampling or distribution not for sale, sale or distribution as including, 15 §4408
 Secretary, definitions, 15 §4408
 Secretary of Education, consultation and development of programs, materials, 15 §4401
 Secretary of Health and Human Services, Secretary as meaning, 15 §4408
 Smokeless tobacco, definitions, 15 §4408
 State and local action, preemption, 15 §4406
 States,
  Commerce as meaning commerce between, 15 §4408
  United States as meaning, 15 §4408
 Television and radio advertising, prohibition, 15 §4402
 United States, definitions, 15 §4408
 Warning, 15 §4402
  Enforcement, violations, 15 §4404
  Injunctions, 15 §4405
Excise tax,
 Definitions, 26 §5702
 Rate of tax, 26 §5701
Interest of Internal Revenue officer in manufacture, 26 §7214
Sales. Comprehensive health education, ante

SMOKEY BEAR
Generally, 16 §580p et seq.
Definitions, Forest Service, 16 §580p
Fees, 16 §580p-2
Injunctions, 16 §580p-4
Manufacturers and manufacturing, reproduction, Smokey Bear, crimes and offenses, 18 §711

SMOKING
Cigarette Labeling and Advertising, generally, this index
Coal and Coal Mines, this index
Federal facilities, smoke-free environment policy, 5 §7301 note, Ex. Ord. No. 13058

Pregnancy, prenatal and postnatal care, 42 §247b-13

SMUGGLING
Generally, 19 §1701 et seq.
Air Carrier Prevention Program, 19 §1584 note
Aircraft, 19 §1584 note
 Supplies, 19 §§1309, 1317
 Unlawful importation or exportation, 19 §1627a
 User fees, customs Services, small airports, seaports, or other facilities, 19 §§58b, 58c
 Withdrawal of articles free of duty to supply aircraft, 19 §1309
 Reports, 19 §§1433, 1436
Aliens, this index
Attempts, 18 §545
Controlled Substances, this index
Evidence, goods, possession, 18 §545
Goods, 18 §545
 International animal quarantine station, application of law, 21 §135a
Immigration, this index
Seamen, 46 §11501
Vessels, 19 §1580

SNAGS
Mississippi River,
 Removal from, 33 §604
 Upper Mississippi River, operation of snag boats on, 33 §605
Ohio River, removal, appropriations, 33 §606
River and harbor improvements, removal, appropriation, 33 §603a

SNAKE INDIANS
Indians, this index

SNAKE RIVER
Administration, 16 §1274 note
Birds of Prey National Conservation Area, 16 §460iii et seq.
Boundaries, 16 §1274 note
Dams and reservoirs, construction, 16 §1274 note
Flows, 16 §460gg-3
Hells Canyon National Recreation Area, 16 §460gg
Studies, 16 §1276
Wild and scenic rivers, 16 §1276

SNAKES
Brown tree snake,
 Eradication, 7 §426; 16 §4728
 Exports and imports, 18 §42
Endangered Species, generally, this index
Mail and mailing, reptiles, 18 §1716

SNOOP (NICKNAME)
Controlled substances, date rape, 21 §§801 note, 802, 812 note, 827, 841, 960

SNOW AND SNOWSTORMS
Ice and Snow, generally, this index

SNOW MOUNTAIN WILDERNESS
Generally, 16 §1132 note

SNOWMOBILES
Alaska national interest lands conservation, 16 §3121
Highways and roads, motor vehicles prohibited on trails and walkways, exception for, 23 §217

turns out not to be covered by federal statutory law, there may be no index entry to be found.

Every volume of the *Statutes at Large* has its own index, and there are also indexes for the annual volumes of *U.S. Code Congressional and Administrative News,* and cumulative indexes in each monthly issue of *USCCAN* and *USCS Advance.* The older indexes in bound volumes can be used to find laws from particular years, and the pamphlet indexes to find the latest laws passed by Congress.

For online research, the *USCA* and *USCS* General Indexes are available. An alphabetical list of all the main index headings can be accessed; you can also retrieve a list of all the references under each main heading. Both online services have features that allow the researcher to move from an index listing to the code section to which it refers.

For access to early federal laws, one can consult the indexes to earlier editions of the *U.S. Code,* the *Revised Statutes,* or individual *Statutes at Large* volumes. Two retrospective indexes to federal law prepared by the Library of Congress are also of occasional use in historical research. These indexes cover the periods indicated in their respective titles: Middleton G. Beaman & Agnus K. McNamara, *Index Analysis of the Federal Statutes, 1789-1873* (1911), and Walter H. McClenon & Wilfred C. Gilbert, *Index to the Federal Statutes, 1874-1931* (1933).[21] These include only general, public and permanent laws.

b. Tables

A researcher often has reference to a particular statute, and does not need to use a subject index. If the reference provides a current *USC* citation, access to the statute is no problem. Frequently, however, the reference gives only the name of a statute or provides an outdated or *Statutes at Large* citation. Two types of tables provide assistance in these situations.

Popular name tables consist of alphabetical lists of statutes, providing citations to their session law and codified locations. For an older statute, "popular name" often means a name with which it has come to be

---

21   The McClenon & Gilbert index superseded George W. Scott & Middleton G. Beaman, *Index Analysis of the Federal Statutes, 1873–1907* (1908).

associated over time, such as "Mann Acts" or "White-Slave Laws." Most modern statutes, on the other hand, specify short titles by which they may be cited. These names, such as "Marine Plastic Pollution Research and Control Act of 1987," are also listed in popular name tables. A person knowing only the name of an act can use these tables to find its Public Law number and its citation in both the *Statutes at Large* and the *USC*. Most codified acts are not printed all in one place, so the table usually lists scattered sections of the *USC* where provisions appear.

As noted above, all three editions of the U.S. Code include popular name tables. The *USC*'s "Acts Cited by Popular Name," printed in the final text volume, is quite thorough, but not as current as those in *USCA* and *USCS*. The *USCA* table is printed in the last general index volume, which is reissued every year; the *USCS* table appears in a bound volume with other tables, updated by an annual pocket part. The *USCA* table is further updated by an "Alphabetical Table of Laws" in the front of each quarterly pamphlet, and a table near the back of each issue of *USCCAN,* which cumulates each month for the entire session of Congress. The *USCS* table is updated in the back of every monthly *Advance* pamphlet and quarterly *Cumulative Later Case and Statutory Service.* The *USCA* and *USCS* popular name tables are available online. Illustration F shows a page from the *USCA* popular name table.

Parallel reference tables are the other tables that allow access to statutes. These tables list one citation for a statute, typically its session law location, and provide a cross-reference to another citation where it may be found, usually as codified.

The *USC*'s Tables volumes contain various parallel conversion tables which provide references between earlier revisions and later texts, and between different forms of statutory publication. Table I covers *USC* titles that have been revised and renumbered since the adoption of the code in 1926, showing where former sections of the title are incorporated into the latest edition. Table II indicates the status of sections of the *Revised Statutes of 1878* within the code, and Table III lists the *Statutes at Large* in chronological order and indicates where each section is incorporated into the code. Other tables cover executive orders, proclamations, reorganization plans, and internal cross-references within the code. The *USC*'s annual bound supplements generally include updates to these tables.

Illustration F
Popular Name Table from the USCA, with an entry for "White Slave Laws"

POPULAR NAME TABLE   1164

White Cane Safety Day Act
Pub.L. 88–628, Oct. 6, 1964, 78 Stat. 1003 (See 36 § 142)
Pub.L. 105–225, § 6(b), Aug. 12, 1998, 112 Stat. 1506 (36 § 169d)

White Charger Act
Pub.L. 86–616, § 10, July 12, 1960, 74 Stat. 395 (10 § 3297 note)

White Clay Creek Study Act
Short title, see 16 USCA § 1271 note
Pub.L. 102-215, Dec. 11, 1991, 105 Stat. 1664 (16 §§ 1271 note, 1276)

White Clay Creek Wild and Scenic Rivers System Act
See, also, Wild and Scenic Rivers Act (WSRA)
Short title, see 16 USCA § 1271 note
Pub.L. 106–357, Oct. 24, 2000, 114 Stat. 1393 (16 §§ 1271 note, 1274)

White-Collar Crime Penalty Enhancement Act of 2002
See, also, Sarbanes–Oxley Act of 2002 (Public Company Accounting Reform and Investor Protection Act)
Short title, see 18 USCA § 1341 note
Pub.L. 107–204, Title IX, July 30, 2002, 116 Stat. 804 (18 §§ 994 note, 1341, 1343, 1349, 1350; 29 § 1131)

White Earth Reservation Land Settlement Act of 1985 (WELSA)
Pub.L. 99–264, Mar. 24, 1986, 100 Stat. 61 (25 § 331 note)
Pub.L. 100–153, § 6(a), (b), Nov. 5, 1987, 101 Stat. 887 (25 § 331 notes)
Pub.L. 100–212, § 4, Dec. 24, 1987, 101 Stat. 212 (25 § 331 note)
Pub.L. 103–263, § 4, May 31, 1994, 108 Stat. 708 (25 § 331 note)

White House Conference for a Drug Free America
Pub.L. 100–138, §§ 1 to 3, Oct. 23, 1987, 101 Stat. 820, 821 (20 § 4601 notes)

White House Conference on Handicapped Individuals Act
Pub.L. 93–516, Title III, Dec. 7, 1974, 88 Stat. 1631 (29 § 701 note)
Pub.L. 93–651, Title III, Nov. 21, 1974, 89 Stat. 2–16 (29 § 701 note)
Pub.L. 94–224, §§ 1, 2, Feb. 27, 1976, 90 Stat. 201 (29 § 701 note)

White House Conference on Productivity Act
Pub.L. 97–367, Oct. 25, 1982, 96 Stat. 1761 (15 § 2401 note)

White House Conference on Small Business Authorization Act
Pub.L. 98–276, May 8, 1984, 98 Stat. 169 (15 § 631 note)
Pub.L. 101–409, Oct. 5, 1990, 104 Stat. 885 (15 § 631 note)
Pub.L. 103–81, § 10, Aug. 13, 1993, 107 Stat. 783 (15 § 631 note)

White House Police Act
Apr. 22, 1940, ch. 133, 54 Stat. 156 (See 3 § 203)

White Phosphorous Matches Act
Apr. 9, 1912, ch. 75, 37 Stat. 81

White Pine Blister Rust Protection Act
Apr. 26, 1940, ch. 159, 54 Stat. 168 (16 § 594a)
July 1, 1978, Pub.L. 95–313, § 13(a)(2), 92 Stat. 374 (16 § 594a)

White Russian Act
June 8, 1934, ch. 429, 48 Stat. 926

White-Slave Laws (Mann Acts) (White-Slave Traffic Act)
Mar. 26, 1910, ch. 128, 36 Stat. 263
June 25, 1910, ch. 395, 36 Stat. 825 (See 18 §§ 2421 to 2424)

White-Slave Traffic Act
See White-Slave Laws

Whitman Mission National Historic Site
Pub.L. 87–471, May 31, 1962, 76 Stat. 90 (16 § 433n)

Wholesome Meat Act (Meat Inspection Acts)
See, also, Federal Meat Inspection Act
Short title, see 21 USCA § 601 note

The most extensive and useful parallel reference tables in federal statutory research are, like the *USC*'s Table III, from Public Law number or *Statutes at Large* citation to the *USC*. The *USCA* and *USCS* versions of these tables are updated in each publication's quarterly and monthly pamphlets. The newer tables add citations for new statutes and update information on older statutes that have been repealed or moved. Illustration G shows a page from the *Statutes at Large* parallel reference table in *USCS*.

Like the *USC*, the *USCA* and *USCS* include other parallel reference tables that provide access from *Revised Statutes* sections to *USC* sections, and explain the disposition of sections of code titles which have been revised. The latter tables can be very handy if one has a reference to a code section from an older case or article, but upon trying to locate the text finds either nothing at all or an unrelated provision.

The *USCS* "Revised Title Table" and "Statutes-at-Large Table" are available in LEXIS. In WESTLAW, the "Revised Statutes," "Public Law," "Executive Orders," "Proclamation" and "Reorganization Plans" tables are available.

2. Updating Statutes

Just as finding decisions is not all there is to case research, finding statutes through indexes, tables, or other means is just the first step of statutory research. Before relying on a statute as authority, one must verify that it is still in force and ascertain how it has been affected by subsequent legislation and by judicial decisions.

a. *USCA* and *USCS*

One reason that annotated codes are such powerful research tools is that they serve two essential functions: they print the text of a primary authority and they provide regularly updated information on its validity and treatment. The frequent and varied supplementation for *USCA* and *USCS* has already been described. These updating materials provide the text of amendments to a statutory provision and include carefully edited, topically arranged annotations of interpretive judicial decisions. A case researcher must do a good deal of work to update a decision, but a statutory researcher finds much of the work already done by the annotated code.

Illustration G
A typical parallel reference table in *USCS*, showing the entry for 88 Stat. 244

| 88 Stat | | STATUTES AT LARGE | | | 93d Cong | |

Pub. L.	Section	Stat. Page	USCS Title	Section	Status	Pub. L.	Section	Stat. Page	USCS Title	Section	Status
		1974 June—Cont'd						*1974 June—Cont'd*			
93-302	1, 2	191, 192	22	2502		93-318	—Cont'd				
							3	245	31	488b-5	
							4	245	31	488b-6	
		1974 June 7					5	245	18	711	
93-303	1	192-					6	245	18	711a	Added
		194	16	460l-6a			7	245	31	488a	
	2	194	16	460l-8			8	245	18	prec 701	
	3	194	16	460l-10a		93-319	1(a)	246	15	791 nt	
							1(b)	246	15	791	
		1974 June 8					2	246	15	792	
93-304		194	Spec.		Un- class.		3	248	42	1857c-10	
93-305		195	Appn.		Un- class.		4	256	42	1857c-5	
							5	258	42	1857f-1	
	101	206	40	174b-1 nt			6(a)(1)- (3)	259	42	1857c-8	
	101	206	40	175 nt			6(a)(4)	259	42	1857c-9	
		207	Appn.		Un- class.		6(b)	259	42	1857d-1	
							6(c)	259	42	1857h-5	
		213	Appn.		Un- class.		7	259	15	793	
							8	260	15	794	
93-306		233	Spec.		Un- class.		9	261	15	795	
							10	261	42	1857f-6, 1857f-7	
93-307	101-302	233- 234	Appn.		Un- class.		11	262	15	796	
							12	264	15	797	
	401	234	10	520 nt			13(a)	265	42	1857b-1	
	402		Appn.		Un- class.		13(b)	265	42	1857f-6e	
							13(c)	265	42	1857l	
93-308		234	Appn.		Un- class.		14	265	15	798	
93-309	1-3	234	Spec.		Un- class.			*1974 June 24*				
						93-320	1	266	43	1571 nt	
93-310	1	235	19	1202			101	266	43	1571	
	2(b)	235	19	1202 nt			102	268	43	1572	
	3(a)	235	26	501			103	269	43	1573	
	3(b)	235	26	501 nt			104	270	43	1574	
93-311		236	15	1026	Rpld.		105	270	43	1575	
93-312	1-8	237	Appn.		Un- class.		106	270	43	1576	
							107	270	43	1577	
	9	238	5	5315, 5316			108	270	43	1578	
	9	238	22	2655a			201	270	43	1591	
93-313		238	16	669b nt			202	271	43	1592	
		238	26	4161 nt			203	271	43	1593	
93-314	1(a)	239	44	910			204	272	43	1594	
	1(b)	239	44	906			205(a), (b)(1)	272	43	1595	
	1(c)	239	44	prec 901			205(b)(2)	273	43	1543	
							205(c)	273	43	1595	
		1974 June 22					205(d)	273	43	620d	
93-315		239	22	2849			205(e)	274	43	1595	
		239	22	2849	Term.		206	274	43	1596	
93-316	1-4	240	Appn.		Un- class.		207	274	43	1597	
							208	274	43	1598	
	5	243	42	2459 nt			209	275	43	1599	
	6	243	42	2473								
	7	243	42	2463				*1974 June 30*				
	8	244	Appn.		Un- class.	93-321		275	Appn.		Un- class.
93-317	1, 2	244	Spec.		Un- class.	93-322		276	Appn.		Un- class.
93-318	1	244	31	488b-3		93-323		280	50 Appx.	2166	
	2	245	31	488b-4		93-324		281	Appn.		Un- class.

b. WESTLAW and LEXIS Databases

The convenient updating features of *USCA* and *USCS*, such as frequent supplementation and extensive annotations, are available in their online formats. The current *USCS* and *USCA* databases on LEXIS and WESTLAW generally update soon after a law takes affect.[22] When you bring up a statutory section, both systems will show a statement of how current the law is. On the LEXIS screen, the statement appears near the top of the document, whereas on WESTLAW it appears at the bottom. Illustrations H and I highlight those statements, which can also be seen when looking at the whole statute in Illustrations E and F. Online statutory research can be further updated by searching for the specific code section or general subject matter in question in the WESTLAW or LEXIS current Public Laws database. This should yield recently enacted legislation directly affecting the relevant code section, and other related matter, such as new statutes or material not yet codified. WESTLAW's *KeyCite* may signal you with a yellow flag if there is pending legislation that may affect for your section.

Finally, citations to statutes in decisions and articles can be found using the online systems by searching in full-text case or periodical databases. Such a search, using either the title or citation of a statute, will find very recent references that have yet to be covered by an annotated code.

3. Interpreting Statutes

The procedures for finding and updating statutes just described constitute the basic methods of statutory research. An essential purpose of such research is to determine what Congress meant by a particular enactment. To do so, one must use resources discussed more fully in other chapters of this book. Because they are treated elsewhere, the following materials are only noted here.

---

22   For example, the U.S. Congress might pass a law today that will not take affect for six months. In a case such as this, LEXIS and WESTLAW will update the text of their *USCS* and *USCA* databases when the law takes affect, not when the law is passed. A law that takes affect immediately will be incorporated into the databases within weeks or days.

Illustration H
Partial Screen Shot of a Statute in LEXIS, Showing Statement of Currentness at the Top of the Screen

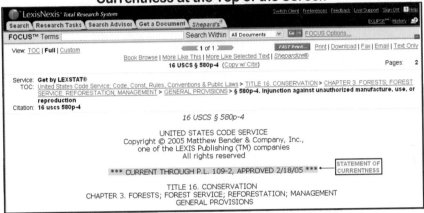

Illustration I
Partial Screen Shot of a Statute in WESTLAW, Showing Statement of Currentness at the Bottom of the Screen

a. Judicial Decisions

Judicial interpretations and constructions of ambiguous or controverted statutory language are often used to establish the meaning of a statute. Such interpretations may have been made in earlier cases dealing with the specific statute, or in cases involving other statutes containing similar provisions or language. Relevant decisions can be located through several methods, including: (1) reading the annotations in *USCA* or *USCS;* (2) Shepardizing or KeyCiting a statutory provision; or (3) searching WESTLAW or LEXIS full-text case databases for references to a statute by citation or name. The publication of judicial decisions and the process of case research have been discussed in Chapters 2 through 4.

b. Legislative History

To determine the meaning of a statutory provision, one can investigate the legislative documents that led to its enactment. Various versions of a bill, reports of Senate and House Committees that considered the proposed legislation, transcripts of floor debates, and other Congressional materials may all be of use in interpreting the text of a statute. These legislative history documents, and the finding aids and research procedures for their investigation, are treated in detail in Chapter 6.

c. Other Resources

Statutes are often discussed in looseleaf services, periodical articles, and treatises. Such discussions may be quite helpful in statutory research and interpretation, and often include references to cases, other statutes, legislative history materials, and regulations. Specialized finding aids of varying quality exist for each of these types of secondary material. Looseleaf services, legal periodicals, and treatises will be discussed in Chapter 10.

Attorney general opinions are an important source of persuasive statutory interpretation on the *state* level, but U.S. Attorney General opinions are not prepared or consulted on such a regular basis. They may be of occasional use, however, and are discussed in Chapter 8.

E. OTHER FORMS OF FEDERAL LEGISLATION

Statutes are not the only form of federal legislation. Most of the following additional legislative materials are discussed elsewhere, but they should be noted in this context.

1. United States Constitution

The federal Constitution is the basic, organic legislation of the United States, and appears in a variety of published sources. These publications, and research in constitutional law generally, are discussed in Chapter 6.

2. Treaties

Treaties are international agreements negotiated between sovereign powers. Article VI of the Constitution provides that treaties made under the authority of the United States have the same legal authority and force as statutes. They are a special kind of federal legislation because they do not follow the usual enactment process through Congress. Under Article II, §2, the President "shall have Power, by and with the Advice and Consent of the Senate to make treaties, provided two thirds of the Senators present concur." Treaty legislation thus arises in the executive branch but requires legislative approval to become law. Research in the law of treaties is a specialized skill. It is treated in depth in *How to Find the Law*.

3. Interstate Compacts

The Constitution, as interpreted by the courts, authorizes agreements between the states, provided they are first approved by Congress.[23] After the compact is agreed upon by the states, it goes to Congress for authorizing legislation. When enacted, each compact thus appears in the *U.S. Statutes at Large* and in the session laws of the states which are parties to it. The Council of State Governments publishes a description of such compacts in *Interstate Compacts & Agencies,* which is revised from time to time and updated between revisions in the Council's annual publication, the *Book of the States.*

Most interstate compacts also appear in the annotated statutory codes of the states enacting them. You can, therefore, use those publications or *Shepard's* or *KeyCite* to locate cases which have applied or interpreted interstate compacts.

4. Reorganization Plans

Reorganization plans are an unusual hybrid form of legislation. They consist of Presidential proposals to reorganize executive agencies below the departmental level, submitted to Congress for approval pursuant to

---

23   Article I, §10 provides: "No state shall, without the Consent of Congress, ... enter into any Agreement or Compact with another State...." For further information, see Federick L. Zimmerman & Mitchell Wendell, *The Law and Use of Interstate Compacts* (1976).

a general authorizing statute. Reorganization plans are treated with other Presidential lawmaking materials in Chapter 8.

F. STATE STATUTES

Statutory research on the state level is quite similar to the federal paradigm already discussed at length. This section will be more brief, and assumes familiarity with principles outlined in the preceding sections on statutory publication generally and federal statutory research.

1. Slip Laws and Session Laws

State statutes are enacted and published in a manner similar to the federal pattern. Most states publish their statutes initially in a slip law form, either on a web site or in paper. All states publish bound session law volumes. The titles of these publications vary from state to state (*e.g., Alaska Session Laws, California Statutes, Acts and Resolves of Massachusetts, Laws of New York*). Like the *U.S. Statutes at Large,* they all print acts chronologically and include non-cumulative subject indexes and tables.

Official state session laws are usually not published until well after the end of a legislative session. In over half of the states, commercially published advance session law services, sometimes known as "legislative services," provide quicker access to current acts. These monthly or bimonthly pamphlets are generally issued by the publisher of a state's annotated code as a form of supplementation to the code. They are similar to Thomson-West's *USCCAN* (but without the legislative history component) and to the *USCS Advance* pamphlets.

For online research, LEXIS provides access to the slip laws or advance legislative services of all fifty states, either in individual files for every state or in a group file. WESTLAW has similar databases for each state's recent and historical legislation, and all the states' legislation combined. Coverage varies by state, so the scope or information screens should be checked before relying on an online search for current information. Generally, coverage begins in the 1990's.

Both WESTLAW and LEXIS offer bill tracking for the fifty states, individually or combined. Both also provide the full text of bills. Remember, however, the official text of bills can often be found, for free, on state legislative web sites.

2. State Codes

State statutory compilations are published in a wide variety of forms and with varying degrees of "official" status. Code provisions in some states are reenacted as positive law, but in most states they are only *prima facie* evidence of the authoritative session laws. Some states have an official, unannotated code, regularly revised and published by the state on an annual or biennial basis. A few small states prepare their own annotated codes. Others have arrangements with commercial publishers to prepare annotated codes, which are legislatively or administratively sanctioned as "official." Many states, however, rarely revise their official codification, so they become obsolete and only of historical interest.[24] In such states, the subject arrangement of an earlier official code is usually retained and updated by a commercial publisher. In most state codes, a certificate or prefatory note in the front of each volume indicates its status as authority.

At least one annotated code is published for every state, and several larger states have two annotated codes issued by competing publishers. While codes vary from state to state in frequency of updating and in editorial quality, they are the most useful and most frequently consulted versions of state statutes.

Most state codes are published in bound volumes with pocket part supplements, although several are published in pamphlets filed in looseleaf binders. In either form, both statutory provisions and annotations are updated at least once a year. Many codes are further updated by pamphlets issued between annual supplements, containing the latest amendments and case notes. Every code is accompanied by an index, and most include parallel reference tables.

---

24   For example, the *Consolidated Laws of New York* have not been officially reissued since 1909.

3. Online Sources

Many states provide access to the state code on a legislative web site. Before relying on a such a web site, you would need to check how often it is updated; many are updated every day and are the source for the commercial services. These web sites will not offer you the annotations that are available in the commercial online services, however.

WESTLAW provides access to the statutes, court rules, and constitutions of all fifty states, as set out in each state's code. Annotated and unannotated code databases are available for all states. Searching in a state's annotated code database provides access to the editorial features, like case annotations and references to secondary materials, included in the print version of the code.

In LEXIS, each state's code file includes the state constitution, the current advance legislative service, and all the titles of the state code. Separate statutory tables of contents files allow the researcher to view the hierarchical structure of each state code, and to then review the desired code section.

In addition to databases for specific codes, both systems offer the ability to search at once in all state codes. Statutory language differs from state to state, but this is nonetheless a powerful capability for someone doing comparative statutory research or interested in finding how a particular word or phrase has been applied in other states.

The frequency of updating varies from state to state. Before relying on an online code as current, a prudent researcher would verify its status by consulting the online database directories or scope screens.

G. STATE STATUTORY RESEARCH

1. Finding State Statutes

Almost all annotated codes include parallel reference tables comparable to those in the three versions of the U.S. Code, and every code has an extensive index. These indexes frequently occupy several volumes, and are either supplemented or reissued each year. WESTLAW includes separate databases for the general index of each state's statutes.

Only a few state codes include tables of acts by name, but comprehensive coverage of state popular name acts is provided in two forms by *Shepard's Citations.* The *Shepard's* citator for each state includes a "Table of Acts by Popular Names or Short Titles." These tables, which are updated in the supplementary pamphlets, generally provide citations only to codes, not session laws. In addition, *Shepard's Acts and Cases by Popular Names: Federal and State,* three volumes published in 1992 and supplemented regularly by cumulative, soft-covered pamphlets, provides one alphabetical listing of statutes from throughout the country, with references to the specific state codes or session laws where the acts or provisions can be found. The nationwide *Acts and Cases by Popular Names* sometimes has more current information than the list in a state citator.[25] It is most useful in situations where the title of an act, but not the state of enactment, is known, or when similar acts from several states are sought.

Multistate statutory searches are not frequently required by practitioners, but they are quite common in scholarly research. Searching fifty state codes is very time-consuming, particularly since different indexes often treat similar subjects in very different ways. Rather than expecting a single search procedure to work for every state, one must approach each index as its own system of classifications and cross-references.

Several resources may help in multistate statutory searches. An online keyword search in the WESTLAW or LEXIS database containing the complete set of every state's statutes may retrieve most relevant documents if terminology is fairly standard. The last volume of the *Martindale-Hubbell Law Directory* contains digests of state laws on a variety of standardized subjects, and provides references to statutory primary sources. Topical looseleaf services in some subject areas reprint state laws; the *Environment*

---

25   For both the state listings and the general *Acts and Cases,* paperback supplements list new acts but take no notice of the recodification or moving of older acts. Such changes are only recognized when a volume is recompiled and reissued. The more current source for a particular state, then, depends on whether the state citator was published before or after the most recent revision of *Shepard's Acts and Cases by Popular Names.*

Reporter, for example, contains state laws and regulations on such issues as air pollution, mining, and waste disposal.

State laws on particular subjects are also collected or surveyed in a variety of other sources, such as treatises, law review articles, and government publications. Some of these sources provide the texts of laws, but even those that only list code citations can save a considerable amount of research time. Extensive guides to these collections and surveys of state laws have been published in recent years. Lynn Foster & Carol Boast, *Subject Compilations of State Laws: Research Guide and Annotated Bibliography* (1981) is arranged by subject, with descriptive annotations and indexes by author and publisher. It is updated by regular supplements under the title, *Subject Compilations of State Laws: An Annotated Bibliography,* authored by Cheryl Nyberg and Carol Boast for 1979-83 (1984), and by Cheryl R. Nyberg for 1983-85 (1986), 1985-88 (1989), and annually since 1991. The *National Survey of State Laws,* edited by Richard Leiter, (5th ed. 2005), collects the texts of statutes on selected topics from all 50 states. Another guide to subject compilations is Jon S. Schultz, *Statutes Compared: A U.S., Canadian, Multinational, Research Guide to Statutes by Subject* (1991-), published in looseleaf format.

2. Updating and Interpreting State Statutes

The primary engine for updating the statutes in any state is its annotated code. The code will be kept current by pocket parts and usually by pamphlets. A common research mistake is to use only the pocket part and to stop. Check and see if the set is updated between the issuance of pocket parts. If so, be sure and use the appropriate temporary pamphlets. Check the advance session law pamphlets as well.

An increasing number of states are making new legislation available via online bulletin boards. Find out if the jurisdiction in question offers such a service. It may be the quickest and most reliable updating available.

If using LEXIS or WESTLAW, be certain of the coverage of the database. How recently has new information been added? Are there files of new legislation that should be checked? Of course you can always run a keyword search that consists of the statutory citation through the relevant case data base (limited to relevant dates of decision) to ascertain if any comment has been made about the statute.

H. UNIFORM LAWS AND MODEL ACTS

For many years, one of the major aspects of the law reform movement in this country has been a drive for the enactment of uniform laws by the several states in those fields in which uniformity would be beneficial. To this end, the National Conference of Commissioners on Uniform State Laws was formed in 1892. The Conference, consisting of representatives from each state, meets annually to draft, promulgate and promote uniform laws, which the states can then adopt as proposed, modify, or reject, as they see fit. Over two hundred uniform laws have been approved by the Conference, of which over a hundred have been adopted by at least one state. The *Uniform Commercial Code*, jointly sponsored by the Conference and the American Law Institute, has been enacted at least in part by every state.[26]

All of the uniform laws which have been adopted by at least one state are compiled in an annotated set published by Thomson-West called *Uniform Laws Annotated* with annual pocket part or pamphlet supplementation and periodic additions. *ULA* includes the Commissioners' notes on each law, explains variations in individual states' enactments, and provides references to law review commentaries and court decisions from all adopting states. The notes of decisions are in the usual Thomson-West format of headnote abstracts. These annotations, reflecting the interpretations of a uniform law in states which have enacted it, are particularly important for research in states which are considering adopting a law or have recently done so.

Tables in each volume and supplementation list states which have adopted each uniform law. In addition, an annual pamphlet accompanying the set provides a directory of uniform acts, lists for each state of enacted uniform legislation, and a brief index covering all acts. Each individual act is indexed in full in the back of its volume.

The *Uniform Laws Annotated* is available in WESTLAW's ULA database, and includes notes of decisions and other editorial features offered in the print version. Another WESTLAW database, HAWKLAND, contains the *Uniform Commercial Code*, along with the full text of *Uniform Commercial Code Series,* a nine-volume treatise by William D. Hawkland.

---

26   Louisiana has adopted only Articles 1, 3, 4, 5, 7, 8, and 9.

The *UCC* is the only uniform law currently available in LEXIS. That company's UCC library includes treatises and secondary materials in addition to the text and official comments on the law, also.

Another important publication on uniform laws is the annual *Handbook of the National Conference of Commissioners on Uniform State Laws.* The *Handbook* contains current information about pending laws under consideration by the Conference and discussions of new and proposed legislation. It is one of the few sources of the texts of uniform laws which have not yet been adopted by any state. Information about pending legislation and the text of draft laws can also be found at the web sites for the NCCUSL.[27]

"Model acts" are drafted for fields where individual states are likely to modify a proposed law to meet their needs, rather than adopt it *in toto.* The National Conference has drafted some model acts, but two of the more influential model acts were developed by the American Law Institute: the Model Penal Code and the Model Business Corporation Act. Research tools for these acts include the American Law Institute, *Model Penal Code and Commentaries* (6 vols., 1980-85), and the American Bar Association, *Model Business Corporation Act Annotated* (4 vols.) (3d ed. 1998).

It should be noted that neither uniform laws nor model acts have any legal effect in a state unless actually adopted by its legislature. When adopted, they appear in the session laws and annotated code. These sources are, of course, invaluable for research purposes, since only they contain the actual text *as enacted,* with whatever changes and variations were made in the form proposed by the National Conference.

I. LOCAL LAW SOURCES

Legal problems and issues are governed not only by federal and state law, but also by the laws of counties, cities, villages, and other local units. Local laws are a form of delegated legislation, based on law-making powers

---

27   <http://www.nccusl.org/> is the home of the NCCUSL, but an official archive <http://www.law.upenn.edu/bll/ulc/ulc_frame.htm> is maintained at the University of Pennsylvania. State bill tracking updates and information can be found at the first site. Texts of the final uniform laws and drafts can be found at the second site.

granted by the state legislatures, or, in the case of Washington, D.C. and other federally controlled areas, by the U.S. Congress.

Despite the trend toward greater centralization of governmental authority over the last fifty years, local laws remain important in many areas of daily life and economic activity. Housing, transportation, social welfare, education, municipal services, zoning, and environmental conditions are all heavily regulated at this level of government. Local taxation is an ever-increasing area of legal activity. Consequently, local law is a frequent subject of research. This research can be very frustrating, since local law sources in general are poorly published, inadequately indexed, and infrequently supplemented. The Internet, however, has made many local laws more accessible and searchable.

1. Municipal Charters and Ordinances

A city's *charter* is its organic law, similar in purpose to a federal or state constitution. An *ordinance* is a measure passed by its council or governing body to regulate municipal matters, and is the local equivalent of a federal or state statute. Most of the larger cities in the United States publish collections of their charter and ordinances in codes of varying quality. Very few municipal codes include annotations to case law. There has been a movement by several small private publishers to prepare codes for smaller cities and towns, and these have greatly improved access to local law in the communities served.

LexisNexis bought one of the larger publishers of local laws, the Book Publishing Company, in 2001 and now maintains a free web site of the municipal codes from this company.[28] Other companies maintaining local laws on the web include General Code[29], Municipal Code Corporation[30] and American Legal Publishing.[31] These companies are paid by the

---

28   <http://www.bpcnet.com/codes.htm> At the time of this writing, there were about 275 local codes on this site. Despite being owned by LexisNexis, these local codes are not available in LEXIS.

29   <http://www.generalcode.com/webcode2.html>

30   <http://www.municode.com/Resources/online_codes.asp>

31   <http://www.amlegal.com/online_library.htm>

municipalities to organize the code and maintain the web site so, for now, access is free. Many localities are mounting the text of local laws themselves on city or county web sites.[32] If searching is available, it is most often a simple keyword match design.

Despite the Internet, however, many local laws are not readily available. Individual ordinances (if their existence is known and they can be identified) must be obtained from the Clerk's Office of the county, city, or town. In larger cities, municipal reference libraries can be very helpful, and some public libraries are useful sources of information on local law.

One of the best sources for information on municipal government is the International Municipal Lawyers Association (IMLA). IMLA consists of professionals who work in the field of municipal law. The Association publishes a bimonthly magazine, the *Municipal Attorney* to help keep its members apprised of the most recent court cases and developments dealing with local laws and ordinances.[33]

State digests, state legal encyclopedias, and local practice sets include references to court decisions on particular local law problems and may discuss local ordinances in point. General legal treatises on municipal law may be helpful for their discussion of broader issues, but are less likely to provide local references.

2. *Ordinance Law Annotations*

Thomson-West publishes a digest of national scope on judicial decisions involving local ordinances, entitled *Ordinance Law Annotations* (13 vols., 1969-date). This service provides brief abstracts of decisions

---

32   For example, the online Berkeley, CA Municipal Code is maintained by the City Clerk's Office. <http://www.ci.berkeley.ca.us/bmc/> One good list of local laws available on the Internet is kept by the Seattle Public Library, <http://www.spl.org/default.asp?pageID=collection_municodes>

33   IMLA was formerly known as NIMLO (National Institute of Municipal Law Officers). From 1946 to 1990, NIMLO published a set called *NIMLO Municipal Law Court Decisions*, which, although outdated, can still be consulted to help find cases concerning municipal law.

under broad subject headings, which are arranged alphabetically and subdivided into more specific subtopics. The set is kept up to date by annual pocket parts, and includes a two-volume table of cases arranged by state and city or county. *Ordinance Law Annotations* allows one to survey municipal lawmaking throughout the country.

J. SUMMARY

Statutory law plays a pivotal role in the modern legal system and in legal research. Most appellate decisions involve the application or interpretation of statutes. Administrative regulations, court rules, and local laws all derive from delegations of power created by statute. The scope of judicial jurisdiction or executive authority is largely determined by legislative enactments. All legal research must therefore include the question: Is there a statute on point?

This chapter can perhaps best be summarized by the following questions applicable to every statutory research problem:

1. What statutory materials are available for the jurisdiction and what is their authority?

2. What statutory research approaches are best suited to this issue in this jurisdiction?

3. Have I found all possible sources of statutory law on this issue?

4. Is what I have found current, reflecting the latest enactments and the most recent judicial interpretations?

5. What other extrinsic aids to statutory interpretation are available on this problem?

K. ADDITIONAL READING

Jack Davies, *Legislative Law and Process in a Nutshell* (2d ed. 1986).

"Dynamic Statutory Interpretation," *Issues in Legal Scholarship* (2002).
    <http://www.bepress.com/ils/iss3>. An on-line symposia in which
    over a dozen recognized scholars in the field of legislation examine
    the theory of dynamic statutory interpretation developed by William
    N. Eskridge, Jr. and ultimately published as a book (see below).

William N. Eskridge, Jr., *Dynamic Statutory Interpretation* (Harvard
    University Press 1994).

William N. Eskridge, Jr., Philip P. Frickey and Elizabeth Garrett, *Cases and
    Materials on Legislation: Statutes and the Creation of Public
    Policy* (3rd ed. 2001). This landmark work on the legislative process
    offers excellent insights.

William J. Keefe and Morris S. Ogul, *The American Legislative Process:
    Congress and the States* (10th ed. 2001).

"Symposium on Statutory Interpretation," 53 *SMU L. Rev.* 3 (2000).

U.S. Office of the Federal Register, *How to Find U.S. Statutes and U.S.
    Code Citations* (3d rev. ed. 1977).

The subject of statutory interpretation has generated much
discussion in academic law scholarship. Accordingly, online indexing tools,
such as *LegalTrac* and *Index to Legal Periodicals* are quite helpful in
gathering the wealth of writing on this topic. Unfortunately, the applicable
subject heading "Law—Interpretation and Construction" is overly broad and
will generate too many articles for an efficient search. Accordingly, one
should try to narrow such a search by jurisdiction, date, etc.

Chapter 6

LEGISLATIVE HISTORY

A. INTRODUCTION

When you have found a statute, your research process often is not complete. Statutory language can be vague or ambiguous, and determining the precise meaning of a provision can be quite a challenge. How to interpret a word or a phrase can determine the outcome of many issues.

Statutes may be difficult to interpret for several reasons. The imprecision of the English language itself is one likely culprit. It is hard to understand what a word like "reasonable" means whether it's used by a legislature or a court. The changes in circumstances caused by the passage of time can bring about entirely new applications of a statute that make it difficult to understand how its language applies. A good example of this is the attempt to apply copyright law to ever-expanding technology such as music and movie downloading from the Internet. Other problems can be caused by poor drafting on the part of the legislature. Sometimes statutes are just ineptly drawn. Finally, confusion can be introduced by a conscious decision on the part of a legislative body to reach an acceptable compromise on a controversial measure by using language ambiguous enough to be acceptable to each contending party.

One way of determining what a statute "really means" is to perform a legislative history. A traditional legislative history is the gathering together of every relevant document that is part of the passage of a piece of legislation. The idea is to find out what the legislative body thought it was doing when it passed the legislation by examining the evidence of what the legislators knew and said at the time. In the matter of federal legislation, this process leads one through a large number of documents of various types.

This method is not without controversy. Can the intent of a legislative body ever really be determined? Isn't it possible that each legislator who voted had a different intent? We know that many members of Congress never actually read the text of the documents that are collected as a part of the legislative history exercise. So how can such documents shed any light on Congressional intent? Such objections are being raised in prominent places. Justice Antonin Scalia of the Supreme Court is quite hostile to the use of legislative histories. He believes that you can find anything you want to in the welter of documents surrounding the passage of legislation. He feels you should just stick to the plain language of the statute to find its meaning. But Justice Scalia's opinion remains a minority view. Legislative histories are cited more and more often in judicial opinions.

Traditional legislative history consists of three steps:

- **First, you must identify the documents that might be relevant.**
- **Second, you must gather the documents.**
- **Third, you must analyze what is found.**

This Chapter will assist with the first two of these functions. Section B will review the documents generated as a part of the federal legislative process. The federal legislative process produces a rich mosaic of materials. Each type of document will be discussed in turn. Section C will discuss methods that can be used to assemble the documents. Analyzing the documents is best addressed in a course on Legislation.

To this point we have spoken of traditional legislative history, a process which uses official documents. In Section D we will talk about contextual legislative history. Contextual legislative history is a more active form of research that will move beyond the normal federal materials. This approach can help one to focus on certain documents, or even parts of documents, making the whole process simpler.

Section E is devoted to state legislative histories. State legislatures do not produce the same wealth of documents that the Congress does. The federal system, with fifty different state legislatures operating in fifty distinct manners, makes any systematic discussion of state tools impossible. We will highlight functional commonalities that can help.

B. THE DOCUMENTS OF THE FEDERAL LEGISLATIVE PROCESS

The documents of a legislative history must be viewed in the context of the parliamentary practices which produce them. Congressional procedures are quite complex. The following brief survey of the normal stages of Congressional action is designed to place the major documents of federal legislative history in their procedural setting. More detailed information about that legislative process can be found in two brief Congressional pamphlets, *How Our Laws Are Made* and *Enactment of a Law: Procedural Steps in the Legislative Process.*[1] Illustration A-1, A-2 &

---

1   Willet, Edward F., *How Our Laws Are Made* (rev. and updated by Charles

A-3 show the text of a federal statute, the Curt Flood Act of 1998, as it appears in the *Statutes at Large*. The illustrations that follow in this chapter show various documents and finding tools relating to the legislative history of that law.

1. Congressional Bills

The bill is the first relevant legislative document. Each bill, when introduced, is printed, assigned a bill number, and then referred to a committee of the house in which it is presented. The bill may be amended at any stage of its legislative progress and some bills are amended many times. The bill number is the key to tracing legislative actions prior to enactment and to locating many of the documents reflecting such actions. The finding tools for such research are called status tables. They usually list bills by number, identify documents relevant to their consideration, and frequently describe significant legislative actions taken. After enactment, similar tables arranged by public law number recapitulate the steps and documents of the legislative history of each enactment. These tables are discussed in Section C below.

Variations in the text of the bill as it is introduced, as it appears in a committee print, as amended, and as passed, may be helpful in determining its meaning. The deletion or insertion of particular language in the text implies a legislative choice and thus may reveal the intent of the legislature. Almost every printing of a bill represents a distinct step in its progress toward enactment and may ultimately be a significant document in its legislative history.

Congressional bills are individually numbered in a separate series for each house and retain that number through both of the annual sessions of each Congress. A citation to a bill includes the number of the Congress and session in which it was introduced or printed, as follows: S. 53, 105th Cong., 1st Sess. (1997). At the end of the two-year term of Congress, pending bills lose their active status and must be reintroduced if they are to be considered.

W. Johnson, 2003) <http://thomas.loc.gov/home/lawsmade.toc.html>; *Enactment of a Law: Procedural Steps in the Legislative Process* (rev. by R.B. Dove, 1997) <http://thomas.loc.gov/home/enactment/enactlawtoc.html>.

Illustration A-1
Beginning of the text of the Curt Flood Act of 1998, as printed in the
U.S. Statutes at Large

112 STAT. 2824   PUBLIC LAW 105–297—OCT. 27, 1998

Public Law 105–297
105th Congress

An Act

Oct. 27, 1998
[S. 53]

To require the general application of the antitrust laws to major league baseball, and for other purposes.

Curt Flood Act of 1998.
15 USC 1 note.

Be it enacted by the Senate and House of Representatives of the United States of America in Congress assembled,

SECTION 1. SHORT TITLE.

This Act may be cited as the "Curt Flood Act of 1998".

15 USC 27a note.

SEC. 2. PURPOSE.

It is the purpose of this legislation to state that major league baseball players are covered under the antitrust laws (i.e., that major league baseball players will have the same rights under the antitrust laws as do other professional athletes, e.g., football and basketball players), along with a provision that makes it clear that the passage of this Act does not change the application of the antitrust laws in any other context or with respect to any other person or entity.

15 USC 27a.

SEC. 3. APPLICATION OF THE ANTITRUST LAWS TO PROFESSIONAL MAJOR LEAGUE BASEBALL.

The Clayton Act (15 U.S.C. § 12 et seq.) is amended by adding at the end the following new section:

"SEC. 27. (a) Subject to subsections (b) through (d), the conduct, acts, practices, or agreements of persons in the business of organized professional major league baseball directly relating to or affecting employment of major league baseball players to play baseball at the major league level are subject to the antitrust laws to the same extent such conduct, acts, practices, or agreements would be subject to the antitrust laws if engaged in by persons in any other professional sports business affecting interstate commerce.

"(b) No court shall rely on the enactment of this section as a basis for changing the application of the antitrust laws to any conduct, acts, practices, or agreements other than those set forth in subsection (a). This section does not create, permit or imply a cause of action by which to challenge under the antitrust laws, or otherwise apply the antitrust laws to, any conduct, acts, practices, or agreements that do not directly relate to or affect employment of major league baseball players to play baseball at the major league level, including but not limited to—

"(1) any conduct, acts, practices, or agreements of persons engaging in, conducting or participating in the business of organized professional baseball relating to or affecting employment to play baseball at the minor league level, any organized

Illustration A-2

PUBLIC LAW 105–297—OCT. 27, 1998   112 STAT. 2825

professional baseball amateur or first-year player draft, or any reserve clause as applied to minor league players;

"(2) the agreement between organized professional major league baseball teams and the teams of the National Association of Professional Baseball Leagues, commonly known as the 'Professional Baseball Agreement', the relationship between organized professional major league baseball and organized professional minor league baseball, or any other matter relating to organized professional baseball's minor leagues;

"(3) any conduct, acts, practices, or agreements of persons engaging in, conducting or participating in the business of organized professional baseball relating to or affecting franchise expansion, location or relocation, franchise ownership issues, including ownership transfers, the relationship between the Office of the Commissioner and franchise owners, the marketing or sales of the entertainment product of organized professional baseball and the licensing of intellectual property rights owned or held by organized professional baseball teams individually or collectively;

"(4) any conduct, acts, practices, or agreements protected by Public Law 87–331 (15 U.S.C. §1291 et seq.) (commonly known as the 'Sports Broadcasting Act of 1961');

"(5) the relationship between persons in the business of organized professional baseball and umpires or other individuals who are employed in the business of organized professional baseball by such persons; or

"(6) any conduct, acts, practices, or agreements of persons not in the business of organized professional major league baseball.

"(c) Only a major league baseball player has standing to sue under this section. For the purposes of this section, a major league baseball player is—

"(1) a person who is a party to a major league player's contract, or is playing baseball at the major league level; or

"(2) a person who was a party to a major league player's contract or playing baseball at the major league level at the time of the injury that is the subject of the complaint; or

"(3) a person who has been a party to a major league player's contract or who has played baseball at the major league level, and who claims he has been injured in his efforts to secure a subsequent major league player's contract by an alleged violation of the antitrust laws: *Provided however,* That for the purposes of this paragraph, the alleged antitrust violation shall not include any conduct, acts, practices, or agreements of persons in the business of organized professional baseball relating to or affecting employment to play baseball at the minor league level, including any organized professional baseball amateur or first-year player draft, or any reserve clause as applied to minor league players; or

"(4) a person who was a party to a major league player's contract or who was playing baseball at the major league level at the conclusion of the last full championship season immediately preceding the expiration of the last collective bargaining agreement between persons in the business of organized professional major league baseball and the exclusive collective bargaining representative of major league baseball players.

Illustration A-3
End of text and legislative history summary for the Curt Flood Act of 1998, in *Statutes at Large*

112 STAT. 2826   PUBLIC LAW 105–297—OCT. 27, 1998

"(d)(1) As used in this section, 'person' means any entity, including an individual, partnership, corporation, trust or unincorporated association or any combination or association thereof. As used in this section, the National Association of Professional Baseball Leagues, its member leagues and the clubs of those leagues, are not 'in the business of organized professional major league baseball'.

"(2) In cases involving conduct, acts, practices, or agreements that directly relate to or affect both employment of major league baseball players to play baseball at the major league level and also relate to or affect any other aspect of organized professional baseball, including but not limited to employment to play baseball at the minor league level and the other areas set forth in subsection (b), only those components, portions or aspects of such conduct, acts, practices, or agreements that directly relate to or affect employment of major league players to play baseball at the major league level may be challenged under subsection (a) and then only to the extent that they directly relate to or affect employment of major league baseball players to play baseball at the major league level.

"(3) As used in subsection (a), interpretation of the term 'directly' shall not be governed by any interpretation of section 151 et seq. of title 29, United States Code (as amended).

"(4) Nothing in this section shall be construed to affect the application to organized professional baseball of the nonstatutory labor exemption from the antitrust laws.

"(5) The scope of the conduct, acts, practices, or agreements covered by subsection (b) shall not be strictly or narrowly construed.".

Approved October 27, 1998.

LEGISLATIVE HISTORY—S. 53:

SENATE REPORTS: No. 105–118 (Comm. on the Judiciary).
CONGRESSIONAL RECORD, Vol. 144 (1998):
    July 30, considered and passed Senate.
    Oct. 7, considered and passed House.
WEEKLY COMPILATION OF PRESIDENTIAL DOCUMENTS, Vol. 34 (1998):
    Oct. 27, Presidential statement.

On occasion, a bill is transmitted to Congress by the President, along with a message. The message may provide useful context for the bill, explaining what the President hopes it will accomplish if enacted. Such statements can be found in *Weekly Compilation of Presidential Documents*[2], and are sometimes reprinted by Congress.

Each session of Congress produces thousands of bills; almost no library can keep them in paper. The federal government provides a number of ways to access the text of bills introduced in Congress. For recent bills, the *Thomas* web site provides the full text of all bills beginning with the 101st Cong. (1989-) and is updated daily. Microfiche sets of the bills are received by libraries that have been designated as federal documents depositories. Most law school law libraries are such depositories. Copies of bills can also be obtained individually from the clerk of the House or Senate, from the legislators who sponsor them, or from the clerk of the committee considering them. The texts of a few bills also appear in the *Congressional Record*, but that is not the regular form of publication for bills. Commercially, the full text of bills is also available online from the 101st Cong. (1989-) from the Congressional Information Service (*CIS/LexisNexis Congressional*)[3], LEXIS and WESTLAW. CIS also has a collection of Congressional bills and resolutions on microfiche beginning with the 74th Congress (1935-36). A more complete discussion of online services will be found in Section C below.

Illustrations B and C represent the first page of different stages of bill number S. 53, which became the Curt Flood Act of 1998. The bill was introduced by Senator Hatch and referred to the Senate Committee on Judiciary. The Committee then issued a report on the bill, and recommended an amendment to it. Reports are discussed in more detail in Section B.3.

---

2   GPO Access has from 1993 forward available for free, <http://www.gpoaccess.gov/wcomp/index.html> and a subscription service, HeinOnline, <http://heinonline.org>, has 1977-2003 and is updating the collection quickly. Presidential documents may also be found on the White House web page, <http://www.whitehouse.gov>.

3   CIS used to be an independent company, and is still widely known by the name "CIS", but it was acquired by Reed Elsevier. Reed Elsevier is also the parent company of LexisNexis. CIS products are available in paper, microfiche and online, but are not always known by the name CIS. With the new ownership, you may find there are name changes. For instance, CIS on the web is now properly known as the "*CIS/LexisNexis Congressional*."

Illustration B
First Page of S.53, As Introduced in the Senate by Senator Hatch

II

105TH CONGRESS
1ST SESSION

S. 53

To require the general application of the antitrust laws to major league
baseball, and for other purposes.

IN THE SENATE OF THE UNITED STATES

JANUARY 21, 1997

Mr. HATCH (for himself, Mr. LEAHY, Mr. THURMOND, and Mr. MOYNIHAN)
introduced the following bill; which was read twice and referred to the
Committee on the Judiciary

A BILL

To require the general application of the antitrust laws to
major league baseball, and for other purposes.

1   *Be it enacted by the Senate and House of Representa-*

2   *tives of the United States of America in Congress assembled,*

3   SECTION 1. SHORT TITLE.

4   This Act may be cited as the "Curt Flood Act of

5   1997".

6   SEC. 2. APPLICATION OF THE ANTITRUST LAWS TO PRO-

7   FESSIONAL MAJOR LEAGUE BASEBALL.

8   The Clayton Act (15 U.S.C. 12 et seq.) is amended

9   by adding at the end the following new section:

Illustration C
First Page of the Report from the Senate Committee on the Judiciary on S. 53

Calendar No. 231

| 105TH CONGRESS | | REPORT |
| 1st Session | SENATE | 105–118 |

CURT FLOOD ACT OF 1997

OCTOBER 29, 1997.—Ordered to be printed

Mr. HATCH, from the Committee on the Judiciary,
submitted the following

REPORT

together with

MINORITY VIEWS

[To accompany S. 53]

The Committee on the Judiciary, to which was referred the bill (S. 53) to require the general application of the antitrust laws to major league baseball, and for other purposes, having considered the same and amendments thereto, reports favorably thereon, with an amendment in the nature of a substitute, and recommends that the bill, as amended, do pass.

CONTENTS

The amendment is as follows:
Strike all after the enacting clause and insert the following:

SECTION 1. SHORT TITLE.

This Act may be cited as the "Curt Flood Act of 1997". .

SEC. 2. PURPOSE.

It is the purpose of this legislation to clarify that major league baseball players are covered under the antitrust laws (i.e., that major league players will have the

59–010

2. Hearings

Hearings are held by standing and special committees of the House and Senate to investigate particular problems or situations of general concern, and also to elicit the views of persons or groups interested in proposed legislation. Hearings may be designed to air a controversial situation, determine the need for new legislation, or bring before the Congress information helpful to its consideration of a pending bill. Hearings do not have to be held on every bill, and occasionally legislation is enacted for which hearings have not been held in one or both houses. But that is unusual and, even then, relevant hearings may be found on similar or related bills which may aid in interpreting the provisions of such an enactment.

The hearings, as published, consist of transcripts of testimony before a particular committee or subcommittee, questions by the legislators and answers by witnesses, exhibits submitted by interested individuals or organizations, and sometimes a print of the bill in question. Not every hearing which is held is published. Those that are published are listed in the *Monthly Catalog of U.S. Government Publications*[4], in *CIS/Index*, and in some of the status tables and legislative services described in Section C below.

Hearings relevant to the interpretation of a particular enactment may have been held and published by a session of Congress prior to the one which enacted the law in question. Sometimes relevant hearings may extend over several sessions and be published in several parts or volumes. Longer hearings sometimes contain indexes which are helpful in locating specific references.

As evidence of legislative intent, hearings rank below committee reports and the variant texts of bills. The testimony they contain may range from the helpful and objective views of disinterested experts to the partisan comments of interest groups. Although careful research can frequently turn up useful material in published hearings, this source must be used with a critical and discriminating view.

---

[4]   Available for free from GPO Access, <http://www.gpoaccess.gov/cgp/>.

Illustration D
First Page of a Hearing Held by the Senate Committee on the Judiciary on S. 53

S. HRG. 105–102

MAJOR LEAGUE BASEBALL ANTITRUST REFORM

HEARING

BEFORE THE

COMMITTEE ON THE JUDICIARY UNITED STATES SENATE

ONE HUNDRED FIFTH CONGRESS

FIRST SESSION

ON

S. 53

A BILL TO REQUIRE THE GENERAL APPLICATION OF THE ANTITRUST
LAWS TO MAJOR LEAGUE BASEBALL, AND FOR OTHER PURPOSES

JUNE 17, 1997

Serial No. J–105–25

Printed for the use of the Committee on the Judiciary

U.S. GOVERNMENT PRINTING OFFICE
WASHINGTON : 1997

42–602 CC

Hearings are generally identified by the number of the Congress and session in which they were held, the name of the committee which held them, the short title which appears on the cover of the published hearing, the number of the bill being discussed, and the dates covered by the hearing. Hearings are not generally published or numbered in consecutive series, but in recent years more committees have begun to employ convenient numbering arrangements for their published hearings. Illustration D shows the title page for the following Senate hearing: *Major League Baseball Antitrust Reform: Hearing before the Committee on the Judiciary of the United States Senate on S. 53*, 105th Cong., 1st Sess. (1997).

While hearings are indexed in the official *Monthly Catalog of U.S. Government Publications*, the most useful listings and indexes appear in the commercial publication, *CIS/Index*. Published by Congressional Information Service since 1970 and now by LexisNexis, *CIS/Index* is a comprehensive finding tool for federal legislative history (described more fully in Section D.1 below). Its annual coverage of hearings includes abstracts of testimony and indexing under the name of each witness. CIS also publishes a detailed retrospective index of hearings held from 1833 to 1969, under the title *CIS US Congressional Hearings Index*. This index provides access to hearings by subject, witness name, bill number, and hearing title. Both the *CIS/Index* and the retrospective index are available online through LEXIS[5] or *CIS/LexisNexis Congressional*.

For unpublished committee hearings, CIS also has two indexes, *CIS Index to Unpublished US Senate Committee Hearings*, presently covering the period 1823 to 1980, and *CIS Index to Unpublished US House of Representatives Committee Hearings* presently covering the period 1833 to 1972. These sets expand as more documents become available. Indexing for unpublished hearings is available online through 1980.

The full-text of all hearings covered in each of these indexes is also available from CIS in microfiche. Some coverage of prepared testimony is available online through LEXIS or *CIS/LexisNexis Congressional* starting in 1988, as well as on WESTLAW. Coverage of full hearing transcripts is very limited in these databases. GPO Access has the official transcripts of hearings beginning with the 105th Cong. (1997-), but they can take up to

---

5   CIS titles on LEXIS are not usually available with an academic subscription. If your campus subscribes to the separate service, *CIS/LexisNexis Congressional*, however, you will have access through LEXIS.

two years to appear. Hearings can be found through *Thomas* as links to House and Senate committees, but coverage is limited to what the committees choose to post, and may be official or unofficial transcripts.

3. Committee Reports

The most important documents of legislative history are the reports of the Congressional committees of each house, and the reports of conference committees held jointly by the two houses. There are two reasons for the importance of Reports. The first is that there is a Report for almost every bill that becomes law. The House and Senate committees generally issue a report on each bill when it is sent to the whole house for consideration, or "reported out of committee." They are thus available for scrutiny. Second, since the Report accompanies the bill when it is returned to the legislative body for debate and a vote, it is presumed that each voting member has read the Report. Thus it is the one systematic, shared evidence of Congressional intent. Of course, many voting members do not actually read each report, but the fact that each one *could* have serves a sort of notice function.

These reports reflect the committee's proposal after the bill has been studied, hearings held, and amendments made. They frequently contain the revised text of the bill, an analysis of its content and intent, and the committee's rationale for its recommendations. Sometimes the report also includes a minority statement if there was disagreement among the committee members. There will only be a Report for bills that make it out of committee. Most bills die quiet deaths.

If different versions of a proposed enactment have been passed by each house, a conference committee is convened, including members from each house. The conference committee reconciles the differences and produces an agreed compromise for return to both houses and final passage. The reports of these conference committees usually contain the text of the compromise bill. Conference committee reports are another very persuasive source for interpretation.

There are other materials that could be even more helpful in interpreting statutory language, such as the transcripts of committee markup sessions, in which legislation is first examined in detail, or of conference committee proceedings. Only rarely, however, are such transcripts published or generally available.[6]

Committee reports may also be issued on special investigations, studies and hearings not related to the consideration or reporting of a specific bill. Reports are issued, for example, on nominations to the executive and judicial branches.

The committee reports of each house are published as single pamphlets in separate numerical series for each session of Congress. They are most easily identified and traced by these report numbers, and their citations include the numbers of the Congress and session which issued them, e.g., "S.Rep. No. 118, 105th Cong., 1st Sess. (1997)." Committee reports are listed and indexed in the *Monthly Catalog of U.S. Government Publications* and the *CIS/Index*. One or more committee reports on major enactments are reprinted selectively in *U.S. Code Congressional and Administrative News*, and a few appear also in the *Congressional Record*.

The reports are also published, together with House and Senate documents (another form of Congressional publication described below), in a bound series of volumes popularly called the *Serial Set*. In that form, they can also be located by the volume numbers in which they appear. A retrospective index to the *Serial Set*, covering the period from 1789 to 1969, is published by the Congressional Information Service under the title *CIS US Serial Set Index* (36 vols., 1975-79). Divided into twelve chronological parts, it provides access by subjects, keywords, and proper names. The *Index* is available online in LEXIS and *CIS/LexisNexis Congressional*. LexisNexis has begun the digitization of the full text contents of the *Serial Set* from 1789 to 1969, and as of this writing over 5.5 million pages have been scanned, but it is only available as a separate subscription and is not found on LEXIS or *CIS/LexisNexis Congressional*. A company called Readex, Inc., also has a digitization project in progress, and plans to scan all the volumes from 1817-1980.[7]

---

6   *See*, Wald, "Some Observations on the Use of Legislative History in the 1981 Supreme Court Term," 68 Iowa L. Rev. 195, 200-203 (1983).

7   A status page for the LexisNexis project, which will ultimately scan over 20 million pages, can be found at:
         <http://www.lexisnexis.com/academic/1univ/serial/status.asp>.
As of December, 2004, the Readex project had scanned over 600,000 pages,

Reports can also be found in full text as a part of LEXIS, *CIS/LexisNexis Congressional* and WESTLAW from the 101st Cong. (1990). The full run of selected Reports printed as a part of *USCCAN* are available on WESTLAW, which takes one back to 1948. *Thomas* has free access to the full text of Reports from the 104th Cong. (1995-) to present.

Illustration C shows the first page of a Committee Report on the the proposed Curt Flood Act of 1997.

Congressional publications also include "committee prints," which like the committee reports are issued generally in consecutive series for each House, with the numbering sequence beginning over in each session of Congress. Some committee prints are not numbered at all, however, and some are reissued subsequently as House or Senate reports or documents. Committee prints usually contain material prepared specifically for the use of a committee, such as studies done by the committee staff or outside experts, or compilations of statutes in particular areas. Others are statements by members of the committee or its subcommittees on a pending bill.

Like other Congressional documents, committee prints since 1970 are covered in the privately published *CIS/Index*. CIS has also published a comprehensive index to earlier committee prints, from 1830 to 1969, *CIS US Congressional Committee Prints Index* (5 vols., 1980). The whole index and the full text of committee prints from the 101st Cong. (1990-) to present are on LEXIS and *CIS/LexisNexis Congressional*.

4. Congressional Debates

Floor debate in Congress on a pending bill can occur at almost any stage of its progress, but typically it takes place after the bill has been reported out by committee. During consideration of the bill, amendments will be proposed and accepted or defeated. Arguments for and against amendments and passage are made, explanations of unclear or controversial provisions are offered, and much of the business of the legislative process is revealed in floor discussion.

Logic would seem to dictate that the spoken words of the legislators should be the most valuable of all evidence concerning legislative intent.

---

representing the years 1817-1859. <http://www.readex.com/scholarl/serlset.html>

Such is not the case. Anyone who has witnessed Congressional debate knows that many members are not present at all. Some remarks are added to the record after the fact. Thus the utility of the transcript of Congressional debate is limited.

The essential source for this form of legislative history is the *Congressional Record*, which is published daily when either house is in session. The *Congressional Record* provides a more or less verbatim transcript of the legislative debates and proceedings, subject, however, to individual legislators' revision of their own remarks.

The *Congressional Record* has been published since 1873, but it has fallen on difficult days. It has always been published in a pamphlet form called the daily edition; then at the end of the particular Congress it would be reissued in bound volumes. The bound set would contain more items, and it would have different pagination. The required citation was to the bound set. Sadly, the bound set has not been complete since 1984. Therefore, everyone has been citing to the pages as they appear in the daily edition despite the *Bluebook*'s preference for citations to bound volumes.

Since the 80th Congress, each issue of the *Congressional Record* contains a "Daily Digest," which summarizes the day's proceedings, and lists actions taken and enactments signed by the President that day, as well as useful committee information. All of the tools in the daily version suffer from the failure to provide a bound, cumulated edition.

Beginning with the 99th Congress in 1985, the *Congressional Record* can be searched full-text online. Both LEXIS, *CIS/LexisNexis Congressional* and WESTLAW have databases with the text of the *Record* since 1985, *Thomas* has it available from 1989 forward, and GPO Access has it from 1995 forward.

5. Presidential Approval or Veto

After a bill is passed by both houses of Congress, it goes to the President for approval. If the President approves a bill, it becomes law. If the President vetoes a bill, to become law it must be re-passed by both houses with a two-thirds majority. The messages or statements issued when the President signs or vetoes particular enactments can shed light on legislative history. Like other Presidential messages to Congress, these documents appear in several places, including the *Congressional Record*, the *Weekly Compilation of Presidential Documents*, the House and Senate Journals, as House and Senate Documents, and on the White House web site while the President in question occupies the Oval Office there. Illustration E shows President Clinton's signing statement for the Curt Flood Act of 1998 as it was published in the *Weekly Compilation of Presidential Documents*.

These statements have been included in *USCCAN's* legislative history section beginning in 1986, both online and in print, although their importance in determining legislative intent is subject to dispute.[8]

6. Other Congressional Documents

Congress publishes many documents as required by law or by special request. These House and Senate Documents are issued in numerical series which run consecutively through both sessions of each Congress. They contain special studies and reports, reprints of Presidential messages, executive agency reports and memoranda, reports of nongovernmental organizations, and a great variety of papers ordered to be printed by either house of Congress. They are listed and indexed in the *Monthly Catalog of U.S. Government Publications*, and, since 1970, in the *CIS/Index*. A document is cited by the name of the house issuing it, the number of the Congress and session, and the document number. House and Senate Documents also appear in the *Serial Set* and can be cited to that form by volume number. The *CIS US Serial Set Index*, referred to above, provides access to House and Senate Documents, as well as House and Senate Reports, issued from 1789 to 1969 (with access to later reports and documents through the *CIS/Index*). The value of House and Senate Documents for legislative history is usually negligible, but occasionally a document will have some relevance to a pending bill.

---

8   *See, e.g.,* Carroll, "Whose Statute is it Anyway? Why and How Courts Should Use Presidential Signing Statements when Interpreting Federal Statutes," 46 Cath. U. L. Rev. 475 (1997), Garber & Wimmer, "Presidential Signing Statements as Interpretations of Legislative Intent: An Executive Aggrandizement of Power," 24 *Harv.J. on Legis.* 363 (1987); Greenhouse, "In Signing Bills, Reagan Tries to Write History," *N.Y. Times,* Dec. 9, 1986, at B14.

Illustration E
Presidential Signing Statement for the Curt Flood Act of 1998, as Printed in the *Weekly Compilation of Presidential Documents*

2150   *Oct. 27 / Administration of William J. Clinton, 1998*

Section 107 requires that the Secretary of State grant U.S. citizens access to U.S. missions abroad for religious activities on a basis no less favorable than that for other nongovernmental activities unrelated to the conduct of the diplomatic mission. State Department policy already allows U.S. Government mission employees access to U.S. facilities for religious services in environments where such services are not available locally. The extension of this practice to U.S. citizens who generally enjoy no privileges and immunities in the host state has the potential to create conflicts with host country laws and to impair the ability of U.S. missions to function effectively. Care also must be taken to ensure that this provision is implemented consistent with the First Amendment. Accordingly, I have asked the Department of State to prepare guidance to clarify the scope of this provision and the grounds on which mission premises are generally available to nongovernmental organizations.

Finally, I will interpret the Act's exception in section 405(d) concerning the provision of medicines, food, or other humanitarian assistance to apply to any loans, loan guarantees, extensions of credit, issuance of letters of credit, or other financing measures necessary or incidental to the sale of such goods. Additionally, I will interpret the license requirements in section 423 regarding specified items to apply only to countries of particular concern.

William J. Clinton

The White House,
October 27, 1998.

NOTE: H.R. 2431, approved October 27, was assigned Public Law No. 105–292. An original was not available for verification of the content of this statement.

Statement on Signing the Curt Flood Act of 1998
October 27, 1998

Today I am pleased to have signed into law S. 53, the "Curt Flood Act of 1998." This legislation is the successful culmination of bipartisan efforts to treat employment matters with respect to Major League Baseball players under the antitrust laws in the same way such matters are treated for athletes in other professional sports.

It is especially fitting that this legislation honors a courageous baseball player and individual, the late Curt Flood, whose enormous talents on the baseball diamond were matched by his courage off the field. It was 29 years ago this month that Curt Flood refused a trade from the St. Louis Cardinals to the Philadelphia Phillies. His bold stand set in motion the events that culminate in the bill I have signed into law.

The Act appropriately limits baseball's special judicially created antitrust exemption by expressly applying the antitrust laws to certain conduct of Major League Baseball; the applicability of the antitrust laws with respect to all other conduct is unchanged. The Act in no way codifies or extends the baseball exemption and would not affect the applicability of those laws to certain matters that, it has been argued, the exemption would legitimately protect (including franchise relocation rules and the minor leagues).

The Act does not in any way limit the standing of the United States to bring an antitrust action. The antitrust laws protect the public's interest in the efficient operation of the free market system, thereby protecting consumers, and the United States has standing to sue to enjoin all violations.

It is sound policy to treat the employment matters of Major League Baseball players under the antitrust laws in the same way such matters are treated for athletes in other professional sports.

William J. Clinton

The White House,
October 27, 1998.

NOTE: S. 53, approved October 27, was assigned Public Law No. 105–297. An original was not available for verification of the content of this statement.

C. TOOLS FOR COMPILING A FEDERAL LEGISLATIVE HISTORY

To compile the legislative history of a pending bill or of an enacted statute, one traces each of the actions taken by the legislature with regard to the bills which became law or which shaped the final enactment. Section B just identified what those documents are. The challenge for the researcher is to find the citation to the documents that she needs, and then to find the documents themselves.

The federal government has been in the information business for more than two centuries. It is not surprising that a wide variety of tools indexing and organizing legislative documents have arisen. The tools produced by the government have the advantage of being low cost, but they have the drawbacks of most government information. They are slow, often hard to use, and sometimes incomplete. The use of these tools is so difficult that legislative histories acquired a reputation for being next to impossible to do. But in recent decades several private publishers have done an excellent job of organizing legislative information. Print tools like CIS and *Congressional Index* take the pain out of the process. Electronic versions of the information also ease the confusion of the researcher. These are the best places to pull information together. Of course, it is even better if the entire job has already been done, so Section 1 will start there.

1. Compiled Legislative Histories

Given the frequency with which legislative histories are used, it stands to reason that many legislative histories have already been compiled. Someone has found the citation to each relevant document and assembled them. Or perhaps someone has assembled those documents or parts of documents judged to be of value. It would be horribly wasteful to ignore all of this work and to re-do it. Thus, before doing anything else, one should check to find out whether a legislative history has already been compiled.

The first step in performing a legislative history should be to check your law library's catalog for a published legislative history. Recently, more of these are being published by companies like Hein for large acts that are thought to be of historical importance. One example would be the five volume set: *USA Patriot Act : a Legislative History of the Uniting and Strengthening of America by Providing Appropriate Tools Required to*

Intercept and Obstruct Terrorism Act, Public Law no. 107-56 (2001), compiled by Bernard D. Reams, Jr. and Christopher T. Anglim. Relatively speaking, there are very few of these published legislative histories. You next best hope is that someone else has already compiled one in the course of his or her work.

One of the next best ways to find a legislative history is the *Sources of Compiled Legislative Histories: a Bibliography of Government Documents, Periodical Articles, and Books : 1st Congress-94th Congress,* by Nancy Johnson, published as a part of the American Association of Law Libraries Publication Series. Ms. Johnson lists, by Congress and Public Law number, all of the already compiled legislative histories that she was able to find, and provides the citation to where to find them. You only need the Public Law number of the statute in question to gain access to this world of information. This reference tool sits at almost every law library reference desk. Checking it will take only a minute, and it might save you hours of effort.

It is also worth checking with the law librarian in your organization to see if there is a bank of existing legislative histories kept locally. Many law firms and government entities build up their own files of legislative histories. This is especially true of organizations that specialize in certain subject areas, where the same pieces of legislation are frequently encountered. Law libraries have been willing to share locally produced legislative histories. The Law Librarians' Society of the District of Columbia has prepared *The Union List of Legislative Histories,* 7th ed. (The Society, 2000-). This offers access to many such private compilations. A local librarian may also know of a relevant interest group that collects legislative histories for laws that are related to its topic. Such a group may be willing to send a complete file on the legislation in question. Never re-do what has been done.

For the quick and dirty precompiled legislative history of every newly enacted federal law since 1947, check *U.S. Code Congressional and Administrative News.* USCCAN serves to update the *U.S. Code* by publishing the text of new laws while Congress is in session. At the end of each Session of Congress, when the pamphlets of the set are bound, an extra feature is added. The editors gather and reprint the most important sections of the most important Congressional Reports on each new piece of legislation. This is hardly comprehensive legislative history, but it is a start. *U.S. Code Congressional and Administrative News* is in almost every law library, so it is easy to find. As a convenient location for some very quick background, it is excellent.

2. Congressional Information Service
   (*CIS/LexisNexis Congressional*)

In 1970 CIS came on the scene and brought order to the chaos of Congressional publication through comprehensive indexing. The *CIS Annual* breaks down the House and Senate into committees and sub-committees. Within each unit it divides publications into Hearings, Reports and Prints. Each one is listed and abstracted. CIS also prepares an index to all of the documents that allows access by subject, bill number and name. Literally each witness at each hearing is indexed. The *CIS Annual* is complete, clear and reliable. It captures each document that is printed. The set is issued monthly in paper form, then at the end of the year appears as bound volumes.[9] There is also a series of retrospective sets of CIS covering periods before 1970.

Online, the CIS indexes are available through LEXIS, or through a separate web site, *CIS/LexisNexis Congressional*. Presently, the *CIS Index* (1970-), the *CIS Legislative Histories* (1984-), the historical *Congressional Indexes* covering congress from 1789-1969 and *Indexes to Unpublished Hearings through 1980*, are all available online. Illustration F shows the opening screen of *CIS/LexisNexis Congressional*, and Illustration G is a copy of the legislative history of the Curt Flood Act of 1998 from CIS.

Libraries can purchase the bound volumes of the *CIS Annual* service alone as finding tools and can also subscribe to an accompanying microfiche set that reprints in full each document abstracted in the set. The microfiche set is keyed to a unique numbering system devised by CIS. This unique identifying number is part of each entry in the Abstracts volume. Thus if the microfiche is available you can go directly from an index or abstract to the full text of the document. Online coverage of the documents is more limited, e.g., the full text of committee reports online begins in 1990. The sections of

---

9   Between 1970-1983, two bound volumes were issued per year: *Abstracts of Congressional Publications and Legislative Histories*, and *Index to Congressional Publications and Public Laws*. Since 1984 it has been issued in three parts: *Abstracts of Congressional Publications, Legislative Histories of U.S. Public Laws*, and *Index to Congressional Publications and Public Laws*.

this Chapter dealing with the particular types of publications will indicate the online coverage.

Illustration F
Screen Capture of *CIS/LexisNexis Congressional*

LexisNexis	Home How Do I? Site Map Help

Congressional Search Forms	· CIS Index	CIS indexing and abstracting of congressional publications and the CIS Legislative Histories (1970-present)
CIS Index		
Historical Indexes	· Historical Indexes	Congressional Indexes, 1789-1969, and Indexes to Unpublished Hearings Through 1980
Publications	· Publications	Full text of congressional reports, documents, prints, bills and the Congressional Record
Testimony		
Bills	· Testimony	Prepared statements and selected question & answer transcripts (1988-present)
Laws	· Bills	Bill tracking reports that follow bills through Congress and the text of bills
Regulations		
Members	· Laws	Public laws, Statutes at Large and the United States Code Service
Committees	· Regulations	The Federal Register and the Code of Federal Regulations
Inside Washington		
Hot Bills/Topics	· Members	Biographical and financial information and voting records
List of Links	· Committees	Rosters, charters and schedules for committees and subcommittees
Search for Other Information	· Inside Washington	An insider's perspective on recent legislative activities
Academic	· Hot Bills/Topics	Relevant publications on key American public policy issues
Government Periodicals Index	· List of Links	Other Web sites with useful information about Congress and American politics
Statistical		

Terms & Conditions Privacy Copyright © 2005 LexisNexis, a division of Reed Elsevier Inc. All Rights Reserved.

Illustration G
CIS Legislative History for the Curt Flood Act of 1998

CIS/Index
Copyright © 1998, Congressional Information Service, Inc.

98 CIS PL 105297; 105 CIS Legis. Hist. P.L. 297

LEGISLATIVE HISTORY OF: P.L. 105-297

TITLE: Curt Flood Act of 1998
CIS-NO: 98-PL105-297
DOC-TYPE: Legislative History
DATE: Oct. 27, 1998
LENGTH: 3 p.
ENACTED-BILL: 105 S. 53 Retrieve Bill Tracking report
STAT: 112 Stat. 2824
CONG-SESS: 105-2
ITEM-NO: 575

SUMMARY:
"To require the general application of the antitrust laws to major league baseball, and for other purposes."

Amends the Clayton Act to apply antitrust laws to labor relations in major league baseball.

The antitrust exemption for major league baseball was based on 1922 Supreme Court decision holding that the business of baseball did not have a sufficient nexus to interstate commerce to provide the fundamental prerequisite for application of antitrust laws.

CONTENT-NOTATION: Professional baseball antitrust immunity repeal

BILLS: 103 H.R. 4994; 103 S. 500; 104 S. 415; 104 S. 416; 104 S. 627; 105 H.R. 21

DESCRIPTORS:
　CURT FLOOD ACT; CLAYTON ACT; BASEBALL; ANTITRUST LAW; PRIVILEGES AND IMMUNITIES; LABOR-MANAGEMENT RELATIONS; FRANCHISES; SUPREME COURT; BUSINESS; INTERSTATE COMMERCE

REFERENCES:

DEBATE:

144 *Congressional Record*, 105th Congress, 2nd Session - 1998
　July 30, Senate consideration and passage of S. 53, p. S9494.
　Oct. 7, House consideration and passage of S. 53, p. H9942.

REPORTS:

103rd Congress

H. Rpt. 103-871 on H.R. 4994, "Baseball Fans and Communities Protection Act of 1994," Nov. 29, 1994.
　CIS NO: 94-H523-41
　LENGTH: 45 p.
　SUDOC: Y1.1/8:103-871

104th Congress

S. Rpt. 104-231 on S. 627, "Major League Baseball Reform Act of 1995," Feb. 6, 1996.
  CIS NO: 96-S523-1
  LENGTH: 31 p.
  SUDOC: Y1.1/5:104-231

105th Congress

S. Rpt. 105-118 on S. 53, "Curt Flood Act of 1997," Oct. 29, 1997.
  CIS NO: 97-S523-4
  LENGTH: 12 p.
  SUDOC: Y1.1/5:105-118

HEARINGS:

102nd Congress

"Baseball's Antitrust Immunity," hearings before the Subcommittee on Antitrust, Monopolies, and Business Rights, Committee on the Judiciary. Senate, Dec. 10, 1992.
  CIS NO: 93-S521-22
  LENGTH: v+440 p. il.
  SUDOC: Y4.J89/2:S.HRG.102-1094

103rd Congress

"Baseball's Antitrust Exemption," hearings before the Subcommittee on Economic and Commercial Law, Committee on the Judiciary. House, Mar. 31, 1993.
  CIS NO: 93-H521-82
  LENGTH: iv+272 p.
  SUDOC: Y4.J89/1:103/6

"Professional Baseball Teams and the Antitrust Laws," hearings before the Subcommittee on Antitrust, Monopolies, and Business Rights, Committee on the Judiciary. Senate, Mar. 21, 1994.
  CIS NO: 95-S521-30
  LENGTH: iii+70 p.
  SUDOC: Y4.J89/2:S.HRG.103-1054

"Key Issues Confronting Minor League Baseball," hearings before the
Committee on Small Business. House, July 20, 1994.
   CIS NO: 95-H721-40
   LENGTH: iii+92 p.
   SUDOC: Y4.SM1:103-95

"Baseball's Antitrust Exemption (Part 2)," hearings before the Subcommittee on
Economic and Commercial Law, Committee on the Judiciary. House, Sept. 22,
1994.
   CIS NO: 95-H521-20
   LENGTH: iv+698 p.+errata. il.
   SUDOC: Y4.J89/1:103/6/PT.2

"Impact on Collective Bargaining of the Antitrust Exemption; H.R. 5095, Major
League Play Ball of 1995," hearings before the Subcommittee on Labor-
Management Relations, Committee on Education and the Workforce. House,
Sept. 29, 1994.
   CIS NO: 95-H341-19
   LENGTH: iii+122 p.
   SUDOC: Y4.ED8/1:103-108

104th Congress

"Court-Imposed Major League Baseball Antitrust Exemption," hearings before
the Subcommittee on Antitrust, Business Rights, and Competition, Committee on
the Judiciary. Senate, Feb. 15, 1995.
   CIS NO: 97-S521-8
   LENGTH: iv+211 p.
   SUDOC: Y4.J89/2:S.HRG.104-682

105th Congress

"Major League Baseball Antitrust Reform," hearings before the Committee on
the Judiciary. Senate, June 17, 1997.
   CIS NO: 97-S521-95
   LENGTH: iii+36 p.
   SUDOC: Y4.J89/2:S.HRG.105-102

MISCELLANEOUS PUBLICATIONS:

Weekly Compilation of Presidential Documents, Vol. 34 (1998): Oct. 27,
Presidential statement.

From 1970 until 1983 the Abstracts volume of the *CIS Annual* for each Session of Congress contained a legislative history table. The table was keyed to each new Public Law. For each new law, the table listed each relevant document. This included Hearings, Reports and Prints, bill numbers, Presidential statements and debates. Thus, for any law enacted since 1970, one need only go to CIS to get a complete listing of documents.

Starting in 1984, CIS began to devote an entire volume to Legislative History. Still keyed to each new Public Law, the set now offered both a listing of each relevant document, and an abstract of what the document covered. This helps the researcher key on what is important. For laws enacted since 1984, the process is thus even simpler.

3. CCH *CONGRESSIONAL INDEX*

Congressional Index, a commercial looseleaf service published since 1937 by Commerce Clearing House, has been a popular finding tools for legislative history. It is especially useful for gathering information about pending legislation. It is issued in two volumes for each Congress, one for the House and one for the Senate. *Congressional Index* offers many different approaches: indexes of all public general bills by subject and by sponsor; digests of each bill; a status table of actions taken on bills and resolutions; an index of enactments and vetoes; a table of companion bills; a list of reorganization plans, treaties, and nominations pending; tables of voting records of members of Congress by bill and resolution number; and a weekly report letter on major news and developments in Congress. Its status table section includes references to hearings, an important feature lacking in some other publications.

It should be noted that this service does not contain the actual text of bills, debates, reports or laws. *Congressional Index* is only a finding tool, but a most useful one, with weekly supplementation and generally good indexing. Illustration G shows a page from the "Status of Senate Bills" section of the *Congressional Index* for S. 53.

Illustration G
A Page from the "Status of Senate Bills" Section of the *Congressional Index* where S. 53 is Listed (The star next to the bill number indicates the bill became law.)

```
21;002                    Status of Senate Bills                   94  11-25-98
                 See also Status at pages 20,101 and 20,501,
                 For digest, see "Bills" and "Resolutions" Divisions.
```

46

Introduced	1/21/97
Placed on S calendar	1/21/97

47

Introduced	1/21/97
Placed on S calendar	1/21/97

48

Introduced	1/21/97
Placed on S calendar	1/21/97

★ 53

Introduced	1/21/97
Ref to S Judiciary Com	1/21/97
Hrgs by Judiciary Com	6/17/97
Ordered reptd w/amdts by Judiciary Com	7/31/97
Reptd w/amdts, S Rept 105-118, by Judiciary Com	10/29/97
Amdts adopted (Voice)	7/30/98
Passed by S (Voice)	7/30/98
Ref to H Judiciary Com	7/31/98
Passed under suspension of rules by 2/3 vote (Voice)	10/7/98
Sent to President	10/15/98
Signed by President	10/27/98
Public Law 105-297 (112 Stat 2824)	10/27/98

54

Introduced	1/21/97
Ref to S Judiciary Com	1/21/97
Hrgs by Judiciary Com	4/23/97

62

Introduced	1/21/97
Ref to S Energy Com	1/21/97
Hrgs by National Parks Subcom	2/12/98

75

Introduced	1/21/97
Ref to S Finance Com	1/21/97
Hrgs by Finance Com	4/10/97

89

Introduced	1/21/97
Ref to S Labor Com	1/21/97
Hrgs by Labor Com	5/21/98

94

Introduced	1/21/97
Ref to S Energy Com	1/21/97
Hrgs by Forests Subcom	5/6/98

98

Introduced	1/21/97
Ref to S Finance Com	1/21/97
Reptd w/amdts, S Rept 105-154, by Finance Com	7/21/97

104

Introduced	1/21/97
Ref to S Energy Com	1/21/97

Hrgs by Com	2/5/97
Com began markup	3/12/97
Ordered reptd w/amdts by Energy Com	3/13/97
Reptd w/amdts, w/o written rept, by Energy Com	3/14/97
Reptd w/o amdts, S Rept 105-10, by Energy Com	3/20/97
Amdts adopted (Voice)	4/10/97
Amdts rejected (24 to 72; S Leg 36)	4/10/97
Amdts adopted (Voice)	4/10/97
Amdts adopted (60 to 33; S Leg 37)	4/10/97
Amdts rejected (24 to 69; S Leg 38)	4/10/97
Amdts adopted (Voice)	4/10/97
Amdts rejected (36 to 56; S Leg 39)	4/10/97
Amdts adopted (Voice)	4/14/97
Amdts rejected (39 to 59; S Leg 40)	4/15/97
Amdts adopted (Voice)	4/15/97
Amdts adopted (Voice)	4/15/97
Amdts adopted (Voice)	4/15/97
Amdts adopted (66 to 32; S Leg 41)	4/15/97
Passed by S (65 to 34; S Leg 42)	4/15/97
H returned bill to S	3/5/98

109

Introduced	1/21/97
Ref to S Indian Affairs Com	1/21/97
Ordered reptd w/amdts by Indian Affairs Com	10/23/97
Reptd w/amdts, S Rept 105-380, by Indian Affairs Com	10/8/98
Amdts adopted (Voice)	10/16/98
Passed by S (Voice)	10/16/98

155

Introduced	1/21/97
Ref to S Energy Com	1/21/97
Hrgs by National Parks Subcom	7/16/98

★ 156

Introduced	1/21/97
Ref to S Energy Com	1/21/97
Energy Com discharged	5/21/97
Ref to S Indian Affairs Com	5/21/97
Hrgs by Indian Affairs Com	10/20/97
Ordered reptd w/amdts by Indian Affairs Com	10/23/97
Reptd w/amdts, S Rept 105-146, by Indian Affairs Com	11/8/97
Passed by S (Voice)	11/9/97
Ref to H Resources Com	11/12/97
Resources Com discharged	11/13/97
Passed by H (Voice)	11/13/97
Signed by President	12/2/97
Public Law 105-132 (111 Stat 2563)	12/2/97

170

Introduced	1/21/97
Ref to S Judiciary Com	1/21/97
Ordered reptd w/o amdts by Judiciary Com	9/18/97
Reptd w/o amdts, w/o written rept, by Judiciary Com	9/18/97
Passed by S (Voice)	11/7/97
Ref to H Judiciary Com	11/8/97

S 46

4. Online Legislative Research Services

The development of a variety of online database services has vastly improved research in legislative history. *Thomas* has developed into one of the best sites for bills and bill tracking. Several others have already been described above, such as the various computer-based approaches to the *Congressional Record* and the online version of *CIS/LexisNexis Congressional*. Several of the specialized federal databases in WESTLAW and LEXIS include selective documents of legislative history of new legislation in those subject fields, with the most comprehensive coverage in federal taxation databases.

Congressional Quarterly (CQ) publishes databases that offer great coverage and analysis. CQ.com has bill text and bill tracking back to 1983, with current bill forecasts and reporting on Congress. If one has access to it, it offers a wealth of information.

A service available through both WESTLAW and LEXIS is Billcast, which summarizes legislation in the current Congress and provides the statistical odds for a bill's success in Committee and on the House or Senate floor. Billcast is archived on both systems with information on earlier terms, beginning with the 99th Congress in 1985.

The electronic sources mentioned above are examples. With the frequent offering of new databases and the demise of others, any description of what is available is soon outdated. The use of current database directories is essential for determining available resources. The best method will be to ask a reference librarian what is current and useful. The librarian can also explain which data bases are available to the researcher.

5. *Statutes at Large*

One of the simplest and most readily available places to find legislative history information for enacted laws is in the *Statutes at Large*. As shown above in Illustration A, at the end of the text for each law there appears a legislative history summary. This summary includes citations of reports from House, Senate, and Conference Committees, lists the dates of consideration and passage in each house, and provides references to presidential statements. It does not, however, provide references to exact *Congressional Record* pages, or to hearings and other relevant documents.

This information has appeared at the end of each law only since 1975. From 1963 to 1974, it appeared at the end of each volume in a table, "Guide to Legislative History." The legislative history summaries in *Statutes at Large* are by no means complete, but they are readily available to a researcher studying the text of an act.

D. CONTEXTUAL LEGISLATIVE HISTORY

One of the reasons that doing a legislative history is such a chore is that the preliminary steps of identifying and gathering the documents can result in a huge stack of material. How is the researcher to cope with thousands of pages of material? Even the assistance of abstracts like those in CIS can only do so much. Flailing about in thousands of pages of Congressional documents can be the worst form of search.

That is why the idea of context can be such a help. Looking to secondary sources that surround the time of a new law's passage, or a bill's introduction and failure can add great insight. Contemporary accounts by knowledgeable sources help the researcher focus on what was especially controversial about the legislation. Such commentary may identify which Hearings or Reports were crucial, why one version of a bill was chosen, or what certain compromises really involved. It can identify who the relevant players were, and what groups cared about the legislation.

There are two types of context that can be of assistance. One comes from sources that monitor all legislative activity. A second comes from sources concerned with the specific issue at hand.

1. Sources for General Context

Several works on Congressional activities are published by Congressional Quarterly, Inc., including an analytical weekly magazine, a daily newsletter, and an online bill-tracking database. Each of these concentrates on what is going in the Congress and why. CQ also publishes a variety of separate reference books relating to Congress, the most comprehensive being *Congressional Quarterly's Guide to Congress*, 5th ed. (1999).

The *Congressional Quarterly Weekly Report* offers weekly reporting of Congressional news, with summaries of major legislation and issues and cumulative indexing. *CQ Weekly Report* includes valuable analysis and background discussion of laws and legislative issues which make it popular with political scientists and many general researchers. This is the kind of context that can help the researcher sort out what to read and why.

CQ also produces an online service, CQ.com, which covers sessions back to 1983 and includes bill-tracking information, daily Congressional schedules, notices of new Congressional publications, and the text of *CQ Weekly* from August 1983 to present. This electronic library also has the CQ Congress Collection, which has information on every member of Congress since the 79th Congress. It includes links for each member's voting record and how various interest groups rate the members.

Another publication which watches the Congress carefully is the *National Journal*.[10] The *National Journal* comes out monthly, and while it also covers the other branches of government, it focuses on the activities of Congress with care. Here one might find a detailed analysis of what really happened behind the scenes.

Since the *Washington Post* and the *Washington Times* are both hometown newspapers for Congress, each can be valuable for background. Checking on newspaper coverage at the time legislation was passed can give one insight and valuable leads. It is an excellent source of shortcuts in determining what Hearing was important. Each is available online.

2. Sources for Specialized Context

Every issue has its constituency. When doing a legislative history or when monitoring pending legislation it is vital to identify what groups or individuals care about the issue. Are there trade groups or professional associations interested in the legislation? Are certain industries lobbying for a particular position? Have public interest groups taken a position? If so, any one of these sources could provide useful background. It may be that they have prepared background papers on the topic, they may even have done a complete legislative history already.

---

10   <http://NationalJournal.com>

The general sources of legislative context discussed in Section 1 may identify such groups. If so, they should be pursued. Many such groups publish newsletters and periodicals and they may even offer online databases. If you are truly lucky, you may find that they have a librarian or information officer who will help. Of course such a group may have a particular take on an issue, but if you are aware of that the work that they have done, the information can still be used. It would be insane to do research on legislation concerning firearms without using the resources of both the National Rifle Association and the gun control advocates.

If one cannot find a relevant group or interested party, check with a reference librarian. There are directories that can be used to find groups interested in any issue. Gale Research's *Encyclopedia of Associations* lists thousands of such groups. This multi-volume set is at most reference desks and is available on WESTLAW.

The work of such groups is not persuasive authority, but it can provide important background. A useful strategy in research is to find someone who cares about the issue and use the work that they have already done.

E. STATE LEGISLATIVE HISTORIES

The use of legislative history in the interpretation of state legislation, and in statutory research at the state level generally, is no less important than in the federal area. However, the sources for state legislative history and the available research tools are much less adequate and the process is often very frustrating. In most states, it is virtually impossible to collect the necessary documents for a simple legislative history outside of the state capitol or its legislative library. Debates are almost never published, bills are usually available only at the legislature and during the session itself, committee reports are published in only a few states, and hearings even less often. Legislative journals are published for most states, but these rarely contain documentation explaining the decision-making process.

Many state legislatures are now covered by commercial legislative services, some of which provide status tables of pending bills. The commercial services often include document ordering options, but they can be quite expensive. In a number of states there are computer-based official or commercial information services for legislative proceedings. A growing number of states have created Internet access that allows free use of a wide range of state materials, some of which were never available in print. These usually include online access to bill tracking and bill digests, and sometimes offer information on legislative documents. For some states, however, there is no convenient method of identifying pending legislation, ascertaining its status, securing copies of documents or abstracts thereof, or tracing legislative proceedings. Recourse must be had to the legislature itself, to the legislative reference library, or to the state library.

Guide to State Legislative and Administrative Materials (W.S. Hein, 2002), by William H. Manz, has vastly improved the process of identifying what documents are available for each state, and from whom they are available. The guide provides detailed information for every state, with addresses and phone numbers of all relevant offices. It also indicates whether each state is covered by a legislative information service, in either printed or online format.

Another useful service, focusing on legislative organization and process generally rather than on specific legislative documents, is the *State Legislative Sourcebook: A Resource Guide to Legislative Information in the Fifty States* (Government Research Service, annual). This tool, first published in 1985, contains eight to ten pages of detailed information on the legislature and legislative process of each state. It also includes references to available information services.

Legal research manuals, describing legislative material, are available for a number of states (see Appendix B at the end of this book), and there are occasional periodical articles describing legislative history research in particular states.[11] The reference staff of a research law library in your state should also be consulted for details as to the local situation.

The Internet has various sources for information. You can check the official state legislative web sites, but there are many sites aggregating information about what is available. The Multistate Associates' State

---

11   *See, e.g.,* Duggan, "Illinois Legislative History," 88 Ill. B.J. 665 (2000); Liebert, "Researching California Ballot Measures," 90 L. Libr. J. 27 (1998); McMahon, "Legislative History in Ohio: Myths and Realities," 46 Clev. St. L. Rev. 49 (1998).

Legislative Presence on the Internet has a chart[12] of the 50 states, describing what materials are available, with links. The Law Librarians' Society of Washington, D.C. has a section "State Legislatures, State Laws and State Regulations"[13] with links.

Some of the annotated state statutory compilations offer legislative session services which, like some looseleaf services with state coverage, include the text of laws enacted during the pending legislative session. These services may also provide some legislative history references, but not on a comprehensive or systematic basis.

Most states now have official or quasi-official agencies devoted to the research and recommendation of new legislation. These include independent law revision commissions, legislatively controlled councils, judicial groups, or academic bodies devoted to legislative study and drafting. The studies and proposals prepared by such agencies frequently result in enactments, although rarely in the exact form proposed. Their publications are an invaluable source of legislative history and may shed considerable light on the interpretation of the resulting enactment.

F. SUMMARY

The many ambiguities in the language of our statutes derive less from the grammatical inadequacies of English prose than from the political compromises necessary to achieve a consensus for enactment. These ambiguities frequently become the focal issues of litigation in both the federal and state courts. Careful research in the documents of legislative history is necessary to ascertain the intent of the legislature in enacting the disputed provisions. Such research also provides sources for the development of arguments for or against particular interpretations.

Research into legislative history is facilitated by the use of a variety of finding tools, indexes and tables, in both official and commercial publications, as well as in an increasing number of online databases. The availability of the legislative documents themselves has been expanded by

---

12   <http://www.multistate.com/site.nsf/state?OpenPage>

13   <http://www.llsdc.org/sourcebook/state-leg.htm>

their inclusion in microfiche collections and computer-based services. Although many of these services are quite expensive the Internet is opening new vistas for the researcher. The work of the skilled researcher in federal legislative history can now be done in smaller libraries and away from large urban centers. For legislative research on the state level, the documentary sources are less adequate, but the finding tools for many states are increasing in numbers and expanding in scope.

G. ADDITIONAL READING

R. Dickerson, *The Interpretation and Application of Statutes* (Little, Brown 1975). The standard text on statutory interpretation.

William N. Eskridge, Jr., Philip P. Frickey and Elizabeth Garrett, *Cases and Materials on Legislation: Statutes and the Creation of Public Policy* (3rd ed. 2001). This casebook is a wonderful analysis of the legislative process. The early chapters, particularly the explanation of the true legislative history of Title IX, is an excellent example of contextual legislative history.

Glen S. Krutz, *Hitching a Ride: Omnibus Legislating in the U.S. Congress* (Ohio State University Press 2001). An exploration and evaluation of omnibus legislating.

Walter J. Oleszek, *Congressional Procedures and the Policy Process* (CQ Press 2004). A close examination of the rules and practice of the U.S. Congress.

P.J. O'Rourke, *Parliament of Whores* (Atlantic Monthly Press 1991). His chapter on the legislative process is an irreverent but refreshing romp. This is how bills really become law.

Norman Singer, *Statutes and Statutory Construction* (Clark Boardman Callaghan 1992-). A looseleaf that updates the classic work by Sutherland of the same title.

Barbara Sinclair, *Unorthodox Lawmaking: New Legislative Processes in the U.S. Congress* (CQ Press 2000). Using illustrative case studies from 1970 onward, the author examines how the contemporary legislative process deviates from the "textbook" model.

To find academic law articles exploring the use of legislative history in statutory interpretation, search LegalTrac using the subject heading "Legislative Histories—Usage" and, more broadly "Law—Interpretation and Construction."

Chapter 7

CONSTITUTIONAL LAW

A. INTRODUCTION

The constitution is the organic document of a political entity and of its legal system. Constitutions set the parameters for governmental action; they allocate power and responsibility among the branches of government and between the central government and its political subdivisions. In addition, they describe the fundamental rules by which the system functions, and, in some jurisdictions, they also define the basic rights of individuals. Constitutions can take any number of forms, ranging from relatively brief and general statements (the United States Constitution can be easily printed in ten pages) to quite lengthy documents of considerable specificity (the Texas Constitution covers about 140 pages).[1]

The United States Constitution defines its own primacy in our legal system. Article VI of the Constitution states: "This Constitution, and the Laws of the United States which shall be made in Pursuance thereof; ... shall be the supreme Law of the Land; ...." Research in constitutional law in the United States is shaped by our concept of judicial review, which was derived in part from that clause of Article VI. This doctrine, established by Chief Justice Marshall's opinion in *Marbury v. Madison*, 5 U.S. (1 Cranch) 137 (1803), established the power of the judicial branch to review actions of the executive and legislature and to rule on their constitutionality. The power has, of course, been extensively used during various periods in our history at both the federal and state levels, and has greatly increased litigation over constitutional issues. Occasionally, it has also created political crises.

Because of the frequent judicial interpretation and application of constitutional provisions, and the vast secondary literature which has been and undoubtedly will be written on the Constitution, only a small part of constitutional law research relates to locating relevant constitutional provisions. The related historical background, judicial interpretations, legislative actions, and scholarly commentaries are a major focus of most research problems. The relationship of federal and state constitutional issues, and the conflict between federal and state jurisdiction and prerogatives introduce further complications in constitutional research. In any event, the constitutional documents of the United States and of the fifty

---

1   You can download a copy of the Texas Constitution in Word format from the Texas State Legislature, <http://www.capitol.state.tx.us/txconst/toc.html>, that runs just over 200 pages with its index.

states represent a separate and distinct literature with their own research procedures and tools.

B. THE UNITED STATES CONSTITUTION

The Constitution of the United States is usually considered the oldest constitutional document in continuous force in the world today. It provides the authority for all federal legislation (i.e., acts, joint resolutions, treaties, and interstate compacts).

The text of the Constitution can be found in a variety of sources. It appears in many pamphlet editions, in standard reference works such as *Black's Law Dictionary*, and in almost all state and federal statutory compilations. Because its text is infrequently amended, obtaining a current version is not difficult. Perhaps the most easily accessible versions are those available on the Internet.[2] It is also included in the official *United States Code*, *USCA* and *USCS*.

Most research into problems of constitutional law requires extrinsic aids, beyond the text of the Constitution. The researcher therefore also needs access to interpretive judicial decisions and the scholarly analysis of commentators. The following sections describe the research tools available for such access -- annotated editions of the Constitution, citators, digests, indexes, databases, and secondary sources.

1. Annotated Texts

An annotated edition of the U.S. Constitution is one that provides notes of judicial decisions which have applied or interpreted its provisions. Three such "annotated" texts of the Constitution are in common use

---

2   There are numerous versions of the Constitution available, so if you look for it on the Internet, make sure you consider the source and whether or not the text is current. An up to date text is available from the GPO, with annotations. <http://www.gpoaccess.gov/constitution/browse.html> The National Archives and Records Association has the text of the original, with image files of the document. <http://www.archives.gov/national_archives_experience/charters/constitution.html>

throughout the country, and many state codes include the Constitution annotated specifically with the decisions of that state's courts.

Two of the most important versions of the Constitution are part of the unofficial, annotated editions of the *U.S. Code*: the "Constitution" volumes of the *United States Code Annotated* (Thomson-West) and of the *United States Code Service* (LexisNexis). The format and use of these sets are similar and have been described in Chapter 5, Statutes. They provide multivolume printings of the U.S. Constitution containing brief abstracts of the relevant cases decided under each clause, section, or amendment.

a. *USCA*

United States Code Annotated, following the traditional Thomson-West approach, provides extensive coverage by including annotations to both federal and state decisions that concern each article or amendment of the U.S. Constitution. As a result, the text of the Constitution, when annotated in *USCA*, requires ten volumes.[3] The annotations to the due process clause of the Fourteenth Amendment alone fill two volumes. The volumes are kept up to date with cumulative annual pocket parts or supplementary pamphlets. As part of the Thomson-West research system, the annotations for each clause include relevant key numbers, providing access to digests covering the Supreme Court, lower federal courts, and all state courts covered by the *National Reporter System*; cross-references to other Thomson-West publications; and citations to periodical articles, attorneys general opinions, and Executive Orders. The case annotations are arranged by subject, and an alphabetical index of the subjects annotated under each section is provided just before the annotations themselves. An index to the Constitution is printed at the end of the final volume, containing Amendments 14 to End. Illustration A shows the page from the bound volume of the *USCA* containing Article II, Section 4, concerning impeachment of the President and other federal officers.

---

3   The *USCA* Constitution volumes were published as a "Bicentennial Edition" in 1987, after a thorough revision which eliminated annotations to many redundant and obsolete cases. The ten new volumes reduced the number of pages almost by half, replacing seventeen volumes and eleven pamphlets or pocket parts.

Illustration A
Article II, §4 as printed in *United States Code Annotated*

Art. II § 3
Note 14

President's right over the office no longer exists, for the right is vested, and is irrevocable; but where the officer belongs to a class removable at any time by the President, there it would seem that the commission, though made out, may be arrested in the office, and the right to the office does not vest. Adams' Case, 1867, 12 Op.Atty.Gen. 306.

Even after confirmation by the Senate the President may, in his discretion, withhold a commission from the applicant, and until a commission to signify that the purpose of the President has been changed, the appointment is not fully consummated. Appointments to Office—

THE PRESIDENT

Case of Lieutenant Cope, 1843, 4 Op.Atty. Gen. 218.

15. Former presidents

Agreement between former president and former national archivist, providing that certain electronic presidential records would be treated as president's personal records, subject to president's control after he left office, conflicted with constitutional provision giving incumbent president authority to direct actions of current executive officials. American Historical Ass'n v. Peterson, D.D.C.1995, 876 F.Supp. 1300. Records ⮜ 30

Section 4. Impeachment

Section 4. The President, Vice President and all civil Officers of the United States, shall be removed from Office on Impeachment for, and Conviction of, Treason, Bribery, or other high Crimes and Misdemeanors.

CROSS REFERENCES

Effect of judgment of impeachment, see USCA Const. Art. I, § 3, cl. 7.
Power of impeachment by House of Representatives, see USCA Const. Art I, § 2, cl. 5.
Power of Senate to try impeachments, see USCA Const. Art. I, § 3, cl. 6.
Treason, see USCA Const. Art. III, § 3, cl. 1.

LAW REVIEW AND JOURNAL COMMENTARIES

Bribery and other not so "good behavior": Criminal prosecution as a supplement to impeachment of federal judges. 94 Colum.L.Rev. 1617 (1994).
Federal judicial impeachment: Defining process due. 46 Hastings L.J. 639 (1995).
Presidential immunity from criminal prosecution. George E. Danielson, 63 Geo. L.J. 1065 (1975).
Removal of the President: Resignation and the procedural law of impeachment. Edwin Brown Firmage and R. Collin Mangrum. 1974 Duke L.J. 1023.
Resignations and removals: a history of federal judicial service—and disservice—1789–1992. Emily Field Van Tassel, 142 U.Pa.L.Rev. 333 (1993).
Spare the rod and spoil the judge? Discipline of federal judges and the separation of powers. Paula Abrams, 41 DePaul L.Rev. 59 (1991).
Treason, bribery, or other high crimes and misdemeanors—A study of impeachment. Jerome S. Sloan and Ira E. Garr, 47 Temp.L.Q. 413 (1974).
Who may discipline or remove federal judges? A constitutional analysis. Peter M. Shane, 142 U.Pa.L.Rev. 209 (1993).

WESTLAW ELECTRONIC RESEARCH

See WESTLAW guide following the Explanation pages of this volume.

254

b. *USCS*

The "Constitution" volumes of the *United States Code Service* serve many of the same functions as those of the *USCA*. The text of each section is printed, followed by annotations of court decisions arranged by subject. The *USCS* volumes also provide cross-references to *Lawyers' Edition* and *ALR* annotations, to other LexisNexis publications such as *Federal Procedure, Lawyers Edition,* and to law review articles. It also includes references to *American Jurisprudence. USCS* includes fewer annotations than *USCA*, so that the Constitution and its amendments, with annotations, are contained in only four volumes. There is an index at the end of the final volume. The four volumes are supplemented annually by cumulative pocket parts or supplementary pamphlets, and in the interim by *USCS*'s "Later Case and Statutory Service" pamphlets. Illustration B shows the impeachment clause as printed in the *USCS* version of the Constitution.

c. The Library of Congress Edition

Despite their usefulness as case finders for decisions under particular clauses of the Constitution, the *USCA* and *USCS* editions of the U.S. Constitution contain no descriptive or explanatory text. Many researchers find them too massive and cumbersome for achieving an understanding of constitutional doctrines, and turn instead to a more compact, single-volume edition which discusses the scope and development of each provision.

The Constitution of the United States of America: Analysis and Interpretation is prepared by the Congressional Research Service of the Library of Congress and published as a Senate Document.[4] This volume, edited by J.H. Killian and George A. Costello and published in 1996, is the ninth annotated edition of the Constitution prepared under Congressional direction. The first, in 1913, merely listed citations of Supreme Court cases after each provision. The work grew in scope with each edition, and adopted much of its present form with the 1953 edition, which was edited by the distinguished constitutional law scholar, Edward S. Corwin. The current edition is the fourth revision since 1953, and discusses Supreme Court cases decided through July 29, 1992. A pocket part supplement, also published in

---

4   S.Doc. No. 6, 103rd Cong., 1st Sess. (1996).

Illustration B
Article II, § 4 as printed in *United States Code Service*

Art II, § 3, n 3

ex rel. Krohn v Sun West Servs. (2000, DC NM) 2000 US Dist LEXIS 17193) and (criticized in United States ex rel. Downy v Corning, Inc. (2000, DC NM) 118 F Supp 2d 1160).

Judicial branch of Federal Government has constitutional duty under Article II, § 3, of Constitution, of requiring executive branch to remain within limits stated by legislative branch; constitutional duty obligating President to "take Care that the Laws be faithfully executed" does not permit President to refrain from executing laws duly enacted by Congress as those laws are construed by judiciary. National Treasury Employees Union v Nixon (1974, App DC) 160 US App DC 321, 492 F2d 587 (criticized in Swan v Clinton (1996, App DC) 321 US App DC 359, 100 F3d 973).

4. Commissioning of officers

Commission is merely evidence of appointment and is not necessary to appointment by President; commission signed by President and sent to Secretary of State for officer not holding office at will of President is not revocable, and appointment is complete. Marbury v Madison (1803) 5 US 137, 2 L Ed 60.

Transmission of commission to officer is not essential to his investiture of office; when commission of postmaster has been signed and sealed, and placed in hands of Postmaster-General, to be transmitted to officer, so far as execution is concerned, it is completed act; and subsequent death of President, by whom nothing remained to be done, could have no effect on such completed act. United States v Le Baron (1856) 60 US 73, 19 How 73, 15 L Ed 525.

Article II § 3, Clause 4 of United States Constitution assigns to the executive branch duty to faithfully execute laws; accordingly, executive branch has discretionary power to control criminal prosecutions and courts may not interfere with this power; order of federal district court making Department of Justice make available to targets of grand jury probe summaries of facts and issues considered by Justice Department in determining whether to indict targets violate separation of powers and endangers grand jury secrecy. In Re Grand Jury (Northside Realty Associates) (3/4/80, Ga ND) 27 Cr L 2001.

Even if alleged agreement between plaintiffs and U.S. attorney by which plaintiffs assisted in government's sting operation to its logical conclusion might comport with public policy, court had no power to second-guess U.S. Attorney's implicit decision in ceasing investigation that case was not prosecutable, since decision whether to prosecute is committed to executive branch and court's review of it, absent allegation of constitutional violation, would violate separation of powers doctrine. Howard v United States (1994) 31 Fed Cl 297.

Section 4. Removal from office.

The President, Vice President and all civil Officers of the United States, shall be removed from Office on Impeachment for, and Conviction of, Treason, Bribery, or other high Crimes and Misdemeanors.

RESEARCH GUIDE

Federal Procedure:
16 Fed Proc L Ed, Government Officers and Employees § 40:707.

Am Jur:
63C Am Jur 2d, Public Officers and Employees §§ 218–222.

Annotations:
Executive privilege with respect to Presidential papers and recordings. 19 ALR Fed 472.
What constitutes conviction within statutory or constitutional provision making conviction of crime ground of disqualification for, removal from, or vacancy in, public office. 10 ALR5th 139.

Law Review Articles:
Franklin. Romanist Infamy and The American Constitutional Conception of Impeachment. 23 Buff L Rev 313.
Firmage; Mangrum. Removal of the President: Resignation and the Procedural Law of Impeachment. 1974 Duke LJ 1023.
McDermott. "The truth": perjury and obstruction as high crimes and misdemeanors. 46 Fed Law 24, January 1999.

712

Illustration C
Article II, § 4 as printed in the Library of Congress edition of the Constitution

ART. II—EXECUTIVE DEPARTMENT   583

Sec. 4—Powers and Duties of the President   Impeachment

areas officials acting in the "outer perimeter" of their duties may be accorded an absolute immunity from liability. [745] Jurisdiction to reach such officers for acts for which they can be held responsible must be under the general "federal question" jurisdictional statute, which, as recently amended, requires no jurisdictional amount. [746]

SECTION 4. The President, Vice President and all civil Officers of the United States, shall be removed from Office on Impeachment for, and Conviction of, Treason, Bribery, or other high Crimes and Misdemeanors.

IMPEACHMENT [747]

Few provisions of the Constitution were adopted from English practice to the degree the section on impeachment was. In Eng-

a Bivens action, the Court distinguished between common-law torts and constitutional torts and denied high federal officials, including cabinet secretaries, absolute immunity, in favor of the qualified immunity previously accorded high state officials under 42 U.S.C. § 1983. In Harlow v. Fitzgerald, 457 U.S. 800 (1982), the Court denied presidential aides derivative absolute presidential immunity, but it modified the rules of qualified immunity, making it more difficult to hold such aides, other federal officials, and indeed state and local officials, liable for constitutional torts. In Mitchell v. Forsyth, 472 U.S. 511 (1985), the Court extended qualified immunity to the Attorney General for authorizing a warrantless wiretap in a case involving domestic national security. Although the Court later held such warrantless wiretaps violated the Fourth Amendment, at the time of the Attorney General's authorization this interpretation was not "clearly established," and the Harlow immunity protected officials exercising discretion on such open questions. See also Anderson v. Creighton, 483 U.S. 635 (1987) (in an exceedingly opaque opinion, the Court extended similar qualified immunity to FBI agents who conducted a warrantless search).

[745] Harlow v. Fitzgerald, 457 U.S. 800, 812 (1982).

[746] See 28 U.S.C. § 1331. On deleting the jurisdictional amount, see P.L. 94–574, 90 Stat. 2721 (1976), and P.L. 96–486, 94 Stat. 2369 (1980). If such suits are brought in state courts, they can be removed to federal district courts. 28 U.S.C. § 1442(a).

[747] Impeachment is the subject of several other provisions of the Constitution. Article I, § 2, cl. 5, gives to the House of Representatives "the sole power of impeachment." Article I, § 3, cl. 6, gives to the Senate "the sole power to try all impeachments," requires that Senators be under oath or affirmation when sitting for that purpose, stipulates that the Chief Justice of the United States is to preside when the President of the United States is tried, and provides for conviction on the vote of two-thirds of the members present. Article I, § 3, cl. 7, limits the judgment after impeachment to removal from office and disqualification from future federal office holding, but it allows criminal trial and conviction following impeachment. Article II, § 2, cl. 1, deprives the President of the power to grant pardons or reprieves in cases of impeachment. Article III, § 2, cl. 3, excepts impeachment cases from the jury trial requirement.

The word "impeachment" may be used to mean several different things. Any member of the House may "impeach" an officer of the United States by presenting a petition or memorial, which is generally referred to a committee for investigation and report. The House votes to "impeach," the meaning used in § 4, when it adopts

1996, updated the text with annotations of cases decided through July, 1 1996.[5] Two subsequent supplements have been published, with the most recent providing annotations of cases through June 28, 2000.[6, 7]

The Library of Congress edition includes the text of the Constitution interspersed with extensive commentary, historical background, legal analysis, and summaries of judicial interpretation of each clause and amendment of the Constitution. The major constitutional decisions of the Supreme Court are discussed in detail, and the footnotes include numerous citations to other relevant cases and scholarly interpretations. Illustration C shows the page on which discussion of the impeachment clause begins.

Unlike the *USCA* and *USCS* indexes to the Constitution, which cover just its text, the Library of Congress edition's index has extensive coverage of topics addressed in its analysis, as well as an alphabetical table listing all cases discussed or noted in the text. The volume also includes the texts of proposed amendments which were not ratified; tables of Acts of Congress, state constitutional and statutory provisions, and municipal ordinances which have been held unconstitutional by the Supreme Court; and a list of Supreme Court decisions overruled by subsequent decisions.

The major shortcoming of this otherwise superb work is its infrequent revision and supplementation. The new volume was already four years out-of-date the day it was published; its most recent supplementation is more than five years old. Unless regular pocket part supplementation is provided, thorough updating will generally require the use of other, more current sources. Although the volume must be used with increasing caution as it ages, it remains an authoritative and useful resource for constitutional research.

d. Annotated State Statutory Codes

State courts frequently apply and interpret the United States Constitution. State laws or governmental actions are often challenged, for

---

5 S.Doc. No. 14, 104th Cong., 2d Sess. (1997).

6 S. Doc. No. 27, 106th Cong., 2d Sess. (2000).

7 The full text and all of the supplements are available through GPOAccess in HTML and PDF format. <http://www.gpoaccess.gov/constitution/browse.html>

example, as being in conflict with the federal constitution. A state court decision is often relevant to research in constitutional issues, particularly as precedent in subsequent litigation in that state. As noted above, the annotations under the provisions of the U.S. Constitution in *USCA* and *USCS* include abstracts of state court decisions, as well as those of the federal courts. In about a dozen states, another valuable source for locating relevant cases is the annotated state code.

Almost every annotated state code contains the text of the U.S. Constitution, in addition to the constitution of that state. While every code annotates the provisions of the state constitution, only a few also annotate the U.S. Constitution. Those that do so provide a valuable service to researchers in their state, by isolating the most relevant case law from the mass of materials found in *USCA* or *USCS*. The annotations include abstracts of both state court decisions and federal cases arising in that state. References to state attorneys general opinions, law review articles, and other publications may also be provided. Notable among these state codes is the *Official Code of Georgia Annotated*, which devotes an entire volume to a thoroughly annotated U.S. Constitution.

2. Shepardizing and KeyCiting the U.S. Constitution

References to court decisions applying and construing the provisions of the Constitution can be found online in *Shepard's* and *KeyCite,* and in the print editions of *Shepard's United States Citations* and in each of *Shepard's* state citators. The first bound volume of the print edition *Shepard's United States Citations, Statute Edition* provides references to all federal court decisions citing or discussing each constitutional clause or amendment. Supreme Court cases are listed first, followed by lower federal court decisions arranged by circuit.[8] The listings also include citations to the Constitution in federal legislation, treaties, American Bar Association Journal articles, and annotations in *ALR*, *ALR Federal*, and *Lawyers' Edition*. Because the Constitution is the subject of much interpretation and litigation, the bound volume's lists of citations under most provisions are lengthy and bewildering. Citations found in recent paperback supplements may be useful, however, in providing references to current cases that have not yet been covered in annotated editions.

---

8   Supreme Court decisions since 1956 which apply or interpret particular constitutional provisions are also listed in the *Lawyers' Edition Desk Book* 's "Table of Federal Laws, Rules and Regulations."

Every *Shepard's* state citator, including those covering the District of Columbia and Puerto Rico, also includes a section listing references to the U.S. Constitution. The citations in these listings are generally limited to decisions of the particular state's courts and, in the past, state legislative acts, although some include state attorneys general opinions. Federal court decisions, even those from District Courts within the state, are not included. These citators can be very useful if one needs to know how a state supreme court or appellate court has applied or interpreted the federal constitution. Since only about a dozen state codes provide state annotations to the U.S. Constitution, *Shepard's* is often the quickest way to find state court decisions. Illustration D shows a screen shot from *Shepard's*, covering the U.S. Constitution, showing the cases where the Colorado Supreme Court has cited to Article 1, §4.

Illustration D
Citations by the Colorado Supreme Court to the U.S. Constitution in
Shepard's

3. Finding Court Interpretations by Subject

Tools such as annotated texts and citators gather references to cases decided under particular constitutional provisions. If one is unsure of the relevant provision or wants a broader perspective, decisions interpreting and applying the Constitution can also be found by using any of the major case-finding methods discussed in Chapter 4.

Digests, including those in Thomson-West's *American Digest System*, arrange headnotes of cases by subject. Although the annotated codes are more effective starting points for constitutional research, the digests can serve as an alternative approach to the same decisions. Thomson-West's digests include sets covering the Supreme Court, the entire federal court system, and nearly every state court system. One of the topics Thomson-West uses is "Constitutional Law," although constitutional issues are also addressed under numerous other topics. One can use the "Descriptive Word Indexes" to find relevant sections, or approach the digest from the key numbers assigned to a known case. Because all of Thomson-West's federal, regional, and state digests follow the same subject outline, it is easy to expand one's research from one jurisdiction to others or to the entire body of published case law. Unlike annotated codes or *Shepard's*, in which references are limited to cases citing a particular constitution, West's digests provide access to all cases with similar themes whether interpreting provisions of the U.S. Constitution or a state constitution.

In the *United States Supreme Court Digest, Lawyers' Edition* (LexisNexis), it is very easy to determine which digest sections are applicable to particular constitutional provisions. The text of the Constitution is set out at the beginning of volume 17 of the set, with references after each provision to relevant digest topics and sections.

Other LexisNexis publishing reference tools also can be used to find cases. Many of the annotations in *ALR, ALR Federal*, and *Lawyers' Edition* contain extensive discussion of federal constitutional issues, including citations to state court decisions where they are relevant. As indicated above, annotations citing particular constitutional provisions are listed in *Shepard's United States Citations*, and access by subject is available in the *Index to Annotations*.

The full-text case databases of WESTLAW and LEXIS can also be very useful in finding case law under the Constitution, especially as one often needs to apply the Constitution's broad language to a particular set of circumstances. A computer search can combine the citation of a constitutional section or amendment with relevant factual or legal terms.

4. Secondary Sources

Research on federal constitutional problems is often aided by the commentary and analysis of legal scholars. The extensive literature of constitutional law in such secondary sources as encyclopedias, treatises, and periodicals includes works that approach the Constitution from both historical and contemporary viewpoints. While later chapters will deal in depth with secondary sources generally, it is appropriate here to mention a few specific sources that can be of particular help to the constitutional researcher.

An excellent beginning point for analysis of constitutional issues is the *Encyclopedia of the American Constitution* (2nd ed., Macmillan 2000). This six volume work, edited by Leonard W. Levy, Kenneth L. Karst and Adam Winkler, includes over two thousand articles, many by leading scholars. It updates the first edition by including original content and then supplementing those existing articles, as well as adding new topics. The arrangement is such that the original text from the first volume will appear, followed by a supplemental article and then an update to the supplement. If you choose to use these volumes, you must remember that the older essays have *not* been revised and keep in mind the context of the time in which they were written. This arrangement of mixing the older and newer text does two things: it allows you to see the change in legal theory over time and it exposes you to different views of the subject matter.

More than half of the encyclopedia discusses doctrinal concepts of constitutional law, but there are also articles on specific people, judicial decisions, statutes, and historical periods. Most articles include numerous cross-references to other articles and a short bibliography of further readings. In the final volume there are chronologies of the Constitution's birth and development, a brief glossary, and indexes by case, name, and subject.[9]

Two current texts should be noted for their broad coverage of the Constitution with a focus on current issues. Laurence H. Tribe's *American*

---

9   Another work attempting comprehensive coverage of major concepts and cases is Ralph C. Chandler, Richard A. Enslen & Peter G. Renstrom, *The Constitutional Law Dictionary* (ABC–Clio, 2 vols., 1985–87). The first volume discusses individual rights provisions and the second covers governmental powers. A supplement to volume one was issued in 1987.

Constitutional Law (3rd ed., Foundation Press 1999-) is probably the most thorough and authoritative treatment of American constitutional law. Ronald D. Rotunda & John E. Nowak, *Treatise on Constitutional Law: Substance and Procedure* (5 vols.) (3rd ed., Thomson-West 1999-) is also an extensive analysis of constitutional issues, with an abridged hornbook version for students published as *Constitutional Law* (7th ed., Thomson-West 2004).

Numerous texts have been devoted to specific aspects of the Constitution and to the interpretative decisions of the Supreme Court. Among the many historical treatments of the Court and the Constitution, perhaps the most ambitious is the *Oliver Wendell Holmes Devise History of the Supreme Court of the United States.* This multivolume, detailed history, with separate authors for each volume, is still incomplete. Nine volumes were published by Macmillan, and the series has now been picked up by Cambridge University Press, which plans four more volumes.[10] Each volume covers the major constitutional issues and decisions in its respective period.

Periodical articles are a rich source of scholarly writing on the Constitution and constitutional issues. Subject access to these articles can be gained through the standard legal periodical indexes, or through one of several bibliographies published in recent years. Two bibliographies worth noting are Kermit L. Hall, *A Comprehensive Bibliography of American Constitutional and Legal History, 1896-1979* (5 vols.) (Kraus International 1984), with a two-volume supplement covering 1980-1987 published in 1991; and Bernard D. Reams, Jr., & Stuart D. Yoak, *The Constitution of the United States: A Guide and Bibliography to Current Scholarly Research* (Oceana 1987) (also published as volume five of *Sources and Documents of*

---

10   The MacMillan volumes are: Julius Goebel, *Antecedents and Beginnings to 1801* (Vol. 1, 1971); George Lee Haskins and Herbert A. Johnson, *Foundations of Power: John Marshall, 1801-1815* (Vol. 2, 1981); *The Marshall Court and Cultural Change, 1815-35* (Vols. 3-4, 1988); *The Taney Period, 1836-64* (Vol. 5, 1974); *Reconstruction and Reunion, 1864-88* (Vols. 6-7, 1971); *Five Justices and the Electorial Commission of 1877* (Vol. 8, 1993); *Troubled Beginnings of the Modern State, 1888-1910* (Vol. 8); *The Judiciary and Responsible Government 1910-21* (Vol. 9, 1984). Cambridge University Press is publishing: William M. Wiecek, *The Birth of the Modern Constitution: The United States Supreme Court, 1941-53* (Vol. 12, 2005). Volumes on the Taft Court, the Hughes Court, the Stone/Vison Court, and the Warren Court are also planned for the series.

United States Constitutions, Second Series (William F. Swindler, ed., Oceana 1982-87)).[11]

In addition to the numerous relevant articles in law reviews of general coverage, there are several periodicals specializing in constitutional issues, such as *Constitutional Commentary, Harvard Civil Rights-Civil Liberties Law Review*, and *Hastings Constitutional Law Quarterly*. The *Supreme Court Review*, published annually by the University of Chicago, includes scholarly articles on important, recent U.S. Supreme Court decisions, many of which deal with constitutional issues. The first issue of each volume of the *Harvard Law Review* usually contains an extensive analysis by its student editors of the activity of the Supreme Court in the preceding term. This survey, always prefaced by a major introductory article written by a noted scholar, is widely read and often cited. Finally, the *Yearbook of the Supreme Court Historical Society*, published annually by the Society, includes articles, usually in a popular tone, on the history of the Court and the Constitution.

C. HISTORICAL BACKGROUND OF THE FEDERAL CONSTITUTION

The events and discussions leading to the adoption of the Constitution and its amendments are preserved in a variety of reports, journals and other documents. These materials are of continuing importance as courts attempt to apply the terms of an eighteenth century document to changing modern circumstances. The significance of the framers' intent, however, is a subject of considerable dispute.[12]

---

11   Other useful bibliographies include Robert J. Janosik, *The American Constitution: An Annotated Bibliography* (Salem Press 1991) and Shelley L. Dowling and Mary C. Custy, *The Jurisprudence of United States Constitutional Interpretation: An Annotated Bibliography* (Rothman, 1999).

12   The opposing viewpoints may best be represented in speeches given in 1985 by Attorney General Edwin Meese III and Justice William Brennan, Jr. *Compare* Edwin Meese, "The Attorney General's View of the Supreme Court: Toward a Jurisprudence of Original Intent," 45 *Pub. Admin. Rev.* 701 (1985) (reprinted with minor changes as "The Supreme Court of the United States: Bulwark of a Limited Jurisdiction," 27 *S. Tex. L. Rev.* 455 (1986)), *with* William J. Brennan, Jr., "The Constitution of the United States: Contemporary Ratification,"

A particularly useful guide to historical research sources on the Constitution and its amendments is Part VI, "Sources for Constitutional Provisions," of Gwendolyn B. Folsom, *Legislative History: Research for the Interpretation of Laws* (University Press of Virginia 1972; reprinted by Rothman 1979).

1. Drafting and Ratification

The Constitution of the United States was drafted in Philadelphia in 1787, and ratified by the states between 1787 and 1790. The Constitutional Convention was called to address deficiencies in the Articles of Confederation, which had been in force since 1781. Although the Constitutional Convention did not issue an official record of its proceedings, extensive notes were kept by James Madison and other delegates. The following sources provide useful documentary background on the drafting and adoption of the Constitution:

- Max Farrand, *The Records of the Federal Convention of 1787* (3 vols.) (Yale University Press 1911) (supplement edited by J.H. Hutson, 1987, supplanting vol. 4, published in 1937). Long the standard source for documents of the constitutional convention, this set includes extensive day-by-day records including notes by major participants and the texts of various alternative plans presented.[13]

- Philip B. Kurland & Ralph Lerner, *The Founders' Constitution* (5 vols.) (University of Chicago Press 1987). This set provides references to and excerpts from primary materials illustrative of the political arguments and reasoning of the adopters of the Constitution. Following a first volume devoted to major themes leading up to the Constitution, the next three volumes are arranged by article, section, and clause of the Constitution. Volume 5 deals with the first twelve amendments.[14]

---

27 S. Tex. L. Rev. 433 (1986). Both speeches are also printed, with others, in *The Great Debate: Interpreting Our Written Constitution* (Federalist Society 1986).

13   The Library of Congress has digitized the first three volumes of this set, and the general index to those volumes. The search mechanism is clunky, but the images are in PDF. <http://memory.loc.gov/ammem/amlaw/lwfr.html>

14   Three earlier, but still extremely useful, compilations of historical

- Wilbourn E. Benton, *1787: Drafting the U.S. Constitution* (2 vols.) (Texas A & M University Press 1986). Less comprehensive in scope than *The Founders' Constitution*, this work also reproduces excerpts from participants' notes, arranged by article and section.

- *The Federalist*, containing the essays of James Madison, John Jay and Alexander Hamilton in support of the adoption of the Constitution, has been issued in many editions since its first collected publication in 1788, and remains an indispensable work for the study of the Constitution.

- The debates concerning ratification of the federal Constitution by the state conventions are recorded in a variety of sources, including Jonathan Elliot's *Debates in the Several State Conventions on the Adoption of the Federal Constitution*, 2nd ed. (5 vols.) (Elliot 183-- 45; reprinted by Ayer 1987). Merrill Jensen's ambitious multivolume set, *Documentary History of the Ratification of the Constitution* (20 vols. to date) (Merrill Jensen, John P. Kaminski & Gaspare J. Saladino, eds., State Historical Society of Wisconsin 1976-), will be, when completed, the most comprehensive compilation of documents on the ratification of the Constitution by the states.[15]

---

documentation are: U.S. Bureau of Rolls and Library, *Documentary History of the Constitution of the United States of America, 1786-1870* (5 vols.) (U.S. Department of State 1894-1905; reprinted by Johnson Reprint 1965); Paul Leicester Ford, *Bibliography and Reference List of the History and Literature relating to the Adoption of the Constitution of the United States, 1887-8* (Brooklyn 1888; reprinted by Lawbook Exchange 2003); and Library of Congress, Legislative Reference Service, *Documents Illustrative of the Formation of the Union of the American States* (Charles C. Tansill, ed.), H.R.Doc. No. 398, 69th Cong., 1st Sess. (1927).

A variety of documents from 1492 to 1977, including major Supreme Court decisions and other primary sources, are reprinted in *Sources and Documents of U.S. Constitutions, Second Series* (5 vols.) (William F. Swindler & Donald J. Musch, eds., Oceana 1982-87).

15   *See*, <http://www.wisconsinhistory.org/ratification/> for information on forthcoming volumes.

2. Amendments

Under the terms of Article V, amendments to the Constitution are proposed by Congress and presented to the states for ratification. The first ten amendments, which are known as the Bill of Rights, were proposed in 1789 and ratified in 1791. Although many other amendments have been suggested over the years, the Constitution has so far been amended only twenty-six times.

Information on the Bill of Rights and other proposed or enacted amendments to the federal Constitution can be found in several sources. *The Complete Bill of Rights: The Drafts, Debates, Sources and Origins* (Neil H. Cogan, ed., Oxford University Press 1997) devotes a chapter to each amendment, presenting each clause in its finished form and tracing it backward to its origins through every draft of the text from all available documentary sources. Volume five of *The Founders' Constitution,* discussed above, covers the first twelve amendments as well as the original seven articles. The texts of major documents relating to the Bill of Rights appear in Bernard Schwartz, *The Bill of Rights: A Documentary History* (2 vols.) (Chelsea House 1971). There are also numerous documentary compilations which focus on the history of individual amendments.

A series of books providing information on amendments proposed during successive time periods all have titles beginning with the words *Proposed Amendments to the Constitution....* The first, covering the Constitution's first century, was prepared by Herman V. Ames, and published as 2 *Am.Hist.A.Ann.Rep.* (1896) and as H.R.Doc. No. 353, Pt. 2, 54th Cong., 2d Sess. (1897). Later volumes published as Senate documents cover the periods 1890-1926, S.Doc. No. 93, 69th Cong., 1st Sess. (1926); 1926-63, S.Doc. No. 163, 87th Cong., 2d Sess. (1963); and 1963-68, S.Doc. No. 38, 91st Cong., 1st Sess. (1969). The latest contribution to the series, covering 1969 to 1984, was edited by R.A. Davis and published in 1985 by the Library of Congress. All these reports, an additional list of proposed amendments through 2001, and a comprehensive index to the whole, were recompiled together in *Proposed Amendments to the U.S. Constitution 1781-2001* (3 vols.) (John R. Vile, ed., William S. Hein & Co., Inc., 2003).

D. STATE CONSTITUTIONS

Each of the fifty states has its own constitution. These documents vary considerably in length and scope, and most address day-to-day activities of state government in a far more detailed manner than that of the U.S. Constitution. State constitutions can also be a vital tool in ensuring citizens' rights; even where the words in a state document mirror those in the federal Constitution, the judiciary of each state can interpret the terms of its own fundamental law.[16] A state constitution cannot deprive persons of federal constitutional rights, but it can guarantee additional protections not found in federal law.[17]

1. Texts

The texts of state constitutions are easily located in any of several sources. Each state's statutory code contains the text of the state's current constitution, along with earlier constitutions and other organic documents. Most useful are the annotated editions of the state codes, which contain annotated texts of the state constitution, similar to those for the U.S. Constitution in *USCA* and *USCS*. These annotated editions usually include references to historical background, attorney general opinions, and legislative history. The Thomson-West state annotated codes can also be used for references, by key numbers, to the Thomson-West digest system. Illustration E shows the section of the New Mexico Constitution concerning grounds for impeachment, as it appears in *New Mexico Statutes Annotated*. Note the cross-references to other constitutional provisions; annotations of

---

16 In an influential article Justice William J. Brennan, Jr. urged the independent consideration and application of state constitutional rights. William J. Brennan, Jr., "State Constitutions and the Protection of Individual Rights," 90 *Harv. L. Rev.* 489 (1977).

17 For example, the U.S. Supreme Court has held that police are not required to inform a criminal suspect of counsel's efforts to provide legal assistance. *Moran v. Burbine,* 475 U.S. 412 (1986). Several state courts have declined to follow *Burbine* and have held that their state constitutions mandate such a duty. *See, e.g., People v. Houston,* 42 Cal.3d 595, 230 Cal.Rptr. 141, 724 P.2d 1166 (1986); *State v. Stoddard,* 206 Conn. 157, 537 A.2d 446 (1988).

cases and New Mexico Attorney General opinions; citations to law review articles; and references to *Am.Jur.2d*, *ALR*, and *CJS*.[18]

Another source for the texts of state constitutions is Oceana's *Constitutions of the United States, National and State Online* or *Constitutions of the United States, National and State*, 2d ed. (7 vols., 1974-date), published by Oceana Publications for the Legislative Drafting Research Fund of Columbia University. This set, whether you use it online or in paper, collects the constitutions of all the states and territories. It is kept current by regular revisions or supplements. Online, full-text searching is available, or there is an alphabetical list of all the states and territories. In print, rather than compiling one comprehensive index for all the constitutions, as it had previously,[19] a series of separate subject indexes are together in a looseleaf binder. Two subject indexes have been issued: "Fundamental Liberties and Rights: A 50-State Index" (1980), and "Laws, Legislature, Legislative Procedure: A Fifty State Index" (1982), both by Barbara F. Sachs.

State constitutions are also available online in WESTLAW or LEXIS. In WESTLAW, constitutions are simply included within each state's statutory database, but in LEXIS one can search in a file containing only a particular state's constitution or in one containing the state's constitution and statutes. Comparative research in constitutional provisions has been greatly facilitated by the ability to search all fifty state constitutions online.

---

18   Note also in Illustration E that Section 37 prohibits legislators from taking free railroad trips, a provision of less impact today than when the New Mexico Constitution was adopted in 1911. Many state constitutions reflect the prevailing political attitudes and concerns of the times in which they were drafted. For earlier examples, see Willi P. Adams, *The First American Constitutions: Republican Ideology and the Making of the State Constitutions of the Revolutionary Era* (Rita & Robert Kimter, trans., University of North Carolina Press 1980).

19   Columbia University, Legislative Drafting Research Fund, *Index Digest of State Constitutions* (2nd ed., Oceana 1959, with pocket part supplementation through 1967), has been discontinued, but is still useful for earlier coverage.

Illustration E
A page from the New Mexico Constitution, in *New Mexico Statutes Annotated*

Art. IV, § 36   LEGISLATIVE DEPARTMENT   Art. IV, § 36

the supreme court shall preside. No person shall be convicted without the concurrence of two-thirds of the senators elected.

Cross-references. — As to officers subject to impeachment, see N.M. Const., art. IV, § 36.

Removal of appointed officer by governor. — State officer appointed by governor, with advice and consent of senate, can be removed by him under N.M. Const., art. V, § 5, regardless of whether he is subject to impeachment. State ex rel. Ulrick v. Sanchez, 32 N.M. 265, 255 P. 1077 (1926).

Comparable provisions. — Idaho Const., art. V, §§ 3, 4.
Iowa Const., art. III, § 19.
Montana Const., art. V, § 13.
Utah Const., art. VI, §§ 17, 18.
Wyoming Const., art. III, § 17.

Law reviews. — For student symposium, "Constitutional Revision — The Executive Branch — Long or Short Ballot?" see 9 Nat. Resources J. 430 (1969).

Am. Jur. 2d, A.L.R. and C.J.S. references. — 63A Am. Jur. 2d Public Officers and Employees §§ 211, 212, 216, 217.

Physical or mental disability as ground for impeachment, 28 A.L.R. 777.

Power of officer as affected by pendency of impeachment proceeding, 30 A.L.R. 1149.

Injunction as remedy against removal of public officer, 34 A.L.R.2d 554.

Removal of public officer for misconduct during previous term, 42 A.L.R.3d 691.

Power of court to remove or suspend judge, 53 A.L.R.3d 882.

67 C.J.S. Officers and Public Employees §§ 179, 181; 81A C.J.S. States §§ 98, 101.

Sec. 36. [Officers subject to impeachment.]

All state officers and judges of the district court shall be liable to impeachment for crimes, misdemeanors and malfeasance in office, but judgment in such cases shall not extend further than removal from office and disqualification to hold any office of honor, trust or profit, or to vote under the laws of this state; but such officer or judge, whether convicted or acquitted shall, nevertheless, be liable to prosecution, trial, judgment, punishment or civil action, according to law. No officer shall exercise any powers or duties of his office after notice of his impeachment is served upon him until he is acquitted.

Cross-references. — As to power of impeachment, and exercise thereof, see N.M. Const., art. IV, § 35.

Legislators. — The impeachment route could be used to handle violation by a legislator of N.M. Const., art. IV, § 28 (relating to appointment of legislators to civil office and interests of legislators in contracts with the state or municipalities) or of art. IV, § 39 (relating to bribery or solicitation involving member of the legislature). 1965 Op. Att'y Gen. No. 65-229.

Judicial officers. — Although the supreme court, upon proper recommendation of the board of bar commissioners, could hold an individual subject to discipline, even though he was a judge, insofar as his activities and standing as a member of the bar association were concerned, recommendation by the board to the court regarding a judge's alleged dishonest, illegal or fraudulent act could not as such affect the individual's capacity as a judge during his term of office, inasmuch as the constitution provides the only method for the removal of a judicial officer. In re Board of Comm'rs of State Bar, 65 N.M. 332, 337 P.2d 400 (1959).

Officers appointed by governor are subject to removal by him, whether or not they may be impeached. State ex rel. Ulrick v. Sanchez, 32 N.M. 265, 255 P. 1077 (1926).

Comparable provisions. — Iowa Const., art. III, § 20.
Montana Const., art. V, § 13.

Utah Const., art. VI, § 19.
Wyoming Const., art. III, § 18.

Law reviews. — For student symposium, "Constitutional Revision — Judicial Removal and Discipline — The California Commission Plan for New Mexico?" see 9 Nat. Resources J. 446 (1969).

Am. Jur. 2d, A.L.R. and C.J.S. references. — 46 Am. Jur. 2d Judges §§ 18, 19; 63A Am. Jur. 2d Public Officers and Employees §§ 213, 214, 218.

Physical or mental disability as ground for impeachment, 28 A.L.R. 777.

Power of officer as affected by pendency of impeachment proceeding, 30 A.L.R. 1149.

Offense under federal law or law of another state or country, conviction as vacating accused's holding of state or local office or as ground of removal, 20 A.L.R.2d 732.

Infamous crime, or one involving moral turpitude, constituting disqualification to hold public office, 52 A.L.R.2d 1314.

Conviction, what constitutes, within statutory or constitutional provision making conviction of crime ground of disqualification for, removal from or vacancy in, public office, 71 A.L.R.2d 593.

Abuse or misuse of contempt power as ground for removal or discipline of judge, 76 A.L.R.4th 982.

48A C.J.S. Judges §§ 42 to 45; 67 C.J.S. Officers and Public Employees §§ 179 to 181; 81A C.J.S. States §§ 99, 101, 129.

The multi-volume *Book of the States*, published biennially by the Council of State Governments, also gives information about proposed state constitutional developments and revisions.

2. Cases and Secondary Sources

State constitutions are covered by *Shepard's* online and in the print volumes, and by *KeyCite* online. Each will provide references to judicial citations of constitutional provisions in that state's courts and in federal courts. Each also includes citations in state session laws, law reviews, and other secondary materials such as *ALR* annotations or legal encyclopedias. In addition, because proposed amendments to state constitutions are included in the state session laws, they can also be checked in the session law sections of the state citators. Many proposed amendments are not ratified, so it is useful to be able to check their status in *Shepard's* or *KeyCite*.

The traditional subject approaches to case-finding can also be used in research on state constitutional law. The topic "Constitutional Law" is used in Thomson-West's digests for issues arising under both federal and state constitutions, and many issues of state governmental powers are digested under the topic "States." Numerous *ALR* annotations discuss matters involving state constitutional issues, and the state case law databases in WESTLAW and LEXIS can be used to find documents combining citations of constitutional provisions with other particular search terms.

Writings on state constitutional law can be found by using the standard periodical indexes or guides for particular states. *State Constitutions of the United States, Second Edition,* by Robert L. Maddex (Congressional Quarterly 2005) profiles every state's constitutions with historical summaries of the constitutions adopted, and summaries of the key provisions in the current constitution with discussion. Two bibliographies of articles and other works are the brief survey "State Constitutional Law Resources," in *Developments in State Constitutional Law* (Bradley D. McGraw, ed., West 1985), and the extensive monograph *The Constitutions of the States: A State-by-State Guide and Bibliography to Current Scholarly Research*, by Bernard D. Reams, Jr., & Stuart D. Yoak (Oceana 1988).

3. Historical Research

Unlike the venerable and rarely amended United States Constitution, state constitutions are subject to frequent amendment and revision. The amendment process in many states has been used for quite mundane matters. The Alabama Constitution of 1901, for example, includes well over 400 amendments. Many states have had several constitutional conventions and a number of corporate revisions. Louisiana has had eleven constitutions in its history. On the other hand, nineteen states still operate under an amended version of their original constitution, and the constitutions for Massachusetts, New Hampshire and Vermont date from the eighteenth century.

The most comprehensive source for documents pertaining to state constitutions is the microfiche collection issued by Congressional Information Service, *State Constitutional Conventions, Commissions, and Amendments*, which includes documents issued from 1776 through 1978 for all fifty states. Access to the microfiche is provided by three bibliographies: Cynthia E. Browne, *State Constitutional Conventions from Independence to the Completion of the Present Union, 1776-1959: A Bibliography* (Greenwood Press 1973); Bonnie Canning, *State Constitutional Conventions, Revisions, and Amendments, 1959-1976: A Bibliography* (Greenwood Press 1977); and the two-volume *State Constitutional Conventions, Commissions, and Amendments, 1959-1978: An Annotated Bibliography* (CIS, 1981), and its successor volume covering 1979-1988 (published in 1989).

The major constitutional documents of every state, including enabling acts, acts of admission, and all enacted constitutions, are reprinted in William F. Swindler, *Sources and Documents of United States Constitutions* (10 vols.) (Oceana 1973-88). Here the past constitutions and other documents are assembled in chronological order for each state, with background notes, editorial comments on provisions of succeeding constitutions, selected bibliographies on the constitutional history of each state, and indexes.[20]

---

20   Two older compilations, still valuable for research in early constitutions, are: Benjamin P. Poore, *The Federal and State Constitutions, Colonial Charters, and Other Organic Laws of the United States* (2 vols.) (Government Printing Office 1877); and Francis N. Thorpe, *The Federal and State Constitutions, Colonial Charters, and Other Organic Laws of the States, Territories and Colonies Now or Heretofore Forming the United States of America* (7 vols.) H.R.Doc. No. 357, 59th

E. SUMMARY

The impact of judicial interpretation and application of constitutional provisions has had and continues to have significant effect on the development of law in the United States. It is therefore important that research problems be closely examined for possible constitutional issues. The extensive literature and research apparatus described in this chapter provides easy access to the texts of the federal and state constitutions, to relevant judicial decisions under each constitutional provision, and to secondary sources. These resources can be used to cut through the bewildering array of constitutional literature and locate further analysis and interpretation.

F. ADDITIONAL READING

Jerome A. Barron and C.Thomas Dienes, *Constitutional Law in a Nutshell* (5th ed. 2003).

Shelley L. Dowling and Mary C. Custy, *The Jurisprudence of United States Constitutional Interpretation: An Annotated Bibliography* (Fred B. Rothman 1999).

Thomas C. Marks and John F. Cooper, *State Constitutional Law in a Nutshell* (2nd ed. 2003).

James T. McHugh, *Ex Uno Plura: State Constitutions and Their Political Cultures* (SUNY Press 2003).

Cong., 2d Sess. (1909).

Albert L. Sturm, *A Bibliography on State Constitutions and Constitutional Revision, 1945-1975* (Kristin Hall, ed., Citizens Conference on State Legislatures 1975), while out of date, contains useful lists of articles and other secondary sources on constitutional revision generally and in each state.

Chapter 8

ADMINISTRATIVE AND EXECUTIVE PUBLICATIONS

A. INTRODUCTION

The third source of primary authority is administrative law. Administrative law is the output of federal and state administrative bodies. These agencies are created by legislation; hence administrative law is technically subordinate to legislation. The volume and importance of administrative law, however, makes its treatment as a separate area both appropriate and necessary.

Research in administrative law can be challenging. The material is not as systematically treated as judicial opinions, nor is it as contained as legislation. There is no equivalent of the digest system or annotated codes for administrative materials. The agencies are numerous, and each has its own practices and publications. In this area the problem that federalism causes for the legal researcher is increased geometrically. Not only are there fifty-one jurisdictions, each jurisdiction has a full complement of administrative bodies issuing rules, regulations and decisions.

Things are made somewhat simpler by the fact that these agency publications tend to resemble the legislative and judicial documents already discussed. The forms will be familiar. Further, the federal level, which will occupy a great deal of the discussion here, has now been well organized. This is an area where the advent of information available in electronic format has been a real boon.

One of the biggest obstacles to successful research using administrative materials is the neophyte researcher's relative unfamiliarity with them. Many law students have little or no contact with administrative materials in law school. Even the law school course titled "Administrative Law" is traditionally about the Administrative Procedure Act, and issues of rulemaking. It touches very little on administrative agency publications. Most law students come to understand the workings of the judicial system while in law school. Most people have at least a basic appreciation of how the legislature works from a high school civics class. But many people have no understanding about how administrative agencies work. Nor is there any template which explains them all. Each is a research universe unto itself. Because this unfamiliarity can be a real barrier, this Chapter first presents some research tips that are applicable to doing research on any administrative law area.

B. RESEARCH STEPS

1. Know the Agency

No one should carry out research using administrative materials until she gains a basic understanding of the administrative agency that regulates the area. Each agency, federal or state, has a mission that it is trying to accomplish. It sets out parameters of operation. This is crucial background. Plunging directly into compilations of regulations without understanding the context in which they were issued is the worst kind of blind research.

If one is dealing with a federal agency, this problem is easily solved. For basic background one can turn to the *United States Government Manual*.[1] This publication of the Office of the Federal Register is a compendium of information about all three branches of government. Along with relatively brief coverage of the legislature and the Courts, there is current information about every bureau, office, agency, commission and board of the Executive Branch. The user can see what an agency is doing and why. It provides the names and telephone numbers of important agency personnel, and it lists resources that the agency offers to the public. It may turn out that there is a regional library for the agency in the researcher's area. If you do not know the name of the relevant agency, there is a subject index. This tool is normally kept at the reference desk of law libraries. Illustration A shows a sample page from the *United States Government Manual*.

A more sophisticated general guide is *The Federal Regulatory Directory* published by Congressional Quarterly. This provides much of the same information as the *United States Government Manual*, but often provides more detail. It concentrates on the large agencies, but gives summary treatment of the others. It is kept more up-to-date and, typical of privately compiled reference tools, its indexing is easier to use.

---

1   The *United States Government Manual* is available for free from GPO Access, <http://www.gpoaccess.gov/gmanual/index.html>.

Illustration A
Page from the 2005-2006 *United States Government Manual*

508   U.S. GOVERNMENT MANUAL

POSTAL RATE COMMISSION
1333 H Street NW., Washington, DC 20268–0001
Phone, 202–789–6800. Fax, 202–789–6886. Internet, www.prc.gov.

Chairman	GEORGE A. OMAS
Vice Chairman	DANA B. COVINGTON
Commissioners	RUTH Y. GOLDWAY, TONY HAMMOND
Special Assistant to the Chairman	MARK ACTON
Chief Administrative Officer and Secretary	STEVEN W. WILLIAMS
General Counsel	STEPHEN L. SHARFMAN
Director, Office of Rates, Analysis and Planning	ROBERT COHEN
Director, Office of the Consumer Advocate	SHELLEY S. DREIFUSS
Deputy Chief Administrative Officer and Personnel Officer	GARRY SIKORA

[For the Postal Rate Commission statement of organization, see the *Code of Federal Regulations*, Title 39, Part 3002]

The major responsibility of the Postal Rate Commission is to submit recommended decisions to the United States Postal Service Governors on postage rates, fees, and mail classifications.

The Postal Rate Commission is an independent agency created by the Postal Reorganization Act, as amended (39 U.S.C. 3601–3604). It is composed of five Commissioners, appointed by the President with the advice and consent of the Senate, one of whom is designated as Chairman.

The Commission promulgates rules and regulations, establishes procedures, and takes other actions necessary to carry out its obligations. Acting upon requests from the U.S. Postal Service or on its own initiative, the Commission recommends and issues advisory opinions to the Board of Governors of the U.S. Postal Service on changes in rates or fees in each class of mail or type of service. It studies and submits recommended decisions on establishing or changing the mail classification schedule and holds on-the-record hearings that are lawfully required to attain sound and fair recommendations. It initiates studies on postal matters, such as cost theory and operations.

The Commission also receives, studies, and conducts hearings and issues recommended decisions and reports to the Postal Service on complaints received from interested persons relating to postage rates, postal classifications, and problems of national scope regarding postal services. It has appellate jurisdiction to review Postal Service determinations to close or consolidate small post offices. The Commission also prepares an annual report on international mail.

Sources of Information

Employment The Commission's programs require attorneys, economists, statisticians, accountants, industrial engineers, marketing specialists, and administrative and clerical personnel to fulfill its responsibilities. Requests for employment information should be directed to the Personnel Officer.

Electronic Access Electronic access to current docketed case materials is available through the Internet, at www.prc.gov. Electronic mail can be sent to the Commission at prc-admin@prc.gov and prc-dockets@prc.gov.

Reading Room Facilities for inspection and copying of records, viewing automated daily lists of docketed

These are only the two most general and basic tools for the federal government. Other specialized directories are devoted to individual agencies and subjects. There are also services, both online and in paper, which track the phone numbers, postal addresses and email addresses of relevant agency personnel such as the *Federal Yellow Book* and the *Federal Regional Yellow Book* by Leadership Directories, Inc.[2] The best advice on available resources in this area is to talk with a reference librarian in the law library and ask what the most current and available source is.

An ever increasing number of federal and state agencies are creating web pages. These pages may include enormously helpful information about the agency, its purpose and its personnel. The agency webpage may also be a seldom updated dud. The upside potential is worth the search.[3]

There are various guides to state agencies and publications. Virtually all of the states publish state manuals, often called "bluebooks" providing basic information about the government, its agencies and its functions. The quality of these publications varies from state to state, but they serve the same basic purpose as the *United States Government Manual*. The privately published *Carroll's State Directory* and the *State Yellow Book* can provide you with names of agency personnel, and information on the organization of the agencies, telephone numbers and both postal and email addresses. If you are working with materials in your own state, a local reference librarian can quickly introduce you to the available state resources. Use whatever is available to get background.

A basic rule of research is not to begin until you have at least a rudimentary understanding of the agency or agencies regulating your area.

2. Know the Legislation

Dean Dan Rodriguez of Boalt Hall Law School once gave a guest lecture in an Advanced Legal Research course on the subject of research in

---

2   The *Yellow Books* (all 14 titles) are available via the Internet with a subscription, <http://www.leadershipdirectories.com/>.

3   A list of Executive branch agencies can be found on the FedWorld page, <http://www.fedworld.gov/gov-links.html>.

administrative law. He said that there are three secrets to performing good research in any administrative area:

> *1. Look to the underlying legislation.*
> *2. Look to the underlying legislation.*
> *3. Look to the underlying legislation.*

This subtle hint is well taken. Administrative agencies are created by legislation. The underlying legislation is the foundation for all that an agency does. By reviewing the legislation itself, you can see the purposes that motivate the agency, and the rules that circumscribe its actions. The wise researcher returns to the original legislation and examines it with care. Since administrative agencies are sometimes challenged for exceeding their charge, this kind of background is essential.

The directories listed in Section A.1., above provide citations to the underlying legislation. It is best to read the legislation as it is found in an annotated code. There you may find references to relevant judicial opinions and other commentary that give useful insight on how the legislation creating the agency has been interpreted.

3. Interactive Research

Administrative agencies are unlike the courts and legislature. Administrative agencies regulate behavior, make judgments, and set limits. Often the agency will interpret its own rules and issue its own opinions. Thus, monitoring the agency is not a static enterprise. If you only use the books and pamphlets on the library shelves or the data in the online systems, you may be missing the boat. It is necessary to interact with an agency. Many of the tools that will be discussed in the balance of this chapter provide telephone numbers and e-mail addresses, where you can get feedback and help.

Use these avenues for interaction. Working on administrative materials in isolation and working out your own theory as to what they mean may be disastrous. The better route is to ask the people who are enforcing the rules what the rules mean. It may turn out that they do not know either, but that is important data too. Be active!

C. REGULATIONS OF FEDERAL ADMINISTRATIVE AGENCIES

The United States Congress enacts detailed legislation on a bewildering variety of subjects. Congress, however, cannot possibly provide for the multitude of possible situations which might arise under its enactments. Members of Congress are not experts in all areas of regulation, and the complexities of the legislative process are not well suited to rational consideration of detailed technical distinctions. Much of the work of creating specific rules to govern conduct is left to agencies specializing in particular activities. These agencies interpret and apply their governing statutes to create highly detailed rules, or regulations, which give specific content to the statutory intent and provide procedures for implementation and enforcement.[4]

Regulations are published by the federal government in the same two basic formats as statutes, first chronologically and later in a subject arrangement. The *Federal Register* is issued every business day. It is the diary of the federal government concerning regulations. Every agency must print every new regulation there. The same regulations are then published in a more accessible format, arranged by issuing agency and subject, in the *Code of Federal Regulations*, or *CFR*.

While the basic method of regulatory publication is analogous to that for statutes, there is little similarity between the research systems. Statutory codes are generally published in bound volumes, with amendments and annotations issued in pocket parts or supplements. Because the great volume of administrative regulations would make such a system impracticable, different methods are employed to update regulations and make current information available. Research in federal regulations has its own unique procedure. The status of a *CFR* section is determined by consulting numerous finding lists for references to *Federal Register* pages.

---

4   The terms "rule" and "regulation" have the same meaning in this context, 1 C.F.R. §1.1 (2005). We use "regulation" more often, since there are numerous other "rules" to be reckoned with in legal research, such as court rules or citation rules.

The process may sound laborious, but most of it is mechanical and quite straightforward.

1. The *Federal Register*

The *Federal Register* is the source for all generally applicable federal rules and regulations. The *Federal Register* is a much more recent creation than either the sources setting out statute law or judicial opinions. Although executive and administrative agencies are as old as our government, it was not until the 1930s that the administrative rules and regulations began to be organized. Roosevelt's New Deal caused a growth in agencies and in their output. No system was in place for publishing this new type of legal information. Hundreds of executive orders, thousands of regulations, and tens of thousands of pages of other documents of legal effect were issued with no regular method of publication. In many instances no attempt at public notice was even made.

Public pressure for reform finally came to a head when two cases concerning New Deal regulation of the oil industry reached the United States Supreme Court, even though they were based on a provision which had been revoked before the lawsuits were begun.[5] The ridiculousness of a system where no one knew what the law really was, accentuated by Chief Justice Hughes' anger about the matter, led to the creation of a new form of publication.

The Federal Register Act[6] was designed to end this chaotic uncertainty by establishing a central repository for the publication of federal proclamations, orders, regulations, notices and other documents of general legal applicability. It initiated a new daily publication, the *Federal Register,* in which documents like those listed above must be published. The first *Federal Register* issue was published on Saturday, March 14, 1936. The

---

5   *United States v. Smith,* 293 U.S. 633 (1934) (appeal dismissed); *Panama Refining Co. v. Ryan,* 293 U.S. 388 (1935).

6   Ch. 417, 49 Stat. 500 (1935).

Federal Register's statutory mandate is to publish the following classes of documents:

> (1) Presidential proclamations and Executive orders, except those not having general applicability and legal effect or effective only against Federal agencies or persons in their capacity as officers, agents, or employees thereof;

> (2) documents or classes of documents that the President may determine from time to time have general applicability and legal effect; and

> (3) documents or classes of documents that may be required so to be published by Act of Congress.

> ... [E]very document or order which prescribes a penalty has general applicability and legal effect.[7]

Publication in the *Federal Register* is deemed to provide any parties affected by a regulation with constructive notice of its contents.[8]

---

7   44 U.S.C. §1505(a) (1982). The Administrative Committee of the Federal Register has further defined "document having general applicability and legal effect" as "any document issued under proper authority prescribing a penalty or course of conduct, conferring a right, privilege, authority, or immunity, or imposing an obligation, and relevant or applicable to the general public, members of a class, or persons in a locality, as distinguished from named individuals or organizations." 1 C.F.R. §1.1 (2005).

8   44 U.S.C. §1507 (1982). Justice Jackson sharply criticized the effects of this notice provision in *Federal Crop Insurance Corp. v. Merrill*, 332 U.S. 380, 387 (1947) (Jackson, J., dissenting):

> To my mind, it is an absurdity to hold that every farmer who insures his crops knows what the *Federal Register* contains or even knows that there is such a publication. If he were to peruse this voluminous and dull publication as it is issued from time to time in order to make sure whether anything has been promulgated that affects his rights, he would never need crop

Despite the substantial improvements in access brought about by the Federal Register Act, the decision-making procedures used by the agencies remained unclear and arbitrary. In 1946 Congress passed the Administrative Procedure Act,[9] which gave the public the right to participate in agency rulemaking and significantly expanded the scope of the *Federal Register*. The act provided that notice of proposed rulemaking be published in the *Federal Register*, affording the public the opportunity to comment on the proposed rules.[10]   In its January 1, 1947 issue, the *Federal Register* inaugurated a new "Proposed Rule Making" section with proposed standards for grades of canned tangerine juice.[11] Further improvements in publication of notices were added by the Freedom of Information Act,[12] which requires agencies to publish organizational descriptions and policy statements,[13] and the Government in the Sunshine Act,[14] which requires agencies to publish notices of most meetings.[15]

In each issue of the *Federal Register*, material is published in the following order:

1. Presidential documents (proclamations, executive orders and other executive documents).

---

insurance, for he would never get time to plant any crops. Nor am I convinced that a reading of technically-worded regulations would enlighten him much in any event.

9   Ch. 324, 80 Stat. 237 (1946).

10   5 U.S.C. §553 (2002).

11   12 Fed.Reg. 32 (1947).

12   Act of July 4, 1966, Pub.L. No. 84-487, 80 Stat. 237.

13   5 U.S.C. §552(a)(1) (2002).

14   Pub.L. No. 94-409, 90 Stat. 1241 (1976).

15   5 U.S.C. §552(e)(3) (2002).

2. Rules and regulations (documents having general applicability and legal effect).

3. Proposed rules (texts of proposed regulations as well as regulatory agendas and notices of hearings).

4. Notices (documents not concerned with rulemaking proceedings, such as announcements of application deadlines or license revocations.

5. Notices of Sunshine Act meetings.

The arrangement of documents in each section of the *Federal Register* is determined by the title of the *Code of Federal Regulations* in which the rules will appear or which they affect. Some documents are published as separate sections at the end of an issue, rather than in their appropriate place, so that issuing agencies can make additional copies available for distribution. Illustration B shows three pages of the January 30, 2003 *Federal Register* in which the Consumer Product Safety Commission exempts some propellant devices for rocket-powered model cars that would otherwise be banned under the Federal Hazardous Substances Act. (Remember Prof. Rodriguez!) The rule amends 16 C.F.R. 1500 by adding a new section 1500.85. Immediately before the printed change is a great deal of information on why the change is being made, the name of a relevant officer of the agency, and even tests of the cars that were used in formulating the change. The *Federal Register* often contains such useful information. It helps put the rule into context.

Each issue of the *Federal Register* also contains a number of finding aids. There is a table of contents arranged by agency name and listing rules, proposed rules, and notices. Illustration C shows one page from the table of contents for the January 30, 2003 *Federal Register* issue, containing the rocket-powered model car rules. Note that cross-references are provided to agency subdivisions if their regulations and notices are listed separately from the agency's.

Illustration B
Three *Federal Register* pages from January 30, 2003 showing a Final Rule from the Consumer Product Safety Commission

Federal Register / Vol. 68, No. 20 / Thursday, January 30, 2003 / Rules and Regulations **4697**

and that the original evidence or copies, as appropriate, are turned over to the appropriate law enforcement authorities.

Information Created Pursuant to an Investigation

§ 270.340 Information created by investigation participants who are not NIST employees.

Unless requested sooner by the Lead Investigator, at the conclusion of an investigation, each investigation participant who is not a NIST employee shall transfer any original information they created pursuant to the investigation to NIST. An investigation participant may retain a copy of the information for their records but may not use the information for purposes other than the investigation, nor may they release, reproduce, distribute, or publish any information first developed pursuant to the investigation, nor authorize others to do so, without the written permission of the Director or their designee. Pursuant to 15 U.S.C. 281a, no such information may be admitted or used as evidence in any suit or action for damages arising out of any matter related to the investigation.

Protection of Information

§ 270.350 Freedom of Information Act.

As permitted by section 7(b) of the Act, the following information will not be released:

(a) Information described by section 552(b) of Title 5, United States Code, or protected from disclosure by any other law of the United States; and

(b) Copies of evidence collected, information created, or other investigation documents submitted or received by NIST, a Team, or any other investigation participant, until the final investigation report is issued.

§ 270.351 Protection of voluntarily submitted information.

Notwithstanding any other provision of law, a Team, NIST, any investigation participant, and any agency receiving information from a Team, NIST, or any other investigation participant, will not disclose voluntarily provided safety-related information if that information is not directly related to the building failure being investigated and the Director finds that the disclosure of the information would inhibit the voluntary provision of that type of information.

§ 270.352 Public safety information.

A Team, NIST, and any other investigation participant will not publicly release any information it receives in the course of an investigation under the Act if the

Director finds that the disclosure might jeopardize public safety.

[FR Doc. 03–2084 Filed 1–29–03; 8:45 am]
BILLING CODE 3510–13–P

CONSUMER PRODUCT SAFETY COMMISSION

16 CFR Part 1500

Exemptions From Classification as Banned Hazardous Substances; Exemption for Certain Model Rocket Propellant Devices for Use With Rocket-Powered Model Cars

AGENCY: Consumer Product Safety Commission.

ACTION: Final rule.

SUMMARY: The Commission is issuing a rule to exempt from the Federal Hazardous Substances Act ("FHSA") certain model rocket propellant devices for vehicles that travel on the ground. The Commission's current regulations exempt motors used for flyable model rockets. The rule exempts certain propellant devices for rocket-powered model cars if they meet requirements similar to those required for flyable model rockets and additional requirements to avoid possible injuries if the cars are operated off of their tether.

DATES: The rule becomes effective on January 30, 2003.

FOR FURTHER INFORMATION CONTACT: James G. Joholske, Office of Compliance, Consumer Product Safety Commission, Washington, DC 20207; telephone (301) 504–0608 ext. 1419.

SUPPLEMENTARY INFORMATION:

A. Background

Section 2(q)(1)(A) of the FHSA bans toys that are or contain hazardous substances that are accessible to a child. 15 U.S.C. 1261(q)(1)(A). However, the FHSA authorizes the Commission, by regulation, to grant exemptions from classifications as banned hazardous substances for:

articles, such as chemistry sets, which by reason of their functional purpose require the inclusion of the hazardous substance involved, or necessarily present an electrical, mechanical, or thermal hazard, and which bear labeling giving adequate directions and warnings for safe use and are intended for use by children who have attained sufficient maturity, and may reasonably be expected to read and heed such directions and warnings.

15 U.S.C. 1261(q)(1)(A). Thus, the Commission may issue an exemption if it finds that the product requires inclusion of a hazardous substance in

order for it to function, has sufficient directions and warnings, and is intended for children who are old enough to read and follow the directions and warnings. *Id.* The Food and Drug Administration, which administered the FHSA before the Commission was established, issued a rule under this authority that exempted from the definition of banned hazardous substances model rocket propellant devices (motors) designed for use in light-weight, recoverable, and reflyable model rockets, if they meet certain requirements. 16 CFR 1500.85(a)(8).

B. The Petition

The Commission received a petition from Centuri Corporation ("Centuri") requesting that the Commission issue a rule exempting certain model rocket propellant devices to be used for model cars that travel on the ground along a tethered line and are propelled in a manner similar to flyable rockets. The petitioner requested an exemption that would allow the sale of both of its two prototype rocket-powered model cars. The smaller car, named "Blurzz," uses an "A" motor, and is shaped like a "rail," a type of custom-made vehicle used in competitive drag racing. The larger prototype, named "Screamin' Eagle," uses a "D" motor, and is shaped like a "Bonneville Speed Record" custom vehicle. The Commission decided to grant the petition in part and propose an exemption for model rocket propellant devices to be used for rocket-powered model cars like the smaller "Blurzz" car only.[1]

C. The Proposed Exemption

On January 30, 2002, the Commission published a notice of proposed rulemaking ("NPR") proposing to exempt model rocket propellant devices for use with smaller rocket-powered model cars like the "Blurzz." 67 FR 4373. As explained in the NPR, the Commission concluded that due to the weight, speed and the height it can reach, the larger "Screamin' Eagle" posed a significant risk of injury to any person downrange from it when it is used in the absence of the tether. The Commission, therefore, denied the petition insofar as it requested an exemption from the FHSA for model rocket propellant devices for cars like the "Screamin' Eagle." However, the Commission concluded that when the smaller "Blurzz" car was ignited

[1] The Commission voted 2–1 to grant the petition with regard to the smaller vehicles and deny it regarding the larger ones. Commissioners Thomas Moore and Mary Sheila Gall voted to take this action. Then-Chairman Ann Brown voted to deny the entire petition.

4698   Federal Register / Vol. 68, No. 20 / Thursday, January 30, 2003 / Rules and Regulations

without the tether, it ordinarily simply flipped onto its back and skittered around on the ground or traveled downrange only a very limited distance, and rose only a few inches in the air, before flipping onto its back. Thus, the Commission concluded that there is a reasonable probability that model rocket propellant devices for rocket-powered model cars like the "Blurzz" present no unreasonable risk of injury even when operated in reasonably foreseeable misuse without the tether. The Commission also preliminarily found that children interested in model rockets and rocket-powered model cars such as the "Blurzz" are of sufficient maturity that they may reasonably be expected to read and heed the directions for use and warnings that accompany model cars like the "Blurzz." The Commission also preliminarily found that those directions and warnings are adequate to guide users in the safe use of the product.

D. Comments on the NPR

The Commission received three comments on the NPR from Centuri, Intertek Testing Services ("Intertek"), and the National Association of Rocketry ("NAR"). Centuri commented on some of the technical statements in the staff's memos that were part of the briefing package concerning Centuri's petition. The comment from Intertek was actually test results submitted by Centuri. Intertek suggested enlarging the safety alert symbol that appears in directions for the model car. Commission staff agrees that the entire warning label should be larger. NAR agreed with the Commission that the exemption should be limited to smaller "A" motors.

E. The Final Rule

When reviewing data for the petition, the Commission's Directorate for Epidemiology found two deaths over a 20-year period involving model airplanes (both involved adult males, 40 and 44 years of age). Centuri provided additional information about these. In one incident, the plane weighed about 5 pounds (compared to 2.7 oz. for a size "A" rocket-powered model car), and was traveling at an estimated 200 mph (compared to the top speed of 28 mph for the size "A" car). Centuri characterized the airplane in the other incident as "quite large and heavy." The staff reviewed data available from the petition briefing package (for the period May 26, 2001 to April 15, 2002) and found no deaths that could be considered comparable to deaths that might involve rocket-powered model cars.

The Commission's Human Factors staff reviewed revised instructions submitted by Centuri and concluded that the revisions were an improvement over previous instructions and would make them easier for users age 10 and up to follow.

The Commission's Engineering staff reviewed results of testing from Intertek. Intertek was primarily concerned with the dangers of launching the engine alone without the vehicle. Because such motors are currently available with other exempted products, the staff does not believe that exempting rocket-powered model cars creates or increases the hazard of igniting motors outside the vehicles. Intertek was also concerned about launching cars from a ramp or vertical support. However, the Engineering staff believes such operation would be similar to launching a model rocket, and injury data do not suggest a problem with model rockets in those types of launches.

The Commission's staff was concerned about possible injuries if rocket powered cars are operated off the tether. As discussed above, when the "Blurzz" was used without the tether it traveled only a limited distance a few inches off the ground and then flipped on its back. Such performance is not likely to injure operators or bystanders. However, Compliance staff was concerned that in the future a company may develop a rocket-powered model car that when operated off the tether could obtain sufficient height, distance and force to injure operators or bystanders. Thus, the final rule contains a limitation that vehicles must be designed so that they either cannot operate off of a track or line (*i.e.*, tether), or if operated off the tether the vehicle will be unstable and will not travel in a guided fashion, so that the car will not strike operators or bystanders. The Commission reminds manufacturers that under section 15 of the Consumer Product Safety Act they have an obligation to report to the Commission if they have information which reasonably supports the conclusion that their product creates an unreasonable risk of serious injury or death or contains a defect which could create a substantial product hazard. 15 U.S.C. 2064(b)(2) & (3). The Commission has the authority to pursue corrective action regarding any toy or other children's article that creates a substantial risk of injury to children. 15 U.S.C. 1274(c)(1).

A small change was made to the final rule in order to correct a cross reference that conflicted with the characteristics of an A motor described in section 1500.85(a)(14)(i)(B) of the rule and to

include appropriate provisions of the cross-reference in the rule itself.

F. Effective Date

This rule exempts certain model rocket propellant devices for rocket-powered model cars that would otherwise be banned under the FHSA. Because the rule grants an exemption, it is not subject to the requirement under the Administrative Procedure Act ("APA") that a rule must be published 30 days before it takes effect. 5 U.S.C. 553(d)(1). The rule lifts an existing restriction and allows a product not previously permitted. Thus, the Commission believes it is appropriate for the rule to become effective upon publication in the **Federal Register**.

G. Impact on Small Business

The NPR discussed the Commission's assessment of the impact that a rule to exempt propellant devices for use with small rocket-powered model cars like the "Blurzz" might have on small businesses. Because the exemption would relieve manufacturers from existing restrictions, the Commission concluded that the proposed exemption would not have a significant impact on a substantial number of small businesses or other small entities. No comments or additional information alter that conclusion.

H. Environmental Considerations

Pursuant to the National Environmental Policy Act, and in accordance with the Council on Environmental Quality regulations and CPSC procedures for environmental review, the Commission assessed the possible environmental effects associated with the proposed exemption. As discussed in the NPR, the Commission concluded that the rule would have no adverse effect on the environment, and therefore, neither an environmental assessment nor an environmental impact statement is required.

I. Executive Orders

According to Executive Order 12988 (February 5, 1996), agencies must state in clear language the preemptive effect, if any, of new regulations.

The FHSA provides that, generally, if the Commission issues a rule under section 2(q) of the FHSA to protect against a risk of illness or injury associated with a hazardous substance, "no State or political subdivision of a State may establish or continue in effect a requirement applicable to such substance and designed to protect against the same risk of illness or injury unless such requirement is identical to

Federal Register / Vol. 68, No. 20 / Thursday, January 30, 2003 / Rules and Regulations 4699

the requirement established under such regulations." 15 U.S.C. 1261n(b)(1)(B). (The FHSA also provides for the state or political subdivision of a state to apply for an exemption from preemption if certain requirements are met.) Thus, the rule exempting model rocket propellant devices for use with certain surface vehicles will preempt non-identical requirements for such propellant devices.

The Commission has also evaluated the rule in light of the principles stated in Executive Order 13132 concerning federalism, even though that Order does not apply to independent regulatory agencies such as CPSC. The Commission does not expect that the rule will have any substantial direct effects on the States, the relationship between the national government and the States, or the distribution of power and responsibilities among various levels of government.

List of Subjects in 16 CFR Part 1500

Consumer protection, Hazardous materials, Hazardous substances, Imports, Infants and children, Labeling, Law enforcement, Toys.

Conclusion

For the reasons stated above, the Commission concludes that, with the requirements stated in the exemption, model rocket propellant devices to propel small rocket-powered cars like the "Blurzz" require inclusion of a hazardous substance in order to function, have sufficient directions and warnings for safe use, and are intended for children who are mature enough that they may reasonably be expected to read and heed the directions and warnings. Therefore, the Commission amends title 16 of the Code of Federal Regulations as follows:

PART 1500—HAZARDOUS SUBSTANCES AND ARTICLES: ADMINISTRATION AND ENFORCEMENT REGULATIONS

1. The authority for part 1500 continues to read as follows:

Authority: 15 U.S.C. 1261–1278.

2. Section 1500.85 is amended by adding a new paragraph (a)(14) to read as follows:

§ 1500.85 Exemptions from classification as banned hazardous substances.

(a) * * *

(14) Model rocket propellant devices (model rocket motors) designed to propel rocket-powered model cars, provided—

(i) Such devices:

(A) Are designed to be ignited electrically and are intended to be operated from a minimum distance of 15 feet (4.6 m) away;

(B) Contain no more than 4 g. of propellant material and produce no more than 2.5 Newton-seconds of total impulse with a thrust duration not less than 0.050 seconds;

(C) Are constructed such that all the chemical ingredients are pre-loaded into a cylindrical paper or similarly constructed non-metallic tube that will not fragment into sharp, hard pieces;

(D) Are designed so that they will not burst under normal conditions of use, are incapable of spontaneous ignition, and do not contain any type of explosive or pyrotechnic warhead other than a small recovery system activation charge;

(E) Bear labeling, including labeling that the devices are intended for use by persons age 12 and older, and include instructions providing adequate warnings and instructions for safe use; and

(F) Comply with the requirements of 16 CFR 1500.83(a)(36)(ii and iii); and

(ii) The surface vehicles intended for use with such devices:

(A) Are lightweight, weighing no more than 3.0 oz. (85 grams), and constructed mainly of materials such as balsa wood or plastics that will not fragment into sharp, hard pieces;

(B) Are designed to utilize a braking system such as a parachute or shock absorbing stopping mechanism;

(C) Are designed so that they cannot accept propellant devices measuring larger than 0.5" (13 mm) in diameter and 1.75" (44 mm) in length;

(D) Are designed so that the engine mount is permanently attached by the manufacturer to a track or track line that controls the vehicle's direction for the duration of its movement;

(E) Are not designed to carry any type of explosive or pyrotechnic material other than the model rocket motor used for primary propulsion;

(F) Bear labeling and include instructions providing adequate warnings and instructions for safe use; and

(G) Are designed to operate on a track or line that controls the vehicles' direction for the duration of their movement and either cannot operate off the track or line or, if operated off the track or line, are unstable and fail to operate in a guided fashion so that they will not strike the operator or bystanders.

* * * * *

3. Section 1500.83(a)(36)(i) is revised to read as follows:

§ 1500.83 Exemptions for small packages, minor hazards, and special circumstances.

(a) * * *

(36) * * *

(i) The devices are designed and constructed in accordance with the specifications in § 1500.85(a)(8), (9) or (14);

* * * * *

Dated: January 27, 2003.

Todd Stevenson,
Secretary, Consumer Product Safety Commission.

Appendix to Preamble—List of Relevant Documents

1. Briefing memorandum from Terrance R. Karels, Directorate for Economic Analysis, to the Commission, "Exemption from Classification as Banned Hazardous Substances Rocket-powered Model Cars, January 13, 2003.

2. Memorandum from Joyce McDonald, Hazard Analysis Division, to Terrance R. Karels, "Model Rocket Car Petition," October 18, 2002.

3. Memorandum from Sharon R. White, Directorate for Engineering Sciences, Division of Human Factors, to Terrance R. Karels, "Responses to Comments on Briefing Package concerning Centuri Corporation's Petition for Exemption of Model Rocket Propellant Devices for Surface Vehicles, HP 01–02," September 6, 2002.

4. Memorandum from Troy W. Whitfield, Directorate for Engineering Sciences, to Terrance R. Karels, "Rocket Powered Model Cars—Public Comment," September 12, 2002.

5. Memorandum from Terrance R. Karels, Directorate for Economic Analysis, to Files, "Rocket powered cars," May 8, 2002.

6. Memorandum from Terrance R. Karels, Directorate for Economic Analysis, to Patricia M. Pollitzer, Office of General Counsel, "Rocket-powered Model Cars—Economic Considerations," December 20, 2002.

7. Memorandum from Jason R. Goldsmith, Ph.D., Division of Health Sciences, to Terrance R. Karels, "Rocket-Powered Model Cars—Response to Comments," October 17, 2002.

[FR Doc. 03–2205 Filed 1–29–03; 8:45 am]

BILLING CODE 6355–01–P

TENNESSEE VALLEY AUTHORITY

18 CFR Part 1301

Revision of Tennessee Valley Authority Freedom of Information Act Regulations

AGENCY: Tennessee Valley Authority (TVA).

ACTION: Final rule.

SUMMARY: The Tennessee Valley Authority is amending its Freedom of

The table of contents is followed by a list of *CFR* parts affected in that day's issue. It places all new regulations into the proper order of the *CFR*. Regular readers of the *Federal Register* can scan this list to see if there are any developments affecting parts of the *Code of Federal Regulations* with which they are concerned.[16] An example can be seen in Illustration D.

At the end of each issue, there are Finding Aids (Illustration E) covering more than that day's issue of the *Register*. First there is a list of telephone numbers in the Office of the Federal Register where one may obtain information and assistance on specific topics. These numbers can be used in the interactive research discussed in Section B. Following this is a table of pages and dates for each *Federal Register* issue published during the current month. This can be helpful since the *Federal Register* is usually cited by page number, but page numbers are not listed on the spine or front cover of an issue. The date does appear in those places, so after using the table one can easily find the needed issue. Next comes a cumulative list of *CFR* parts affected during the current month. This list is updated each day to include the developments in that issue, and hence incorporates the items listed in the front of the issue. This table is an important tool for updating regulations, as will be explained in Section C.4 below. Following the table of *CFR* parts there are a list of public laws received by the Office from Congress and a weekly checklist of current *CFR* volumes.

Each year's output comprises a new volume of the *Federal Register*, with continuous pagination throughout the year. The first volume in 1936 contained 2,400 pages. The size expanded to a peak of 86,405 pages in 1980, and has since leveled off at around 70,000 pages a year. It reached 78,851 in 2004. The legal presumption is that every citizen is on notice for

---

16   To a person first confronting the *Federal Register,* it may seem absurd that anyone would regularly read "this voluminous and dull publication," to quote Justice Jackson in *Federal Crop Insurance Corp. v. Merrill, supra* note 8. Lawyers dealing closely with particular agencies or specializing in specific areas of administrative law, however, would be poorly serving their clients if they were unaware of proposed changes that could affect those clients' interests. Examining each issue of the *Federal Register* is the best and most thorough way to stay informed.

every rule at appears in the *Federal Register*. 78,851 pages of bureaucratic rules boggles the mind.

Illustration C
A *Federal Register* Table of Contents Page from January 30, 2003

III

Contents

Federal Register

Vol. 68, No. 20

Thursday, January 30, 2003

Agriculture Department
See Food and Nutrition Service
See Forest Service
See Rural Utilities Service

Air Force Department
NOTICES
Meetings:
  Community College Board of Visitors, 4767

Census Bureau
NOTICES
Agency information collection activities:
  Proposed collection; comment request, 4755–4756

Civil Rights Commission
NOTICES
Meetings; State advisory committees:
  Arizona, 4755
  Texas, 4755

Commerce Department
See Census Bureau
See Foreign-Trade Zones Board
See International Trade Administration
See National Institute of Standards and Technology
See National Oceanic and Atmospheric Administration

Consumer Product Safety Commission
RULES
Federal Hazardous Substances Act:
  Model rocket propellant devices used with lightweight
    surface vehicles; exemptions, 4697–4699

Copyright Office, Library of Congress
PROPOSED RULES
Copyright Arbitration Royalty Panel rules and procedures:
  Digital performance of sound recordings by preexisting
    subscription services; reasonable rates and terms
    determination, 4744–4747

Defense Department
See Air Force Department
PROPOSED RULES
Federal Acquisition Regulation (FAR):
  Commercially available off-the-shelf items, 4873–4874
  Depreciation cost principle, 4875–4877
  Insurance and pension costs, 4879–4883
NOTICES
Agency information collection activities:
  Proposed collection; comment request, 4766
  Submission for OMB review; comment request, 4766–
    4767

Education Department
NOTICES
Grantback arrangements; award of funds:
  Illinois; compromise of claim intent; comment request,
    4767–4768
Grants and cooperative agreements; availability, etc.:
  Special education and rehabilitative services—
    Technical Assistance ALLIANCE for Parent Centers
      Program, 4768–4769

Employment Standards Administration
NOTICES
Agency information collection activities:
  Proposed collection; comment request, 4797–4798

Energy Department
See Federal Energy Regulatory Commission
NOTICES
Defense Nuclear Facilities Safety Board recommendations:
  Defense nuclear complex; weapons laboratory support,
    4769

Environmental Protection Agency
RULES
Air quality planning purposes; designation of areas:
  Missouri and Illinois, 4835–4841
PROPOSED RULES
Air quality implementation plans; approval and
    promulgation; various States; air quality planning
    purposes; designation of areas:
  Missouri and Illinois, 4846–4860
Air quality implementation plans; approval and
    promulgation; various States:
  Missouri, 4841–4847
NOTICES
Meetings:
  Science Advisory Board, 4775–4777
Reports and guidance documents; availability, etc.:
  Enforcement and Compliance History Online Web site,
    4777
Toxic and hazardous substances control:
  New chemicals—
    Receipt and status information, 4777–4785

Executive Office of the President
See Presidential Documents

Federal Aviation Administration
PROPOSED RULES
Airworthiness directives:
  Boeing, 4731–4737
  Bombardier, 4737–4739
  Dassault, 4739–4741
  Empresa Brasileira de Aeronautica S.A. (EMBRAER),
    4725–4727
  Honeywell, 4730–4731
  McDonnell Douglas, 4727–4729
Colored Federal airways, 4741–4742
VOR and colored Federal airways, 4742–4743
NOTICES
Meetings:
  RTCA, Inc., 4811–4812
Reports and guidance documents; availability, etc.:
  Transport category airplanes—
    Strengthened flightdeck doors; certification, 4812

Federal Election Commission
NOTICES
Meetings; Sunshine Act, 4785

Illustration D
A *Federal Register* CFR Parts Affected page from January 30, 2003

Federal Register / Vol. 68, No. 20 / Thursday, January 30, 2003 / Contents   VII

CFR PARTS AFFECTED IN THIS ISSUE

A cumulative list of the parts affected this month can be found in the Reader Aids section at the end of this issue.

3 CFR
Proclamations:
7643................................4887

5 CFR
550................................4681
2641................................4681

7 CFR
1738................................4684

14 CFR
Proposed Rules:
39 (6 documents) ...4725, 4727,
            4730, 4731, 4737, 4739
71 (2 documents) 4741, 4742

15 CFR
270................................4693

16 CFR
1500................................4697

17 CFR
210................................4862
228................................4820
229................................4820
244................................4820
249................................4820

18 CFR
1301................................4699

20 CFR
404................................4700

21 CFR
510................................4712
524................................4712

23 CFR
Proposed Rules:
973................................4744

37 CFR
Proposed Rules:
260................................4744

39 CFR
111................................4713

40 CFR
81................................4836
Proposed Rules:
52 (2 documents) 4842, 4847
81................................4847

48 CFR
Proposed Rules:
2 (2 documents) 4874, 4876
12................................4874
31 (2 documents) 4876, 4880
52 (2 documents) 4874, 4880

49 CFR
1420................................4718

50 CFR
660................................4719
Proposed Rules:
216................................4747

Illustration E
A *Federal Register* Reader Aids page from January 30, 2003

i

Reader Aids

Federal Register

Vol. 68, No. 20

Thursday, January 30, 2003

CUSTOMER SERVICE AND INFORMATION

Federal Register/Code of Federal Regulations

General information, indexes and other finding aids 202–741–6000

Laws 741–6000

Presidential Documents

Executive orders and proclamations 741–6000

The United States Government Manual 741–6000

Other Services

Electronic and on-line services (voice) ... 741–6020

Privacy Act Compilation 741–6064

Public Laws Update Service (numbers, dates, etc.) 741–6043

TTY for the deaf-and-hard-of-hearing ... 741–6086

ELECTRONIC RESEARCH

World Wide Web

Full text of the daily Federal Register, CFR and other publications is located at: http://www.access.gpo.gov/nara

Federal Register information and research tools, including Public Inspection List, indexes, and links to GPO Access are located at: http://www.archives.gov/federal_register/

E-mail

FEDREGTOC-L (Federal Register Table of Contents LISTSERV) is an open e-mail service that provides subscribers with a digital form of the Federal Register Table of Contents. The digital form of the Federal Register Table of Contents includes HTML and PDF links to the full text of each document.

To join or leave, go to http://listserv.access.gpo.gov and select *Online mailing list archives, FEDREGTOC-L, Join or leave the list (or change settings)*; then follow the instructions.

PENS (Public Law Electronic Notification Service) is an e-mail service that notifies subscribers of recently enacted laws.

To subscribe, go to http://hydra.gsa.gov/archives/publaws-l.html and select *Join or leave the list* (or change settings); then follow the instructions.

FEDREGTOC-L and PENS are mailing lists only. We cannot respond to specific inquiries.

Reference questions. Send questions and comments about the Federal Register system to: info@fedreg.nara.gov

The Federal Register staff cannot interpret specific documents or regulations.

FEDERAL REGISTER PAGES AND DATE, JANUARY

1–254	2
255–458	3
459–662	6
663–994	7
995–1142	8
1143–1358	9
1359–1512	10
1513–1792	13
1793–1954	14
1955–2174	15
2175–2408	16
2409–2678	17
2679–2868	21
2869–3162	22
3163–3370	23
3371–3802	24
3803–4074	27
4075–4360	28
4361–4680	29
4681–4888	30

CFR PARTS AFFECTED DURING JANUARY

At the end of each month, the Office of the Federal Register publishes separately a List of CFR Sections Affected (LSA), which lists parts and sections affected by documents published since the revision date of each title.

3 CFR

Proclamations:

6641 (See Proc. 7641) 3163

7636 995

7637 1951

7638 2173

7639 2409

7640 2869

7641 3163

7642 3169

7643 4887

Executive orders:

10865 (Amended by 13284) 4075

11423 (Amended by 13284) 4075

11958 (Amended by 13284) 4075

12260 (Amended by 13284) 4075

12333 (See EO 13283) 3371

12333 (Amended by 13284) 4075

12543 (See Notice of January 2, 2003) 661

12544 (See Notice of January 2, 2003) 661

12590 (Amended by 13284) 4075

12829 (See 13284) 4075

12859 (Amended by 13284) 4075

12881 (Amended by 13284) 4075

12947 (Continued by Notice of January 20, 2003) 3161

12958 (See 13284) 4075

12968 (See 13284) 4075

12992 (Amended by 13284) 4075

13011 (Amended by 13284) 4075

13048 (Amended by 13284) 4075

13099 (Continued by Notice of January 20, 2003) 3161

13122 (Amended by 13284) 4075

13151 (Amended by 13284) 4075

13224 (Amended by 13284) 4075

13228 (Amended by 13284) 4075

13231 (Amended by 13284) 4075

13234 (Amended by 13284) 4075

13249 (Superseded by 13282) 1133

13282 1133

13283 3371

13284 4075

Administrative orders:

Memorandums:

Memorandum of January 17, 2003 3157

Notices:

Notice of January 2, 2003 661

Notice of January 20, 2003 3161

Presidential Determinations:

No. 2003-09 of January 7, 2003 1513

No. 2003-10 of January 10, 2003 2411

No. 2003-11 of January 10, 2003 2419

No. 2003-12 of January 17, 2003 3803

5 CFR

532 .... 459, 460, 1515

550 4681

831 2175

837 2175

842 2175

843 2175

844 2175

847 2175

2641 4681

Proposed Rules:

735 1987

2606 2923

6 CFR

Ch. 1 4056

5 4056

7 4056

7 CFR

97 1359

301 .... 1360, 2679, 3373

318 2681

319 .... 2681, 2684

354 3375

905 4361

906 1362

989 .... 1143, 4079, 4085

996 1145

997 1145

998 1145

999 1145

1208 .... 1364, 2108

1738 4684

Proposed Rules:

56 1169

300 69

723 1556

1464 1556

Although the texts of most final rules are arranged by subject in the *CFR,* much of the other material in the *Federal Register* never appears elsewhere.[17]   Proposed rules, agency policy statements, discussion of comments received, and descriptive statements on agency organization give the *Federal Register* a permanent reference value, and most large law libraries have a complete backfile, either bound or in microfilm or microfiche editions.

Access to the *Federal Register* is provided through several different indexes, tables, and computer databases. The *Federal Register* also appears in electronic forms that will be discussed below. If you are concerned with the actions of a specific agency it is worth monitoring each day's *Federal Register* for actions by that agency. Skimming the table of contents of the *Federal Register* is part of many legal researchers' daily routine.[18]

For purposes of keeping current, the *Federal Register* is available on WESTLAW and LEXIS. The online version is often more up to date than the print version found in your law library or office. The *Federal Register* is also available daily on the Internet from a variety of sources. These include both free and fee-based systems.[19] Your library may also subscribe to an online backfile, such as the one from HeinOnline, which has made the *Federal Register* available in PDF format from the very first volume, and is working to bring the database up to date. As of this writing, the database contained every page of the *Federal Register* through 1993.

---

17   In *Wiggins Bros., Inc. v. Department of Energy,* 667 F.2d 77 (Temp.Emer.App.1981), *cert. denied,* 456 U.S. 905 (1982), the court reversed a district court ruling that excluded consideration of *Federal Register* material not published in *CFR* in construing an agency regulation. The court held that the agency's failure to include a preamble in the codified regulation did not mean that the preamble should be disregarded.

18   You can sign-up to receive a daily email of the *Federal Register* Table of Contents from the GPO Access page, <http://listserv.access.gpo.gov/>.

19   The *Federal Register* is available in PDF format from GPO Access, for free, from 1994 forward. <http://www.gpoaccess.gov/fr/index.html>

Because most research in administrative regulations requires use of both the *Register* and the *Code of Federal Regulations,* however, we must first introduce the latter publication.

2. *Code of Federal Regulations*

When Congress sought to control the chaos of administrative rules through the Federal Register Act, it understood the need for a subject arrangement of regulations in force. Section 11 of the act required each agency to compile and publish in the *Register* its then current body of regulations.[20] It was not until an amendment in 1937,[21] however, that a regular form of codification was established. The first edition of the new *Code of Federal Regulations* was published in 1939, and contained regulations in force as of June 1, 1938.

The *CFR* is to contain "documents of each agency of the Government having general applicability and legal effect, ... relied upon by the agency as authority for, or ... invoked or used by it in the discharge of, its activities or functions."[22] The regulations are codified in a subject arrangement of fifty titles somewhat similar to those employed for federal statutes in the *United States Code.* For example, 26 USC is the Internal Revenue Code and 26 CFR contains tax regulations, and Title 7 of each code is concerned with agriculture. The titles do not always match, however. Education statutes are in 20 USC but corresponding regulations are in 34 CFR; and 40 CFR, dealing with protection of the environment, has no direct statutory counterpart. The real difference lies in the fact that instead of truly grouping administrative rules together by subject, the *CFR* groups the agencies together by subject. This keeps all of one agency's rules and regulations together. Regulations on a single topic, such as tobacco, may be spread through several agencies, hence several titles of the *CFR.*

Each title is divided into *chapters,* each of which is devoted to the

---

20   Ch. 417, §11, 49 Stat. 500, 503 (1935).

21   Act of June 19, 1937, ch. 369, 50 Stat. 304.

22   44 U.S.C. §1510(a) (2002).

regulations of a particular agency. Chapters are numbered with Roman numerals,[23] and sometimes are divided into subchapters designated by capital letters. In the back of every *CFR* volume there is an alphabetical list of federal agencies indicating the *CFR* title and chapter of each agency's regulations.

The regulations of a particular agency are divided into *parts,* each of which consists of a body of regulations on a particular topic or agency function. (Each *Federal Register* issue, you may recall, includes lists of *CFR* parts affected in that issue and during that month.) Parts are further divided into *sections,* the basic unit of the code. A section "is a short, simple presentation of a single regulatory function."[24] The citation identifying a *CFR* section shows the title, the part and the section (but not the chapter), so that 1 C.F.R. §1.1 is title 1, part 1, section 1.

Before 1967 the *CFR* appeared in various cumulations. Since that date it has been totally republished in paperbound pamphlets each year. This schedule of annual republication of the whole set is very ambitious. The colors of the volume covers change each year, so annual editions can be readily distinguished from each other. The cover of each volume of the *CFR* explains exactly what it covers. Illustration E shows the cover of Title 16, Parts 100-end. Note how it states that it represents all the rules as of January 1, 2005.

The current code consists of about two hundred volumes. Rather than reissue the entire set at one time, the Office of the Federal Register revises the set on a quarterly basis. Titles 1-16 contain regulations in force as of January 1 of the cover year; titles 17-27 as of April 1; titles 28-41 as of July 1; and titles 42-50 as of October 1. Because one year's edition gradually supplants the previous year's, a current *CFR* set almost always

---

23   Chapters in Title 41, Public Contracts and Property Management, and Title 48, Federal Acquisition Regulations System, are designated by Arabic, not Roman, numeral.

24   Office of the Federal Register, *Document Drafting Handbook §1-12* (October 1988 revision).

Illustration F
Cover of 16 CFR Parts 1000-End, Commercial Practices

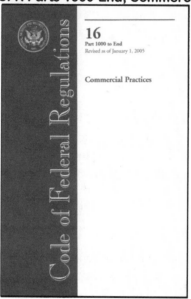

consists of volumes of two or more colors. The republication schedule is a goal that is not always met. Be sure and check the cover for the dates of coverage.

The table of contents for each title lists its chapters; that for each chapter, its parts; and for each part, its sections. In addition, at the beginning of each part the agency provides notes showing the statutory or executive authority under which the regulations in that part are issued. This *authority note* is followed by a *source note,* providing the citation and date of the *Federal Register* in which the part was last published in full. Illustration F shows the beginning of 16 CFR 1500, with authority and source notes following the table of sections. If an individual section is based on a different authority a separate authority or source note follows that section. Illustration H shows the pages where 1500.85 is printed.

Illustration G
The Beginning of 16 CFR 1500 (2005) with Authority and Source Notes

SUBCHAPTER C—FEDERAL HAZARDOUS SUBSTANCES ACT REGULATIONS

403

§ 1500.1   16 CFR Ch. II (1-1-05 Edition)

AUTHORITY: 15 U.S.C. 1261-1278.

SOURCE: 38 FR 27012, Sept. 27, 1973, unless otherwise noted.

§ 1500.1 Scope of subchapter.

Set forth in this subchapter C are the regulations of the Consumer Product Safety Commission issued pursuant to and for the implementation of the Federal Hazardous Substances Act as amended (see § 1500.3(a)(1)).

§ 1500.2 Authority.

Authority under the Federal Hazardous Substances Act is vested in the Consumer Product Safety Commission by section 30(a) of the Consumer Product Safety Act (15 U.S.C. 2079(a)).

§ 1500.3 Definitions.

(a) *Certain terms used in this part.* As used in this part:

(1) *Act* means the Federal Hazardous Substances Act (Pub. L. 86-613, 74 Stat. 372-81 (15 U.S.C. 1261-74)) as amended by:

(i) The Child Protection Act of 1966 (Pub. L. 89-756, 80 Stat. 1303-05).

(ii) The Child Protection and Toy Safety Act of 1969 (Pub. L. 91-113, 83 Stat. 187-90).

(iii) The Poison Prevention Packaging Act of 1970 (Pub. L. 91-601, 84 Stat. 1670-74).

(2) *Commission* means the Consumer Product Safety Commission established May 14, 1973, pursuant to provisions of the Consumer Product Safety Act (Pub. L. 92-573, 86 Stat. 1207-33 (15 U.S.C. 2051-81)).

(b) *Statutory definitions.* Except for the definitions given in section 2 (c) and (d) of the act, which are obsolete, the definitions set forth in section 2 of the act are applicable to this part and are repeated for convenience as follows (some of these statutory definitions are interpreted, supplemented, or provided with alternatives in paragraph (c) of this section):

(1) *Territory* means any territory or possession of the United States, including the District of Columbia and the Commonwealth of Puerto Rico but excluding the Canal Zone.

(2) *Interstate commerce* means (i) commerce between any State or territory and any place outside thereof and (ii) commerce within the District of Co-

lumbia or within any territory not organized with a legislative body.

(3) *Person* includes an individual, partnership, corporation, and association.

(4)(i) *Hazardous substance* means:

(A) Any substance or mixture of substances which is toxic, corrosive, an irritant, a strong sensitizer, flammable or combustible, or generates pressure through decomposition, heat, or other means, if such substance or mixture of substances may cause substantial personal injury or substantial illness during or as a proximate result of any customary or reasonably foreseeable handling or use, including reasonably foreseeable ingestion by children.

(B) Any substance which the Commission by regulation finds, pursuant to the provisions of section 3(a) of the act, meet the requirements of section 2(f)(1)(A) of the act (restated in (A) above).

(C) Any radioactive substance if, with respect to such substance as used in a particular class of article or as packaged, the Commission determines by regulation that the substance is sufficiently hazardous to require labeling in accordance with the act in order to protect the public health.

(D) Any toy or other article intended for use by children which the Commission by regulation determines, in accordance with section 3(e) of the act, presents an electrical, mechanical, or thermal hazard.

(ii) *Hazardous substance* shall not apply to pesticides subject to the Federal Insecticide, Fungicide, and Rodenticide Act, to foods, drugs, and cosmetics subject to the Federal Food, Drug, and Cosmetic Act, nor to substances intended for use as fuels when stored in containers and used in the heating, cooking, or refrigeration system of a house. "Hazardous substance" shall apply, however, to any article which is not itself a pesticide within the meaning of the Federal Insecticide, Fungicide, and Rodenticide Act but which is a hazardous substance within the meaning of section 2(f)(1) of the Federal Hazardous Substances Act (restated in paragraph (b)(4)(i) of this section) by reason of bearing or containing such a pesticide.

404

Illustration H
16 CFR 1500.85

Consumer Product Safety Commission   **§ 1500.85**

section 2(p)(1) of the act (repeated in §1500.3(b)(14)(i)) insofar as such requirements would be necessary because the articles are flammable or generate pressure, provided that:

(i) The devices are designed and constructed in accordance with the specifications in §1500.85(a)(8), (9) or (14);

(ii) Each individual device or retail package of devices bears the following:

(A) The statement "WARNING— FLAMMABLE: Read instructions before use";

(B) The common or usual name of the article;

(C) A statement of the type of engine and use classification;

(D) Instructions for safe disposal; and

(E) Name and place of business of manufacturer or distributor; and

(iii) Each individual rocket engine or retail package of rocket engines distributed to users is accompanied by an instruction sheet bearing complete cautionary labeling and instructions for safe use and handling of the individual rocket engines.

(37) Glues with a cyanoacrylate base in packages containing 3 grams or less are exempt from the requirement of §1500.121(d) that labeling which is permitted to appear elsewhere than on the main label panel must be in type size no smaller than 6 point type, provided that:

(i) The main panel of the immediate container bears both the proper signal word and a statement of the principal hazard or hazards associated with this product, as provided by §1500.121 (a) and (c);

(ii) The main panel of the immediate container also bears an instruction to read carefully additional warnings elsewhere on the label and on any outer package, accompanying leaflet, and display card. The instruction to read additional warnings must comply with the size, placement, conspicuousness, and contrast requirements of §1500.121; and

(iii) The remainder of the cautionary labeling required by the act that is not on the main label panel must appear elsewhere on the label in legible type and must appear on any outer package, accompanying leaflet, and display card. If there is no outer package, accompanying leaflet, or display card,

then the remainder of the required cautionary labeling must be displayed on a tag or other suitable material that is securely affixed to the article so that the labeling will remain attached throughout the conditions of merchandising and distribution to the ultimate consumer. That labeling which must appear on any outer package, accompanying leaflet, tag, or other suitable material must comply with the size, placement, contrast, and conspicuousness requirements of §1500.121(d).

(38) Rigid or semi-rigid writing instruments and ink cartridges having a writing point and an ink reservoir are exempt from the labeling requirements of section 2(p)(1) of the act (repeated in §1500.3(b)(14)(i) of the regulations) and of regulations issued under section 3(b) of the act (§1500.14(b)(1, 2)) insofar as such requirements would be necessary because the ink contained therein is a "toxic" substance as defined in §1500.3(c)(2)(i) and/or because the ink contains 10 percent or more by weight ethylene glycol or diethylene glycol, if all the following conditions are met:

(i) The writing instrument or cartridge is of such construction that the ink will, under any reasonably foreseeable condition of manipulation and use, emerge only from the writing tip.

(ii) When tested by the method described in §1500.3(c)(2)(i), the ink does not have an LD–50 single oral dose of less than 2.5 grams per kilogram of body weight of the test animal.

(iii) If the ink contains ethylene glycol or diethylene glycol, the amount of such substance, either singly or in combination, does not exceed 1 gram per writing instrument or cartridge.

(iv) The amount of ink in the writing instrument or cartridge does not exceed 3 grams.

[38 FR 27012, Sept. 27, 1973; 42 FR 33026, June 29, 1977, as amended at 43 FR 32745, July 28, 1978; 43 FR 47176, Oct. 13, 1978; 44 FR 42678, July 20, 1979; 46 FR 11513, Feb. 9, 1981; 48 FR 16, Jan. 3, 1983; 68 FR 4699, Jan. 30, 2003]

§ 1500.85 Exemptions from classification as banned hazardous substances.

(a) The term *banned hazardous substances* as used in section 2(q)(1)(A) of the act shall not apply to the following articles provided that these articles

§ 1500.85

bear labeling giving adequate directions and warnings for safe use:

(1) Chemistry sets and other science education sets intended primarily for juveniles, and replacement components for such sets, when labeled in accordance with § 1500.83(a)(23).

(2) Firecrackers designed to produce audible effects, if the audible effect is produced by a charge of not more than 50 milligrams (.772 grains) of pyrotechnic composition. (See also § 1500.14(b)(7); § 1500.17(a) (3), (8) and (9); and part 1507).

(3) [Reserved]

(4) Educational materials such as art materials, preserved biological specimens, laboratory chemicals, and other articles intended and used for educational purposes.

(5) Liquid fuels containing more than 4 percent by weight of methyl alcohol that are intended and used for operation of miniature engines for model airplanes, boats, cars, etc.

(6) Novelties consisting of a mixture of polyvinyl acetate, U.S. Certified Colors, and not more than 25 percent by weight of acetone, and intended for blowing plastic balloons.

(7) Games containing, as the sole hazardous component, a self-pressurized container of soap solution or similar foam-generating mixture provided that the foam-generating component has no hazards other than being in a self-pressurized container.

(8) Model rocket propellant devices designed for use in light-weight, recoverable, and reflyable model rockets, provided such devices:

(i) Are designed to be ignited by electrical means.

(ii) Contain no more than 62.5 grams (2.2 ounces) of propellant material and produce less than 80 newton-seconds (17.92 pound seconds) of total impulse with thrust duration not less than 0.050 second.

(iii) Are constructed such that all the chemical ingredients are preloaded into a cylindrical paper or similarly constructed nonmetallic tube that will not fragment into sharp, hard pieces.

(iv) Are designed so that they will not burst under normal conditions of use, are incapable of spontaneous ignition, and do not contain any type of explosive or pyrotechnic warhead other than a small parachute or recovery-system activation charge.

(9) Separate delay train and/or recovery system activation devices intended for use with premanufactured model rocket engines wherein all of the chemical ingredients are preloaded so the user does not handle any chemical ingredient and are so designed that the main casing or container does not rupture during operation.

(10) Solid fuel pellets intended for use in miniature jet engines for propelling model jet airplanes, speed boats, racing cars, and similar models, provided such solid fuel pellets:

(i) Weigh not more than 11.5 grams each.

(ii) Are coated with a protective resinous film.

(iii) Contain not more than 35 percent potassium dichromate.

(iv) Produce a maximum thrust of not more than 7½ ounces when used as directed.

(v) Burn not longer than 12 seconds each when used as directed.

(11) Fuses intended for igniting fuel pellets exempt under subparagraph (10) of this paragraph.

(12) Kits intended for construction of model rockets and jet propelled model airplanes requiring the use of difluorodichloromethane as a propellant, provided the outer carton bears on the main panel in conspicuous type size the statement "WARNING—Carefully read instructions and cautions before use."

(13) Flammable wire materials intended for electro-mechanical actuation and release devices for model kits described in paragraph (12) of this section, provided each wire does not exceed 15 milligrams in weight.

(14) Model rocket propellant devices (model rocket motors) designed to propel rocket-powered model cars, provided—

(i) Such devices:

(A) Are designed to be ignited electrically and are intended to be operated from a minimum distance of 15 feet (4.6 m) away;

(B) Contain no more than 4 g. of propellant material and produce no more than 2.5 Newton-seconds of total impulse with a thrust duration not less than 0.050 seconds;

Consumer Product Safety Commission   **§ 1500.86**

(C) Are constructed such that all the chemical ingredients are pre-loaded into a cylindrical paper or similarly constructed non-metallic tube that will not fragment into sharp, hard pieces;

(D) Are designed so that they will not burst under normal conditions of use, are incapable of spontaneous ignition, and do not contain any type of explosive or pyrotechnic warhead other than a small recovery system activation charge;

(E) Bear labeling, including labeling that the devices are intended for use by persons age 12 and older, and include instructions providing adequate warnings and instructions for safe use; and

(F) Comply with the requirements of 16 CFR 1500.83(a)(36)(ii and iii); and

(ii) The surface vehicles intended for use with such devices:

(A) Are lightweight, weighing no more than 3.0 oz. (85 grams), and constructed mainly of materials such as balsa wood or plastics that will not fragment into sharp, hard pieces;

(B) Are designed to utilize a braking system such as a parachute or shock absorbing stopping mechanism;

(C) Are designed so that they cannot accept propellant devices measuring larger than 0.5″ (13 mm) in diameter and 1.75″ (44 mm) in length;

(D) Are designed so that the engine mount is permanently attached by the manufacturer to a track or track line that controls the vehicle's direction for the duration of its movement;

(E) Are not designed to carry any type of explosive or pyrotechnic material other than the model rocket motor used for primary propulsion;

(F) Bear labeling and include instructions providing adequate warnings and instructions for safe use; and

(G) Are designed to operate on a track or line that controls the vehicles' direction for the duration of their movement and either cannot operate off the track or line or, if operated off the track or line, are unstable and fail to operate in a guided fashion so that they will not strike the operator or bystanders.

(b) [Reserved]

[38 FR 27012, Sept. 27, 1973, as amended at 41 FR 22935, June 8, 1976; 42 FR 43391, Aug. 29, 1977; 48 FR 16, Jan. 3, 1983; 68 FR 4699, Jan. 30, 2003]

§ 1500.86 Exemptions from classification as a banned toy or other banned article for use by children.

(a) The term *banned hazardous substance* as used in section 2(q)(1)(A) of the act (repeated in § 1500.3(b)(15)(i)(A)) of the act shall not apply to the following articles:

(1) Toy rattles described in § 1500.18(a)(1) in which the rigid wires, sharp protrusions, or loose small objects are internal and provided that such rattles are constructed so that they will not break or deform to expose or release the contents either in normal use or when subjected to reasonably foreseeable damage or abuse.

(2) Dolls and stuffed animals and other similar toys described in § 1500.18(a)(3) in which the components that have the potential for causing laceration, puncture wound injury, or other similar injury are internal, provided such dolls, stuffed animals, and other similar toys are constructed so that they will not break or deform to expose such components either in normal use or when subjected to reasonably foreseeable damage or abuse.

(3) [Reserved]

(4) Any article known as a "baby-bouncer," "walker-jumper," or "baby-walker" and any other similar article (referred to in this paragraph as "article(s)") described in § 1500.18(a)(6) provided:

(i) The frames are designed and constructed in a manner to prevent injury from any scissoring, shearing, or pinching when the members of the frame or other components rotate about a common axis or fastening point or otherwise move relative to one another; and

(ii) Any coil springs which expand when the article is subjected to a force that will extend the spring to its maximum distance so that a space between successive coils is greater than one-eighth inch (0.125 inch) are covered or otherwise designed to prevent injuries; and

(iii) All holes larger than one-eighth inch (0.125 inch) in diameter and slots, cracks, or hinged components in any portion of the article through which a child could insert, in whole or in part a finger, toe, or any other part of the anatomy are guarded or otherwise designed to prevent injuries; and

477

In addition to the regulations which form the main contents of the code, Title 3 consists of the texts of proclamations, executive orders and other presidential documents. These materials will be separately described below in Section E.

Among the *CFR* volumes revised and reissued each year is an "Index and Finding Aids" volume. This volume is just one of several indexes and means of access to the *Code of Federal Regulations,* and will be discussed in the next section.

3. Finding Regulations

There are several methods of finding federal agency regulations. Both the *Federal Register* and the *Code of Federal Regulations* have indexes prepared by the Office of the Federal Register and by commercial publishing companies. Both are available in full text on WESTLAW and LEXIS where keyword searching can be especially helpful.

Ordinarily research into the regulations of a federal agency begins with the *Code of Federal Regulations,* rather than the daily *Federal Register.* Since the *CFR* pulls all the regulations together into one place and it is updated on an annual basis, it is the logical starting place.

If you know the name of the agency in which you are interested, the list of agencies and the location of their rules in the back of each volume can point out where to look. Given Section B's emphasis on starting research with context, the researcher should at least know the name of the agency.

For more specific searches, the *Code* is accompanied by an annually revised volume entitled *Index and Finding Aids,* most of which consists of an index of subjects and agencies. The index provides references to *parts,* rather than sections, so it is not always as specific as would be desired. It also covers a very broad area in relatively terse fashion, so it is not very specific and is sometimes difficult to use. Of course, someone who is following the research suggestions set out in Section B would already know an agency, and should come to the set with full citation in hand. Starting a new search in any subject index is a bad idea.

For those who do need a subject index, there are two commercial annual indexes of the *CFR*. The LexisNexis Congressional Information Service publishes an *Index to the Code of Federal Regulations* (*ICFR*). In four annual volumes, updated quarterly, it provides very detailed indexing of the *CFR* by subject and by geographic location. As in the official index, however, its entries refer to parts rather than to specific sections. Unlike many commercial publications which appear much more quickly than official works, this index is published rather slowly. The index for one year's *CFR* edition generally does not appear until the following autumn.

The *United States Code Service* publishes a one volume paperbound index of *CFR* materials. It is a reprint of the *CFR*'s Finding Aids volume. It is shelved as part of the *USCS* set.

The *Federal Register* also has an official index published monthly, consisting of a consolidation of the entries in each issue's table of contents. Entries are arranged by agency, not by subject. Within each agency's listing, rules, proposed rules and notices are listed alphabetically by subject. Each month's index cumulates those earlier in the year, so the January-February index replaces the January index, and the January-December index serves as the final annual index. A table of *Federal Register* pages and dates, similar to that in each daily issue, appears in the back of each index for the months covered. The index usually does not appear until several weeks after its period of coverage ends.[25]

An increasingly important means of access to both the *Code of Federal Regulations* and the *Federal Register* is provided by full-text coverage in both WESTLAW and LEXIS. *Federal Register* issues since the summer of 1980 are searchable on both systems, and each new issue is

---

25   A much more thorough index to the *Register* was published between 1984-98 by the Congressional Information Service. The *CIS Federal Register Index* was published weekly, within two or three weeks of the period covered. The weekly issues were cumulated periodically, until the publication of permanent bound semiannual volumes. The index provided thorough coverage of all *Federal Register* documents except Sunshine Act notices, and was divided into four sections: a calendar of effective dates and comment deadlines, and indexes by subjects and names, by *CFR* section numbers affected, and by agency docket numbers. It may still be useful if you have to research within that time period.

available online the day of its publication. The current edition of the *Code of Federal Regulations* is also available online, and both systems also have archival databases containing previous years' editions of *CFR*. LEXIS also has a combined file of both *Register* and *Code*. WESTLAW has combined files in six major topical areas including tax, bankruptcy & securities. Keyword searching can be especially effective for some searches in these databases. When you are doing research in federal administrative regulations, you often have the name of a very specific product or topic. If you wanted to find regulations on the "Guadalupe fur seal" (50 CFR 223.201) a keyword search would be just the ticket. The *CFR* and the *Federal Register* appear at various Internet sites as well, such as the GPO Access page. This site is also updated daily, and allows keyword searching in current and archival issues.

Often one has a statute or presidential document and would like to find regulations promulgated under its authority or related to it. A "Parallel Table of Authorities and Rules" in the *Index and Finding Aids* volume provides access. It lists every statute and presidential document cited by an agency as authority for its rules, taken from the rulemaking authority citation in *CFR*. The table consists of separate sections for *United States Code* sections, *Statutes at Large* pages, public law numbers, and presidential documents. Authority citations are provided by the agencies, and may follow different formats; the same statute may be cited by code section by one agency and by public law number by another agency. The table does not reconcile inconsistencies, so it may be necessary to check more than one section to find all references to a statute. The table in the *Index and Finding Aids* volume is current as of January 1st of each year. During the course of the year, both additions to and removals from the list are printed in the monthly pamphlet *LSA: List of CFR Sections Affected.* These monthly lists cumulate until the next annual edition.

One of the simplest ways to find relevant regulations may be to use a looseleaf service or other resource which collects and reprints agency regulations in a particular subject area. If relevant regulations are already collected, there may be no need to search through indexes or computer databases. Topical looseleaf services focusing on the work of particular agencies (such as the Internal Revenue Service or the National Labor Relations Board) provide currently supplemented and well annotated texts of both substantive and procedural regulations in their subject agencies.

In addition, procedural regulations of over two dozen agencies are printed in the "Administrative Rules of Procedure" volume of *United States Code Service.* Like the rest of *USCS,* the administrative rules volumes include annotations of interpretive agency and court decisions and references to relevant forms, *ALR* annotations, and other research tools, and are updated by annual pocket parts and interim supplements. Pike and Fischer's *Administrative Law, Third Series, Deskbook* also contains the texts of eight major agencies' procedural regulations under the Administrative Procedure Act.

4. Updating and Verifying Regulations

Even though the *Code of Federal Regulations* is reissued every year, at some point during the year each volume will be up to a year or more out of date. Administrative regulations change frequently, and researchers must be able to determine their current status. To make sure that a *CFR* section is still current, and to find any new or proposed rules affecting it, there is a straightforward routine to be followed. It consists of several steps, different and often simpler than the ways cases and statutes are updated.

The first step in updating a *CFR* section is to check for references in a monthly pamphlet entitled *LSA: List of CFR Sections Affected.*[26] Like the daily and monthly lists in each issue of the *Federal Register, LSA* indicates *Register* pages of any new or proposed rules affecting the *Code.* Under each *CFR* title, there are separate listings for final actions and for proposed rules. Except for proposed rules, references are to exact sections and include a descriptive word or phrase indicating the nature of the change, such as "amended," "removed," or "revised." Illustration I shows a page from the January, 2003 *LSA* indicating that 16 *CFR* 1500.85 (a) (14) was added. The *LSA* volumes physically resemble the *CFR* volumes and are normally shelved at the end of the set.

---

26   Available   from   GPO   Access,   from   1986   forward, <http://www.gpoaccess.gov/lsa/index.html>.

Illustration I
An *LSA* page, showing Title 16 *CFR* sections affected

20   LSA—LIST OF CFR SECTIONS AFFECTED

CHANGES JANUARY 2, 2003 THROUGH JANUARY 31, 2003

TITLE 15

Chapter VII—Bureau of Industry and Security, Department of Commerce (Parts 700—799)

744 Authority citation revised 1797
744.17 Added 1797
744 Supplement No. 1 added 1797
    Supplement No. 1, Category 3
    (ECCN 3A001) amended...............1798

Chapter VIII—Bureau of Economic Analysis, Department of Commerce (Parts 800--899)

806.15 (h)(1) and (2) revised 3813
806.17 Revised...................................1532

Chapter IX—National Oceanic and Atmospheric Administration, Department of Commerce (Parts 900—999)

902 Technical correction 2636
902.1 (b) table amended (OMB
    numbers) 209, 2192

TITLE 16—COMMERCIAL PRACTICES

Chapter I—Federal Trade Commission (Parts 0—999)

303.7 (m) amended 3816
310 Revised......................................4669
801.1 (h) revised 2430
801.21 Introductory text revised
   2430
803.9 (a) Examples 7 and 8 added;
    (c) revised 2431
803.20 (c) and example revised.........2431
803 Appendix revised 2431

Chapter II—Consumer Product Safety Commission (Parts 1000--1799)

1500.85 (a)(14) added 4699

Proposed Rules:

0—999 (Ch. I).....................................2465

The coverage of *LSA* reflects changes back to the last revision of each title. Because *CFR* volumes are updated as of four different dates during the year, this means that the dates covered for each title will vary. Fortunately, the cover of each issue of the *LSA* lists exactly what it covers. Because *LSA* cumulates every month, it is not necessary to examine more than the most recent pamphlet to find out about changes since the latest *CFR* revision.

The second step in updating sends us back to the *Federal Register.* Because the latest *LSA* pamphlet does not bring a search completely up to date, a similar list must be consulted in the last *Federal Register* issue of each month not covered in the pamphlet. This list is by part rather than section. A researcher in late October who has examined a September *LSA* pamphlet need only check the "List of CFR Parts Affected in October" in the latest available *Federal Register* issue to be assured that no changes in the regulation have been promulgated.

Finally, updating takes us beyond administrative materials to judicial decisions. There is a chance that the regulation has been challenged in court or interpreted in litigation. *CFR,* however, does not include annotations to decisions construing or applying regulations, and no publisher issues a comprehensive annotated set of federal regulations. In specialized areas, looseleaf services include annotations to regulations

However, the best sources for updating and checking the judicial treatment of regulations are the *KeyCite* and *Shepard's* online systems.[27]

---

27   In paper, *Shepard's Code of Federal Regulations Citations,* however, is the best source for checking for judicial treatment of regulations. It includes citations of regulations in federal courts since about 1949, in state courts and selected law reviews since 1977, and in *ALR* annotations. Abbreviations similar to those used in *Shepard's* statutory citators are used to indicate, for example, when a regulation has been found constitutional (C), valid (Va), void or invalid (V), or void or invalid in part (Vp). *Shepard's Code of Federal Regulations Citations* (in paper as well as online) also covers presidential proclamations, executive orders, and reorganization plans, as will be discussed below in section D. Several of the topical *Shepard's* units include coverage of regulations in their subject areas. Some, such as *Shepard's Federal Tax Citations,* include citations to regulations in topical reporters, such as *American Federal Tax Reports,* but coverage unfortunately does not extend to administrative agency decisions applying or interpreting regulations.

These will show when regulations have been amended, or cited in the state and federal courts and law reviews.

Illustration J
A screen shot from LEXIS showing results from *Shepard's*
for 16 CFR 1500.85

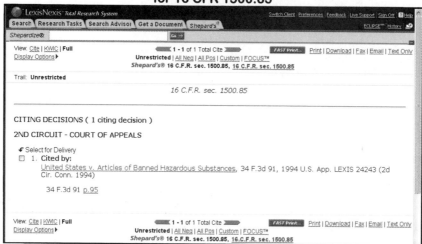

Occasionally a researcher will have a citation to a *CFR* section no longer appearing in the current code. The section or its part might have been repealed or simply transferred to another location in the code. In order that one can determine just what has happened to missing sections, each *CFR* volume contains a list of all changes occurring in its contents since January 1, 2001. These changes are listed by year, at the back of the volume. The entries are the same as those appearing in *LSA* pamphlets, but are limited to the sections in each particular volume. Changes in the entire code before 2001 are listed in eleven separate, hardbound volumes, entitled *List of CFR Sections Affected, 1949-1963*, *1964-1972*, *1973-1985* and *1986-2001*.

5. Using the *Federal Register* System

The Federal Court has said that attorneys "may be presumed to understand how to use the *Federal Register* system."[28] This presumption

---

can be satisfied by a familiarity with the standard means of finding and verifying the status of agency regulations. A basic search for current regulations ordinarily covers the following steps:

(a) Using the general index to the *Code of Federal Regulations* or one of the commercial indexes to the code, or searching the *CFR* database on either LEXIS or WESTLAW, to determine the titles and sections of relevant regulations.

(b) Examining the text of the regulations in the latest revised edition of its *CFR* volume.

(c) Inspecting the latest monthly pamphlet of *LSA: List of CFR Sections Affected* to determine whether the relevant sections have been affected by later changes. The latest *LSA* pamphlet includes all changes from the current *CFR* edition through the end of the month indicated on its cover.

(d) Examining the cumulative "List of CFR Parts Affected" in the most recent issue of the *Federal Register*. This list updates *LSA* and indicates all changes published during the current month. (Depending on how current the latest *LSA* pamphlet is, it may also be necessary to check the final issue of the previous month.)

(e) Checking the citations found in steps (c) and (d) in the *Register* itself to evaluate the substance of the changes.

(f) Using *KeyCite*, *Shepard's* online, or *Shepard's Code of Federal Regulations Citations* to determine whether the current status of the regulation has been affected by any court decisions.

169-70 (D.D.C.1984). At issue was whether a supplemental *CFR* volume had to be published when the 1984 edition of Title Five included Office of Personnel Management regulations which had been barred by Congress and declared void before ever taking effect. While noting that a *Federal Register* notice was sufficient to apprise attorneys of what regulations were in force, the court held that a supplemental volume was necessary "to assure that less sophisticated users of the Code are able to have ready access to the regulations currently in effect. Nonattorney users of the Code cannot be expected to be able to engage in legal research such as that done by an attorney." *Id.* at 170.

There are ways to save some of these steps. A looseleaf service reprinting regulations in a particular subject area should frequently update and cumulate *CFR* changes appearing in the *Federal Register,* so that its subject arrangement of regulations would be more current than the latest *CFR* edition. A LEXIS or WESTLAW search in the *Federal Register* database for citations of particular *CFR* parts would retrieve changes and proposed changes and eliminate the need to examine *LSA* or the *Register*'s lists of *CFR* parts affected.

D. DECISIONS OF FEDERAL ADMINISTRATIVE AGENCIES

Among the functions of most administrative agencies is the exercise of quasi-judicial power in determining cases and questions arising under their statutes and regulations. These adjudications usually involve a fact-finding process and the application of agency regulations to particular situations or problems. Agency decisions may follow lengthy formal hearings or consist of rulings on specific submitted inquiries.

As administrative agencies grew during the 1930's and assumed more decision-making authority, they came under increasing attack as to their fairness, efficiency, and procedural methods. In 1939 President Roosevelt asked the Attorney General to appoint a committee to study agency procedures, and in 1941 the extensive final report of the Attorney General's Committee on Administrative Procedure was submitted to Congress.[29] The pressure for reform culminated in enactment of the Administrative Procedure Act in 1946.[30] The Act strengthened procedural safeguards, established minimum standards to ensure fairer hearings, and provided a framework for judicial review of agency action.

---

29   *Administrative Procedure in Government Agencies: Report of the Committee on Administrative Procedure, Appointed by the Attorney General, at the Request of the President, to Investigate the Need for Procedural Reform in Various Administrative Tribunals and to Suggest Improvements Therein,* S.Doc. No. 8, 77th Cong., 1st Sess. (1941).

30   Ch. 324, 80 Stat. 237 (1946).

Under the Administrative Procedure Act, most agency hearings are conducted by an administrative law judge, who has a role very similar to that of a trial judge and issues the initial decision of the agency. That decision can be appealed to a higher authority within the agency, such as the secretary of the department or the commission, and review of a final agency decision can generally be sought in federal court. The statutes creating and empowering most major agencies provide that actions for review be brought in the United States Court of Appeals.[31]

Most federal agencies write formal opinions to justify or explain their decisions, and these are often published in both official and unofficial sources. Such opinions are very much like those issued by courts, both in form and method of publication. An agency decision can be an important document in interpreting a regulation or statute, or in applying regulations to particular facts. Although most agencies do not consider themselves strictly bound by their prior decisions under the doctrine of *stare decisis*, the decisions do have considerable precedential value for attorneys practicing before an agency or appealing an agency decision. Whenever you are working in an area within the cognizance of a federal agency, that agency's decisions are an important primary legal source.

1. Official Reports

Over two dozen federal agencies, including all the major regulatory commissions, publish official reports of their decisions, in a form very similar to official court reports. Most decisions are first published in various preliminary forms such as Internet releases, printed slip decisions, and advance pamphlets. Usually these are cumulated after a considerable time lag into permanent bound volumes in numbered series. As time passes, agencies are producing official documents in Internet, microform or compact disk formats as well as paper. There is great variation.

When official reports are published, they almost always contain tables of cases and other aids to provide access to their contents. Some contain tables of statutes or regulations cited, and most have indexes of some sort, although their quality and depth vary widely. *Federal Trade*

---

31   The model for these provisions is the Federal Trade Commission Act of 1914, ch. 311, §5, 38 Stat. 717, 720 [current version at 15 U.S.C. §45(c) (2000)].

Commission Reports has a very brief index in each volume, while *Decisions of the Employees' Compensation Appeals Board* has an extensive digest with lengthy descriptive entries. Just as lawyers in each state must familiarize themselves with the resources of their jurisdiction, those practicing before a particular agency need to learn the resources it offers.

2. Unofficial Sources

An increasing number of agency decisions are available online from agency websites[32] and in WESTLAW and LEXIS. Recent decisions of most major regulatory commissions are included in topical databases. This is the most centralized place to find administrative decisions. New agencies are continually being added to the systems, and older materials to existing databases. When beginning research in a specialized area, it is often worthwhile to determine whether there is a suitable topical database or library and, if so, to learn about its contents. Illustration K shows a menu page from WESTLAW, introducing the user to resources available in Environmental law. LEXIS has similar topical screens of available resources.

In addition to the various official reports, the decisions of many agencies are also published commercially, either in looseleaf services or in numbered series of bound volumes. Looseleaf editions have several advantages over the official reports. They are issued much more quickly, are better indexed, and are often supplemented by editorial discussion or integrated into other relevant source materials. A more extensive discussion of looseleafs is contained in Chapter 10.

---

32   An extensive list of agency decisions that can be found on the Internet is maintained by the University of Virginia:
<http://www.lib.virginia.edu/govdocs/fed_decisions_agency.html>.

Illustration K
Page from a WESTLAW Menu Screen

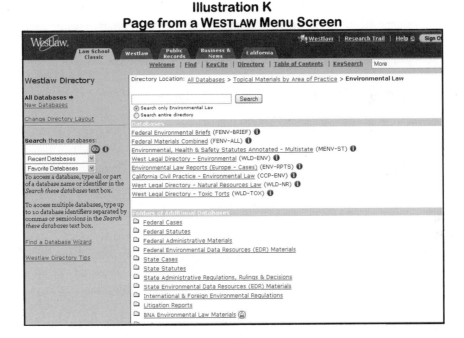

3. Finding Agency Decisions

One doing research that touches on the decisions of federal administrative agencies should either possess expertise in the area or at least understand its context. Each agency is a whole new story, and it is often a complicated one. The best bet is a looseleaf service. Most administrative subject areas are covered by a looseleaf service or text that helps define and sort information. The topical databases on LEXIS and WESTLAW are helpful since they pull together administrative cases, rules and documents. But you need to know the ropes. Talk to a senior lawyer or a librarian to get a feel for how the information in a specific topic area is used.

Some administrative decisions can be found by using standard legal research tools. Citators include agency citations of federal court cases. A researcher who has found a relevant Court of Appeals case, for example, can use *Shepard's* or *KeyCite* online, or *Shepard's Federal Energy Law Citations* to find citations to it in *F.E.R.C. Reports* and *N.R.C. Issuances*. The citators do *not* include agency citations of statutory provisions, but *United States Code Service* includes administrative decisions among its case annotations.   Illustration L shows a page of *USCS* with numerous annotations from *Agriculture Decisions.*   Finally, scholarly secondary sources such as law review articles will frequently combine discussion of agency and court decisions, providing both citations and commentary.

4. Updating and Verifying Agency Decisions

Precedent may not have a determinative role in administrative adjudication, but it is always important to know if a decision has been overturned in judicial review or disapproved by a later agency decision. Although methods of finding agency decisions are not as standard and readily accessible as case-finding methods, updating techniques are becoming increasingly uniform.

Most major agencies receive coverage online in *KeyCite, Shepard's* online or in one of *Shepard's* specialized citators or in *Shepard's United States Administrative Citations,* which consists of a compilation of citations to decisions and orders of a dozen federal administrative departments, courts, boards and commissions.   The citators will indicate when decisions of agencies such as the Federal Communications Commission or the Interstate Commerce Commission have been cited in later agency reports, in federal court opinions, and in selected law reviews.   Signal references indicate the precedential effect of later agency and court decisions.   In addition, there will be cross-references between several series of official agency reports and commercial looseleaf services.   Parallel citations for FCC decisions, for example, are provided in *Public Utilities Reports* and *Radio Regulation.*

For some agencies there are other tools besides *KeyCite* or *Shepard's* for updating and verifying decisions. *Decisions and Orders of the National Labor Relations Board* and several Internal Revenue Service publications are covered by Auto-Cite, a alternative citation verification system available through LEXIS which will cost you less than a *Shepard's* search. Selected other administrative decisions are also included, if they are published in one of the several looseleaf reporters within Auto-Cite's coverage.   One can use Auto-Cite to verify a Federal Trade Commission decision, for example, only if it is published in the CCH *Trade Cases.*

Illustration L
A *USCS* page, including annotations of administrative decisions

AGRICULTURAL ADJUSTMENT   7 USCS § 608c, n 11.5

INTERPRETIVE NOTES AND DECISIONS

11.5. Miscellaneous

I. IN GENERAL; ISSUANCE OF ORDERS

1. Constitutionality

In conducting referendum to determine whether or not to continue certain marketing orders imposed on orange producers, provision of Agriculture Marketing Agreement Act of 1937 (7 USCS § 608c) that requires Secretary of Agriculture to consider vote of producer-cooperative association as representing votes of all of association's member producers did not violate Constitutional free speech rights of plaintiff orange producers. Harris Farms v United States Dep't of Agriculture'ricultural Mktg. Serv. (1993, CA9 Cal) 10 F3d 616, 93 CDOS 8584, 93 Daily Journal DAR 14782.

Excessive Fines Clause of Eighth Amendment applies to civil penalties set forth in Agricultural Marketing Agreement Act of 1937 (7 USCS § 608c(14)(B)). Saulsbury Enterprises v USDA (1999, ED Cal) 58 Ag Dec 19.

Department of Agriculture's almond marketing program that was promulgated pursuant to almond marketing order violated almond handlers' First Amendment rights, since creditable advertising regulations were more extensive than necessary to serve interest of increasing almond sales. Cal-Almond, Inc. v U.S. Department of Agriculture (CA9, 1993) 52 Ag Dec 831.

Almond Order requirement that almond handlers pay assessments for advertising does not violate handlers' First Amendment right to freedom of speech. In re Cal-Almond (1998) 57 Ag Dec 24.

5. Notice and hearing on proposed order [7 USCS § 608c(3)]

Claim of orange handler challenging validity of marketing orders governing California navel and Valencia oranges is partially granted summarily, where amended marketing orders issued by Secretary of Agriculture were invalid because Secretary failed to comply with provisions of Administrative Procedures Act (APA), pre-amendment marketing orders could not be reinstated without Secretary's compliance with Court of Appeals decision directing Secretary to address his 1984 tendency finding in compliance with notice and comment provisions of APA. United States v Sunny Cove Citrus Ass'n (1994, ED Cal) 854 F Supp 669, 94 Daily Journal DAR 13092.

Secretary cannot hold hearing on amendment unless Secretary has reason to believe that amendment will tend to effectuate declared policy of Act (7 USCS § 608c(3), (17)); cannot issue amendment to order without finding, set forth in amendment, that issuance of amendment will tend to effectuate declared policy of Act (7 USCS § 608c(4), (17)), and cannot issue amendment to order without determining that it is approved by requisite number of producers (7 USCS § 608c(9), (17)); thus, before Secretary submits proposed amendment to producers to determine their approval or disapproval, Secretary is required to find that proposed amendment tends to effectuate declared policy of Act. In re Stark Packing Company (1992) 51 Ag Dec 993.

6. Findings and issuance of order [7 USCS § 608c(4)]

Secretary cannot hold hearing on amendment unless Secretary has reason to believe that amendment will tend to effectuate declared policy of Act (7 USCS § 608c(3), (17)), cannot issue amendment to order

without finding, set forth in amendment, that issuance of amendment will tend to effectuate declared policy of Act (7 USCS § 608c(4), (17)), and cannot issue amendment to order without determining that it is approved by requisite number of producers (7 USCS § 608c(9), (17)); thus, before Secretary submits proposed amendment to producers to determine their approval or disapproval, Secretary is required to find that proposed amendment tends to effectuate declared policy of Act. In re Stark Packing Company (1992) 51 Ag Dec 993.

7. Termination and suspension of orders [7 USCS § 608c(16)]

Act requires public access to list of those eligible to vote in referendum on continuation of marketing order. Cal-Almond, Inc. v United States Dept. of Agriculture (1992, CA9 Cal) 960 F2d 105, 92 CDOS 2654, 92 Daily Journal DAR 4221.

Formal, on-the-record rulemaking hearing pursuant to 7 USCS § 608c(18) was not required with respect to Secretary's order terminating base-excess plan of milk marketing order regulating handling of milk in central Arkansas, since termination order, which was executed pursuant to 7 USCS § 608c(16)(A), did not amend or fix minimum prices to be paid by handlers. Arkansas Dairy Cooperative Assn. y Espy (1994, DC Ark) 53 Ag Dec 1012.

8. Amendments of orders [7 USCS § 608c(17)]

Secretary cannot hold hearing on amendment unless Secretary has reason to believe that amendment will tend to effectuate declared policy of Act (7 USCS § 608c(3), (17)), cannot issue amendment to order without finding, set forth in amendment, that issuance of amendment will tend to effectuate declared policy of Act (7 USCS § 608c(4), (17)), and cannot issue amendment to order without determining that it is approved by requisite number of producers (7 USCS § 608c(9), (17)); thus, before Secretary submits proposed amendment to producers to determine their approval or disapproval, Secretary is required to find that proposed amendment tends to effectuate declared policy of Act. In re Stark Packing Company (1992) 51 Ag Dec 993.

Hearing requirement in 7 USCS § 608c(17) is not constitutional requirement, and Congress may amend such statutory hearing requirement or exempt Secretary of Agriculture from hearing requirement at any time. In re Lamers Dairy, Inc. (2001) 60 Ag Dec 406.

11.5. Miscellaneous

Small Business Regulatory Enforcement Fairness Act of 1996 (SBREFA) (Act March 29, 1996, P.L. 104-121, Title II, 110 Stat. 857, which appears as 5 USCS § 601 note) does not apply to actions brought under Agricultural Marketing Agreement Act of 1937 (7 USCS § 608c), since SBREFA does not contain any indication that its substantive provisions were directed at administrative agencies acting in their adjudicative capacity; instead, Congress intended that agencies comply with SBREFA when engaging in rulemaking. Balice v U.S. Department of Agriculture (1998, ED Cal) 57 Ag Dec 841.

Creditable advertising regulations contained at 7 CFR § 981.444 (promulgated pursuant to § 608c(6)(I) and which deal with crediting for marketing promotion including paid advertising) do not directly conflict with prohibition on regulation of advertising set forth in § 608c(10). Cal-Almond, Inc. v U. S. Department of Agriculture (1992) 51 Ag Dec 79.

13

It is important to keep in mind when working with administrative materials, whether decisions or regulations, that agency actions are reviewable by the courts. Judicial decisions may set standards and determine limitations on administrative action. Many of the most important procedural safeguards of agency rulemaking and adjudication have resulted from decisions of the Supreme Court and the U.S. Courts of Appeals. Methods of access and updating discussed in this chapter focus specifically on the regulations and decisions of the agencies themselves, but should not be used to the exclusion of case-finding techniques discussed in earlier chapters. Substantive and procedural areas can be researched through digests or *ALR* annotations, and case databases on LEXIS or WESTLAW can be searched for references to a specific administrative regulation or decision.

E. PRESIDENTIAL DOCUMENTS

Thus far we have discussed the regulations and decisions of administrative agencies, which are part of the executive branch of the federal government and operate under the supervision of the President. In addition, the President has the power to veto legislation passed by Congress and the duty to enforce enacted laws. The President also has a wide-ranging lawmaking authority in his or her own right, as the nation's agent of foreign relations and its military commander. In fulfilling these roles and functions, the President issues executive orders, proclamations, and other documents of legal effect.

1. Executive Orders and Proclamations

Two basic forms of executive fiat are used to perform presidential functions pursuant to statutory authority or inherent powers. These are *executive orders* and *proclamations.* Proclamations are general announcements of policy issued to the nation as a whole, and are commonly associated with ceremonial occasions such as observance of National Safe Boating Week, 2003,[33] or Lief Erikson Day, 2003.[34] A few substantive

---

33   Proclamation No. 7677, 3 C.F.R. 66 (2004).

34   Proclamation No. 7718, 3 C.F.R. 122 (2004).

proclamations deal with trade policy or tariff issues. Executive orders cover a wide range of issues and are generally issued to government officials. The two types of document have substantially the same legal effect.[35]

Executive orders and proclamations are effective upon publication in the *Federal Register*. The Office of the Federal Register assigns a number to each, in separate series for orders and proclamations. This number is the official and permanent means of identifying the document. Presidential documents are the first items appearing in each *Federal Register* issue, in a larger typeface and more legible format than any of the other material. Their titles are listed under the alphabetical heading "Presidential Documents" in the table of contents and in the monthly indexes, and their numbers are listed in the tables of *CFR* parts affected in the particular issue and for the month. They are also listed by number in the monthly pamphlet *LSA: List of CFR Sections Affected.*

At the end of each year executive orders and proclamations are compiled and published in Title 3 of the *Code of Federal Regulations,* which becomes the standard source for these documents. Because each annual edition of Title 3 is a unique set of documents rather than an updated codification, older volumes remain part of the current *CFR* set. Documents from the years 1936 to 1975 have been recompiled into multiyear hardcover editions.[36]

All executive orders and proclamations published in the *Federal Register* are also published in the *U.S. Code Congressional and Administrative News* and *USCS Advance*. *USCCAN* bound volumes have reprinted all orders and proclamations since 1943. In both monthly pamphlets and bound volumes of *USCCAN,* Table 7 lists proclamations and Table 8 executive orders, and the index lists documents both by subject and under the headings "executive orders" and "proclamations."

---

35   For an historical overview of the development of the use of these presidential documents, *see* House Committee on Government Operations, 85th Cong., 1st Sess., *Executive Orders and Proclamations: A Study of a Use of Presidential Powers* (Comm. Print 1957).

36   There is also a two-volume set, *Proclamations and Executive Orders: Herbert Hoover, March 4, 1929 to March 4, 1933,* compiling pre-*Federal Register* documents for one president.

Proclamations back to 1846, but *not* executive orders, are printed in *Statutes at Large.* Some proclamations and orders issued under the specific authority of a statute are also published in the *United States Code* (and its annotated editions, *USCA* and *USCS*), following the text of the authorizing section.

Proclamations and executive orders are also available on LEXIS, WESTLAW and GPO Access.[37] LEXIS has all presidential documents since January 20, 1981, WESTLAW has executive orders dating back to 1936 and other presidential documents since 1984, and GPO Access has from 1995 forward.

The Office of the Federal Register publishes a useful volume, *Codification of Presidential Proclamations and Executive Orders,* which arranges proclamations and orders by subject in fifty titles similar to those in *CFR.* It contains executive orders and proclamations of general applicability and continuing effect issued from January 20, 1961 to January 20, 1989, with amendments incorporated into the texts of documents. Orders and proclamations are printed in numerical order within each of the fifty titles. The volume also includes valuable disposition tables, listing all proclamations and orders issued from 1961 to 1985 and indicating their current status. Amendments and revocations are listed, as well as the title and page locations of documents included in the codification.

Judicial and law review citations to proclamations and executive orders are included in the coverage of *Shepard's,* but not *KeyCite* at this time. Presidential documents receive treatment similar to regulations, with symbols indicating the effect of court decisions on the documents' validity.

2. Other Presidential Documents

While executive orders and proclamations are the most usual forms of presidential documents, the President does issue a variety of other documents of legal effect. The President issues administrative orders, transmits messages to Congress, and makes executive agreements with other

---

37   These documents are available through the Federal Register, and are most easily searched from the advanced search page: <http://www.gpoaccess.gov/fr/advanced.html>.

countries. While these documents may be less common than executive orders and proclamations, some familiarity with them is often necessary.

Administrative orders: A variety of other documents are printed in the *Federal Register* along with executive orders and proclamations, but not included in either numbered series. These documents, such as memoranda, notices, letters, and presidential determinations, are treated similarly to orders and proclamations. They are included in the table of contents and indexes under "Presidential documents," and are cited by date under Title 3 in the lists of *CFR* parts affected and in *LSA*. They are also reprinted in the annual cumulation of 3 *CFR* in a separate section following executive orders. Table 3 in each annual volume lists these documents by date. Unlike proclamations and executive orders, however, they are generally not reprinted in *USCCAN,* and because there is no standardized numbering system they are not covered in *Shepard's* or *KeyCite* citators.

Reorganization plans: A reorganization plan consists of a presidential proposal for changes in the form of agencies, and can abolish or transfer agency functions. Until recently a plan became law automatically unless either chamber of Congress passed a resolution disapproving it, and so was a powerful means of executive action. In 1983, however, the Supreme Court found such one-house legislative vetoes to be unconstitutional,[38] and a reorganization plan must now be approved by both houses of Congress to take effect.[39] Perhaps because it is no longer as efficient a device, the reorganization plan has fallen into disuse.

Reorganization plans are designated by year and plan number within that year, and published in several places. Upon taking effect they appear in the *Federal Register,* in Title 3 of *CFR,* in the *Statutes at Large,* and unofficially in *USCCAN.*[40] They are also published in Title 5 of the *United States Code,* following the particular Reorganization Act under which they were authorized. *USCA* and *USCS* include notes, presidential messages, and

---

38   *Immigration and Naturalization Service v. Chadha,* 462 U.S. 919 (1983).

39   Reorganization Act Amendments of 1984, 5 U.S.C. §906 (1988).

40   When submitted to Congress, reorganization plans are printed in the *Congressional Record* and in the House and Senate documents series. These are the best sources for plans that have not passed Congress.

executive orders relating to the plans, and are therefore often the most useful research sources. Reorganization plans, like proclamations and executive orders, can be traced in *Shepard's* online, and in *Shepard's Code of Federal Regulations Citations.* They can also be traced in *Shepard's United States Citations* under their *Statutes at Large* or *U.S. Code* citations.

Messages to Congress: Communications to Congress by the President are typically made in the form of presidential messages. They may propose new legislation, explain vetoes, transmit reports or other documents, or convey information about the state of national affairs or some matter of concern. Most messages are printed as Congressional documents. They are also printed and indexed in the *Congressional Record* and in the House and Senate journals. A few important ones appear in *USCCAN.* These documents have some value in developing legislative histories of particular statutes.

Presidential statements upon signing legislation into law may also have some relevance in legislative history research. These signing statements, which since 1986 are printed in *USCCAN,* are discussed in Chapter 6, Legislative History.

Executive agreements: The President makes executive agreements with other countries, under the authority to conduct foreign affairs. Unlike treaties, they do not require the advice and consent of the Senate. In recent years, more and more diplomatic arrangements have been made through these convenient methods. Because their purposes and publication methods are basically the same as treaties, the two forms of international agreements are discussed in detail in *How to Find the Law*.

3. Compilations of Presidential Papers

The most comprehensive source for current presidential documents is the *Weekly Compilation of Presidential Documents,* which has been published by the Office of the Federal Register since 1965.[41] The *Weekly Compilation* includes nominations, announcements, and transcripts of

---

41   Available on GPO Access from 1993 to present: <http://www.gpoaccess.gov/wcomp/index.html>.

speeches and press conferences, as well as orders, proclamations, and other legally significant documents. Each weekly issue contains an index to all material in the current quarter, and there are cumulated annual indexes.

An annual volume, *Public Papers of the President,*[42] has since the beginning of the Carter presidency cumulated all material in the *Weekly Compilation* in a final, bound format. Earlier, somewhat more selective *Public Papers* volumes have been published for Presidents Hoover, Truman, Eisenhower, Kennedy, Johnson, Nixon, and Ford.[43] The official set contains only annual indexes, but the commercially published *Cumulated Indexes to the Public Papers of the Presidents of the United States* (K.T.O. Press, 1977-79; Kraus International, since 1979) provides single-volume coverage of each administration.

The papers of earlier presidents are available in various forms. Congress created a Joint Committee on Printing in 1895,[44] and one of its first projects was a comprehensive collection of presidential papers. The resulting ten-volume set, *A Compilation of the Messages and Papers of the Presidents, 1789-1897,* was edited by James D. Richardson and published in 1896-97. The Bureau of National Literature and Art reissued the set in numerous later editions, supplementing it into the 1920's.

F. UNPUBLISHED INFORMATION

While the focus of this book is material that is generally published or available, the government has a vast store of additional documentation that it does not publish, such as internal records, data collected on

---

42   Available on GPO Access from 1992 to present: <http://www.gpoaccess.gov/pubpapers/index.html>.

43   While Franklin D. Roosevelt's papers have not been included in the official series, they have been edited by S.I. Rosenman and commercially published as *The Public Papers and Addresses of Franklin D. Roosevelt,* (Random House, 13 vols., 1938–50).

44   Act of January 12, 1895, ch. 23, 28 Stat. 601.

individuals, and staff studies. The Freedom of Information Act[45] and the Privacy Act[46] have dramatically expanded access to government files. Although government resistance to applications and suits under the acts has increased since their passage, these laws have been quite effective in opening new areas of fact-finding for those involved in legal research.

Several books explain the procedures for gaining access to government records under these laws. They discuss the history and interpretation of the acts, explain procedures for filing requests and suing to compel disclosure, and provide the citations of relevant regulations and sample forms. Among these are:

J.D. Franklin & R.F. Bouchard, *Guidebook to the Freedom of Information and Privacy Acts,* 2nd ed. (Clark Boardman, 2 vols., 1987-date).

Freedom of Information Act Guide and Privacy Act Overview (Government Printing Office 2000).

J.T. O'Reilly, *Federal Information Disclosure: Procedures, Forms and the Law* 2nd Edition (Shepard's/McGraw-Hill, 2 vols., 1990-date).

A concise handbook on the acts is *A Citizen's Guide on Using the Freedom of Information Act and the Privacy Act of 1974 to Request Government Records,* H.R.Rep. No. 172, 108th Cong., 1st Sess. (2003). The guide includes sample request forms.

G. STATE ADMINISTRATIVE MATERIALS

State administrative publications receive only brief treatment in this chapter for two reasons. First, because the availability of these materials varies widely from state to state, any discussion must necessarily be quite general. Second, state administrative documents tend to emulate the patterns

---

45   5 U.S.C. §552 (2000).

46   5 U.S.C. §552a (2000).

of federal administrative publication, so a person familiar with federal research can usually adapt readily to a particular state's materials.

The regulatory bodies of the various states affect their citizens no less profoundly than the federal bureaucracy. State agencies set and enforce public health and housing standards, fix and regulate utility rates and practices, govern labor and business activities, and perform many other functions. Unfortunately problems of access and control are not always met with sufficient resources or interest to make administrative materials regularly available.

Many states have administrative codes and registers similar to the *CFR* and *Federal Register,* but some states publish neither. Some states publish decisions of selected agencies, or issue other documents of legal significance. A large part of the process of doing state administrative research is determining just what publications exist for a particular state. One place to learn about the situation in individual states is a state-specific legal research guide. Appendix B, at the end of this volume, lists available guides.

For a survey of the officers, agencies, functions, practices and statistics in all the states, *The Book of the States* (Council of State Governments, biennial) is very helpful. A thorough reference tool on state governmental operations, it includes legal, political and statistical information from every state. The *Municipal Year Book* (International City Management Association, annual) performs a similar function for governments on a local level.

Names and addresses of state administrative personnel are available in the *Municipal Yellow Book* (Monitor Publishing Co., biannual) or *State Administrative Officials Classed by Function* (Council of State Governments, annual).

1. Regulations

The availability of state rules and regulations has improved considerably in recent years. In 1965 only fourteen states published administrative codes.[47] Over forty states and territories and the District of Columbia now publish subject compilations of administrative regulations, more or less resembling *CFR*.[48] Many of these are issued in a looseleaf format with periodic updating. Some of these codes are very easily accessible, but the arrangement and indexing of others can be cumbersome and confusing even to experienced users.

In California a private publisher, Barclays, purchased the rights to the administrative code. The company cleaned up what had been a grossly messy administrative code. They provided a good index, and make most of the code available online.[49] Using on-demand printing technology, they supply subscribers with whatever parts of the code they wish to purchase. This wonderful streamlining came at a cost to consumers, as the code went from relatively inexpensive to being fairly costly. Most judge the trade to be a fair one. Barclay's and other companies are now trying to get rights to the codes in other states. As they do, one can expect to see improved information at a higher cost. This process of privatizing state information represents a trend.

WESTLAW and LEXIS each contain the text of over forty state administrative codes. State administrative websites might also have texts available. Specific agencies may have their own regulations on the Internet, even if the whole of the regulatory code does not appear online.

---

47   Cohen, "Publication of State Administrative Regulations-Reform in Slow Motion," 14 *Buffalo L.Rev.* 410, 421 (1965).

48   Like the *CFR*, these codes can be highly detailed. California's regulations include a Board of Corrections recipe for a "disciplinary isolation diet," that may be served to inmates. *Cal. Code Regs.* tit. 15, §1247 (2001).

49   The state of California did not sell the whole administrative code to Barclay's. Certain parts were sold separately to other publishers, including the fire, electrical, plumbing, energy, building, mechanical, and building standards codes. It was thought these particular codes would sell well and therefore be highly profitable. These codes are neither included in *Barclay's Official California California Code of Regulations*, nor are they available online.

2. Decisions

Some state agencies publish official reports of their decisions, similar to those of federal bodies. The most common are the reports of state tax commissioners, public utility commissions, banking commissions, insurance commissions, and labor agencies. Advance sheets are quite rare, although some agencies issue their decisions *only* in separate slip form. Occasionally state administrative decisions may be found in specialized subject reporters and looseleaf services, and a growing number of state agency decisions are included on WESTLAW and LEXIS.

State attorney general opinions are often an important resource in interpreting and applying statutory provisions. These opinions are similar in form and purpose to those of the United States Attorney General, but in most states they are used much more frequently.[50] They are typically published in annual or biennial volumes by the state (with a considerable time lag), and are also available currently on microfiche from Hein. For several states, *Shepard's* and *KeyCite* citators include attorney general opinions as citing material, so one can find opinions discussing particular cases or statutes. Many of the annotated state codes also include references to relevant opinions. Both LEXIS and WESTLAW have databases containing state attorney general opinions, with coverage in most states beginning in 1977.

3. Other Documents

Like the federal government, state governments publish a variety of documents such as reports, studies, and periodicals. A few states issue periodic lists of recent publications, and some issue annual catalogs. The most complete source for all states is the *Monthly Checklist of State Publications,* which was published between 1910-1994. Publications are listed by state and indexed by subject.

---

50   State attorney general practices are surveyed in Heiser, "The Opinion Writing Function of Attorneys General," 18 *Idaho L.Rev.* 9 (1982).

H. SUMMARY

The development of administrative agencies on both federal and state levels has added a massive literature of administrative regulations and decisions to the essential resources of legal research. With the growth of the executive branch generally, the legal documentation flowing from the exercise of Presidential powers has further enlarged the range of these materials. The increased sophistication of indexing and access aids in the *Federal Register* and the *Code of Federal Regulations,* commercial publication of administrative documents such as looseleaf services, and online access through WESTLAW and LEXIS have made these materials easily available to the researcher. Even state regulations and decisions are now more accessible through the proliferation of state administrative codes and registers, and their partial coverage in looseleafs and databases. What had been a wilderness of confusion and frustration has blossomed into a fertile field for the astute researcher.

I. ADDITIONAL READING

Alfred C. Aman, Jr. and William T. Mayton, *Administrative Law* (2nd ed. 2001). This is the Horn Book on administrative law.

Scott Larson, "Federal Environmental Administrative Law Pathfinder," 22 *Legal Reference Serv.Q.* 19 (2003).

Richard J. Pierce and Kenneth Culp Davis, *Administrative Law Treatise* (4th ed. 2002). A three volume set updated by supplements.

Cheryl Rae Nyberg, *State Administrative Law Bibliography: Print and Electronic Sources* (Twin Falls, Idaho: Carol Boast and Cheryl Rae Nyberg 2000).

Selected Federal and State Administrative and Regulatory Laws (William F. Funk et al. eds., 2002).

Kenneth F. Warren, *Administrative Law in the Political System* (4th ed. 2004).

Chapter 9

COURT RULES AND PRACTICE

A. INTRODUCTION

While much of legal literature focuses on substantive rights, an equally important aspect of the law deals with the processes under which parties come before courts to settle disputes. These processes are the focus of law school classes on civil procedure and of the burgeoning body of material on court rules and practice. Neither substance nor procedure would serve much purpose without the other. As Roscoe Pound succinctly explained: "Procedure is the means; full, equal and exact enforcement of substantive law is the end."[1]

For centuries the rules governing court proceedings were developed piecemeal through case law, eventually creating the arcane and formalistic pleading rituals of the Court of Chancery in Dickens' *Bleak House*. Reforms within the past century have considerably changed court procedures, making them simpler and more flexible.[2] In any area of thought shaped by lawyers and judges, however, there are bound to be unforeseen complexities and differences of interpretation. Rules that may appear straightforward must be applied in light of the large body of case law that has developed. An extensive secondary literature also exists to guide litigants through the intricate maze of court proceedings, and form books provide the proper format for pleadings and other court documents. This chapter surveys the sources available for finding the texts of court rules and the judicial and secondary reference materials that can aid one's passage through the courts. Much of this chapter is devoted to sets that generally play little role in the law school curriculum, though they may shed light on courses like Civil Procedure. But these tools are the bread and butter of anyone who works in the area of litigation.

---

[1]   Roscoe Pound, "The Etiquette of Justice," 3 *Proc. Neb. St. B.A.* 231, 231 (1909).

[2]   "The practically universal trend of reform has been in favor of less binding and strict rules of form enforced upon the litigants and their counsel and with a large measure of discretion accorded to the trial judge in directing the course of a particular lawsuit." Charles E. Clark, "The Handmaid of Justice," 23 *Wash. U. L.Q.* 297, 308 (1938).

B. COURT RULES

Court rules regulate the conduct of business before the courts. They range from purely formal details, such as the format to be followed in preparing a brief, to matters of substantial importance, such as grounds for appeal, time limitations, and the types of motions and appeals which will be heard. Court rules may specify or limit available remedies, and may thus affect rights in significant ways.

Each jurisdiction has its own requirements and procedures for the promulgation of court rules. Some involve action by special conferences of judges; others require action or approval by the highest court of the jurisdiction. Some court rules are statutory and are created by legislatures, while some require a combination of judicial action and legislative approval. While courts are traditionally considered to have inherent power to control the conduct of their affairs, court rules are generally promulgated under authority granted by the legislature and are considered a form of delegated legislation.

Federal procedure is discussed here first for two reasons. Not only does it affect more people than the procedure of any individual state, but its forms and methods of publication have been very influential on the states. An increasing number of states have chosen to model their procedural rules on those established for the federal courts in the past half-century.

1. Federal Rules

Since its first session, Congress has expressly given the federal courts power to make rules governing their procedures.[3] It took until well into the twentieth century, however, for the Supreme Court to promulgate extensive general rules of procedure for the federal courts. The Federal Rules of Civil Procedure, adopted by the Supreme Court in December 1937

---

3   Section 17 of the Judiciary Act of 1789 gave the new federal courts the power "to make and establish all necessary rules for the orderly conducting [of] business in the said courts, provided such rules are not repugnant to the laws of the United States." Ch. 20, §17, 1 Stat. 73, 83. The Supreme Court's first rules, at its first meeting in February 1790, dealt mostly with qualification of attorneys who wished to practice before it. Appointment of Justices 2 U.S. (2 Dall.) 399 (1790). A rule five years later ordered that "the Gentlemen of the Bar be notified, that the Court will hereafter expect to be furnished with a statement of the material points of the Case, from the Counsel on each side of a Cause." 3 U.S. (3 Dall.) 120 (1795).

and effective September 16, 1938,[4] successfully modernized federal civil practice. The Federal Rules of Criminal Procedure followed on March 21, 1946.[5]

The new criminal rules governed proceedings both before and after trial, but appeals in civil cases continued to be handled differently in each circuit. In 1966, Congress empowered the Supreme Court to prescribe rules for the Courts of Appeals in civil actions.[6] The Federal Rules of Appellate Procedure, governing both civil and criminal proceedings, took effect on July 1, 1968.[7]

The last of the four major sets of rules governing federal court proceedings had a rather different origin. In 1972, the Supreme Court submitted proposed Federal Rules of Evidence to Congress, which passed a law preventing them from taking effect until expressly approved.[8] One problem was that the proposed rules covering evidentiary privileges were seen as substantive rather than procedural in nature, and thus outside the scope of the Court's rulemaking authority.[9] Congress adopted its own amended version of the rules, which became law on July 1, 1975.[10]

---

4   308 U.S. 645 (1938). The Supreme Court acted under a 1934 Act of Congress that had given it the authority to combine equity and law into one federal civil procedure, and to make and publish rules governing federal actions. Act of June 19, 1934, ch. 651, 48 Stat. 1064. Previously, the Supreme Court had promulgated its first set of procedural rules in equity in 1822, 20 U.S. (7 Wheat.) (1822), but had not issued general rules for actions at law.

5   327 U.S. 821 (1946). Congress had given the Supreme Court authority to promulgate rules governing criminal appeals in 1933, Act of Feb. 24, 1933, ch. 119, 47 Stat. 904, as amended by Act of Mar. 8, 1934, ch. 49, 48 Stat. 399; in 1940 it passed a law providing for rules with respect to criminal trial court proceedings, Act of June 29, 1940, ch. 445, 54 Stat. 688.

6   Act of Nov. 6, 1966, Pub. L. No. 89-773, 80 Stat. 1323.

7   389 U.S. 1063 (1968).

8   Act of Mar. 30, 1973, Pub.L. No. 93-12, 87 Stat. 9.

9   The then-governing statutory provision contained the same language as the current provision, 28 U.S.C. §2072 (2000), specifying that rules promulgated by the Supreme Court "shall not abridge, enlarge or modify any substantive right." *See*

In 1988, Congress enacted the Judicial Improvements and Access to Justice Act,[11] and consolidated the Supreme Court's authority to promulgate "general rules of practice and procedure and rules of evidence for cases in the United States district courts (including proceedings before magistrates thereof) and courts of appeal."[12] As a result of this consolidation, scattered sections of the United States Code which previously had given the Court power to prescribe rules of procedure and evidence were repealed.[13] The Court's authority to promulgate rules is now concentrated in Sections 2072-2075 of 28 USC.

In addition to the four major sets of federal rules, the Supreme Court also has issued rules for more limited circumstances. For example, rules governing bankruptcy proceedings were first promulgated under the authority of the Bankruptcy Act of 1898,[14] and have undergone several revisions and changes. The current Federal Rules of Bankruptcy Procedure were promulgated by the Supreme Court in 1983.[15]

An important resource in applying federal court rules is the accompanying commentary by the Advisory Committee that drafted the original rules or a later committee that drafted and proposed an

---

Arthur J. Goldberg, "The Supreme Court, Congress, and Rules of Evidence," 5 *Seton Hall L.Rev.* 667 (1974).

10   Act of Jan. 2, 1975, Pub.L. No. 93-595, §2(a)(1), 88 Stat. 1926, 1948.

11   Act of Nov. 19, 1988, Pub. L. No. 100-702, 102 Stat. 4642 (codified as amended in scattered sections of 28 U.S.C.). The part of the act dealing with court rules (the Rules Enabling Act) can be found at §§ 401-407, 102 Stat. 4648-4652.
12   28 U.S.C. §2072(a) (2000).

13   Before being repealed by the 1988 Act, 28 U.S.C. §2072 had provided for rules of civil procedure; § 2076 had governed rules of evidence; and 18 U.S.C. §§3771-3772 had provided for rules of criminal procedure.

14   Ch. 541, §30, 30 Stat. 544, 554. This section was repealed in 1964, when the Supreme Court's rulemaking power in bankruptcy was brought into conformity with its power to make other court rules. Act of Oct. 3, 1964, Pub.L. No. 88-623, §1, 78 Stat. 1001, 1001 (codified as amended at 28 U.S.C. §2075 (2000)).

15   461 U.S. 977 (1983).

amendment.[16] These notes usually consist of a few paragraphs discussing the history of procedure under prior law and the purpose of the new rule or amendment, and provide a sort of "legislative history" analogous to congressional committee reports. Advisory Committee notes are often an invaluable first step in interpreting rule provisions. In most versions of the major sets of rules, these important notes are printed immediately following the text of each rule.

Finally, in addition to the sets of rules applying to the federal courts in general, there are rules governing proceedings in particular courts. The Supreme Court and specialized courts such as the Claims Court have their own sets of rules, and individual Courts of Appeals and District Courts promulgate supplementary rules for local practice. Any federal court can establish local rules for the conduct of its business, as long as they are not inconsistent with Acts of Congress or rules prescribed by the Supreme Court.[17] These local rules are important.

These various rules governing federal court proceedings are rarely far from hand in any law library. They can be found in online databases and in numerous publications, both unannotated and annotated. The sheer number of resources about to be described may be bewildering at first, but different versions serve different purposes. The proper source to use depends on the research needs in a particular situation. Sometimes you need to consult the text of a set of rules, but often it is necessary to have references to judicial decisions or expert commentary. Table 1 lists the locations of rules in the tools discussed below.

---

16   Under a 1958 Act, a permanent Committee on Rules of Practice and Procedure of the Judicial Conference of the United States studies the federal rules on a continuous basis and recommends changes as necessary. Act of July 11, 1958, Pub. L. No. 85-513, 72 Stat. 356 (codified as amended at 28 U.S.C. §331 (2000).

17   28 U.S.C. §2071 (2000). The Judicial Conference reviews for consistency with federal law rules prescribed under this provision by courts other than the Supreme Court and the district courts, and is empowered to modify or abrogate any rule found to be inconsistent. 28 U.S.C § 331 (2000). The Supreme Court may also exercise its inherent supervisory power to ensure that local rules are consistent with principles of right and justice. *See, e.g., Frazier v. Heebe,* 482 U.S. 641 (1987), *on remand,* 825 F.2d 89 (5th Cir.1987) (prohibiting Eastern District of Louisiana from requiring that a member of its bar live or maintain an office in Louisiana).

a. Unannotated Texts

(1) Major Rules

A variety of resources contain the texts of federal court rules. The *United States Code* publishes both the rules and Advisory Committee notes for the major sets of rules. An appendix to Title 28, Judiciary and Judicial Procedure, contains the Federal Rules of Civil Procedure, Appellate Procedure, and Evidence, as well as rules governing proceedings in the Supreme Court and several specialized courts.[18] The Federal Rules of Criminal Procedure appear in an appendix to Title 18, Crimes and Criminal Procedure. The official *USC,* however, is always at least two or three years out of date when it is published, so it cannot be relied upon for more recent developments or changes.

Several commercially published sources also contain the texts of the major rules, updated on a more timely basis. The text and Advisory Committee notes for all major rules are published annually in the "National Volume" of the *Federal Procedure Rules Service,* with updates provided in a cumulative pocket part issued quarterly. This title is published by Thomson-West.

Two other references include the major federal rules. The "Finding Aids" volume of *Federal Rules Service* contains the Rules of Civil Procedure and Appellate Procedure; the Rules of Evidence can be found in the corresponding volume of *Federal Evidence Rules Service.*[19] The *Cyclopedia of Federal Procedure*, Volume 16A, "Rules," (1995 rev.) contains the text of the major rules, but does not include Advisory Committee notes.

Many law students first encounter the Federal Rules of Civil Procedure in one of several available soft-cover editions that usually contain the other major rules as well. For example, Thomson-West's *Federal Rules of Civil Procedure* (2004-05 Educational Edition) includes the texts of the Rules of Civil Procedure, Appellate Procedure, and Evidence, along with the

---

18   Bankruptcy Rules and Official Forms are in an appendix to Title 11, Bankruptcy.

19   These very useful resources for research on judicial decisions relating to the rules will be discussed below in Section C.

text of Title 28 of the *USC*.[20] Foundation Press publishes a similar volume aimed at law students, the *Cermont's Judicial Code and Rules of Procedure in the Federal Courts*, which includes the Rules of Criminal Procedure.

(2) Local Court Rules

While not as widely applicable as the major sets of rules discussed above, rules for specific federal courts can be just as important in the day-to-day practice of law. For example, the Rules of the United States Supreme Court can be found in the *USC* and several of the other sources discussed above.

The rules of individual lower federal courts are not quite as widely published as rules promulgated by the Supreme Court. The most comprehensive source for all circuit and district court civil practice rules is *Federal Local Court Rules*, a set of updated looseleaf volumes published by Thomson-West. Most of the set consists of rules for individual U.S. District Courts, arranged by state; the last volume includes rules and internal operating procedures for the Courts of Appeals.

The rules of individual courts are also available in several other places. For example, eleven separate "Circuit Volumes," corresponding to the eleven numbered U.S. Courts of Appeals, are published as part of *Federal Procedure Rules Service*. Each volume contains the rules of its circuit and of each district within the circuit. Rules for the District of Columbia Circuit appear in the Third and Fourth Circuit volumes, and Federal Circuit rules are in the Second, Third and Fourth Circuit volumes. The "Rules" volume of the *Cyclopedia of Federal Procedure* also includes rules of the federal circuit, but not district, courts.

The handiest source for rules of the district courts in a particular state, and of the circuit within which that state lies, will frequently be a state court rules pamphlet published by Thomson-West or LexisNexis. These pamphlets, published for over thirty states to accompany annotated state codes, contain rules of both state and federal courts, and will be discussed further in the "state rules" section, below.

---

20   Thomson-West also publishes annually the soft-covered *Federal Civil Judicial Procedure and Rules* and *Federal Criminal Code and Rules*. As the titles indicate, these books contain the texts of relevant statutes as well as numerous sets of court rules.

Table 1 – Published Locations of Various Sets of Federal Court Rules Annotated Editions

	United States Code Annotated (WESTLAW)	*United States Code Service* (LEXIS)	*Supreme Court Digest, L.Ed.* (LEXIS)	*Moore's Rules Pamphlets* (LEXIS)
Federal Rules of Civil Procedure	Title 28 Appendix	Rules volumes	Vol. 18	Vol. 1
Federal Rules of Criminal Procedure	Title 18 Appendix	Rules volumes	Vol. 19	Vol. 3
Federal Rules of Appellate Procedure	Title 28 Appendix	Rules volumes	Vol. 17	Vol. 1 (unannotated)
Federal Rules of Evidence	Title 28 Appendix	Title 28 Appendix	Vol. 20	Vol. 2
Bankruptcy Rules and Official Forms	Title 11 Appendix	Rules volumes	Vol. 17	
Rules of the Supreme Court of the United States	Title 28 Appendix	Rules volumes	Vol. 21	
Rules of the Individual U.S. Courts of Appeals	Title 28 Appendix	Rules volumes	Vol. 21	
Rules for the Trial of Misdemeanors before U.S. Magistrates	Title 18 Appendix	Rules volumes	Vol. 19	

Table 1 – Published Locations of Various Sets of Federal Court Rules Annotated Editions, con't.

	United States Code Annotated (WESTLAW)	United States Code Service (LEXIS)	Supreme Court Digest, L.Ed. (LEXIS)	Moore's Rules Pamphlets (LEXIS)
Rules Governing Sections 2254 and 2255 (habeas corpus) Proceedings	Title 28 following §§ 2254, 2255	Rules volumes	Vol. 22	
Rules of the Judicial Panel on Multidistrict Litigation	Title 28 following § 1407	Rules volumes	Vol. 22	Vol. 1
Rules of the U.S. Claims Court	Title 28 Appendix	Rules volumes	Vol. 22	
Rules of the U.S. Court of International Trade	Title 28 Appendix	Rules volumes	Vol. 22	
Rules of the U.S. Tax Court	Title 26 following §7453	Rules volumes	Vol. 22	
Rules of the U.S. Court of Military Appeals	Title 10 following § 867	Rules volumes	Vol. 22	

**Table 2 – Published Locations of Various Sets
of Federal Court Rules
Unnnotated Editions**

United States Code	Federal Procedure Rules Service	Cyclopedia of Federal Procedure
Title 28 Appendix	National volume	Vol. 16A
Title 18 Appendix	National volume	Vol. 16A
Title 28 Appendix	National volume	Vol. 16A
Title 28 Appendix	National volume	Vol. 16A
Title 11 Appendix		
Title 28 Appendix	National volume	Vol. 16A
	Individual circuit volumes	Vol. 16A
Title 18 Appendix	National volume	Vol. 16A
Following Title 28 §§ 2254, 2255	National volume	Vol. 16A
Following Title 28 § 1407	National volume	
Title 28 Appendix	3d and 4th Circuit volumes	Vol. 16A
Title 28 Appendix	2d Circuit volume	
Title 26 Appendix		
Title 10 Appendix		

b. Annotated Texts

Annotated editions of the federal rules contain not only Advisory Committee comments but headnotes of relevant cases. Both commercially published annotated versions of the U.S. Code provide comprehensive coverage of rules.

The *United States Code Annotated* and *United States Code Service* treat the rules in similar fashion to statutes and provide extensive annotations of relevant decisions. In *USCA,* the eighty-six Federal Rules of Civil Procedure fill ten volumes, and in *USCS* they occupy almost eight volumes. The rules are located in the sets in different places: *USCA* includes the rules at the same place they appear in the *U.S. Code,* following the code titles to which they are most closely related (for example, the Federal Rules of Civil Procedure, Appellate Procedure, and Evidence follow Title 28, Judiciary and Judicial Procedure, while the Federal Rules of Criminal Procedure appear in a volume after Title 18, Crimes and Criminal Procedure). *USCS* publishes several unnumbered "Court Rules" volumes, which are generally shelved at the end of the set. The one exception is the Federal Rules of Evidence;

because they were enacted by Congress, *USCS* prints them as an appendix volume to Title 28. Both *USCA* and *USCS* also include annotated editions of the rules of the Supreme Court, of the thirteen individual circuits, and of specialized federal courts. Like the rest of the sets, the volumes of court rules are updated by annual pocket parts and by interim pamphlets.

As it does with statutes, *USCA* includes extensive cross-references to related material such as other federal rules, the publisher's treatise *Federal Practice and Procedure,* and *West's Federal Forms* (discussed below in Sections D.1 and E, respectively). The notes to each section also provide relevant digest key numbers and *C.J.S.* section numbers. The bulk of each volume consists of case headnotes, arranged by subject after each rule. Illustration A shows the *USCA* version of Federal Rules of Evidence, Rule 802, concerning the admissibility of hearsay.

USCS provides the same rules text and Advisory Committee notes, along with cross-references to other rules and statutes and to its publisher's other works. These references include *Federal Procedure, Lawyers' Edition,* as well as *Am.Jur.2d* and annotations in *ALR* and *U.S. Supreme Court Reports, Lawyers' Edition.* The notes following some rules also include references to other texts and to law review articles. Illustrations B-1 and B-2 show Rule 802 of the Federal Rules of Evidence as it appears in *USCS.*

Federal rules are also available online in both LEXIS and WESTLAW. LEXIS has individual files in its library containing the four major sets of rules (Civil Procedure, Criminal Procedure, Appellate Procedure, and Evidence), as published in *USCS.* Historical notes and Advisory Committee comments are included as well as texts. Also available are the rules for several federal courts, including the U.S. Supreme Court, the U.S. Tax Court, the U.S. Claims Court, and the eleven circuit courts. A group file combines these individual files with other specialized federal rules. WESTLAW's database includes the texts of rules printed in *USCA*, along with annotations. A separate database of federal rules contains the four major sets of rules and the Bankruptcy Rules as they appear in the *USC* or an appendix to the *USC.* WESTLAW also provides numerous specialized sets of rules in their related topical areas.

Illustration A-1
Federal Rules of Evidence, Rule 802, in *USCA*

HEARSAY   **Rule 802**

ARTICLE X. CONTENTS OF WRITINGS, RECORDINGS AND PHOTOGRAPHS

Rule
1001. Definitions.
1002. Requirement of Original.
1003. Admissibility of Duplicates.
1004. Admissibility of Other Evidence of Contents.
1005. Public Records.
1006. Summaries.
1007. Testimony or Written Admission of Party.
1008. Functions of Court and Jury.

ARTICLE XI. MISCELLANEOUS RULES

Rule
1101. Applicability of Rules.
1102. Amendments.
1103. Title.

ARTICLE VIII. HEARSAY

Rules 802 to 807 appear in this Volume

Rule
801. Definitions.
802. Hearsay Rule.
803. Hearsay Exceptions; Availability of Declarant Immaterial.
804. Hearsay Exceptions; Declarant Unavailable.
805. Hearsay Within Hearsay.
806. Attacking and Supporting Credibility of Declarant.
807. Residual Exception.

Rule 802. Hearsay Rule

Hearsay is not admissible except as provided by these rules or by other rules prescribed by the Supreme Court pursuant to statutory authority or by Act of Congress.

(Pub.L. 93–595, § 1, Jan. 2, 1975, 88 Stat. 1939.)

ADVISORY COMMITTEE NOTES

1972 Proposed Rules

The provision excepting from the operation of the rule hearsay which is made admissible by other rules adopted by the Supreme Court or by Act of Congress continues the admissibility thereunder of hearsay which would not qualify under these Evidence Rules. The following examples illustrate the working of the exception:

3

Illustration A-2
Rule 802 in *USCA*, con't.

Rule 802 RULES OF EVIDENCE

Federal Rules of Civil Procedure

Rule 4(g): proof of service by affidavit.

Rule 32: admissibility of depositions.

Rule 43(e): affidavits when motion based on facts not appearing of record.

Rule 56: affidavits in summary judgment proceedings.

Rule 65(b): showing by affidavit for temporary restraining order.

Federal Rules of Criminal Procedure

Rule 4(a): affidavits to show grounds for issuing warrants.

Rule 12(b)(4): affidavits to determine issues of fact in connection with motions.

Acts of Congress

10 U.S.C. § 7730: affidavits of unavailable witnesses in actions for damages caused by vessel in naval service, or towage or salvage of same, when taking of testimony or bringing of action delayed or stayed on security grounds.

29 U.S.C. § 161(4): affidavit as proof of service in NLRB proceedings.

38 U.S.C. § 5206: affidavit as proof of posting notice of sale of unclaimed property by Veterans Administration.

CROSS REFERENCES

Affidavits—
> Motion on facts not appearing of record, see Fed.Rules Civ.Proc. Rule 43, 28 USCA.
> Motions, determination of issues of fact on, see Fed.Rules Cr.Proc. Rule 12, 18 USCA.
> Process, proof of service, see Fed.Rules Civ.proc. Rule 4, 28 USCA.
> Proof of posting notice of sale of unclaimed property by Veterans' Administration, see 38 USCA § 8506.
> Proof of service in National Labor Relations Board proceedings, see 29 USCA § 161.
> Summary judgment proceedings, see Fed.Rules Civ.Proc. Rule 56, 28 USCA.
> Temporary restraining order, see Fed.Rules Civ.Proc. Rule 65, 28 USCA.
> Unavailable witnesses in actions for damages caused by vessel in naval service, or towage or salvage of same, when taking of testimony or bringing of action delayed or stayed on security grounds, see 10 USCA § 7730.
> Warrants, issuance upon showing grounds, see Fed.Rules Cr.Proc. Rule 4, 18 USCA.
Depositions, admissibility of in court proceedings, see Fed.Rules Civ.Proc. Rule 32, 28 USCA.

AMERICAN LAW REPORTS

Admissibility, as against hearsay objection, of report of tests or experiments carried out by independent third party. 19 ALR3d 1008.

Admissibility in evidence of sound recording as affected by hearsay and best evidence rules. 58 ALR3d 598.

Admissibility of tape recording or transcript of "911" emergency telephone call. 3 ALR5th 784.

Consideration, in determining facts, of inadmissible hearsay evidence introduced without objection. 79 ALR2d 890.

Written recitals or statements as within rule excluding hearsay. 10 ALR2d 1035.

Admissibility of statement under Rule 801(d)(2)(B) of Federal Rules of Evidence, providing that statement is not hearsay if party-opponent has manifested his adoption or belief in its truth. 48 ALR Fed 721.

Exception to hearsay rule, under Rule 803(3) of Federal Rules of Evidence, with respect to statement of declarant's mental, emotional, or physical condition. 75 ALR Fed 170.

Treatises, periodicals, or pamphlets as exception to hearsay rule under Rule 803 (18) of the Federal Rules of Evidence. 64 ALR Fed 971.

What information is of type "reasonably relied upon by experts" within Rule 703, Federal Rules of Evidence, permitting expert opinion based on information not admissible in evidence. 49 ALR Fed 363.

4

Illustration B-1
Rule 802 in *USCS*

HEARSAY   **Rule 802**

In prosecution for conspiracy to commit bribery in regard to illegal issuance of Section 8 housing subsidies, there was independent evidence of defendant's and declarant's participation in conspiracy so as to support introduction of coconspirator's statements against defendant under coconspirator exception to hearsay rule. United States v Gatling (1996, App DC) 321 US App DC 63, 96 F3d 1511, 45 Fed Rules Evid Serv 1041.

In action for damages due to rape in prison infirmary, plaintiff's letter written to defendant warden a few days after incident would be admitted under Rule 801(d)(1)(B) as prior consistent statement to rebut implied accusation by defendants that plaintiff fabricated story of rape since he did not report rape immediately to authorities. Redmond v Baxley (1979, ED Mich) 475 F Supp 1111, 5 Fed Rules Evid Serv 708.

In order for statement by creditor to be admissible as statement of co-conspirator in action against another creditor for conspiracy to drive debtor out of business, there must be independent evidence of conspiracy and creditor's connection to and knowing participation in conspiracy. Prudential Ins. Co. v Curt Bullock Builders, Inc. (1985, ND Ill) 626 F Supp 159.

Rule 802. Hearsay Rule

Hearsay is not admissible except as provided by these rules or by other rules prescribed by the Supreme Court pursuant to statutory authority or by Act of Congress.

(Jan. 2, 1975, P. L. 93-595, § 1, 88 Stat. 1939.)

HISTORY; ANCILLARY LAWS AND DIRECTIVES

Other provisions:

Notes of Advisory Committee on Rules. The provision excepting from the operation of the rule hearsay which is made admissible by other rules adopted by the Supreme Court or by Act of Congress continues the admissibility thereunder of hearsay which would not qualify under these Evidence Rules. The following examples illustrate the working of the exception:

FEDERAL RULES OF CIVIL PROCEDURE

Rule 4(g): proof of service by affidavit.
Rule 32: admissibility of depositions.
Rule 43(e): affidavits when motion based on facts not appearing of record.
Rule 56: affidavits in summary judgment proceedings.
Rule 65(b): showing by affidavit for temporary restraining order.

FEDERAL RULES OF CRIMINAL PROCEDURE

Rule 4(a): affidavits to show grounds for issuing warrants.
Rule 12(b)(4): affidavits to determine issues of fact in connection with motions.

ACTS OF CONGRESS

10 U.S.C. § 7730: affidavits of unavailable witnesses in actions for damages caused by vessel in naval service, or towage or salvage of same, when taking of testimony or bringing of action delayed or stayed on security grounds.
29 U.S.C. § 161(4): affidavit as proof of service in NLRB proceedings.
38 U.S.C. § 5206: affidavit as proof of posting notice of sale of unclaimed property by Veterans Administration.

COMMENTARY

by Stephen A. Saltzburg, Daniel J. Capra, and Michael M. Martin

Basic rule

Rule 802 provides for the standard exclusion of hearsay evidence;

327

Illustration B-2
Rule 802 in *USCS*, con't.

Rule 802

hearsay is simply inadmissible unless an exception is applicable. The significant thing about the Rule, however, is that hearsay exceptions can only be provided by "other Rules prescribed by the Supreme Court pursuant to statutory authority or by Act of Congress." The Rule is plain, therefore, that unless an exception to the hearsay rule is provided by statute or in these Rules or in other Court rules, the Supreme Court and lower Federal Courts are not free to create new categorical hearsay exceptions without engaging in rulemaking. In other words, whereas Rule 501 explicitly permits the law of privilege to be changed by adjudication, hearsay rules can only be changed by rulemaking.

It must be kept in mind that Rule 801(d) provides exemptions from the ban on hearsay evidence. Thus, one must consult that Rule, in addition to Rules 803, 804, and 807, to ascertain whether out-of-court statements offered for their truth may be admitted.

Statutory exceptions

In order to be admissible under Rule 802, evidence does not have to be explicitly exempted from the hearsay rule. Rather, Congress can provide for admissibility of evidence by stating in a statute that certain evidence is admissible for a specified purpose. For example, 18 USCS § 4245 provides that a certificate by the Director of the Bureau of Prisons stating that there is probable cause to believe that a convict is mentally incompetent at the time of trial "shall be prima facie evidence of the facts and conclusions certified therein." It does not matter that the word hearsay is not used; Congress has made its will known with respect to the admissibility of the evidence. Federal statutes are replete with provisions that certain evidence is admissible for specified purposes.

CROSS REFERENCES

Agricultural certificates, 7 USCS §§ 54, 79(d), 94, 511f, 1622(h).

Immigration records, 8 USCS §§ 1284(b), 1360(d), 1439(b), 1440(c).

Maritime matters, 10 USCS § 7730.

Copyright records, 17 USCS § 410(c).

Extradition proceedings, 18 USCS § 3190.

Foreign trade and commerce, 19 USCS § 1509(b).

District Courts, 28 USCS § 753(b).

Workers' compensation proceedings, 33 USCS § 923(a).

Bills of health for foreign vessels, 42 USCS § 269(b).

Social Security and Medicare, 42 USCS § 405(c)(3).

Destitute seamen, 46 USCS § 11104.

FCC, 47 USCS § 412.

Accused's right to confront witnesses, USCS Constitution, Amendment 6.

Depositions, USCS Rules of Civil Procedure, Rule 32.

Temporary restraining orders, USCS Rules of Civil Procedure, Rule 65(b).

Arrest warrants and probable cause, USCS Rules of Criminal Procedure, Rule 4(a).

Pretrial motions, USCS Rules of Criminal Procedure, Rule 12.

Depositions, USCS Rules of Criminal Procedure, Rule 15.

Posttrial motions, USCS Rules of Criminal Procedure, Rule 33.

Finally, multivolume treatises on the federal rules, such as *Federal Practice and Procedure* and *Moore's Federal Practice* (to be discussed below in Section D), can also be considered annotated editions of the rules. They are frequently arranged by rule number, and include the rule texts and Advisory Committee notes as well as extensive analyses of interpretive cases.[21]

2. State Rules

The publication of state court rules vary from state to state. In states where legislative acts determine court procedures, these "rules" appear as part of the state's statutory code. In states where rules are promulgated by the judiciary alone, until recently they often appeared only in elusive pamphlets or in the state reports. Increasingly, however, publishers of annotated codes recognize the importance of court rules and include them within their scope of coverage. Even when court rules are not legislative in nature, they receive the same treatment as statutes and are published in a fully annotated, regularly supplemented format. For many state codes, the rules volumes are published in a softcover format and reissued annually.

In many states, court rules are also issued in annual, *unannotated* pamphlets designed for ready desktop reference. Thomson-West publishes such pamphlets for virtually every state in which it publishes an annotated code, and for several other states as well. Each state has competing publishers performing the same task. As noted earlier, these rules pamphlets are valuable sources not only for state court rules but for the rules of federal courts sitting in that state. In some states, annotated editions of court rules are also published separately as part of practice treatises.

State court rules are available online through WESTLAW or LEXIS, usually in a state's code or statute database, but also in a separate rules-only database.

---

21   Three of the major sets of rules are published by Clark Boardman in shorter, one-volume, looseleaf format or annual paperback editions. For each rule, the text and Advisory Committee notes are accompanied by "practice comments" discussing the rule and its application. The volumes are: Thomas A. Coyne, *Federal Rules of Civil Procedure* (2d ed., 1994-date); Michelle G. Hermann, *Federal Rules of Criminal Procedure* (annual); and Paul F. Rothstein, *Federal Rules of Evidence* (3d ed., 2002-date).

To learn about available sources for state court rules other than statutory compilations, it may help to consult Betsy Reidinger & Virginia T. Lemmon, "Sources of Rules of State Courts," 82 *Law Libr. J.* 761 (1990), or one of the state legal research guides listed in Appendix B. Once the set of rules is in hand, pinpointing applicable provisions depends on the quality of organization and indexing. A steadily increasing number of states, however, have rules modeled on the various federal rules, particularly the Federal Rules of Civil Procedure and the Federal Rules of Evidence. A researcher who knows the relevant rules provision in federal court can easily check the comparable provision in another state.

For civil matters, you can use the Federal Rules of Civil Procedure numbers to find relevant state provisions even if the state rules bear no relation to the Federal Rules. Each Circuit Volume of *Federal Procedure Rules Service* includes a "Comparator," which correlates the provisions of the Federal Rules of Civil Procedure to the court rules or statutory provisions for each state within the circuit.[22]

A rule-by-rule comparison of federal and state evidence provisions can be found in the "State Correlation Tables" in *Federal Rules of Evidence Service* (Thomson-West), "Finding Aids" volume.

C. UPDATING AND INTERPRETING RULES

1. Finding Amendments to Federal Rules

It is important that practitioners be aware of and be able to find proposed and recent amendments to rules. For the major rules sets, the Supreme Court submits newly adopted amendments to Congress. The texts of the amendments, accompanied by Judicial Conference Advisory Committee notes, are printed by Congress as House Documents. The same material is reproduced in full in advance sheets for Thomson-West's *Supreme Court Reporter, Federal Reporter, Federal Supplement,* and *Federal Rules Decisions,* with its inclusion prominently noted on the pamphlet covers. Any attorney monitoring the advance sheets for current

---

22   The civil procedural systems of all fifty states and the District of Columbia were surveyed in John B. Oakley & Arthur F. Coon, "The Federal Rules in the State Courts: A Survey of State Court Systems of Civil Procedure," 61 *Wash. L. Rev.* 1367 (1986).

case developments should thus be on notice of any prospective change in the rules.   The advance sheets for the *Federal Reporter* also include amendments to the rules of individual Courts of Appeals. The monthly pamphlets for *U.S. Code Congressional and Administrative News* and *United States Code Service Advance* contain not only all these amendments, but those for other federal courts and administrative tribunals as well.

2. Judicial Interpretations of Rules

While annotated editions of rules provide references to judicial decisions, there are other tools for finding cases construing and applying court rules. Some of these tools have already been introduced in earlier chapters, but their specific focus on court rules is discussed at greater length here.

a. Citators

The "statutes" unit of all jurisdictional *Shepard's* citators can be used to determine the current status and judicial treatment of federal and state court rules online or in print. For example, Illustration C-1 shows a screen shot of *Shepard's* for Federal Rule of Evidence 802, and C-2 shows the Florida Statutes, §90.802, the evidence rule covering hearsay. Like Shepard's coverage for cases, courts citing to rules will be listed from the highest court to the lowest, with citations to secondary sources listed at the very end. *KeyCite* also provides history notes and citing references to cases and secondary materials for state and federal court rules. Citing references on *KeyCite* are broken down by subject, as if you were looking at the annotations in the *USCA*, for example. Illustration D shows the citing references from *KeyCite* for FRE 802.

In print, *Shepard's United States Citations, Statute Edition,* provides coverage of every set of federal rules listed in Table 1 above (except U.S. Court of Military Appeals rules, which are in *Shepard's Military Justice Citations*). It also includes citations to the rules of several other specialized courts and of individual United States Court of Appeals and District Courts. Since annotated editions of very few district court rules are published, this may be the only way to find interpretive cases.

Shepard's Federal Rules Citations (print) covers the four major sets of federal rules. It also covers the rules of various federal courts, such as the Rules of the Supreme Court of the United States and the rules of the individual United States District Courts. For the Federal Rules of Civil Procedure, Criminal Procedure, Evidence, and Appellate Procedure, it provides citations in both federal and state courts. The coverage includes state court decisions that are citing either to the federal rule or to state rules that are identical or similar to the federal rule. Also included are citations to the federal rule taken from articles in selected leading law reviews.

Coverage of state court rules is contained in full in each of *Shepard's* print state citators as well as online. Changes in rules are noted, as well as citations in federal and state court decisions, selected law reviews, annotations, and (in some states) attorney general opinions.

Illustration C-1
Screen Shot of the Beginning of *Shepard's* Coverage for FRE 802

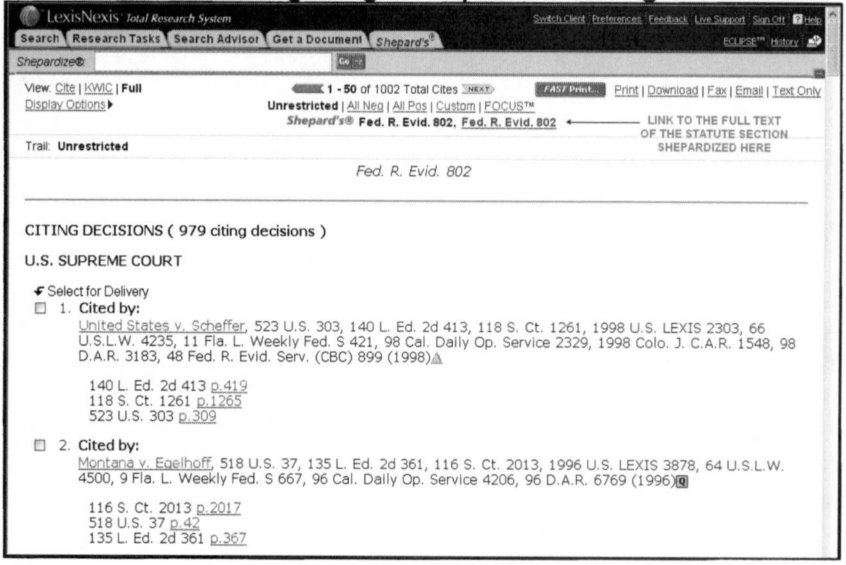

Illustration C-2
Screen Shot of the Beginning of *Shepard's* Coverage for Florida Statutes, §90.802

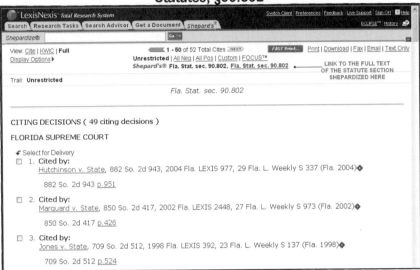

Illustration D
Screen Shot of the Beginning of *KeyCite* Citing References for FRE 802

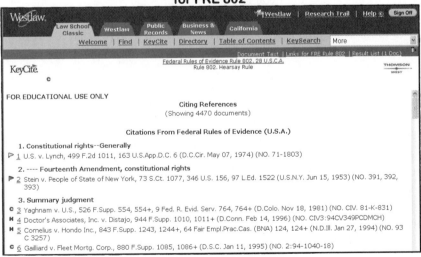

b. Reporters and Digests

While standard case reporters such as official reports and the components of the National Reporter System include many decisions dealing with the application of court rules, there are also specialized reporters for cases decided under the federal rules. Thomson-West's *Federal Rules Decisions* (cited as F.R.D.) began publication in 1940 as an offshoot of the *Federal Supplement,* and provides the texts of U.S. District Court decisions that construe the Federal Rules of Civil Procedure and Criminal Procedure.

Cases appearing in *F.R.D.* are not included in the *Federal Supplement.* *F.R.D.* is by no means an exclusive source of procedural opinions, however, since many *F.Supp.* opinions also involve procedural issues and since neither Supreme Court nor Courts of Appeals decisions are included. *Federal Rules Decisions* is just an additional component of Thomson-West's National Reporter System,[23] sharing coverage of the U.S. District Courts with the voluminous *Federal Supplement.* It differs from most reporters in that it includes not just cases but also relevant articles, speeches, and the proceedings of judicial conferences.

Federal Rules Service (cited as Fed. R. Serv.) is a competing commercial reporter for decisions construing federal rules. *Federal Rules Service* provides the texts of court decisions interpreting the Federal Rules of Civil Procedure and the Federal Rules of Appellate Procedure. Cases are published first in looseleaf format and then in bound volumes. The looseleaf cases are accompanied by current case and digest tables and a "Current Material Highlights" pamphlet, summarizing the holdings of important recent cases.

Federal Rules Service includes cases from all levels of the federal court system, not just district courts. Most of the decisions also appear in one of Thomson-West's reporters, but some are not published anywhere but *Fed. R. Serv.* Each case is given one or more headnotes assigned to specific rules and numbered subject subdivisions within each rule, and these headnotes are arranged numerically in the accompanying *Federal Rules Digest.* A "Finding Aids" volume includes cumulative tables of cases and the outline of the publisher's classification system for each rule, known as the "Federal Index" or "Findex." The second edition of the *Federal Rules*

---

23   As part of the National Reporter System, decisions appearing in *Federal Rules Decisions* are digested in West's *Federal Practice Digest* and other digests.

Digest covers the years 1938-54, and the current third edition covers cases from 1954 to date. Because the digest is arranged by rule, and within the rule by subject, its purpose is similar to that of the case annotations in *USCA* or *USCS:* a comprehensive collection of headnotes for cases decided under each provision.

In 1979 a separate reporting service for the new evidence rules, the *Federal Rules of Evidence Service,* was begun providing similar coverage of evidentiary issues. As with the *Federal Rules Service,* most cases are also published in one of the Thomson-West federal reporters, although a few appear only in *Fed. Rules Evid. Serv.* The service is accompanied by the *Federal Rules of Evidence Digest,* which arranges the case headnotes by subject within each rule. A "Finding Aids" volume includes the text of the rules, a table of cases, the "Findex" or digest classification system, and state correlation tables providing information on state rules of evidence based on or similar to the Federal Rules. In addition to recent cases, the "Current Material" volume contains finding aids and a monthly "Current Material Highlights."

3. Secondary Sources

The general secondary sources in legal literature, such as law review articles and encyclopedias, contain a great deal of information on procedural matters. There are also numerous specialized resources dealing specifically with the intricacies of court rules and practice.

a. Federal Practice

The technical nature of the various federal rules and their importance in legal practice has led to the development of a number of excellent commentaries on the rules. These include two comprehensive treatises by distinguished scholars in the fields of federal courts and procedure: *Federal Practice and Procedure* and *Moore's Federal Practice.*

Federal Practice and Procedure (31 vols. to date) (Thomson-West 1969-date) is an extensive treatment of federal procedural and jurisdictional issues. The set consists of four components covering the Federal Rules of Criminal Procedure, the Federal Rules of Civil Procedure, jurisdiction and related matters, and the Federal Rules of Evidence. The volumes covering the rules sets are organized by rule. The entire set is commonly referred to as *"Wright & Miller,"* after two of its principal authors, Professors Charles

Alan Wright of the University of Texas and Arthur R. Miller of Harvard Law School.[24]

For each rule, *Federal Practice and Procedure* provides extensive discussion of its history, purpose, and application generally and in specific situations. The text includes copious footnotes to cases and other materials. The set is updated by annual pocket parts, and third edition volumes have since 1998 been supplanting second edition volumes. There is one index covering the civil and jurisdictional components, but the other parts are separately indexed.

The other major treatise, *Moore's Federal Practice* (29 vols.) (3d ed., Matthew Bender 1997-date), is published in a looseleaf format, revised annually by replacement pages and supplements. The set is named after its primary author, Professor James William Moore of Yale Law School, who has had numerous coauthors at different times and on various volumes. Like *Federal Practice and Procedure, Moore's* devotes several volumes to a rule-by-rule analysis of the Federal Rules of Civil Procedure, with other volumes focusing on other matters such as jurisdiction, the Federal Rules of Criminal Procedure, the Federal Rules of Evidence, and Supreme Court practice. The set includes a detailed index and one volume of tables listing statutes and rules cited.[25]

Two other multivolume treatments of federal practice are organized not by specific rule but more generally, by subject. An encyclopedia similar in format to its *Am.Jur.2d* but designed specifically for federal practice is *Federal Procedure, Lawyers' Edition* (1982-date). It consists of eighty alphabetically arranged chapters, some of which focus on procedural issues

---

24   In actuality, each component is the work of a different set of authors. The criminal volumes were written by Wright alone, but are now updated by Nancy J. King and Susan R. Klein; the civil volumes by Wright, Miller, Mary K. Kane, and Richard L. Marcus; the jurisdiction volumes by Wright, Miller, Edward H. Cooper, and Richard D. Freer, Patrick J. Schiltz, Vikram David Amar, and Joan E. Steinman; and the evidence volumes by Wright, Kenneth W. Graham, Jr., Victor J. Gold, and Michael H. Graham.

25   A similar but less voluminous work is also available from the same publisher. James W. Moore, Allan D. Vestal & Phillip B. Kurland, *Moore's Manual: Federal Practice and Procedure* (3 vols.) (1962-date) is arranged by subject rather than by rule, but contains much of the same text as the larger work. Each section in the *Manual* provides cross-references to more comprehensive treatment in *Moore's Federal Practice.*

(Access to District Courts, New Trial) and some on topical areas of federal law (Atomic Energy, Job Discrimination). The chapters deal with civil, criminal and administrative practice, and include checklists, synopses of law review articles, and texts of relevant statutes. The text also includes references to *Federal Procedural Forms, Lawyers' Edition* and other titles available from the publisher. The set is updated by annual pocket parts, and includes a three-volume index and a table of statutes, rules and regulations cited.

Thomson-West recently assumed publication of another comprehensive work, *Cyclopedia of Federal Procedure*. The *Cyclopedia* is arranged topically rather than alphabetically; it is divided into five parts (courts and jurisdiction; civil trial practice; criminal procedure; appeal and review; and particular actions and proceedings) and organized topically within each part. Like most of the other works described in this section, its text summarizes the ruling law and its footnotes provide extensive references to cases. Both text and footnotes are updated in annual pocket parts. In addition to an index, the set includes volumes containing the texts of relevant statutes and court rules, as mentioned earlier.

A number of works focus on the Federal Rules of Evidence. One of the principal drafters of the rules, Judge Jack B. Weinstein, wrote, with Margaret A. Berger, a multi-volume treatise explaining the intent and application of each provision, *Weinstein's Evidence: Commentary on Rules of Evidence for the United States Courts and Magistrates* (7 vols.) (Matthew Bender 1975-1996). It includes both a subject index and an author/title index (of works cited in the text), as well as tables of cases and of statutes and rules. While it may not be up to date, it still may give insight. A similar multivolume rule-by-rule analysis is Christopher B. Mueller & Laird C. Kirkpatrick, *Federal Evidence 2d* (5 vols.) (Thomson-West 1994-date), which is updated with annual pocket parts.[26]

Procedural guides for particular courts are also published. One work designed specifically for attorneys practicing before the United States Supreme Court is Robert L. Stern, et. al., *Supreme Court Practice: for Practice in the Supreme Court of the United States* (8th ed., Bureau of National Affairs 2002). The book includes extensive discussions of the

---

26   Less comprehensive but handier treatments include Michael H. Graham, *Handbook of Federal Evidence* (4 vols.) (5th ed., Thomson-West 2000), and Stephen A. Saltzburg, Michael M. Martin & Daniel J. Capra, *Federal Rules of Evidence Manual* (5 vols.) (8th ed., LexisNexis 2001).

Court's policies and procedures, and also contains forms, checklists and Supreme Court Building floor plans.

b. State-Specific Materials

State practice manuals and procedural aids, containing such material as the text of court rules, commentaries on the rules, annotations of court decisions, and model forms keyed to the rules, are published for virtually every state. Some of the larger states have two or more competing publications of this kind. The best of these are updated regularly, either with looseleaf filings, pocket part supplements, or complete annual revisions. They provide useful, current information regarding the local rules of practice, and are essential tools for the lawyer's daily work.

Thomson-West and several other publishers offer multi-volume sets on practice in particular states. Some of these are commentaries on procedural rules, while others are series of individual subject treatises in a uniform format, with legal forms and practice checklists. Usually, these works are regularly updated by either pocket parts or looseleaf supplements.

Another source for practical information on state practice is through continuing legal education materials. Many states publish materials from their C.L.E. programs, often in a looseleaf format. These books often provide clear, step-by-step assistance for practitioners in a particular jurisdiction. They are usually updated or replaced periodically, although not always as frequently as works from major commercial publishers.

One of the easiest ways to learn about available treatises, practice manuals, and C.L.E. materials in a particular state is to consult a reference librarian.

c. General Works

Procedural manuals and treatises published for a general national audience can also be of immense practical value, although they are related to no specific procedural rules. Among these are the practice adjuncts to *American Jurisprudence*, such as *Am.Jur. Trials* and *Am.Jur. Proof of Facts*. Both of these multi-volume sets contain articles on specific issues in litigation, and contain numerous cross-references to other products.

The first six volumes of *Am.Jur. Trials* constitute an extensive treatise on general aspects of trial preparation and procedure. Ensuing volumes, which are issued periodically, consist of "Model Trials." Individual articles in each volume describe unique aspects of specific types of litigation, on issues from compensation for multiple sclerosis to defective automobile door latches. There are almost ninety volumes of "Model Trials," and the set has a three-volume index.

Am.Jur. Proof of Facts, now in its third series, contains articles on specific evidentiary issues, and provides sample interrogatories and examinations in over eighty volumes. Individual articles describe the elements of proof required for establishing particular facts in judicial proceedings, and outline useful procedures. A four-volume index covers all three series.

A similar collection of articles on trial practice in very specific areas is *Causes of Action, 2d* (Thomson-West, 1993-date), which includes extensive references to law review articles, legal encyclopedias, digests, and annotations. Works such as these may be little used in academic research, but they are important time-saving resources for practicing lawyers.

D. PRACTICE FORMS

Many writings must follow certain conventions to have legal significance or to have a desired effect. This is true not only of documents such as contracts and wills, but also of forms used in court practice such as briefs or pleadings. The publication of model forms has evolved and is today a major component of legal literature. Forms are included as part of many procedural treatises, and are published separately in comprehensive collections. Some jurisdictions even have prescribed official forms that must be used for certain pleadings or motions.

For federal practice, several multi-volume collections of forms are published in conjunction with the practice treatises described in the preceding sections. Some are arranged by rule, some by subject, all provide useful cross-references to other sources. Table 3 lists practice sets and their companion form books.

Table 3
Federal Practice Treatises and Form Books

Practice Treatise	Form Book	Arrangement
Federal Practice & Procedure (Wright & Miller)	*West's Federal Forms*	By rule
Moore's Federal Practice	*Bender's Federal Practice Forms*	By rule
Moore's Manual	*Federal Practice Forms*	By rule
Federal Procedure, Lawyer's Edition	*Federal Procedural Forms, Lawyer's Edition*	By subject
Federal Local Court Rules	*Federal Local Court Forms*	By court

Legal forms are an essential part of most state practice manuals discussed above. In addition, many states have separate, commercially published collections of forms. Some states have officially promulgated forms, such as *California Judicial Council Forms,* published annually as an adjunct to *West's Annotated California Codes.*

Although not keyed to the practice of any particular jurisdiction, general formbooks can still be very useful in preparing for litigation. *American Jurisprudence Pleading and Practice Forms,* rev. ed. (Thomson-West 1967-date) is an extensive collection of over 36,5000 forms for such matters as complaints, motions, and orders. Its forms are accompanied by explanatory text, case annotations, and cross-references to other publications, as well as tables providing statutory and rules references for each jurisdiction. It is arranged alphabetically by subject, and has a multi-volume paperback index which is replaced every few years. Other series are designed for specific stages of litigation, such as *Bender's Forms of Discovery* (16 vols.) (1963-date), which includes ten volumes of sample interrogatories by subject. Practice forms appear as well in many specialized treatises and manuals.

E. MODEL JURY INSTRUCTIONS

Publications of jury instructions are an important aid to both practicing trial lawyers and judges. Before a jury is sent out to weigh the evidence, the judge instructs its members on the applicable law. Proposed instructions are frequently drafted and submitted to the judge by opposing counsel, and the outcome of a case may turn on which instructions are chosen. Collected examples of jury instructions have been published since the late nineteenth century.[27]

Cases have frequently been overturned on appeal due to inadequate or erroneous instructions. To reduce the chances of error, many states have prepared standardized, approved instructions to be used in common situations. These instructions are known by various designations, including *model, pattern,* or *approved* jury instructions. The first published set of these instructions was in California, *Book of Approved Jury Instructions,* in 1938. By now there are model instructions for practically every state.[28] In some states model jury instructions are used by judges only as guides, but in others the instructions must be read verbatim if applicable. Some sets of model instructions are promulgated by the state supreme courts, while others are unofficial products of bar or judicial associations.

For the federal courts there is no general set of approved instructions, although some sets of pattern instructions have been published for individual circuits. There are, however, two sets of commercially published, unofficial instructions covering both criminal and civil cases: Kevin F. O'Malley, Jay E. Grenig & William C. Lee, *Federal Jury Practice and Instructions* (3 vols.) (5th ed., Thomson-West 1987-date) is an authoritative work with explanatory comments and notes of relevant cases; Leonard B. Sand et al., *Modern Federal Jury Instructions* (4 vols.) (Matthew Bender 1985-date) is a looseleaf work, consisting of sample instructions, comments, and case notes.

---

27   Frederick Sackett, *Instructions and Requests for Instructions from the Court to the Jury in Jury Trials* (Jameson & Morse 1881). A book published the previous year concluded with an example of an instruction *not* to be followed. It began: "Gentlemen of the Jury: The investigation of guilt and the punishment of crime are a painful, but a highly important duty. God has so ordered it, and we worms of the dust must recognize what He has ordered." Seymour D. Thompson, *Charging the Jury: A Monograph* 176 (W.H. Stevenson 1880).

28   Comprehensive listings of published jury instructions, arranged by state, are: Cheryl R. Nyberg & Carol Boast, "Jury Instructions: A Bibliography Part I: Civil Jury Instructions," *Legal Reference Services Q.,* Spring/Summer 1986, at 5; and Cheryl R. Nyberg, Jane Williams & Carol Boast, "Jury Instructions: A Bibliography Part II: Criminal Jury Instructions," *Legal Reference Services Q.,* Fall/Winter 1986, at 3.

F. SUMMARY

Access to court rules, both federal and state, is available in a variety of sources. The most useful forms of publication are those which provide commentary and citations to court decisions interpreting and applying the rules. The extensive literature of practice manuals and formbooks is closely related to court rules. These materials describe the procedures to be followed in litigation and usually include the texts of rules as well as forms, commentary, and annotations to court decisions. They are an essential component of the working library of every practitioner.

The literature of court rules and practice is sometimes seen as dry and overly concerned with technical minutiae. This is a valid criticism, particularly when rules prescribe rigid and formalistic processes to be followed in all cases. Even so, a lawyer must be familiar with governing rules and procedures in order to avoid compromising clients' interests. As Justice Hugo Black complained thirty-five years ago: "Judicial statistics would show, I fear, an unfortunately large number of meritorious cases lost due to inadvertent failure of lawyers to conform to procedural prescriptions having little if any relevancy to substantial justice."[29] Simplification and flexible application of rules, however, can allow them to achieve the salutary purpose Justice Black enunciated: "The principal function of procedural rules should be to serve as useful guides to help, not hinder, persons who have a legal right to bring their problems before the courts."[30]

---

29   Order Adopting Revised Rules of the Supreme Court of the United States, 346 U.S. 945, 946 (1954) (Black, J., dissenting).

30   *Id.*

Chapter 10

SECONDARY AUTHORITY

A. INTRODUCTION

Legal information is traditionally divided into two broad categories: primary authority and secondary authority. Primary authority is a statement of the law itself. The holding in a judicial decision from your jurisdiction, the enactment of your legislature, a rule or regulation promulgated by your jurisdiction's administrative agencies are primary authorities. Everything else is secondary. Sources that comment upon the law, index the law or summarize the law are all secondary in nature. Even the words of a judge from your jurisdiction are only secondary authority when they are not part of the holding of a case.

Some secondary sources can be used as *persuasive authority*. Those sources can be used to persuade a court to accept your argument. A law review article by a famous law professor or a judicial decision from another jurisdiction can be used to buttress your argument when the primary authority is against you. Or perhaps there is no primary authority at all. Perhaps a question is new or unresolved. In many situations courts will seek guidance and secondary sources can provide it.

For new legal researchers secondary sources offer explanation. Even sources that would never be cited to a court as persuasive authority can be of great help in understanding an area of the law. Often the most useful sources to a beginner will be the least weighty ones. Think of how law students use commercial outlines to understand Torts and you will get the idea.

In this Chapter we will introduce the wide spectrum of secondary tools that you might use in your research and perhaps in your law school courses. Because a bibliographic description of such tools is inevitably a bit abstract and dry we also included Appendix A. This is a Wisconsin State Supreme Court case written by Justice Shirley Abrahamson. It is a case that called for interpretation of Wisconsin legislation and the meaning of the *Uniform Commercial Code*. In Appendix A we point out the use Justice Abrahamson, a former law professor and noted judicial craftsperson, makes of secondary sources. Take a look at it while reading this Chapter and both the Chapter and the opinion should make more sense.

B. BOOKS ENCOUNTERED IN LAW SCHOOL

1. Hornbooks

Hornbooks grew out of the casebook method of teaching in law school. Recall from Chapter 1 that Dean Langdell believed that the best way to learn about law was to read cases and let the points emerge. Langdell's first casebook contained nothing but cases. Times have changed, and the modern casebook contains a lot more than just edited cases. In spite of the changes, though, most casebooks are still filled with questions and conundrums, not answers.

The casebook method is linked to the use of the Socratic teaching method in law schools. When employing the Socratic method, a professor teaches by posing questions. Even when asked a question by a student, the professor may answer with a question. There are no "right" answers, each answer is questioned. This process, so archly portrayed in the movie, *The Paper Chase*, is designed to force one to think like a lawyer. It can also produce great anxiety in the student who wants to know the correct answer to a question. Students feel a need to know what the answer to a question is, not just each of the possible answers. Simple answers to legal questions that baldly laid out the rule became known as **black letter** law. Such treatment was -- and still is -- much scorned by legal academics as overly simplistic. But the demands by students for such a treatment created a market.

The first response was the development of hornbooks. Hornbooks are texts that address the major questions in a particular legal field, invariably a field that is the focus of a law school course. These texts are authored by one or more law school professors who teach in the field. The authors lay out legal principles in a simple, straightforward manner. A hornbook makes it a point to discuss important cases, often cases that are covered in a law school course on the subject, except the hornbook explains the case and puts it in context. The hornbook will have an index and a Table of Cases. The latter is an alphabetic listing of each case that is discussed in the text. This allows pin point location of the discussion of a confusing case. Where appropriate there is also a Table of Statutes. Hornbook indexing is usually pretty low level, and, except in rare cases, they are not kept up-to-date.

As time passed, some hornbooks assumed a role far beyond that of a study aid. Probably the first hornbook to break out of the mold was William Prosser's, *The Law of Torts*. Prosser was a giant in the field of Torts and his book not only described what the law was, it laid out what the law ought to be. It wove all of the cases into a readable, sensible fabric and had profound effect on the development of tort law. Prosser's book was cited thousands of times in the courts. Prosser has been dead for decades, but his book lives on a version revised by four other scholars. It is not uncommon for famous books to be carried on after the death of the original author.

Prosser's *The Law of Torts* is a classic, but there were other hornbooks that took on a life of their own beyond assisting students. Today hornbooks occupy a somewhat ambiguous position. A hornbook can be pedestrian or influential. Some can be cited as persuasive authority in a brief to a court, but to use others in a such a manner would be foolish. As the potential stature of the books has grown, their simplicity and black letter tone have faded. Some hornbooks are now quite complex, having moved a long way from simple statements of the black letter law.

Several publishers produce hornbooks. The most established are the Thomson-West hornbook series (the hard copy version of this book is a member of that series) and the Foundation Press University Textbook Series. One of the questions most frequently asked of law librarians is, "What hornbook should I use?" There is no easy answer. For the law student, the best idea to ask the professor in the relevant course. He or she may find one book's approach more useful. For general research the best course is to ask the reference librarian in your law library. Hornbooks rise and fall in stature, and their influence varies from place to place, so the counsel of an expert is advised.

2. Nutshells

As hornbooks became more and more complicated in content, the need for a simple, straightforward discussion of legal topics re-opened. The void was filled by Thomson-West"s *Nutshell* series. A *Nutshell* is a paperback volume, inexpensive by law book standards and written in an even more simplified manner. Each volume in the *Nutshell* series focuses on a topic, sometimes a quite specific topic. The treatment is general and the text is usually readable. The author does not buttress each point with citations as he would if he were writing a scholarly work. Nutshells are rarely cited by the courts, so they remain a student's tool, although a practitioner venturing into a new subject area can find helpful background in them. One rule for resesearch in a new area is that you should not begin a subject search until you have at least the sophistication of the *Nutshell* in that area. *Nutshells* can point one toward important cases and introduce one to crucial terminology, both key elements in any search.

Most *Nutshells* have a section entitled "Table of Cases" that allow syou to see if a particular case is discussed within the text. The indexing is primitive. There is no supplementation, though *Nutshells* on hot topics may be revised with some frequency. It is always a good idea to check the copyright date.

3. Outlines

Study outlines for law school courses have proliferated in recent years. Outlines provide a very straightforward approach to a specific legal topic that is the subject of a law school course. Outlines may even be keyed to a particular textbook in a particular course. Outlining a law school course is a practice commonly urged upon students, either alone or as a part of a study group. Thus the form is well known. Several of the best known outline series, *Gilberts* and *Emmanuels*, grew from the notes of one student. Others grew out of an outline prepared by a particularly great study group. Because the outline form requires condensation of often confusing material, it inevitably runs the risk of oversimplifying. Despite all of that, they are quite helpful, though they are still frowned upon by some professors. A wide variety of study aids are now available in electronic form. This market is just developing and changes will be quick.

Some of the companies that offer the bar review courses that prepare recent law school graduates to take the state bar now sell variations of their bar review outlines to students for use in preparing for law school exams. Bar review outlines are often of quite high quality, though the titles vary and some courses are far better than others.

How to know what outline to use? Once again, checking with professors and reference librarians, as well as students who have taken a particular professor may be the best method. There is a great deal of money to be made in this market so competition is quite keen and new products appear frequently. Outlines can never be thought of as persuasive authority; they are the least sophisticated of the black letter law tools.

C. DICTIONARIES

In the first Chapter the problem of legal jargon was discussed as one of the impediments to research in the law. Words that are used in common discourse, words like "liability" or "reasonable," may take on a special meaning when used in the law, other words, for example "*renvoi*", are unique to law. A substantial part of the law school experience lies in learning legal vocabulary. A correspondingly large part of legal research concerns the interpretation and manipulation of language. Many of the indexes and digests that we have introduced are dependent on legal jargon. It is crucial to be as precise as possible in one's use of terms.

This problem has been recognized for centuries. Dictionaries are one of the oldest forms of legal research tool. The modern versions offer a broad coverage of possible research needs. One should take care to consult dictionaries frequently. There are three ways of looking up words in the law.

1. Legal Dictionaries

Traditional legal dictionaries function much like any dictionary. A legal dictionary is an alphabetic arrangement of legal words and phrases with a definition provided for each. The difference is that in a legal dictionary, each definition is cited to a source. Complying with the law's requirement for authority, a citation backs up each assertion of meaning. These citations are to judicial opinions where possible.

The best known legal dictionary is *Black's Law Dictionary*. *Ballentine's Law Dictionary* is found in many collections as well. These two are massive single volume works, and are expensive. *Black's*, however, is available to you on WESTLAW and *Ballentine's* (and others[1]) are available on LEXIS. You are well advised to use them either online or at the law library, at least until you determine that a purchase of one of them is absolutely necessary. There are a large variety of paperback legal dictionaries on the market; some are keyed to specific subject fields. Paperback dictionaries should be used with care, but they are very convenient for classroom use. The critical question is who compiled the dictionary and why should you rely on that person or person's expertise.

2. *Words and Phrases*

Thomson-West publishes the set *Words and Phrases Judicially Defined*. When the editors at Thomson-West prepare the text of cases for the *National Reporter System*, they note when the judge defines any word or phrase in the text of the opinion. A citation to each such definition is listed in a table in the front of each advance sheet listing any such citations. The citations are collected into *Words and Phrases*. The set currently consists of

---

1   LEXIS allows you to search all of the legal dictionaries that system has at one time so that you can compare a definition by *Ballentine's* with one from *Modern Legal Usage*, for example.

75 volumes which are kept up-to-date with annual pocket parts. Entries are arranged in alphabetical order. The set covers all jurisdictions and lists each time a court defines a term. Thus some terms may have dozens of definitions listed while others will have none at all.

The set is an odd one, seldom used by many researchers, but on occasion it can provide an interesting entry into a research system via a specific term. It is, as you might have guessed, available on WESTLAW.

3. LEXIS and WESTLAW

WESTLAW and LEXIS are full text databases, containing each word of each document. Therefore, if you wish to find how a particular word has been used, or if a word or phrase has been defined, you can simply pull each use from the database. In the case of an exotic word, this might yield useful references. In most cases, such a search will simply dump a huge mass of gibberish onto the researcher. But wise use can be made of these systems. If you can limit the term's usage to a particular court, or to a particular time period, perhaps even to a specific judge, you may be able to find relevant information. At this juncture the traditional style of dictionary searching and the intelligent use of Boolean operators merge.

D. LEGAL ENCYCLOPEDIA AND RESTATEMENTS

The common law, with its thousands of cases and its unavoidable lack of clarity quite naturally has lead to the production of tools that try to explain it all. From the late 17th Century through the early part of the 20th Century, great legal scholars labored to produce treatises that covered entire legal topics. Often filling many volumes, these works relied upon the eminence of the author for their authority and many defined whole fields. This monumental treatise form has declined in recent decades. The researcher will still find versions of many of these old warhorses on the shelves, but they now resemble reference tools, kept up to date by editorial staffs. They are used almost as encyclopedia; they are rarely read from beginning to end. In part this is due to the proliferation of cases and the breakdown of law into separate specialties. Simply put, no one could write a credible treatise covering every aspect of a field like Contracts today. Today's legal information is presented in sets that lack the intellectual ambition (or presumption) of the old treatises. They are simpler, and do not qualify as persuasive authority. Two types worth discussing are encyclopedia and *Restatements*.

1. Legal Encyclopedia

The most imposing sets are legal encyclopedia. Not unrelated in basis to the hornbooks and *Nutshells* discussed in Section B, these multi-volume sets are grander attempts to encompass everything. A legal encyclopedia arrays significant legal topics in alphabetical order, and attempts to discuss each relevant issue. It is inevitable that in trying to describe everything they fall quite short of precisely describing anything. The most curious are the national legal encyclopedia. Given the federal nature of the United States, no one set could possibly describe everything. Only a fool cites to legal encyclopedia as persuasive authority.

But for all of their flaws, legal encyclopedia have virtues. They can provide useful background, they can inform you of the landmark cases in an area and they can acquaint you with the important jargon. Perhaps best for the legal researcher, the modern legal encyclopedia pulls you into a research universe. It will provide citations to relevant cases, hints for other places to look for information. If you are using a Thomson-West product, relevant Topics and Key numbers are provided. If using a LexisNexis product, the reference will be to the Total Research System. Each is the gateway to many related sources.

There are two national legal encyclopedia: *Corpus Juris Secundum* and *AmJur 2d*.

a. *Corpus Juris Secundum (CJS)*

This huge Thomson-West set is bound in dark blue volumes or found on WESTLAW. It consists of an alphabetic arrangement of legal terms and topics. The discussion is often terse. *CJS* provides the user with relevant Topics and Key Numbers as reference points into the Thomson-West digests and through them into the *National Reporter System*, as well as citations to relevant cases. The set is kept up to date with pocket parts. In some cases, volumes have been split into two parts. This is done when the supplementation of a volume grows too large, leading to the necessary insertion of an entirely new volume into the set.

This set was constructed with the Thomson-West philosophy as its underpinning. The original intent was to cite the researcher to every relevant case on the topic being discussed. This goal has been abandoned as unrealistic, but *CJS* still cites to many, many cases. Pages filled with only a little bit of text and great dollops of footnotes are normal. *CJS* is rather dated, and the pocket parts are extremely important in some volumes.

Always check the copyright date of the volume that is being used. Pocket parts can only do so much.

CJS has a multi-volume general index at the end, and a separate index for each major topic. The index is easy to use, and this set is popular with non-lawyers. One could actually think of *CJS* as a case finding tool since the index leads one to discussion with cases and entry points into the Key Number System. Occasionally this makes it a great place to start when looking for that one good case.

b. *AmJur 2d*

This set was begun in the 1970s and is a more open-textured attempt at describing the law. The narrative is often more clearly presented than in *CJS*. Writing clearly and simply means that sometimes the set is not as precise as one might want. It is also kept up-to-date with pocket parts. It too has a general index at the end as well as topic indexes. The user receives citations to other practice sets, form books and primary sources that are linked into a research system. Find one useful source and one is immediately linked to others. *AmJur 2d* is found on both LEXIS and WESTLAW. The major components of the *AmJur* family are:

- *ALR* and *ALR Federal*
- *AmJur Forms*
- *AmJur Pleading and Practice Forms*
- *AmJur Trials*
- *Proof of Facts*
- *Federal Procedure*

AmJur 2d has a New Topics binder at the end of the set in which entirely new topics can be introduced. This solves the problem of how to fit an entirely new topic into the existing alphabetical arrangement without reconfiguring the whole set.

AmJur 2d also contains a volume called the *AmJur Deskbook*. This is a one volume compilation of facts and figures that are of use to legal researchers. A surprising number of answers to questions like, "What is the address of the Secretary of State of Wyoming?" can be answered by the *Deskbook*.

c. State Legal Encyclopedia

A number of states have a state legal encyclopedia. Some are done by Thomson-West or LexisNexis, and not surprisingly these follow the format of the national sets, including entries into each company's research system. A few states have encyclopedia produced by other publishers. But each can be used for background and research leads. A state encyclopedia has the advantage of being able to focus on the unique nature of a state's legal system. This can result in a more coherent focus on legal questions. But be forewarned, state legal encyclopedia are viewed with disdain in many quarters, and should never be relied on as persuasive authority. They can still be the starting places for research and sources for basic background, but should be handled with care.

2. *Restatements*

The *Restatements* represent an attempt to bring order to the development of the common law. The *Restatement* movement sprang from the dismay of leaders of the Bar in the early years of this century. They were upset by the proliferation of contradictory cases that were appearing. How could the common law grow if poorly drafted decisions were appearing in great droves? How to focus attention on the really important cases in a legal system that had chosen comprehensive publication? In part this dilemma is the product of the West Publishing Company's decision to publish everything so many years ago.

The American Law Institute, an offshoot of the American Bar Association, was set up in part to deal with this problem. *Restatements* of the law in specific fields began when the ALI commissioned a reporter, a major figure in the field, to prepare a systematic summary of the best cases. The roster of these Reporters constitutes a list of great legal thinkers of the early part of the 20th Century. Consider the implications of being asked to summarize an entire field like Contracts or Torts. The Reporter's work was reviewed by different levels within the ALI and was eventually voted on by the whole body. The ALI is comprised of lawyers, legal scholars and judges. Membership in it is an honor. There was a great deal of back and forth as the various review committees made suggestions for changes. The process took decades.

In the end the first series of *Restatements* was born. They stated general principles and used anonymous cases as examples. The hope was that the *Restatements* would come to be viewed as authoritative. No one would ever have to go back to the original cases. No actual case names were used in the first series of *Restatements* for that reason.

The *Restatements* did prove to be quite influential, and were cited by the courts with great frequency, but in the end, they became just another research source. Indeed, as the importance of the common law has faded in this era of legislation and administrative activity, the *Restatements* have become even less central. But new editions of the *Restatements* continue to appear, these days including the citations to cases used. In line with the modern trend toward specialization in the law, they are taking on narrower topics.[2] *Restatements* can be used as persuasive authority, but only with care. Titles can be found on both LEXIS and WESTLAW.

E. LAW REVIEWS

Law reviews are peculiar institutions. They have long been the dominant form of publication for law professors and other legal scholars, and they are the repository of much of the best contemporary legal scholarship. What makes them so distinctive is that they are student-edited. Rather than having panels of editors drawn from the ranks of distinguished professionals, the editorial choices as to what gets published is made by groups of third year law students. These same students edit the articles.

This strange situation arises because law reviews are seen as part of the law school pedagogical process. Those students lucky enough to serve on a law review get extensive experience with the process of legal writing and argumentation. (Membership on a law review is also an excellent ornament for the resume.) Debates rage from time to time about the value of law reviews, and the faculties at some prestigious law schools may look down upon the form, but the primacy of place of the law school law review can hardly be challenged.

Law reviews come in two types. The most common is the law

---

2   *Restatements* are now written for the following topics: *Agency, Conflict of Laws, Contracts, Foreign Relations Law of the United States, Judgments, The Law Governing Lawyers, Property (Landlord & Tenant, Wills and Other Donative Transfers, Mortgages, Servitudes), Restitution, Suretyship and Guaranty, Torts (Apportionment of Liability, Products Liability, Trusts (Prudent Investor Rule), and Unfair Competition.*

review that bears the name of its school of origin: the *Harvard Law Review*, the *Yale Law Journal, etc.*, can be thought of as generic law reviews. Such reviews have no particular subject focus, they publish articles on various subjects. You can find an article about the First Amendment next to another on Corporate Securities. The one thing all such articles have in common is a "law review" style. Law review articles consist of a closely analyzed, heavily footnoted, very technically written exploration of a topic. Each assertion made by the author must be rooted in authority. It is not unusual to find a sixty page law review article with 500 footnotes.[3]

Such a law review article may be citable as persuasive authority. Persuasive authority is authority that does not state the law, but instead states what the law should be. It can be used to convince a court to move into a new area or to change an old one. The power of any persuasive authority in the form of a law review article is determined by both the prestige of the article's author and the prestige of the law review in which the article appears. Any article by a famous figure like Lawrence Tribe will carry power. Any article in the *Harvard Law Review*, by far the most widely read and influential law review, will carry power. Thus an article by someone like Lawrence Tribe in the *Harvard Law Review* is the best cite of all. Of course sometimes the only help one find to bolster an argument comes in the form of an article by an unknown assistant professor in an obscure law review. Such an article can still be used, but understand that it is a slimmer reed to lean on.

Even if an article is not useful as persuasive authority, it can serve a second function as a mother lode of research sources. The author, and the students who served as the editors of the article, will cite to every possibly relevant source in the footnotes. The footnotes are pure gold to the researcher interested in the topic. The author of this text reads the footnotes of a law review article first. Even if the text is useless, the footnotes are often rich. Besides, the accepted "law review" style of writing also dooms

---

3   In 2005, the *Harvard Law Review* changed its policy regarding the length of articles submitted as a result of a December 2004 survey conducted by the *HLR* of 800 law professors. The *HLR* and ten other schools are joining in an attempt to moderate the length of the law review articles.
<http://www.harvardlawreview.org/articles_length_policy.pdf>

The policy now reads, "The *Review* will give preference to articles under 25,000 words in length -- the equivalent of 50 law review pages -- including text and footnotes. The *Review* will not publish articles exceeding 35,000 words -- the equivalent of 70-75 law review pages -- except in extraordinary circumstances." <http://www.harvardlawreview.org/manuscript.shtml>.

most interesting speculation to the footnotes. But interesting or not, the combined labor of the author and the student editors will introduce the researcher to a universe of legal information.

Law reviews may also contain student comments and student notes. These are articles written by students. Generally this diminishes their value as persuasive authority, but such student pieces can provide the same level of research assistance.

The second form of law review is the subject specialty review. Such reviews focus on a particular field: *e.g.*, *Ecology Law Quarterly*. They are often started by students with an interest in exploring one special topic. They also serve the purpose of allowing more students to gain experience as law review editors.

Many law schools have a generic review and one or more subject specialty reviews. In the 2004-2005 school year the law school at Boalt Hall, the University of California at Berkeley, had eleven law reviews. This is a bit extreme, but it shows the proliferation of law reviews. The *California Law Review* served as the generic review, and there were ten other specialty reviews. In large measure the specialty reviews follow law review style -- heavy footnoting and careful discussion. Specialty reviews are generally less prestigious than the generic reviews, though some have attained significant status.

One of the best things about law review articles is that they are easy to find by topic. One can find law review articles in a number of ways. The print indexes to legal periodicals are arranged by topic and author, by cases discussed and by statutes. They are kept current by paper supplements. Online systems make searching even easier by putting all of the information in one place (no more looking through annual indexes) and offering searching alternatives.

The H.W. Wilson Company produces the *Index to Legal Periodicals and Books*. This is the oldest index to legal periodicals, dating back to 1908. Only in 1993 was the "*and Books*" added to its title, and most people use it for periodicals. The *Index* comes out in paper issues, and cumulates into annual and sometimes tri-ennial volumes. It features a joint author/title list, and also has tables that allow one to search for articles that have focused on a specific case or statute. Since H.W. Wilson has published a variety of periodical indexes for years, it is part of the research system in many libraries. *Index to Legal Periodicals* is also online via LEXIS (from 1978 forward) and WESTLAW (from 1981 forward), and the Wilson company has its own online version with a retrospective database going back to 1908.

The Gale Group (also a part of Thomson) produces *Current Law Index* (*CLI*), a paper index of legal periodicals and books. It began in 1980, so its historical coverage is much more limited. It uses the subject headings developed by the Library of Congress, which are much more specific than those used in the *Index to Legal Periodicals*. It also covers a wider range of periodicals and newspapers, as well as some books. *CLI* comes out twelve times a year and then is republished in annual volumes. There is an online version of *CLI* called *Legal Resources Index* that is available on LEXIS and WESTLAW.

The Gale Group also produces an online system called *LegalTrac*. This system takes the information from the *CLI* database, augments it with coverage of many more sources, and sells it to law libraries as a separate subscription database.

Because both WESTLAW and LEXIS publish the full text of many law reviews and journals, you can use Boolean searching techniques to locate articles. You can search for relevant law review articles by using keywords and phrases, in combination. The language of law review authors is as difficult to predict as that of judges, but in those cases where one is seeking a very specific term, case name or citation, this method can be a real short cut.

F. PRACTICE MATERIALS

The practice of law is about solving real problems. This is a very different enterprise than the labors of the law school to make one think like a lawyer. The tools that have developed to serve lawyers in the real world reflect the needs and interests of lawyers in the real world. Such tools are often more focused on a particular topic and are much more likely to offer advice and direction to the busy professional. The tools used in legal education must carefully weigh all arguments, with the researcher urged to go back to the beginning of the problem and review all sources in a blissful paranoid compulsive exercise. By contrast, the practicing lawyer often wants help and a short cut. Whether she is in a large corporate law firm with her hours being billed by the minute serving a client who demands efficiency, or in a public interest practice with a massive overload of files and no time for anything but the basics, the modern lawyer needs help. Each research problem is a matter of available time and resources. These are the principles that inform the discussion of the tools described below.

1. Looseleaf Services

The term looseleaf service can be applied to any set of books that are issued in looseleaf binders. This format allows information to be added to the original publication. Indeed, the binder format allows the substitution of new pages for old, producing a book in which the process of revision never ends.

The first looseleaf services tracked federal administrative agencies. The traditional legal information system, based on court reports, did not cover these prolific agencies well. Agencies produce many documents that would never fall into the *National Reporter System*. Lawyers who worked in the very specialized subject areas covered by the administrative agencies needed specialized indexing. They both understood and needed the use of jargon particular to the field. They also put a premium on timeliness. Information was needed quickly.

Looseleaf services filled these needs. The looseleaf publishers could assemble panels of specialists, devoted to the subject area being covered. They could follow developments closely and issue new releases of information with great frequency, even daily. The new information could be put directly into the binder. The looseleaf publishers could create multiple indexes. One especially useful variation was the printing of cases, statutes, administrative rules and regulations, practice forms, practice tips and much more, all in the same set. Some of these looseleaf services are truly universes of information.

In addition to the myriad of titles by Thomson-West and LexisNexis, Commerce Clearinghouse (CCH) is a major looseleaf publisher known for its practice sets. CCH products are often rich in detail and structurally complex, with layers of indexes and frequent supplementation. The Bureau of National Affairs (BNA) is another major publisher in the area. BNA sets are often more narrowly focused, and tend to be additive, i.e., new information is added at the end of the binder. CCH and BNA are established publishers, but there are many others. This is a field that lends itself to small companies operating in specialized areas. Many of these other publishers have titles that appear on LEXIS or WESTLAW, and many of them also have their own online systems.

There are two survival tips to keep in mind when using looseleaf services. The first is to be sure that one is using the correct looseleaf service. It is likely that the first time a law student will encounter a need to use a looseleaf service will be in practice. Looseleaf services are quintessential practice tools. Many legal fields may be served by several looseleaf sets produced by competing publishers, but there may be one intellectually dominant looseleaf service, *i.e.*, one looseleaf service that everyone uses. If everyone working in a certain area views one looseleaf set as authoritative, that is the one to use. To determine what set is dominant, ask lawyers who work in the area or check with the law librarian in the organization. This first step is crucial.

The second survival tip is to read the directions. Each looseleaf service will have a section on how to use it. In the larger sets this section may be a dozen pages long. Reading this will explain the algorithm that the editors of the set used to put the set together. The "How To Use This Set" section will explain the information included in the set, the lay out, the indexing and the various aids. Spend the twenty minutes needed to read this section and any looseleaf service can be yours. There is an axiom that as a set gains more tools to help its user, as it strives to be more current, the set becomes less intuitive to use. Thus as the publisher works to make it easier to use, it grows harder to approach without guidance. The more that the set tries to help the user, the more the user needs to read the "How To" section.

Looseleaf services have always offered expertise, good indexing, integration of materials and timely delivery. These are all functions that can be delivered equally well, perhaps better, by electric information. At the very least, looseleaf services were always hard to maintain. Finding someone to reliably file the flimsy sheets of paper into the binders is a challenge to every library. Thus, many looseleaf services are now appearing online and as a part of WESTLAW and LEXIS. As such they will function exactly the same, though hypertext links may make them even more useful. As always, innovations designed to make the researcher's life easier will only make it more difficult if you don't read the directions.

2. Legal Newspapers and Journals

Legal newspapers have long been a part of the lawyer's universe. Each metropolitan area had a legal newspaper that listed court dockets, published legal notices, *etc*. In the 1970's this universe was changed when several publishers recognized that there was a market for legal newspapers that carried stories about legal issues, law firms and practice. This idea proved quite perspicacious, and some think that it profoundly changed the way law is practiced. Though there were a number of players who participated, it was Steve Brill who truly led the change.

Legal newspapers now provide coverage of hot issues, big cases, professional developments and often the text of recent cases. Because they are published with great frequency, they are timely, able to spread both news of new legal developments and gossip. Some of them print copies of decisions in paper form before any other source. Find the legal newspaper that is read by lawyers in the area where one is practicing and one has entry to a deep pocket of information.

There are three national legal newspapers. Two weeklies, *The National Law Journal* and the *Legal Times of Washington*, combine coverage of national stories with practice tips and some primary source materials. The latter obviously has a Washington, D.C. focus, hence covering federal agencies in more depth. A third national paper is the *American Lawyer*. This is a monthly that has long feature articles often prepared by investigative reporters. It tracks hot issues and provides good background.

American Lawyer is indexed in *CLI*. Other legal newspapers make no appearances in the print indexes to periodicals. All three national papers are part of the *Legal Resources Index* database on WESTLAW and LEXIS. *LegalTrac* covers the national and regional legal newspapers. Legal newspapers are topical, of the moment current awareness tools. In the time compressed universe of the modern lawyer this makes them potentially very useful.

3. Form Books and Practice Sets

For the practicing lawyer, form books frequently are a way of life. These tools supply forms that are approved by the courts in the relevant jurisdiction, and aid the lawyer in doing her business. Form books also contain practice tips that can assist the practitioner in focusing on issues related to the issue at hand.

There are some national form book sets, the most elaborately articulated being the elements of the LexisNexis *AmJur* universe already dealt with in an earlier section. For the average lawyer, however, form books are local in scope. Each state, indeed each court, may prefer a certain set of forms. This is a Tinker Bell phenomenon. One wants to use the set that everyone believes in. The researcher should find out what set is preferred in her specialty or jurisdiction. Ask an experienced lawyer or law librarian for guidance. Once a set is located, the standard questions should be applied to analyzing it. Is it a part of larger research system? Does it provide references into other sets? How is it kept up to date? Remember that form books are not primary source material. Always recall that the authority of such materials only goes so far as the quality of the set. Use them with a healthy inquisitiveness.

Forms are increasingly appearing as word processing or PDF files available online. In states like California there are dozens of firms fighting for the market. Only time will tell what sets will win a significant market, and survive. Compatibility with an organization's internal information system will decide which format is most convenient in many cases. Forms are being included on some state disks that also have cases and legislation on them. No matter the format, the same questions posed at the end of the preceding paragraph should be applied.

Practice sets are functionally distinct from form books, but in practice the two are often combined. Some looseleaf sets that dominate a practice area are really combinations of a practice book, a form book and learned commentary. What we mean here by practice set are multi-volume sets geared to day-to-day legal activity. Practice sets are produced by private publishers and continuing legal education bodies, and give practical advice on dealing with legal practice. Most states have a practice set that is dominant. If there is such a set, lawyers and judges view it as reliable and correct. At the national level there are a number of sets designed for practice. The two best known national practice sets are built around the *Federal Rules of Civil Procedure* and are discussed at length in Chapter 9.

The growing number of lawyers who need assistance has brought many organizations into the business of providing practice aids. Such concerns may be national in scope, or they may be quite small. The two oldest and best known continuing legal education providers are Practicing Law Institute (PLI) and California Continuing Education of the Bar (CEB). These two traditional providers of continuing legal education materials issue a variety of publications. Some are no more than outlines of seminars, others are quite substantial texts, often with forms attached. Each now has plenty of competition.

Local companies are producing products in a wide range of media. Interactive video, satellite conferencing and compact disk programs are only the edge of the technological innovation that will be seen in years to come. There is substantial money to be made in the continuing education field, this means innovation will follow. Checking with an experienced lawyer or law librarian would be the best way to assess what is accepted locally.

G. LEGAL DIRECTORIES

Finding information about a person can often be crucial to the legal research task. There are a wide variety of tools that list biographical and directory information for individuals. A good reference librarian can find information about almost anyone. Presented here are the standard sources for finding names and basic information about lawyers and judges.

1. *Martindale-Hubbell Law Directory*

There are over 1,000,000 lawyers in the United States. The problem of how to find one has brought forth a series of answers. The traditional tool for finding information on a lawyer or firm is *Martindale-Hubbell Law Directory*. This annual set is built around a state by state listing of attorneys, but lists by specialty are now a part of it as well. Any lawyer can be listed in the set by simply filling in a form. You also can pay for a display advertisement that prints much more information. In the basic listing one finds the name, address, legal education and telephone number of any lawyer. The display advertisements, listed by firm and city, include more information. Because *Martindale-Hubbell* has become the standard set, most lawyers choose to list in it. It is a primary source of information for law students interviewing for jobs. Here is where you can find out about the partner who is interviewing at your school.

Martindale-Hubbell contains many other features, including useful summaries of state and foreign laws. The heart of the set remains its listings. It is published annually and is available online via LEXIS or at <http://www.martindale.com>.

2. *West's Legal Directory*

This element of the WESTLAW database lists information about law firms, lawyers, law schools and legal organizations. It is updated frequently, and is especially useful in job hunting. In part because West has made a portion of the database available for free on the Internet, <http://www.wld.com>, it is growing rapidly. Success for a directory flows from its acceptance.

3. *Who's Who in American Law*

This segment of the Marquis *Who's Who* family of products covers men and women who have distinguished themselves in American law.

Marquis is the most respected of the general biographical directory publishers. *Who's Who in American Law* is a good place to find background on judges, prominent lawyers and politicians. In such directories, the information that appears is produced by the person listed, so that one finds both long and short entries and veracity is never guaranteed.

H. CONCLUSION

Secondary sources contain a world of information. Using them intelligently can save an enormous amount of time. As long as you understand what you are doing, and are careful about the distinction between persuasive and binding authority, research background, and good citations, you can prosper using them. New formats, that is, moving from a paper to an online source, should not throw you. To date, a change in format has never altered the functional workings of any of the tools. The same old caveats and blessings apply.

Chapter 11

RESEARCH STRATEGIES

A.   Introduction.
B.   The Nature of the Search.
     1.   The Fresh Search.
          a.   Defining the Question.
          b.   Understanding the Territory.
     2.   The Incremental Search.
          a.   Creating a Research Plan.
          b.   Looking at a Legal Information Tool.
               (1)   Structure.
               (2)   Timeliness.
               (3)   Research Links.
C.   Finishing and Economics.
D.   Summary.

A. INTRODUCTION

Legal research takes many forms. Some research involves only a simple look-up. For example, you may be called upon to find a statute, or perform a single run through *KeyCite* or *Shepard's* to confirm a citation's validity. This chapter is not about that type of research. This chapter concerns the integrated research process. By this we mean the situation where you begin with a complex problem, sort it, and search for an answer. What follows is an attempt to help you approach such problems. There is no one right way to carry out such research; each problem has its own dynamic. Most problems can be approached in many different ways. As you become a more experienced researcher, you will develop your own rules and methods for approaching research. The following chapter contains a set of generic guidelines that should fit most situations. Use them if they are helpful.

B. THE NATURE OF THE SEARCH

Before approaching the question of strategy, you must recognize that there are two different kinds of searches. The first type of search is the incremental search; the second is the fresh search. The incremental search occurs when you already have data or expertise -- or both -- concerning the problem when you start. You may be a specialist in a subject area, already deeply familiar with the legal information that describes it. If so, the need is to find out if what you have is correct and up-to-date. The incremental search is just another layer of knowledge.

In the fresh search, you know very little about the topic. This type of search must be constructed from the ground up. Because the fresh search is more difficult, and because it is more frequently encountered by newer researchers, it will be dealt with first.

1. The Fresh Search

a. Defining the Question

When approaching a complex research problem in an area where you have little or no expertise, you must define the question with care. The process of definition can involve the subject matter of the search itself or the kind of materials you should use to find an answer. Thinking of the *Bonds* case used earlier in the text, it could involve conceptualizing the legal questions that are posed by the problem of prenuptial contracts or the kind of tools where you can find discussion of the problem.

When embarking on a fresh search you should answer a list of questions. What is the exact topic of the search? Can it be refined? What is the context of the answer? Will the information be used by a lawyer or a client? Does the requesting party want an answer to a query or a set of alternatives? Does the source of the question want you to find a case, a statute, a regulation, some secondary authority or a relevant form? Is the problem a federal one or a state one? Without a full understanding of questions like these, no real progress can be made.

The source of the research question may be a problem here. If you are a lawyer in solo practice, it might be crucial to determine the relevant facts of a problem by interviewing the client. If you are a lawyer in a large firm, the problem may come from a senior associate or partner. If you work for the government problem may come from a supervisor. There are other variations, but consider those three. In each case, the person who is framing the problem may possess only partial or confused knowledge of it. The client may have trouble expressing himself. He may have only a fuzzy grasp of the facts involved. The senior lawyer may be uncertain of what he is asking. If he is busy he may not explain the problem as clearly as he might. If he is uncertain about much of the problem, he may mask his ignorance by being brusque, hoping that you will solve everything. In the government situation, your supervisor could have received the assignment after it has passed through many hands. If he does not understand the question, he may be unwilling to expose that fact.

It is beyond the scope of this book to help you with interviewing your client, or dealing with the office politics of your boss. Learning to extract as much information as possible is a difficult skill to teach. The bottom line is that you must determine what the expectation is. What type of answer does he want? If he cannot tell you that, it is important to have it acknowledged at the start.

Thus, you sometimes begin with only a fraction of the information needed. Given the fact that you may be beginning with something of a data deficit, it is vital to lay out exactly what you do know and what you think that you are looking for in your search. No search should ever be begun until you have a clear goal in mind. (Being finished does not count as a goal!) Far too often the researcher wants to charge into the library, fling books about, and leap from database to database. With 5,000,000+ cases and 750,000+ statutory sections out there you can do a lot of flailing. Stop and invest time now. Write out the question, be explicit about what you expect to find. Understand what information is missing from the question and compensate where possible.

b. Understanding the Territory

Once you have a feel for the question, you must look at the topic that it covers. In a fresh search this often means unknown territory. Before you can conduct an effective search within the literature of a topic you must have a baseline familiarity with it. Legal tools are organized around concepts and jargon. If you don't know the buzz words, you may never be able to find anything. Some areas are dominated by a statute or a set of regulations, and all the information may be organized around these lodestars. Or, an area may be based in a common law topic where judicial opinions developed over decades form the information base. It could be that one multi-volume looseleaf service dominates the area and is used by everyone. Maybe the topic of your search is one that is in great turmoil, with several competing theories currently doing battle. You must know these things before seriously beginning.

If the topic is one of legal doctrine, you should acquire enough background to feel comfortable. This level of background can be attained by use of the relevant *Nutshell*, a current law review article or a perhaps a law school outline. Needed expertise may reside in a research pathfinder that has been published or one that is maintained within your law firm or legal organization's local information structure. Someone may have passed this way before. Here is where a law librarian can be a godsend. The librarian will have the best understanding of your information resources. Needed background might best come from a meeting with a senior lawyer or supervisor. In a face to face meeting, an experienced researcher can impart more background about a topic than any text. Spending a few minutes with a human being at this point is better than days spent laying siege to indexes.

How much background is needed? One guideline is that you should have a grasp of a new topic that is roughly equal to the familiarity you would have if you had taken a law school course in the relevant topic. Put another way, you should have the sophistication to read the *Nutshell* on the topic with ease. Purists might scoff that this is not enough expertise, but lawyers in practice have to learn new topics all the time. Efficiency in research, *i.e.* doing just as much as is needed, is often the highest virtue.

Until such familiarity is gained, you should stay away from the large databases like WESTLAW, LEXIS and the Topic and Key Number System. These tools are massive information universes. They can help you if you know what you are doing, but they are no place to learn about the background of a topic. You come to them with information in hand. You need to know jargon, a conceptual framework and have a background or you will just stumble through a jungle of pages. To attempt an online search without it is a waste of time and money.

A word must be added about research in non-legal areas. Much of the real research work of the attorney is about non-legal matters. Whether a lawyer works primarily in litigation or in transactions, lawyers are constantly being called upon to master the intricacies of new subject areas. The same need for background applies. In the hard-bound version of this book, *How to Find the Law*, an entire chapter is devoted to working with non-legal materials. The best rule is to learn the concepts and the jargon that is needed by getting the right background, by locating the "Tinker Bell"[1] in the factual area. Once again, a few minutes spent with an experienced librarian is a good way to start.

Having reached this point, the fresh search becomes the same as an incremental search. You should now have sufficient familiarity with the topic and its literature to proceed. The following sections apply to all searches.

2. The Incremental Search

a. Creating a Research Plan

Before beginning any research *write down a research plan*. The emphasis is added for a reason. Writing down a research plan is essential.

---

[1]   Everyone believes in Tinker Bell, so this is Bob's word for the one source (looseleaf, practice guide) that every practitioner in the field believes in. If everyone else is using it, you should know what it is and use it also.

The first issue to be considered in creating your research plan is resources. How much is the question worth in terms of time and money? Not knowing this is a dealbreaker. In the real world time is money and money is everything. (This is true in public sector as well as the private.) One of the most frequent complaints made by senior lawyers about recent law school graduates is that they do not know how to budget time. To budget, you must know what is available. Therefore, the foundation question is how much time are you supposed to spend on the problem?

The next question is how much in the way of resources can you expend? In the world of electronic information, the available funds are a defining element. Will you be authorized to use WESTLAW and LEXIS? Does your organization subscribe to proprietary websites that you can use in lieu of online services? How should you balance the equation between saving your time and spending money on resources? In some situations your time is irrelevant. Law school is like that. Your professors can give you endless conflicting assignments that can only be completed if food and interpersonal relationships are mostly abandoned. But in the real world your time may be in demand. There may be competing priorities. How much is that worth in terms of resources? Find out before you act. Put it in the plan.

Once the resource questions are sorted out, prepare the guts of the plan. Point them toward your deadline. Allocate your time and then list what steps your research will take. It is imperative that you list which research tools you expect to use. This allows you to plan realistically. Just as important is the need to list out search terms that you will use in indexes. Think them through before the rough and tumble of the search begins. Also, write out likely searches for use with search engines. Of course such lists will have to be modified as your research progresses, but you must have a base to work from as you go. Make notes of new ideas as you get them. This will save time and pain later. One law librarian at a large firm in San Francisco reminds the attorneys working there that they shouldn't spend more than ten minutes in an electronic database (LEXIS, WESTLAW, even Google) looking for what they want, otherwise they are wasting too much time (and money).

Look at your list to see if you will have access to everything that you need. Will you have to leave the library or office in which you normally work? Do you need some printed source or database that is not available to you? A good first step is to go over the tools you plan to use and terms that you plan to employ with a law librarian. She can give you tips and new ideas. As a general matter, you should be aware of the information resources of your organization. Take a look at them sometime when you are not in the middle of a research crisis. Increasingly organizations are developing internal information files, files that may save the work of the past, or draw upon the work of other specialists. Sit down with the librarian and find this out. You will also find that the librarian is a part of a network of librarians. She often can get to information sources that you cannot. She may also know about individuals or groups that can help you. As discussed in Chapter 6, finding someone who cares about the issue can save you time. Make a list of people or organizations that may already have done some of your work for you.

You will have to vary from this plan, but it will guide you. The budget element is the one to watch. A research job done adequately, on-time and on-budget is infinitely better than one done perfectly but completed three days late at a cost no one can pay. A good friend in a very big law firm tells us that what he misses most about law school is the opportunity to do as much research as he would like on a complicated problem. In practice he can only do as much as the client authorizes – that is, only as much as the client will pay for.

The most important thing is to write down the plan before beginning. We suggest that every plan contain at least the following:

1. Deadline for project
2. Time that should be spent on the project
3. Amount of resources that can be used
4. Steps Anticipated in Research Process
5. Research tools to be used
6. Likely Search Terms
7. Possible Boolean search terms
8. People who can help.

b. Looking at a Legal Information Tool

Now that you are embarked on the search, the focus shifts to the tools that you will use. If you are already familiar with a subject area, you probably have mastery of the jargon and concepts that are at play. You are something of a personal expert on the topic. Such familiarity should never lead to complacency. Each day, each hour, new cases are being decided, new statutes are being enacted, new rules are appearing. New fact situations are pushing and pulling at the most settled of doctrines. You must keep up, keep open and never stop looking. Perhaps it is an unfortunate metaphor in a book for law students, but legal research is a bit like a shark, it has to keep moving or it will die.

But whether you are new to a topic or an experienced hand, you must be efficient. You will have to get the most possible out of every tool that you use. To do this you must understand how to use each legal information tool. This applies both to printed sources and to electronic information. Look for the functions that the tool serves, how it is designed. In today's rich information environment, you must understand the research tool as well as the topic.

Listed below are some general pieces of advice on evaluating research tools. They are a necessary part of every research process, but they are especially critical for the incremental researcher.

(1) Structure

The most common mistake that you can make in using any research tool is to use it blindly. Far too often people search intuitively, trying a generic method, or guessing at how to exploit a book. It is a very common human trait to try to search by the "seat of your pants." It can even be contended that when the legal research universe consisted largely of cases and the finding tools built around them, and when the database of cases was small, that such a method was workable. The information environment of the 21st Century, with oceans of information being produced and highly sophisticated tools being built by various vendors, is very different. In this world, you can never take information for granted. Legal research has become a much more active process.

The first time you use any research tool, you must look at it critically. What features does it have? How is it put together? When was it compiled? When was it last updated? What is the publisher trying to tell you? Is there a section that explains how to use it? If it's electronic information, have you looked at the user's manual? Can you bring yourself to use the "help" links? Amazing resources are devoted to creating manuals and "help" links, yet folks are reluctant to use them. If you do so you will look like a genius.

Books on research like this one can attempt to describe what certain tools contain, but the researcher will never make any sense of the tool until he sits down to use. Hold the work in your hands, or look at it on the terminal, and be sure that you understand it. Skip this step and the work is lost. The dumbest kind of research is "A to B" research where the person using a tool only knows how to look up one thing in one way. Invest the minutes to scope out the set. If the structure seems too difficult or obscure, ask for help from the nearest reference librarian. Listen and learn now and you will look like a star later.

(2) Timeliness

One of the most salient questions to ask about a research tool today is how timely it is. Getting current information is a matter of economics. In the information world of today, you can get information almost instantaneously, if you want to pay for it. It is important to understand the worth of a research problem in terms of both time and money, so that you can calculate the equation of how much time and money can be spent on the search in comparison with how current the information must be to be valuable.

The question is how current the information has to be to meet the researcher's needs. Any good law librarian can tell you that if someone has the resources to pay for it, any information can be found. You must make an informed calculation how much to spend in this particular case.

Knowing the costs is not enough. You must be certain to exhaust the full extent of the timeliness built into the tool. When was the database last updated? How recently has the website been modified? Check the copyright date of any book that you use. Given production schedules the information is probably a year older than that date. Check when the pocket part or pamphlet supplement that keeps the set up-to-date was issued. You must know how good your source is on timing.

(3) Research Links

Every research tool is part of a larger research universe. A source may cite to cases, statutes, regulations, other works, other sets, other authors. Think of each research tool as the center of a great cross-hatching of information. Most of the citations referenced are obvious, but the deeper connections are sometimes the most useful. WESTLAW and LEXIS will refer you to practice sets and commentaries when you use their systems. Sometimes a researcher will sniff at such references, seeing them as mere puffing of products. They are that, but they may also be useful research tools. Each can be exploited by the researcher to find more information. Each leads to a new location. These are not persuasive authority, but they can represent considerable spade work already done. With experience you may find that one set of books, or the works of one publisher's system, is superior. But at the beginning of your research career, especially when you are working in the relatively rich and varied environment of a law school library, it is worthwhile to try them all.

C. FINISHING AND ECONOMICS

The great zen koan of legal research is "When is legal research complete?" Can you ever read every relevant document? Can you ever follow every trail through *KeyCite* to its end? If you *KeyCite* every case found and then *KeyCite* every case found by *Keyciting* those cases, and then *Shepardize* those, will you slip into an M. C. Escher spiral? Can you ever really be up-to-date? As soon as the ink on your last print job is dry things are changing. The law will not stand still. It seems that real closure is never reached. When can you stop?

The simplest answer is that you stop when the deadline arrives. In the real world reality intervenes. That is why the section on creating a research plan emphasizes cost so much. If you have budgeted your time, you come to a natural end. When they are pounding on your door demanding the answer you are done. But beyond hitting the wall, how can you know when the job is really done?

One way to know that research is complete is to return to the original question and the original research plan. Is the question answered? Have you checked everything on your list? Another way is to look at the information that further research is producing. Are you running into the same citations? Frequently an area will be filled with unresolved questions and uncertainties. Are you being circled back to the same dilemmas? You should apply the law of diminishing returns. Are you getting back very little that is new for your investment of time? This probably means that you are on top of the field.

As a way to check yourself, you can consult an "end source." An end source is one of the last documents in the research stream, *i.e.* one of the most recent. For example, read the latest judicial opinion on the topic. Are you comfortably informed about all the issues raised and the sources cited? If the problem is in a legislative area, do you know why the latest legislation was passed and what areas are currently in dispute? If one is working in a regulatory area, do you know who issued the relevant regulations and why? Can you identify the Tinker Bell set, the set that everyone believes to be the most authoritative, in the topic area? If you can answer these questions, you understand the dynamics of the issue. You must of course continue to update as time passes. But if you truly understand the issues in an end source document, you are done.

As a last check, return to the original economic equation. Be certain that you have carried both your updating and your level of detail to the point required by the economics of the problem.

D. SUMMARY

Legal research is a means to an end. No one ever made a living just knowing how to use research tools. One must be able to take the product of legal research and analyze it. The real joy of being a lawyer is to be able to use your own intelligence, to take the sources and create an answer out of them. The point of this Chapter, and this book, is to make sure that you can find all the sources that you need. A good researcher can gather in all of the relevant sources so that the really good part can begin. The required first step to good lawyering is good research. Good luck!

A Few Words at the End

Here are a few things Bob thought worth mentioning, even if some of them aren't traditional legal research sources:

1.   I still like Findlaw. <www.findlaw.com> For me it is like a Target or a Walmart store. There is too much stuff on display and I sometimes get lost, but there are really a lot of treasures there. And it's free. Good current events source too. Makes for fine reading during a boring class.

2.   Wikipedia is a great resource. <www.wikipedia.org> This is an open access web-based encyclopedia into which anyone may add information. A great way to find factual information and fun getting there.

3.   Prof. Brian Leiter at the University of Texas Law School maintains a blog that covers legal education. It is a place to go to if you want to get the skinny on the world of law schools. Prof. Leiter can be provocative, but that is half the fun. <www.leiterreports.typepad.com>

4.   Prof. Bernard Hibbits of the University of Pittsburgh Law School maintains the Jurist website. This is a great resource with a wide range of items covering legal and non-legal matters. Prof. Hibbits was an early proponent of digital information and he remains in the forefront. <www.jurist.law.pitt.edu>

5.   Sabrina Pacifici is a pioneer librarian who edits a site called LLRX. Here law librarians doing cutting edge research gather to share secrets. The site is very strong in international sources and in research guides. If you are a serious researcher you have to check this out. <www.llrx.com>

6.   I still love <www.imdb.com> A great place to run down movies and movie stars and it is still free.

Appendix A

THE FLAMBEAU CASE

Part I: Reading a Case

In order to illustrate the principles of legal research and legal information discussed in the text of *Finding the Law*, we have decided to use an example from the real world. Therefore, we are reprinting the case of *Flambeau v. Honeywell*, 116 Wisc. 2d 95, 341 N.W.2d 655, (1984). No one case demonstrates all of the things discussed in this book, or even all of the things discussed about judicial opinions, but *Flambeau* is a wonderful example of many points of legal information. The *Flambeau* opinion is selected from the opinions of the Wisconsin Supreme Court. Justice Shirley Abrahamson, a very able jurist, writes the decision. At issue in the case is the common law of contract, specifically the doctrine of accord and satisfaction, and how the adoption of the *Uniform Commercial Code* changes one part of it. The case appears in some casebooks used in Contracts in the first year of law school.

First, we reprint the entire opinion. Read it straight through. The casebooks used by first year law students reprint parts of cases, often artfully edited to make them mysterious. Look at the full case as created by Justice Abrahamson and augmented by the publisher. Read it with an eye for the features of case reporting and the hooks for case finding that are discussed in Chapters 2 and 4 of the text. Note the types of information sources that Justice Abrahamson uses, and how she uses them. What is the primary authority? What persuasive sources does she use?

Second, we reprint the case one more time. To help you understand the case, this time we will precede it with a diagram showing how it arrived at the Wisconsin Supreme Court. This time we present the text of the decision as it would appear if you were using WESTLAW, and we include a running commentary alongside the text of the case. In the commentary we point out the various parts of the case. We will also point out what sources Justice Abrahamson uses, and how she uses them. You will see materials mentioned in almost every chapter come to light. At the end of the case we will print out a *KeyCite* and a *Shepard's* search based on the citation of the *Flambeau* case. Each point that we discuss is covered in the text, but here, in context, it may make more sense. We will also try to make a few points about legal argumentation.

We hope that this exercise leads you to view all cases critically. Any judicial opinion is a universe of information. It should be read as one point on a vector of legal argument. The opinion summarizes the law as viewed by one particular court at one particular point in time. Perhaps other courts will cite to it, leading it into the future. Do not view opinions as static, they are part of a process. But give them credit for being attempts at stating the law as a sensible whole. Not all Judges are as skilled as Justice Abrahamson is, but what she does is in many ways what every judge is attempting to do.

Part II: The *Flambeau* Case

Supreme Court of Wisconsin.
FLAMBEAU PRODUCTS CORPORATION, a Wisconsin corporation,
Plaintiff-Respondent-
Petitioner,
v.
HONEYWELL INFORMATION SYSTEMS, INC., a foreign
corporation, Defendant-
Appellant.
No. 82-307.

Argued Oct. 31, 1983.
Decided Jan. 4, 1984.

Debtor buyer of computer equipment sought declaratory judgment against creditor seller to effect that debtor had no additional obligations to obligation already paid and that creditor had no security interest in equipment. The Circuit Court, Sauk County, Howard Latton, J., granted summary judgment in favor of debtor, and creditor appealed. The Court of Appeals, 97 Wis.2d 759, 295 N.W.2d 834, reversed and remanded. On remand, the Circuit Court, Sauk County, Howard Latton, J., entered an order for an interlocutory judgment extinguishing debtor's obligations under contract and discharging creditor's security interest, and creditor again appealed. The Court of Appeals, Cane, J., 111 Wis.2d 317, 330 N.W.2d 228, again reversed and remanded. On review, the Supreme Court, Abrahamson, J., held that: (1) Uniform Commercial Code section, providing that party who with explicit reservation of rights assents to performance in manner offered by other party does not prejudice rights reserved, does not alter common-law rule of accord and satisfaction as it relates to full payment checks, and (2) debtor's good-faith claim of offset for value of computer programming services included in purchase price but only partially used by debtor rendered entire claim as to amount of debt under contract disputed, and thus creditor's claim against debtor was discharged upon creditor's cashing check tendered by debtor in full payment of debt and retaining proceeds.

Decision of the Court of Appeals reversed; order for judgment of the circuit court affirmed and cause remanded.

Steinmetz and William A. Bablitch, JJ., filed dissenting opinions.

West Headnotes

[1] Accord and Satisfaction ☞11(2)
8k11(2) Most Cited Cases
Under common-law rule of accord and satisfaction, if check offered by debtor as full payment for disputed claim is cashed by creditor, creditor is deemed to have accepted debtor's conditional offer of full payment notwithstanding any reservations by creditor.

[2] Accord and Satisfaction ☞11(2)
8k11(2) Most Cited Cases
Under common-law rule of accord and satisfaction, if check offered by debtor as sole payment for disputed claim is cashed by creditor, creditor's cashing of check constitutes accord and satisfaction which discharges entire debt.

[3] Accord and Satisfaction ☞11(2)
8k11(2) Most Cited Cases
Uniform Commercial Code section, providing that party who with explicit reservation of rights assents to performance in manner offered by other party does not prejudice rights reserved, is not applicable to full payment check and does not alter common-law rule of accord and satisfaction as it relates to full payment checks. W.S.A. 401.207; U.C.C. § 1-207.

[4] Accord and Satisfaction ☞1
8k1 Most Cited Cases
"Accord and satisfaction" is agreement to discharge existing disputed claim, and constitutes a defense to action to enforce claim.

[5] Accord and Satisfaction ☞1
8k1 Most Cited Cases

[5] Accord and Satisfaction ☞5
8k5 Most Cited Cases
Accord and satisfaction requires offer, acceptance, and consideration.

[6] Accord and Satisfaction ☞11(1)
8k11(1) Most Cited Cases

Payment in full settlement of claim which is disputed as to amount discharges entire claim.

[7] Accord and Satisfaction ⚿5
8k5 Most Cited Cases

Resolution of actual controversy involving some subject of pecuniary value and interest to parties is sufficient consideration of an accord and satisfaction.

[8] Accord and Satisfaction ⚿7(1)
8k7(1) Most Cited Cases

Payment of part of debt which is not disputed as to amount does not discharge debt altogether, even when it is expressly agreed that partial payment is received in full satisfaction.

[9] Accord and Satisfaction ⚿10(1)
8k10(1) Most Cited Cases

Debtor's mere refusal to pay full claim does not make it a disputed claim as to which debtor's partial payment in full settlement of claim will discharge debt altogether.

[10] Accord and Satisfaction ⚿11(1)
8k11(1) Most Cited Cases

Where debtor's refusal to pay full claim is arbitrary and debtor knows it has no just basis, payment of less than full amount claimed does not operate as accord and satisfaction, even though it is tendered and received as such.

[11] Accord and Satisfaction ⚿10(1)
8k10(1) Most Cited Cases

When amount of debt is undisputed but offset is claimed arising directly out of contract of sale of goods and not out of any collateral transaction, debt is single claim which is disputed in amount, and payment in full settlement of less than amount claimed operates as accord and satisfaction.

[12] Accord and Satisfaction ⚿10(1)
8k10(1) Most Cited Cases

Question whether offset arising directly out of contract of sale of goods renders claim as to amount of debt under contract disputed, for purpose of determining whether payment in full settlement of less than amount claimed operates as accord and satisfaction, depends not on whether offset is legally valid but on whether it is asserted in good faith.

[13] Accord and Satisfaction ☞10(1)
8k10(1) Most Cited Cases

Debtor's good-faith claim of offset under contract for sale of computer equipment for value of computer programming services included in purchase price but only partially used by debtor rendered entire claim as to amount of debt under contract disputed, and thus creditor's claim against debtor was discharged upon creditor's cashing check tendered by debtor in full payment of debt and retaining proceeds.

**657 *97 Clyde C. Cross, Baraboo, argued, for plaintiff-respondent-petitioner; there were briefs by Karen A. Mercer and Cross, Mercer & Maffei, Baraboo, on brief.

J. Leroy Thilly, Madison, argued, for defendant-appellant; Barbara L. Block, James E. Bartzen and Boardman, Suhr, Curry & Field, Madison, on brief.

ABRAHAMSON, Justice.

This is a review of a published decision of the court of appeals, *Flambeau Products Corp. v. Honeywell Information Systems,* 111 Wis.2d 317, 330 N.W.2d 228 (1983) (*Flambeau II*), reversing an order of the circuit court for Sauk county, ***98** Howard W. Latton, circuit judge. The circuit court entered an order for an interlocutory judgment extinguishing the obligations of Flambeau Products Corporation to Honeywell Information Systems, Inc., under an installment purchase contract and discharging Honeywell's security interest in the purchased equipment. [FN1] The circuit court concluded that sec. 401.207, Stats. 1981-82, was not applicable to this case in which Flambeau tendered a check in full satisfaction of Honeywell's claim and that Honeywell's acceptance of Flambeau's check constituted an accord and satisfaction discharging the balance of Honeywell's claim, notwithstanding Honeywell's reservation of rights to claim the balance due. The court of appeals reversed the judgment of the circuit court, holding that sec. 401.207 is applicable to Flambeau's check offered in full payment of the claim and that Honeywell effectively reserved its rights under sec. 401.207. Because we agree with the circuit court's interpretation of sec. 401.207 and its application of the common law doctrine of accord and satisfaction, we reverse the decision of the court of appeals and affirm the circuit court's order for an interlocutory judgment.

FN1. The judgment is interlocutory because Flambeau's second cause of action seeking damages from Honeywell for Honeywell's failure to supply a termination statement discharging the lien has not yet been tried.

I.

The facts are set forth in detail in the decision of the court of appeals in *Flambeau II,* and it is sufficient for us to summarize them briefly here.

Flambeau Products Corporation (plaintiff-buyer) entered into purchase contracts with Honeywell Information Systems, Inc. (defendant-seller) in September 1975 for the acquisition of computer equipment. Under the purchase contracts Flambeau was obligated to pay 60 ***99** monthly installments over a period of five years and had the right to prepay the entire amount at any time. In connection with the equipment purchase and as part of the purchase price, Flambeau was to receive $14,000 worth of computer programming services that Flambeau could use until October 1, 1976. Flambeau used part of these services prior to October 1, 1976 but stopped requesting programming services when it unilaterally decided they were not helpful.

In late 1976 or early 1977, at Flambeau's request, Honeywell advised Flambeau that the amount due to prepay the contract was ****658** $109,412. Without further discussion, Flambeau sent Honeywell a check for $95,412. On the back of the check were the words "in full payment of liability to you for equipment...." Flambeau's check was accompanied by a letter which stated that the "check in the amount of $95,412 [is] in full settlement of notes we owe to Honeywell in connection with purchase of our computer system." The calculations set forth in the letter show that $14,000 for "unused programming" was deducted from the sum of $109,412 to arrive at the net payment. Honeywell cashed the check, retained the proceeds, notified Flambeau that the check was not accepted as payment in full, and requested Flambeau to remit the balance due plus interest. Honeywell does not on this review assert that the check cashing or retention of the proceeds was unauthorized.

Flambeau sought a declaratory judgment that it had no further obligations to Honeywell and that Honeywell had no valid security interest in its equipment. Honeywell counterclaimed for $14,000. The circuit court granted summary judgment to Flambeau on the ground that there was an accord and satisfaction. On appeal the court of appeals reversed the circuit court in an unpublished decision, 97 Wis.2d 759, 295 N.W.2d 834, filed on June 17, 1980 (*Flambeau I*). It is not entirely clear whether the court of appeals *100 held that summary judgment was not appropriate because there was a dispute of material facts or that as a matter of law Flambeau could not, on the basis of the facts presented in the record on summary judgment, claim an accord and satisfaction. In any event on remand a trial was held on the issue of accord and satisfaction.

After trial to the court, the circuit court held that sec. 401.207 was not applicable to this case and that the offer and acceptance of Flambeau's check constituted an accord and satisfaction discharging the balance of Honeywell's claims. The circuit court ordered judgment in favor of Flambeau. In *Flambeau II*, the court of appeals reversed the circuit court's order, addressing only the issue of the applicability of sec. 401.207 to this case, not the issue of accord and satisfaction. [FN2]

> FN2. Honeywell argues on review that since the same facts were presented in the trial as in the summary judgment *Flambeau I* established as the law of the case that Flambeau is not entitled to claim an accord and satisfaction. Honeywell made this same argument to the court of appeals. We are not persuaded by Honeywell's argument. The holding in *Flambeau I* is subject to interpretation, and the court of appeals in *Flambeau II* apparently interpreted its decision in *Flambeau I* as not requiring reversal of the circuit court's order on the issue of accord and satisfaction.

Two issues are raised on review:

(1) Does the Uniform Commercial Code sec. 1-207 (sec. 401.207, Stats. 1981-82) alter the common law rule of accord and satisfaction as it relates to full payment checks? [FN3]

> FN3. We use the term "full payment check," but there are other terms used to describe a situation in which the check is offered upon a condition and the payee understands that cashing the check constitutes an assent to the conditions. For example: check in full settlement, conditional check, conditioned check. See Rosenthal, *Discord and Dissatisfaction: Section 1-207 of the Uniform*

Commercial Code, 78 Colum.L.Rev. 48, 49-50 (1978); 6 Corbin, *Contracts* sec. 1277, pp. 122-23 (1962).

*101 (2) If sec. 401.207, Stats. 1981-82, does not alter the common law rule, may Flambeau claim an accord and satisfaction in this case?

II.

[1][2] Under the common law rule of accord and satisfaction, if a check offered by the debtor as full payment for a disputed claim is cashed by the creditor, the creditor is deemed to have accepted the debtor's conditional offer of full payment notwithstanding any reservations by the creditor. In other words, the creditor's cashing the full payment check constitutes an accord and satisfaction which discharges the entire debt.

The common law rule of accord and satisfaction promotes fairness by protecting the ****659** bona fide expectations of a debtor who tenders payment on condition that it will be accepted as payment in full. The rule also provides a method of settling disputes without litigation.

Honeywell argues that sec. 1-207 of the Uniform Commercial Code (UCC) (sec. 401.207, Stats. 1981-82) alters the common law rule of accord and satisfaction and permits the seller-creditor to accept and cash the check offered as payment in full and to explicitly reserve the right to obtain payment from the buyer-debtor of the balance due.

Sec. 1-207 (sec. 401.207, Stats. 1981-82) provides as follows:
"A party who with explicit reservation of rights performs or promises performance or assents to performance in a manner demanded or offered by the other party does not thereby prejudice the rights reserved. Such words as 'without prejudice', 'under protest' or the like are sufficient."

Sec. 1-207 of the UCC became sec. 401.207 of the law of Wisconsin on July 1, 1965. Although the language ***102** of sec. 1-207 can be read to apply to a full payment check, the words of sec. 1-207 do not compel this conclusion. It is generally conceded that the scope and meaning of sec. 1-207 are unclear, Farnsworth, *Contracts* sec. 4.23, p. 283 (1982), and courts and commentators are divided as to whether sec. 1-207 has changed the common law principles relating to full payment checks. [FN4] The issue of the applicability of sec. 1-207 (sec. ***103** 401.207, Stats. 1981-82) to the full payment check is one of first impression in this state.

FN4. For authorities that sec. 1-207 has altered the common law of accord and satisfaction, see *Bivins v. White Dairy,* 378 So.2d 1122, 1124 (Ala.Civ.App.1979) (dictum); *Miller v. Jung,* 361 So.2d 788, 789 (Fla.App.1978); *Kilander v. Blickle Co.,* 280 Or. 425, 429, 571 P.2d 503 (1977) (dictum); *Braun v. C.E.P.C. Distributors, Inc.,* 77 App.Div.2d 358, 433 N.Y.S.2d 447, 449-50 (1980); *Scholl v. Tallman,* 247 N.W.2d 490, 492 (S.D.1976); White & Summers, *Handbook of the Law Under the Uniform Commercial Code* sec. 13-21 (2d ed. 1980); Calamari & Perillo, *Contracts* sec. 5-16, p. 197 (2d ed. 1977).

For the view that sec. 1-207 does not affect the common law of accord and satisfaction, see *Chancellor, Inc. v. Hamilton Appliance Co., Inc.,* 175 N.J.Super. 345, 352, 418 A.2d 1326 (1980); *Brown v. Coastal Truckways, Inc.,* 44 N.C.App. 454, 458, 261 S.E.2d 266 (1980); *State Department of Fisheries v. J-Z Sales Corporation,* 25 Wash.App. 671, 681-82, 610 P.2d 390 (1980); *Jahn v. Burns,* 593 P.2d 828, 830 (Wyo.1979); 6 Corbin, *Contracts* sec. 1979 (Supp.1982, pt. 2); 2 Restatement (Second), *Contracts* sec. 281, comment *d,* p. 384 (1979) (sec. 1-207 "need not be read as changing" the common law rules); Hawkland, *The Effect of U.C.C. § 1-207 on the Doctrine of Accord and Satisfaction by Conditional Check,* 74 Comm.L.J. 329, 331 (1969); McDonnell, *Purposive Interpretation of the Uniform Commercial Code: Some Implications for Jurisprudence,* 126 U.Pa.L.Rev. 795, 824-28 (1978); Rosenthal, *Discord and Dissatisfaction: Section 1-207 of the Uniform Commercial Code,* 78 Colum.L.Rev. 48 (1978); Comment, *U.C.C. Section 1-207 and the Full Payment Check: The Struggle Between the Code and the Common Law--Where Do the Debtor and Creditor Fit In,* 7 U. Dayton L.Rev. 421, 422-23, 435 (1982); Comment, *Accord and Satisfaction: Conditional Tender by Check Under the Uniform Commercial Code,* 18 Buffalo L.Rev. 539, 549 (1969); Note, *Does U.C.C. Section 1-207 Apply to the Doctrine of Accord and Satisfaction by Conditional Check,* 11 Creighton L.Rev. 515, 527 (1977).

See also Fritz v. Marantette, 404 Mich. 329, 273 N.W.2d 425 (1978), which refused to decide the question. This case has been criticized in Harris, *Commercial Transaction, 1979 Annual Survey of Michigan Law,* 26 Wayne L.Rev. 469 (1980).

For other discussions of sec. 1-207, see Quinn, *Uniform*

Commercial Code Commentary and Law Digest sec. 1-207[A][1][2] (1983 Cum.Supp. No. 1); Caraballo, *The Tender Trap: U.C.C. § 1-207 and Its Applicability to an Attempted Accord and Satisfaction by Tendering a Check in a Dispute Arising from a Sale of Goods,* 11 Seton Hall L.Rev. 445 (1981).

Since the language of sec. 1-207 does not provide an answer to the question of whether the section redefines the common law of accord and satisfaction as it applies to full payment checks, we attempt to determine the drafters' intent [FN5] by examining **660 the official comments to sec. 1-207 and the legislative history and by applying the rules of interpretation set forth in the UCC.

> FN5. As Dean Rosenthal wisely explains, "Any assertion of the 'intention' of one legislature, much less that of all the enacting legislatures [of the UCC, namely the American Law Institute and the National Conference of Commissioners on Uniform State Laws] collectively, in such circumstances, requires wondrous confidence." Rosenthal, *Discord and Dissatisfaction: Section 1-207 of the Uniform Commercial Code,* 78 Colum.L.Rev. 48, 58 (1978).

The official UCC Comments generally point out any significant changes which a section makes in existing law. If the drafters of the UCC intended sec. 1- 207 to effect a change in the full payment check rule, one would suppose that the official UCC Comment and commentary of the Commercial Code Committee [FN6] of the *104 Wisconsin Legislative Council would have described such a significant change. They do not. Professor Hawkland notes that "a strong argument can be made that the failure of the comment to 1-207 to mention such a sweeping change as would be caused by the application of the section" to the full payment check, indicates that no such result was intended. Hawkland, *The Effect of U.C.C. Section 1-207 on the Doctrine of Accord and Satisfaction by Conditional Check,* 74 Comm.L.J. 329, 331 (1969).

> FN6. A commentary entitled Summary of Changes or Clarifications was prepared by the Commercial Code Committee of the Wisconsin Legislative Council in its section-by-section analysis of the Uniform Commercial Code (UCC) prior to the adoption of the UCC in Wisconsin. The commentary was

designed to be used with the official text and official comments of the UCC. See Introduction, 1961 Report of the Wisconsin Legislative Council, vol. III, part 2, reproduced in 40A, West's Wis.Stats., Annot. vii (1964).

Significantly both the official UCC Comment to sec. 1-207 and the commentary of the Commercial Code Committee of the Wisconsin Legislative Council to sec. 401.207 suggest that sec. 1-207 does not apply to a full payment check.

The official UCC Comment to sec. 1-207 reads as follows:
"1. This section provides machinery for the continuation of performance along the lines contemplated by the contract despite a pending dispute, by adopting the mercantile device of going ahead with delivery, acceptance, or payment 'without prejudice,' 'under protest,' 'under reserve,' 'with reservation of all our rights,' and the like. All of these phrases completely reserve all rights within the meaning of this section.
    The section therefore contemplates that limited as well as general reservations and acceptance by a party may be made 'subject to satisfaction of our purchase,' 'subject to acceptance by our customers,' or the like.
"2. This section does not add any new requirement of language of reservation where not already required by law, but merely provides a specific measure on which a party can rely as he makes or concurs in any interim adjustment in the course of performance. It does not affect or impair the provisions of this Act such as those under which the buyer's remedies for defect survive acceptance without being expressly claimed if notice of the defects is given within a reasonable time. Nor does it disturb the policy of those cases which restrict the effect of a waiver of a defect to reasonable limits under *105 the circumstances, even though no such reservation is expressed.
"The section is not addressed to the creation or loss of remedies in the ordinary course of performance but rather to a method of procedure where one party is claiming as of right something which the other feels to be unwarranted."

Various interpretations of sec. 1-207 and the official comment have been suggested. Professor Hawkland and Dean Rosenthal conclude that the official comment indicates that sec. 1-207 is not applicable to full payment checks. Professor Hawkland reaches this conclusion by focusing on the phrase "performance along the lines contemplated by the contract" in the comment. [FN7] The official UCC Comment, according to Professor Hawkland, suggests that sec. 1-207 was intended to apply to ongoing **661 contracts, not to full payment checks that terminate the contractual arrangement. Hawkland, *The Effect of U.C.C. § 1-207 on the Doctrine of Accord and Satisfaction by Conditional Check,* 74 Comm.L.J. 329, 331 (1969).

> FN7. One commentator suggests that those who support the idea that sec. 1-207 overrules the common law have not offered any satisfactory explanation why payment and performance are treated separately in sec. 1- 208 but performance should be viewed as including payment in sec. 1- 207. 6 Corbin, *Contracts* sec. 1279, p. 396 (Supp.1982, pt. 2).

Dean Rosenthal suggests an alternative interpretation of sec. 1-207 and the official UCC Comment. He suggests that sec. 1-207 applies "only where one party's acquiescence in the other's performance or demand might, *by operation of law,* result in a waiver or other basis for prejudicing his rights.... Under this interpretation, sec. 1-207 would not apply where the challenge was *expressly* communicated, as in a check offered in satisfaction of an obligation on a clear take-it-or-leave-it basis." Rosenthal, *Discord and Dissatisfaction: *106 Section 1-207 of the Uniform Commercial Code,* 78 Colum.L.Rev. 48, 63-64 (1978).

The commentary to the Wisconsin Commercial Code Committee also suggests that sec. 401.207 was intended to apply to fact situations other than full payment checks. [FN8]

> FN8. The Committee's summary of changes or clarifications of the law made by sec. 401.207 states:
> *"Summary of changes or clarifications*
> [Sec. 401.207] provides a method of procedure whereby one party claiming a right which the other party feels to be unwarranted can make certain that the fact that he proceeds with or promises or assents to performance will not operate as a waiver of his claim to such right; there is no similar general provision in the present law, though the policy of Wis.Stat. sec. 121.49 is similar." See sec. 401.207, West's Wis.Stat.Annot. (1964).
> Sec. 121.49, Stats.1961, provided:

"Acceptance does not bar action for damages. In the absence of express or implied agreement of the parties, acceptance of the goods by the buyer shall not discharge the seller from liability in damages or other legal remedy for breach of any promise or warranty in the contract to sell or the sale. But, if, after acceptance of the goods, the buyer fails to give notice to the seller of the breach of any promise or warranty within a reasonable time after the buyer knows, or ought to know, of such breach, the seller shall not be liable therefor."

While the official UCC Comment and the Wisconsin Commercial Code Committee's commentary indicate that sec. 401.207 should not be interpreted to apply to a full payment check, they do not conclusively settle the question. We therefore turn to the legislative history of sec. 1-207 for guidance in deciding the issue before us. The legislative history offers conflicting inferences.

One piece of legislative history suggests that sec. 1-207 should be read as not being applicable to full payment checks. When sec. 1-207 first appeared in the UCC it coexisted with another provision, sec. 3-802(3), which substantially codified the common law rule of the effect of the full payment check. Sec. 3-802(3) provided:
   *107 "Where a check or similar payment instrument provides that it is in full satisfaction of an obligation the payee discharges the underlying obligation by obtaining payment of the instrument unless he establishes that the original obligor has taken unconscionable advantage in the circumstances." [FN9]

   FN9. The official UCC Comment to sec. 3-802(3) reads:
   "5. Checks are frequently given with a term providing that they are "in full payment of all claims," or similar language. The holder who obtains payment of such a check takes its benefits subject to the drawer's stipulation that he releases the original obligation. Even where the obligation is for an undisputed and liquidated debt there is no unfairness in the tender and acceptance of an accord and satisfaction; and in this respect subsection (3) changes the law in a number of states.
   "The exception stated as to unconscionable advantage taken by the obligor has been recognized in a considerable number of decisions. A genuine accord and satisfaction is to be found only where the

parties are dealing at arm's length and on fair terms of bargaining equality, without unfair advantage taken by either party. The following cases illustrate the application of the exception:

"a. The debtor sends the creditor a false statement of their account with a check which stipulates that it is in full payment. The creditor cashes the check in good faith reliance on the statement of account. The original obligation is not discharged.

"b. The debtor, knowing that it is the practice of the creditor's clerks to put through checks without examining accounts, sends a check for half the amount due which states that it is in full payment. The check is cashed without examining the account. The obligation is not discharged.

"c. The debtor sends a check for less than the amount due which states that it is in full payment. The creditor insists that the amount is not correct, and finally cashes the check as the only available means of obtaining any payment. The original obligation is not discharged.

"d. An employer hands an employee a check for less than the full amount of wages due which states that it is in full payment, and threatens to fire the employee if he does not accept the amount. When the employee cashes the check the original obligation is not discharged.

"e. An employer hands an employee a check for less than the full amount of wages due which states that it is in full payment. He refuses the employee's demands for the proper amount, and the employee cashes the check in order to obtain money for subsistence. The obligation is not discharged."

662 *108 Since sec. 3-802(3) expressly recognized that acceptance of a full payment check was effective to create an accord and satisfaction, it creates an inference that sec. 1-207 was intended to apply to a different fact situation. Sec. 3-802(3) was ultimately dropped from the UCC, but the fact that secs. 1-207 and 3-802(3) both were part of the UCC at the same time suggests that sec. 1-207 should not be read to change the common law recognizing the effectiveness of the full payment check.

On the other hand, another piece of legislative history suggests that sec. 1-207 was intended to change the common law rule. The 1961 Report of the New York Commission on Uniform State Laws, in its section-by-section annotations reflecting the relationships between the

UCC and then existing New York law, viewed sec. 1-207 as changing the common law rules governing payments tendered in full settlement. The New York report stated as follows:

"[Section 1-207] permits a party involved in a Code-covered transaction to accept whatever he can get by way of payment, performance, etc. without losing his rights ... to sue for the balance of the payment, so long as he explicitly reserves his rights.... The Code rule would permit ... the acceptance of a part performance or payment tendered in full settlement without requiring the acceptor to gamble with his legal right to demand the balance of the performance or payment."

The New York report is of some significance since New York took a lead in studying the UCC and suggesting revisions during the drafting of the Code, and the report was highly influential in bringing about the adoption of the UCC in that key state. Rosenthal, *supra,* 78 Colum.L.Rev. 48, 58, 61, 62. Not surprisingly New York courts have concluded that sec. 1-207 does apply ***109** to full payment checks. [FN10] The New York report has no binding effect, however, on our interpretation of the UCC as passed by the Wisconsin legislature, and there is no evidence that this state intended to follow the New York interpretation or was aware of it. [FN11] Because the legislative history is subject to conflicting inferences, it does not aid us in interpreting sec. 1-207.

> FN10. See, *e.g., Braun v. C.E.P.C. Distribs., Inc.,* 77 App.Div.2d 358, 433 N.Y.S.2d 447 (1st Dept.1980); *Continental Information Sys. Corp. v. Mutual Life Ins. Co. of N.Y.,* 77 App.Div.2d 316, 432 N.Y.S.2d 952 (4th Dept.1980); *Ayer v. Sky Club, Inc.,* 70 App.Div.2d 863, 418 N.Y.S.2d 57 (1st Dept., 1979), *appeal dismissed,* 48 N.Y.2d 705, 422 N.Y.S.2d 68, 397 N.E.2d 758 (1979).

> FN11. The contract provided that it was governed by the laws of Massachusetts. Massachusetts has, like Wisconsin, adopted sec. 1-207 of the UCC. Honeywell's brief advises the court that Massachusetts has no reported decision resolving the issue presented in the instant case. Because the commentary in the Massachusetts annotation to sec. 1-207 is similar to the New York commentary, Honeywell argues that we should assume the Massachusetts court will follow the New York cases. We are not persuaded that Massachusetts would necessarily adopt the New

York courts' interpretation of sec. 1-207.   We assume
Massachusetts would adopt the same reasoning this court does.

Since we are not aided by the language of the Code, the official comments,
or the legislative history, we look to the rules of construction set forth in
the UCC.   One rule of construction set forth in the UCC itself is that the
UCC is to be liberally construed and applied to promote its underlying
purposes and policies.   Sec. 1-102, UCC;   sec. 401.102, Stats. 1981-82.
The underlying purposes and policies of the UCC as set forth in the UCC
are as follows:
  "(a) To simplify, clarify and modernize the law governing commercial
  transactions;
  663 "(b) To permit the continued expansion of commercial practices
  through custom, usage and agreement of the parties;
  110 "(c) To make uniform the law among the various jurisdictions."
Sec. 1-102(2), UCC;   sec. 401.102(2), Stats. 1981-82.

Applying sec. 1.207 to the full payment check would not necessarily serve
to "simplify," or "clarify," or "modernize the law governing commercial
transactions."   Nor would an application of sec. 401.207 promote the
purpose and policy of the UCC of permitting "the continued expansion of
commercial practice through ... agreement of the parties."   All that would
be accomplished would be the elimination of the simple technique of the
full payment check; sophisticated parties might still arrange their affairs
to achieve the benefits of the full payment check.   See Rosenthal, *Discord
and Dissatisfaction: Section 1-207 of the Uniform Commercial Code,* 78
Colum.L.Rev. 48, 71-74 (1978).

As to the purpose of achieving uniformity among the jurisdictions adopting
the UCC, we note that the state courts have not been uniform in their
interpretation of sec. 401.207, and the developing trend appears to be to
interpret sec. 401.207 as not changing the common law rule applicable to
full payment checks.

The official UCC Comment to sec. 1-102(2) advises that "the text of each
section should be read in the light of the purpose and policy of the rule or
principle in question...." We should therefore consider the purposes of the
common law rule of accord and satisfaction and full payment checks and
the effect on commercial practices of interpreting sec. 401.207 as
overriding the common law rule to determine how sec. 401.207 should be

interpreted.

The common law rule that acceptance of a full payment check is an accord and satisfaction discharging the entire debt is a long-standing doctrine resting not *111 only on principles of contract law but on principles of sound public policy, that is, interests of resolving disputes informally without litigation and of fairness. Use of the full payment check by parties bargaining at arm's length is a convenient and valuable way of resolution of dispute through agreement of the parties. The interests of fairness dictate that a creditor who cashes a check offered in full payment should be bound by the terms of the offer. The debtor's intent is known, and allowing the creditor to keep the money disregarding the debtor's conditions seems unfair and violative of the obligation of good faith which the UCC makes applicable to every contract or duty. Sec. 1-203, UCC; sec. 401.203, Stats. 1981- 82. The doctrine of accord and satisfaction includes safeguards designed to protect a creditor from an overreaching debtor: there must be a good faith dispute about the debt; the creditor must have reasonable notice that the check is intended to be in full satisfaction of the debt. One commentator called the rule binding the creditor upon cashing a full payment check "a short cut to complete justice." 6 Corbin,Contracts sec. 1279, p. 130 (1962). [FN12] Another commentator noted:

> FN12. In contrast, the full payment check has been described as follows: "Offering a check for less than the contract amount, but in 'full settlement' inflicts an exquisite form of commercial torture on the payee." White and Summers, *Handbook of the Law Under the Uniform Commercial Code,* sec. 13-21, p. 544 (2d ed. 1980).
> As we discuss later, if there is "undue advantage" in the settlement, there will be no discharge. *Kercheval v. Doty,* 31 Wis. 476, 485 (1872).

"It is unfair to the party who writes the check thinking that he will be spending his money only if the whole dispute will be over, to allow the other party, knowing of that reasonable expectation, to weasel around the deal by putting his own markings on the other person's checks. There is no reason why s. 1-207 should be interpreted as being an exception to the basic duty of good *112 faith, when it is possible to interpret the two sections consistently. The academic writers who support this result offer no analysis, to the current knowledge of this treatise, which would justify licensing the recipient of the check to so deceive the drawer." **664 6

Corbin, *Contracts* sec. 1279, p. 396-97 (1982 Supplement).

[3] Inasmuch as there is no clearly expressed legislative direction in sec. 401.207, we are reluctant to impair the long-recognized settlement tool of the full payment check.   Accordingly we hold that sec. 401.207 is not applicable to the full payment check.

III.

Since we conclude that sec. 401.207 is not applicable to the full payment check, we must decide whether there was a valid discharge by an accord and satisfaction in this case.

[4][5] An "accord and satisfaction" is an agreement to discharge an existing disputed claim; it constitutes a defense to an action to enforce the claim. 6 Corbin, *Contracts* sec. 1276, p. 114 (1962). Like other contracts, an accord and satisfaction requires an offer, an acceptance, and consideration.

The parties do not dispute that Flambeau offered the check as full payment and that Honeywell's retention of the proceeds constituted an acceptance of the terms of the offer. The sole issue in contention between the parties in this case as to whether there was a valid accord and satisfaction is whether there was consideration for the discharge of the claim.   The requirement of consideration tends to offer protection against unfairness, but several courts have tended to move away from conceptual abstractions of consideration in commercial contexts and to consider directly the issues of duress, unconscionability, *113 bad faith or fraud.   Rosenthal, *Discord and Dissatisfaction: Section 1-207 of the Uniform Commercial Code,* 78 Colum.L.Rev. 48, 53 (1978).   In any event, the parties have addressed the issue of consideration in traditional terms.

Three rules relating to consideration and accord and satisfaction come into play. [FN13]

> FN13. As noted previously, the contract provided that it was governed by the law of Massachusetts.   The parties took the position that the law of Massachusetts and the law of Wisconsin are the same on the question of accord and satisfaction until shown otherwise.   The parties' briefs relied almost exclusively on Wisconsin cases, treating the common law of the two states the

same. Following the parties' lead, we have examined Wisconsin cases, not Massachusetts cases, and we have deemed Massachusetts law to be the same as Wisconsin's since there was no showing that Massachusetts law is different.

[6][7] First, the law in Wisconsin has long been that payment in full settlement of a claim which is disputed as to amount discharges the entire claim.   Resolution of an actual controversy involving some subject of pecuniary value and interest to the parties is sufficient consideration of an accord and satisfaction. *Superior Builders, Inc. v. Large,* 52 Wis.2d 563, 566, 190 N.W.2d 901 (1971); *Kercheval v. Doty,* 31 Wis. 476, 485 (1872).

[8][9][10] A second rule, also of long-standing, is that payment of part of a debt which is not disputed as to amount does not discharge the debt altogether, even when it is expressly agreed that the partial payment is received in full satisfaction. The debtor's mere refusal to pay the full claim does not make it a disputed claim.   Where the refusal is arbitrary and the debtor knows it has no just basis, the payment of less than the full amount claimed does not operate as an accord and satisfaction even though it is tendered and received as such.   This **114 rule is based on the principle that a part payment furnishes no consideration for relinquishing the balance of the debt. *Robinson v. Marachowsky,* 184 Wis. 600, 606-607, 200 N.W. 398 (1924); *Holman Mfg. Co. v. Dapin,* 181 Wis. 97, 99, 100, 193 N.W. 986 (1923), citing *Pinnel's Case,* 3 Coke's Rep. 238; *Otto v. Klauber,* 23 Wis. 471 (1868). [FN14]

> FN14. This rule has been criticized by the commentators.   See, *e.g.,* Farnsworth, *Contracts* sec. 4.21-4.23 (1983).   Although this court has not directly discarded the common law rule allowing the creditor to accept a check offered as payment in full and to then sue for the balance of the claim on the ground that the release was void for want of consideration, it has not viewed the rule requiring consideration with favor. *Herman v. Schlesinger,* 114 Wis. 382, 400, 401, 90 N.W. 460 (1902), quoted with approval in *Petersime Incubator Co. v. Klinke,* 248 Wis. 166, 21 N.W.2d 377 (1946).

**665 [11][12] The third rule, also of long duration, is that when the amount of a debt is undisputed but an offset is claimed arising directly out of the contract of sale of goods and not out of any collateral transaction, the debt is a single claim which is disputed in amount.   Payment in full settlement of less than the amount claimed operates as an accord and satisfaction.   The question whether an offset renders the claim disputed depends not on whether the offset is legally valid but on whether it was asserted in good faith.   *Lange v. Darling & Co.,* 233 Wis. 520, 525, 290 N.W. 188 (1940); *Robinson v. Marachowsky,* 184 Wis. 600, 606, 607, 200 N.W. 398 (1924); *Holman Mfg. Co. v. Dapin,* 181 Wis. 97, 101, 193 N.W. 986 (1923); *Thomas v. Columbia Phonograph Co.,* 144 Wis. 470, 129 N.W. 522 (1911).

The parties disagree as to whether this case falls under the second or third rule.   Honeywell claims that Flambeau's payment is nothing more than a part payment of an undisputed debt and that this case comes within the second rule, the undisputed debt rule.   On the other hand, ***115** Flambeau asserts that its good faith claim of offset rendered the entire debt disputed as to amount and that this case comes within the third rule, the "offset" rule.

[13] The circuit court made a finding that although there was no dispute about the account known to Honeywell until the check for $95,412 was tendered by Flambeau, when Honeywell received the check it was faced with an offer by Flambeau to satisfy a disputed claim. [FN15] The circuit court further found that Flambeau's claim to the $14,000 offset "had sufficient support to make it bona fide rather than dishonest or fraudulent." Because our review of the record leads us to conclude that these findings are not clearly erroneous we shall not set them aside.   Sec. 805.17, Stats. 1981-82.   In light of these findings, we conclude that the good faith claim of offset rendered the entire claim disputed.

> FN15. Honeywell cites no authority for its assertion that a dispute must have been manifest before the settlement offer is made.

Nevertheless Honeywell asserts that Flambeau's payment of $95,412, the undisputed amount, is not sufficient consideration for a discharge of the disputed claim.   Honeywell urges that where there are disputed and undisputed portions of a claim, payment of the undisputed portion by a full payment check is not consideration for settlement of the disputed portion. In other words, Honeywell is saying that there was no dispute between the parties that $95,412 was owed.   The only dispute concerned what, if any, part of the sum of $14,000 in excess of the $95,412 was due.   According to Honeywell, since Flambeau only paid the claim then undisputed, Flambeau has not offered a compromise and Honeywell is being asked to surrender the whole part of the disputed claim without getting anything in return.   Honeywell claims that since there was no consideration for settlement of the $14,000 disputed portion of the claim, there was no discharge of this disputed portion.

*116 Honeywell relies on three cases to support its position: *Karp v. Coolview of Wisconsin, Inc.,* 25 Wis.2d 299, 130 N.W.2d 790 (1964); *O'Leary v. Hannaford,* 258 Wis. 146, 44 N.W.2d 908 (1950); *Kendall v. Sump,* 204 Wis. 514, 235 N.W. 544 (1931).   We conclude that these cases are inapposite.

In *Karp v. Coolview of Wisconsin, Inc., supra,* 25 Wis.2d 299, 130 N.W.2d 790, a creditor extended credit to a debtor for thirteen airline tickets. The debtor claimed it was not responsible for six of these tickets and sent the creditor a check for seven of the tickets marked "paid in full" which the creditor cashed.   The creditor sued for payment for the six tickets.   The debtor pleaded accord and satisfaction.   The court held for the creditor. Honeywell asserts that the case stands for the rule that there was no accord and satisfaction because the debtor admitted liability for seven tickets and its payment could not be consideration **666 for settlement of the dispute over the remaining six.   We do not read the case this way.   The check specifically referred only to the seven tickets, the undisputed portion of the claim.   The check made no reference to the six disputed tickets.   It would be unreasonable to interpret a notation on a check as full payment of seven tickets as being full payment for thirteen tickets.   This court concluded that since the debtor had not offered to settle the entire debt, the cashing of the check did not constitute an acceptance of an offer of accord.

In *O'Leary, supra,* 258 Wis. 146, 44 N.W.2d 908, unlike in this case, the amount due was liquidated and not disputed.   Consequently the court held that the "amounts due the plaintiff were certain and stated ... [and] cashing a check marked 'in full' did not constitute an accord and satisfaction."

In *Kendall v. Sump, supra,* 204 Wis. 514, 517, 235 N.W. 544, a farm tenant brought an action for his share of produce.   There *117 was no dispute as to his right to certain amounts for certain produce less certain credits. However, the landlord claimed an offset of $150.08 which was disputed and which left the farm tenant with an amount due of only $6.04. The landlord sent the tenant a check for the sum of $6.04 which the tenant cashed.   In *Kendall,* unlike in the instant case, the check was not marked "paid in full." There was no evidence that the tenant was told that the check was intended as full settlement. As the court said, "There is no evidence that the [tenant] ever agreed to this as a final settlement."

Weidner v. Standard Life and Accident Ins. Co., 130 Wis. 10, 15, 110 N.W. 246 (1906), has been viewed by one commentator as supporting the position Honeywell is asserting. [FN16] In *Weidner,* the creditor, the insurance company, issued a check in full in the sum of $300 in settlement of a $3,000 claim by a widow under her husband's life insurance policy. *Weidner* is also distinguishable from the instant case. *Weidner* has been viewed as a case in which there were two separate and distinct claims and the acceptance of payment in full on one claim did not constitute an accord and satisfaction as to the other claim. *Sprinkmann Sons Corp. v. Bishopric Prods. Co.,* 340 F.Supp. 148, 149 (E.D.Wis.1972). See also 1 Restatement (Second), *Contracts* sec. 74, comment *c,* p. 186 (1979). Perhaps *Weidner* can best be explained by noting that a purported accord and satisfaction will not be given effect where there is overreaching by the debtor. The plaintiff offered evidence that she was suffering from nervous exhaustion at the time she signed a full payment receipt from the insurance ***118** company less than three weeks after her husband died from injuries sustained in an assault.

> FN16. 6 Corbin, *Contracts* sec. 1289, p. 163, n. 89 (1962). Corbin also cites *Schulz Co. v. Gether,* 183 Wis. 491, 198 N.W. 433 (1924), for this proposition. There is language in *Schulz* supporting the citation but it appears that the court also viewed the two claims as separate and independent. See 183 Wis. at 494, 496. See 1 Restatement (Second), *Contracts* sec. 74, comment c, p. 186 (1979).

The position Honeywell urges this court to adopt has been criticized by commentators [FN17] and courts. The majority rule apparently is that where the total claim is disputed, payment of the amount the debtor admits to be due supports the creditor's discharge of the entire debt on the cashing of the full payment check. [FN18]

> FN17. See, *e.g.,* 6 Corbin, *Contracts* sec. 1289, pp. 163-66 (1962).

> FN18. 6 Corbin, *Contracts* sec. 1289, p. 165 (1962). See also Calamari & Perillo, *Contracts* sec. 4-12, p. 155 (2d ed. 1977).

We find unpersuasive Honeywell's assertion that the payment of the undisputed portion of a disputed claim by a check marked "paid in full" is not consideration for the disputed portion of the claim. Honeywell does not explain why we should treat a single contract out of which a dispute as to the performance of one party arises as if it were two divisible contracts, each of which must be negotiated separately. Furthermore, as the Oregon Supreme Court explained, "It would be too technical ****667** a use of the doctrine of consideration to release a well-counseled debtor who tenders a nominal amount beyond his admitted debt but to trap one less sophisticated who is induced to pay the undisputed amount in return for his creditor's illusory promise to forgive the rest." *Kilander v. Blickle Co.*, 280 Or. 425, 571 P.2d 503, 505 (1977).

Honeywell's argument raises the spectre of overreaching if the court allows a debtor to force a creditor to discharge a debt when the debtor is paying only the undisputed portion. There can, of course, be overreaching by a debtor who tenders a full payment check. But overreaching can be policed through the doctrine of good faith. See 1 Restatement (Second), *Contracts* sec. 74, comment *c,* p. 186 (1979); Hillman, *Policing Contract *119 Modification under the U.C.C.: Good Faith and the Doctrine of Economic Duress,* 64 Iowa L.Rev. 849 (1979).

In this case, however, the circuit court found that Flambeau asserted its offset in good faith. The parties dealt with each other at arm's length with mutual understandings as to the effect of usual commercial practices. Under these circumstances, we conclude it would be unfair to allow Honeywell to accept Flambeau's money which was offered on condition of full settlement and then to turn around and claim the right to sue Flambeau for the balance of its asserted claim.

For the reasons set forth we conclude that Honeywell's claim against Flambeau was discharged upon Honeywell's cashing the full payment check and retaining the proceeds. Accordingly we reverse the decision of the court of appeals and remand the matter to the circuit court for proceedings on Flambeau's claim against Honeywell not inconsistent with this opinion.

Decision of the court of appeals reversed; order for judgment of the circuit court affirmed and cause remanded.

STEINMETZ, Justice (dissenting).

I disagree with the majority that the check presented and cashed in this case was an accord and satisfaction.

The $14,000 worth of computer programming services was an inducement to enter into the purchase of the equipment. There is nothing in this record nor the opinion to be persuasive that the services had a separate value above and in addition to the value of the equipment purchased. The programming services appear to be a "throw-in" incentive to sell the equipment. The services may have been listed as a $14,000 value to the purchaser of the equipment, Flambeau; however, there is no evidence in the record as to the cost to Honeywell to provide those services or their actual value.

*120 Flambeau did not disagree with the value of the equipment or the amount still owed on it. Its check paid for the amount due on the equipment which was not disputed minus the $14,000 for the unused programming services. It paid less than it owed on the equipment while not disputing the amount it owed on the equipment and therefore there was no accord and satisfaction.

Flambeau was not under the contract expected to pay $14,000 for programming services since it was a sales inducement only and therefore the unused services should not have been deducted from the undisputed equipment debt still owed.

I would hold that payment of part of the debt for the equipment which was not disputed did not discharge the debt altogether. The issue of $14,000 as a possible offset should have been tried to determine whether it had value independent of the equipment contract price.

WILLIAM A. BABLITCH, Justice (dissenting).

I dissent because I conclude that sec. 401.207, Stats., applies in this case. Section 401.102(2) delineates the underlying purposes and policies of the Uniform Commercial Code, including the policy of simplifying, clarifying and modernizing the law governing commercial transactions. Sec. **668 401.102(2)(a). Under sec. 401.102(1), chs. 401 to 409 must be liberally construed and applied to promote the underlying purposes and policies set forth in sec. 401.102(2).

I conclude that interpreting sec. 401.207, Stats., to allow a creditor to accept a conditional check under protest and reserve the right to obtain payment for any balance due is supported by the language of sec. 401.207. I also conclude that this interpretation promotes the policy of simplifying, clarifying and modernizing the law governing commercial transactions. As White and Summers note in *Handbook of the Law Under the Uniform *121 Commercial Code,* sec. 13-21 at 544 (2d ed. 1980), "... offering a check for less than the contract amount, but 'in full settlement' inflicts an exquisite form of commercial torture on the payee." Under the common law doctrine of accord and satisfaction, the payee may have to refuse the check, even if both parties agree that the amount tendered is due, in order to reserve the right to pursue a claim for any additional amount that the payor owes. [FN1] This commercially unreasonable result can be avoided by interpreting sec. 401.207 to allow the payee to cash the check and still retain the right to sue for the balance owing if the payee has reserved his or her rights.

> FN1. This case presents a perfect example of this dilemma. In order to avoid the result that would occur under the common law doctrine of accord and satisfaction, Honeywell would be forced to return Flambeau's check for $95,412, an amount Flambeau concedes it owes Honeywell, in order to reserve the right to pursue its claim for $14,000 that it contends Flambeau still owes under the purchase contracts.

In this case, Honeywell reserved its rights under sec. 401.207, Stats., by the letter it sent to Flambeau disputing Flambeau's assertion that Flambeau had satisfied all of its obligations under the purchase contracts. Because I conclude that sec. 401.207 applies in this case, and because Honeywell reserved its rights under that provision, I would hold that Honeywell reserved its right to demand full performance of Flambeau's obligations under the purchase contracts.

Part III: How the Case Got to the Wisconsin Supreme Court

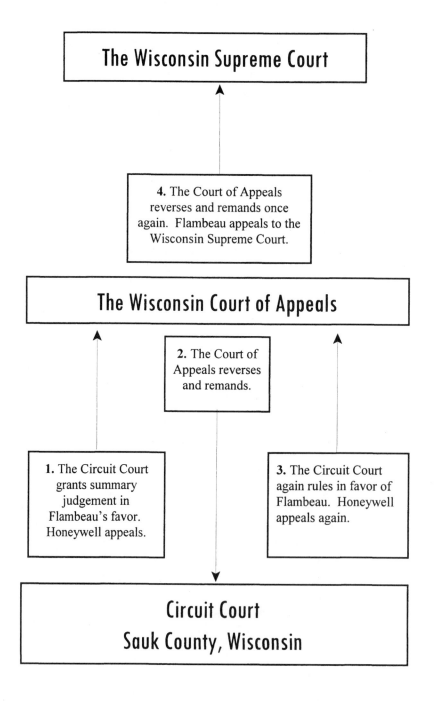

The Wisconsin Supreme Court

4. The Court of Appeals reverses and remands once again. Flambeau appeals to the Wisconsin Supreme Court.

The Wisconsin Court of Appeals

2. The Court of Appeals reverses and remands.

1. The Circuit Court grants summary judgement in Flambeau's favor. Honeywell appeals.

3. The Circuit Court again rules in favor of Flambeau. Honeywell appeals again.

Circuit Court
Sauk County, Wisconsin

Part IV: *Flambeau*, with a Gloss

341 N.W.2d 655

116 Wis.2d 95, 341 N.W.2d 655, 37 UCC Rep.Serv. 1441

(Cite as: 116 Wis.2d 95, 341 N.W.2d 655)

Here are examples of parallel citations. Within the parenthesis you see the official and the National Reporter *citation. Above these citations is a citation to the* UCC Reporter Service, *a specialty reporter.*

▷

A yellow flag warns you that subsequent cases have commented on the case, with potential negative consequences.

Supreme Court of Wisconsin.
FLAMBEAU PRODUCTS
CORPORATION, a Wisconsin
corporation, Plaintiff-Respondent-
Petitioner,

v.

HONEYWELL INFORMATION
SYSTEMS, INC., a foreign corporation,
Defendant-
Appellant.
No. 82-307.

Note the captions. The Uniform System of Citation explains how to shorten party names. In this case the first party is plaintiff-respondant-petitioner, the second is defendant-appellant.

The docket number, the court's own internal system, may grow in importance as citation systems change to format-neutral styles.

Argued Oct. 31, 1983.
Decided Jan. 4, 1984.

Relevant dates are listed. In a citation, it is the "decided" date that is important.

Debtor buyer of computer equipment sought declaratory judgment against creditor seller to effect that debtor had no additional obligations to obligation already paid and that creditor had no security interest in

This is a syllabus, or synopsis, of the case. This one is written by the editors at Thomson-West, not the Justice. This summary is not part of the opinion, but is designed to

equipment. The Circuit Court, Sauk County, Howard Latton, J., granted summary judgment in favor of debtor, and creditor appealed. The Court of Appeals, 97 Wis.2d 759, 295 N.W.2d 834, reversed and remanded. On remand, the Circuit Court, Sauk County, Howard Latton, J., entered an order for an interlocutory judgment extinguishing debtor's obligations under contract and discharging creditor's security interest, and creditor again appealed. The Court of Appeals, Cane, J., 111 Wis.2d 317, 330 N.W.2d 228, again reversed and remanded. On review, the Supreme Court, Abrahamson, J., held that: (1) Uniform Commercial Code section, providing that party who with explicit reservation of rights assents to performance in manner offered by other party does not prejudice rights reserved, does not alter common-law rule of accord and satisfaction as it relates to full payment checks, and (2) debtor's good-faith claim of offset for value of computer programming services included in purchase price but only partially used by debtor rendered entire claim as to amount of debt under contract disputed, and thus creditor's claim against debtor was discharged upon creditor's cashing check tendered by debtor in full payment of debt and retaining proceeds.

Decision of the Court of Appeals reversed; order for judgment of the circuit court affirmed and cause remanded.

outline the history of the case, to tell you how it got to the Supreme Court. It is a snapshot, designed to assist the reader. Note that this case has traveled up and down the ladder of the courts.

Here is the editor's summary of the holding, the decisive point where the Court rules and the substantive issue is made as simple as possible. Once again, this is not to be quoted or cited, but it can help you understand what happened.

Here is the final disposition.

Steinmetz and William A. Bablitch, JJ., filed dissenting opinions.

The reader is alerted that there will be two dissents following the opinion.

West Headnotes

These are the headnotes. An editor at Thomson-West has summarized each point of law in the case. The headnote's lead number, [1], will be placed next to the part of the text summarized in the headnote so that you can go right to it. Again, these headnotes may not be quoted.

[1] Accord and Satisfaction ☜11(2)
8k11(2) Most Cited Cases
Under common-law rule of accord and satisfaction, if check offered by debtor as full payment for disputed claim is cashed by creditor, creditor is deemed to have accepted debtor's conditional offer of full payment notwithstanding any reservations by creditor.

[2] Accord and Satisfaction ☜11(2)
8k11(2) Most Cited Cases
Under common-law rule of accord and satisfaction, if check offered by debtor as sole payment for disputed claim is cashed by creditor, creditor's cashing of check constitutes accord and satisfaction which discharges entire debt.

These are Thomson-West headnotes, so each one is keyed into the American Digest system. Headnote [2] is assigned to the topic Accord and Satisfaction. Key Number 11(2), Accord and Satisfaction is a venerable common law topic. It is covered in the first year of law school. You might want to skim the whole topic sometime and see how Thomson-West has broken it down. It shows one way of looking at the whole issue.

[3] Accord and Satisfaction ☜11(2)
8k11(2) Most Cited Cases
Uniform Commercial Code section, providing that party who with explicit reservation of rights assents to performance in manner offered by other party does not prejudice rights reserved, is not applicable to full payment check and does not alter common-law rule of accord and satisfaction as it relates to full payment checks. W.S.A. 401.207; U.C.C. § 1-207.

Note at the end of Headnote [3] there is a citation to the Wisconsin Statutes Annotated. *There is also a cite to the* UCC. *These cross-references allow you to go directly to the proper place in those sets. Online, there is a hyperlink to them.*

[4] Accord and Satisfaction 🔑1
8k1 Most Cited Cases
"Accord and satisfaction" is agreement to discharge existing disputed claim, and constitutes a defense to action to enforce claim.

[5] Accord and Satisfaction 🔑1
8k1 Most Cited Cases

[5] Accord and Satisfaction 🔑5
8k5 Most Cited Cases
Accord and satisfaction requires offer, acceptance, and consideration.

[6] Accord and Satisfaction 🔑11(1)
8k11(1) Most Cited Cases
Payment in full settlement of claim which is disputed as to amount discharges entire claim.

[7] Accord and Satisfaction 🔑5
8k5 Most Cited Cases
Resolution of actual controversy involving some subject of pecuniary value and interest to parties is sufficient consideration of an accord and satisfaction.

[8] Accord and Satisfaction 🔑7(1)
8k7(1) Most Cited Cases
Payment of part of debt which is not disputed as to amount does not discharge debt altogether, even when it is expressly agreed that partial payment is received in full satisfaction.

[9] Accord and Satisfaction 🔑10(1)
8k10(1) Most Cited Cases
Debtor's mere refusal to pay full claim does

Note that all of the headnotes in this case have been assigned to this topic. This is not typical, sometimes many different topics will be covered in a single case.

If you clicked on the referenced Topic and Key Number in the online version of the case, you would find other cases with the same headnote reference.

not make it a disputed claim as to which debtor's partial payment in full settlement of claim will discharge debt altogether.

[10] Accord and Satisfaction 🔑11(1)
8k11(1) Most Cited Cases
Where debtor's refusal to pay full claim is arbitrary and debtor knows it has no just basis, payment of less than full amount claimed does not operate as accord and satisfaction, even though it is tendered and received as such.

[11] Accord and Satisfaction 🔑10(1)
8k10(1) Most Cited Cases
When amount of debt is undisputed but offset is claimed arising directly out of contract of sale of goods and not out of any collateral transaction, debt is single claim which is disputed in amount, and payment in full settlement of less than amount claimed operates as accord and satisfaction.

[12] Accord and Satisfaction 🔑10(1)
8k10(1) Most Cited Cases
Question whether offset arising directly out of contract of sale of goods renders claim as to amount of debt under contract disputed, for purpose of determining whether payment in full settlement of less than amount claimed operates as accord and satisfaction, depends not on whether offset is legally valid but on whether it is asserted in good faith.

The headnotes move through Accord and Satisfaction theory, but stay on this one topic. If you read the opinion without seeing these footnotes, you might expect a wider range of topics, but in Contract theory it is all about this one major topic.

The headnotes seem repetitive because the editors are struggling to sift out each separate legal issue. Think of yourself as a researcher interested only in one aspect of accord and satisfaction.

[13] Accord and Satisfaction 🔑➼**10(1)**
8k10(1) Most Cited Cases
Debtor's good-faith claim of offset under contract for sale of computer equipment for value of computer programming services included in purchase price but only partially used by debtor rendered entire claim as to amount of debt under contract disputed, and thus creditor's claim against debtor was discharged upon creditor's cashing check tendered by debtor in full payment of debt and retaining proceeds.

**657 *97 Clyde C. Cross, Baraboo, argued, for plaintiff-respondent-petitioner; there were briefs by Karen A. Mercer and Cross, Mercer & Maffei, Baraboo, on brief.

J. Leroy Thilly, Madison, argued, for defendant-appellant; Barbara L. Block, James E. Bartzen and Boardman, Suhr, Curry & Field, Madison, on brief.

ABRAHAMSON, Justice.

This is a review of a published decision of the court of appeals, *Flambeau Products Corp. v. Honeywell Information Systems,* 111 Wis.2d 317, 330 N.W.2d 228 (1983) (*Flambeau II*), reversing an order of the circuit court for Sauk county, ***98** Howard W. Latton, circuit judge. The circuit court entered an order for an interlocutory judgment extinguishing the obligations of Flambeau Products Corporation to Honeywell Information Systems, Inc., under

This is an example of star paging. The WESTLAW & LEXIS *versions of the case will let you know what page you would be reading if you were looking at the official, printed sets, i.e., the Wisconsin Reports and the Northwestern Reporter, in front of you. Therefore, you can cite to the written sets. Citation of legal materials has always been based on references to the volume and page of an authoritative set, but citation reform may change the need for this.*

The names of the lawyers who carried the appeal forward.

This is the name of the Justice who wrote the opinion. Justice Abrahamson is a former law professor and respected jurist. She authored the opinion and persuaded five of her colleagues to join her.

an installment purchase contract and discharging Honeywell's security interest in the purchased equipment. [FN1] The circuit court concluded that sec. 401.207, Stats. 1981-82, was not applicable to this case in which Flambeau tendered a check in full satisfaction of Honeywell's claim and that Honeywell's acceptance of Flambeau's check constituted an accord and satisfaction discharging the balance of Honeywell's claim, notwithstanding Honeywell's reservation of rights to claim the balance due. The court of appeals reversed the judgment of the circuit court, holding that sec. 401.207 is applicable to Flambeau's check offered in full payment of the claim and that Honeywell effectively reserved its rights under sec. 401.207. Because we agree with the circuit court's interpretation of sec. 401.207 and its application of the common law doctrine of accord and satisfaction, we reverse the decision of the court of appeals and affirm the circuit court's order for an interlocutory judgment.

Often a Justice will begin an opinion with a detailed procedural history of the case. This will describe how the case worked its way through the court system. Decisions of the lower courts are summarized. This helps set the stage for the case. Reading the lower court version of the case is often useful, and the case's whole citation history is set out here.

FN1. The judgment is interlocutory because Flambeau's second cause of action seeking damages from Honeywell for Honeywell's failure to supply a termination statement discharging the lien has not yet been tried.

Footnotes are often used in judicial opinions, although the number often depends on the author. Online, footnotes are set off like this. Each opinion is its own universe of information: the Justice's best shot at describing the state of the law at the point in time when the decision is written. The Justice and her clerks have pulled together every relevant source. Read opinions in this context.

I.

The facts are set forth in detail in the decision of the court of appeals in *Flambeau II,* and it is sufficient for us to summarize them briefly here.

Flambeau Products Corporation (plaintiff-buyer) entered into purchase contracts with Honeywell Information Systems, Inc. (defendant-seller) in September 1975 for the acquisition of computer equipment. Under the purchase contracts Flambeau was obligated to pay 60 ***99** monthly installments over a period of five years and had the right to prepay the entire amount at any time. In connection with the equipment purchase and as part of the purchase price, Flambeau was to receive $14,000 worth of computer programming services that Flambeau could use until October 1, 1976. Flambeau used part of these services prior to October 1, 1976 but stopped requesting programming services when it unilaterally decided they were not helpful.

In late 1976 or early 1977, at Flambeau's request, Honeywell advised Flambeau that the amount due to prepay the contract was ****658** $109,412. Without further discussion, Flambeau sent Honeywell a check for $95,412. On the back of the check were the words "in full payment of liability to you for equipment...." Flambeau's check was accompanied by a letter which stated that the "check in the amount of $95,412 [is] in full settlement of notes we owe to Honeywell in connection with purchase of our computer system." The

Note that Justice Abrahamson refers the reader to the lower court opinion for extensive facts. This is a way of saving space. It is worth noting that she goes on to provide a rather detailed summary of the case.

calculations set forth in the letter show that $14,000 for "unused programming" was deducted from the sum of $109,412 to arrive at the net payment. Honeywell cashed the check, retained the proceeds, notified Flambeau that the check was not accepted as payment in full, and requested Flambeau to remit the balance due plus interest. Honeywell does not on this review assert that the check cashing or retention of the proceeds was unauthorized.

Flambeau sought a declaratory judgment that it had no further obligations to Honeywell and that Honeywell had no valid security interest in its equipment. Honeywell counterclaimed for $14,000. The circuit court granted summary judgment to Flambeau on the ground that there was an accord and satisfaction. On appeal the court of appeals reversed the circuit court in an unpublished decision, 97 Wis.2d 759, 295 N.W.2d 834, filed on June 17, 1980 (*Flambeau I*). It is not entirely clear whether the court of appeals ***100** held that summary judgment was not appropriate because there was a dispute of material facts or that as a matter of law Flambeau could not, on the basis of the facts presented in the record on summary judgment, claim an accord and satisfaction. In any event on remand a trial was held on the issue of accord and satisfaction.

After trial to the court, the circuit court held that sec. 401.207 was not applicable to this case and that the offer and acceptance of Flambeau's check constituted an accord and satisfaction discharging the balance of

Note that even when a state supreme court justice reads a lower court order, she cannot always determine just what it says. This sort of mention is not a pleasant one for the lower court judge, but it should make you feel better about not always understanding what a court is saying.

It is worth realizing how long it takes an astute Justice to briefly summarize a case. When you are asked to brief a case in law school, recall how hard this can be.

Honeywell's claims.   The circuit court ordered judgment in favor of Flambeau. In *Flambeau II,* the court of appeals reversed the circuit court's order, addressing only the issue of the applicability of sec. 401.207 to this case, not the issue of accord and satisfaction. [FN2]

> FN2. Honeywell argues on review that since the same facts were presented in the trial as in the summary judgment *Flambeau I* established as the law of the case that Flambeau is not entitled to claim an accord and satisfaction. Honeywell made this same argument to the court of appeals. We are not persuaded by Honeywell's argument.
>
> The holding in *Flambeau I* is subject to interpretation, and the court of appeals in *Flambeau II* apparently interpreted its decision in *Flambeau I* as not requiring reversal of the circuit court's order on the issue of accord and satisfaction.

This footnote is used to dispose of the "law of the case" argument raised by Honeywell's lawyers. Justice Abrahamson relegates it to death in a footnote.

Two issues are raised on review:

(1) Does the Uniform Commercial Code sec. 1-207 (sec. 401.207, Stats. 1981-82) alter the common law rule of accord and satisfaction as it relates to full payment checks? [FN3]

> FN3. We use the term "full payment check," but there are other terms used to describe a situation in which the check is offered upon a condition and the payee understands that cashing the check constitutes an

If only more jurists were this clear. Justice Abrahamson sets out exactly what the issues are. So, we have seen a procedural history, a summary of the facts, and now the simple statement of the two issues that the Court must decide. Note that each issue is concerned with statutory interpretation. The Court is being asked to determine just what a statute means. A large

assent to the conditions. For example: check in full settlement, conditional check, conditioned check. See Rosenthal, *Discord and Dissatisfaction: Section 1-207 of the Uniform Commercial Code,* 78 Colum.L.Rev. 48, 49-50 (1978); 6 Corbin, *Contracts* sec. 1277, pp. 122-23 (1962).

number of judicial opinions concern statutory and administrative interpretation, not the common law.

*101 (2) If sec. 401.207, Stats. 1981-82, does not alter the common law rule, may Flambeau claim an accord and satisfaction in this case?

Note that Justice Abrahamson is citing to §401.207, Stats. 1981-1982. The headnote sent you to WSA §401.207. The Justice is sending you to the official state code, the editor to the more helpful annotated code.

II.

[1][2] Under the common law rule of accord and satisfaction, if a check offered by the debtor as full payment for a disputed claim is cashed by the creditor, the creditor is deemed to have accepted the debtor's conditional offer of full payment notwithstanding any reservations by the creditor. In other words, the creditor's cashing the full payment check constitutes an accord and satisfaction which discharges the entire debt.

Here is a straightforward statement of the common law rule. This is "black letter law," or hornbook law, an accepted statement of traditional principle.

The common law rule of accord and satisfaction promotes fairness by protecting the ****659** bona fide expectations of a debtor who tenders payment on condition that it will be accepted as payment in full. The rule also provides a method of settling disputes without litigation.

Honeywell argues that sec. 1-207 of the Uniform Commercial Code (UCC) (sec. 401.207, Stats. 1981-82) alters the common law rule of accord and satisfaction and

Here we have Honeywell's initial position. They content that legislation has changed the common law rule. The Justice reprints the text of the

permits the seller-creditor to accept and cash the check offered as payment in full and to explicitly reserve the right to obtain payment from the buyer-debtor of the balance due.

Sec. 1-207 (sec. 401.207, Stats. 1981-82) provides as follows:

"A party who with explicit reservation of rights performs or promises performance or assents to performance in a manner demanded or offered by the other party does not thereby prejudice the rights reserved.   Such words as 'without prejudice', 'under protest' or the like are sufficient."

Sec. 1-207 of the UCC became sec. 401.207 of the law of Wisconsin on July 1, 1965. Although the language ***102** of sec. 1-207 can be read to apply to a full payment check, the words of sec. 1-207 do not compel this conclusion. It is generally conceded that the scope and meaning of sec. 1- 207 are unclear, Farnsworth, *Contracts* sec. 4.23, p. 283 (1982), and courts and commentators are divided as to whether sec. 1-207 has changed the common law principles relating to full payment checks. [FN4]   The issue of the applicability of sec. 1-207 (sec. ***103** 401.207, Stats. 1981-82) to the full payment check is one of first impression in this state.

FN4. For authorities that sec. 1-207 has altered the common law of accord and satisfaction, see *Bivins v. White Dairy*, 378 So.2d 1122, 1124 (Ala.Civ.App.1979) (dictum); *Miller v. Jung*, 361 So.2d 788, 789 (Fla.App.1978); *Kilander v. Blickle*

statute for your consideration. Online you could link directly to the whole statute, but Justice Abrahamson is making it easier for folks using the books to see what she is doing.

Here Justice Abrahamson notes the point at which the UCC was enacted into law in Wisconsin.   She goes on to point out that the language of this section is considered to be unclear.   Note that she cites Farnsworth's hornbook on contract law to buttress her point.

Footnote 4 is a spectacular piece of judicial handiwork, and we must admire it. Justice Abrahamson is faced with language that has been the subject of varying interpretation.   She uses this footnote to set out cases and

Co., 280 Or. 425, 429, 571 P.2d 503 (1977) (dictum); *Braun v. C.E.P.C. Distributors, Inc.*, 77 App.Div.2d 358, 433 N.Y.S.2d 447, 449-50 (1980); *Scholl v. Tallman*, 247 N.W.2d 490, 492 (S.D.1976); White & Summers, *Handbook of the Law Under the Uniform Commercial Code* sec. 13-21 (2d ed. 1980); Calamari & Perillo, *Contracts* sec. 5-16, p. 197 (2d ed. 1977).

For the view that sec. 1-207 does not affect the common law of accord and satisfaction, see *Chancellor, Inc. v. Hamilton Appliance Co., Inc.*, 175 N.J.Super. 345, 352, 418 A.2d 1326 (1980); *Brown v. Coastal Truckways, Inc.*, 44 N.C.App. 454, 458, 261 S.E.2d 266 (1980); *State Department of Fisheries v. J-Z Sales Corporation*, 25 Wash.App. 671, 681-82, 610 P.2d 390 (1980); *Jahn v. Burns*, 593 P.2d 828, 830 (Wyo.1979); 6 Corbin, *Contracts* sec. 1979 (Supp.1982, pt. 2); 2 Restatement (Second), *Contracts* sec. 281, comment *d*, p. 384 (1979) (sec. 1-207 "need not be read as changing" the common law rules); Hawkland, *The Effect of U.C.C. § 1-207 on the Doctrine of Accord and Satisfaction by Conditional Check*, 74 Comm.L.J. 329, 331 (1969); McDonnell, *Purposive Interpretation of the Uniform Commercial Code: Some Implications for Jurisprudence*, 126 U.Pa.L.Rev. 795, 824-28 (1978);

commentary on each side of the issue as well as some interpretations that fall in between. She cites you to cases from other jurisdictions which have no legal power, but are persuasive, as well as the work of law professors and law review commentary. If you were online, you could link to many of them. What she has done is sketched out the architecture of a legal argument by making powerful points on each side. This is an excellent example of how argument can be joined. Often when a justice authors an opinion she crafts it to lead almost inevitably to her conclusion. Justice Abrahamson is playing fair and showing both sides.

Rosenthal, *Discord and Dissatisfaction: Section 1-207 of the Uniform Commercial Code,* 78 Colum.L.Rev. 48 (1978); Comment, *U.C.C. Section 1-207 and the Full Payment Check: The Struggle Between the Code and the Common Law--Where Do the Debtor and Creditor Fit In,* 7 U. Dayton L.Rev. 421, 422-23, 435 (1982); Comment, *Accord and Satisfaction: Conditional Tender by Check Under the Uniform Commercial Code,* 18 Buffalo L.Rev. 539, 549 (1969); Note, *Does U.C.C. Section 1-207 Apply to the Doctrine of Accord and Satisfaction by Conditional Check,* 11 Creighton L.Rev. 515, 527 (1977).

A "Comment" is a student authored article in an academic law review. Student authored pieces carry less weight than those written by an established legal scholar, but the Justice is citing to several student pieces.

See also Fritz v. Marantette, 404 Mich. 329, 273 N.W.2d 425 (1978), which refused to decide the question. This case has been criticized in Harris, *Commercial Transaction, 1979 Annual Survey of Michigan Law,* 26 Wayne L.Rev. 469 (1980).

The Justice refers to a case, then shows how commentators have criticized it.

For other discussions of sec. 1-207, see Quinn, *Uniform Commercial Code Commentary and Law Digest* sec. 1-207[A][1][2] (1983 Cum.Supp. No. 1); Caraballo, *The Tender Trap: U.C.C. § 1-207 and Its Applicability to an Attempted Accord and Satisfaction by Tendering a Check in a Dispute Arising from a Sale of Goods,* 11 Seton Hall L.Rev. 445 (1981).

Since the language of sec. 1-207 does not provide an answer to the question of whether the section redefines the common law of accord and satisfaction as it applies to full payment checks, we attempt to determine the drafters' intent [FN5] by examining ****660** the official comments to sec. 1-207 and the legislative history and by applying the rules of interpretation set forth in the UCC.

> FN5. As Dean Rosenthal wisely explains, "Any assertion of the 'intention' of one legislature, much less that of all the enacting legislatures [of the UCC, namely the American Law Institute and the National Conference of Commissioners on Uniform State Laws] collectively, in such circumstances, requires wondrous confidence." Rosenthal, *Discord and Dissatisfaction: Section 1-207 of the Uniform Commercial Code,* 78 Colum.L.Rev. 48, 58 (1978).

Legislative intent is a tricky business. There is a fashionable dismissal of legislative history these days and Professor Rosenthal makes the point well here. Yet, many opinions still use it as a device, and despite her use of this footnote, Justice Abrahamson will do so, too.

The official UCC Comments generally point out any significant changes which a section makes in existing law. If the drafters of the UCC intended sec. 1- 207 to effect a change in the full payment check rule, one would suppose that the official UCC Comment and commentary of the Commercial Code Committee [FN6] of the ***104** Wisconsin Legislative Council would have described such a significant change. They do not. Professor Hawkland notes that "a strong argument can be made that the failure of the comment to 1-207 to mention such a sweeping change as would be caused by the

The UCC was written by the leading legal minds of their time. It was meant to simplify commercial law among the states, offering a uniform statute on commercial law that each jurisdiction could adopt. All jurisdictions have done so, although there are often local modifications introduced when a state enacts its version into law. In order to assist state legislator and lawyers, the drafters of the UCC included Official Comments and

application of the section" to the full payment check, indicates that no such result was intended.   Hawkland, *The Effect of U.C.C. Section 1-207 on the Doctrine of Accord and Satisfaction by Conditional Check,* 74 Comm.L.J. 329, 331 (1969).

Examples with each section. In other words, they worked as hard as they could to be as clear as to what it was they were doing. Yet, you will see, even that did not suffice.

FN6. A commentary entitled Summary of Changes or Clarifications was prepared by the Commercial Code Committee of the Wisconsin Legislative Council in its section-by-section analysis of the Uniform Commercial Code (UCC) prior to the adoption of the UCC in Wisconsin.   The commentary was designed to be used with the official text and official comments of the UCC.   See Introduction, 1961 Report of the Wisconsin Legislative Council, vol. III, part 2, reproduced in 40A, West's Wis.Stats., Annot. vii (1964).

When Wisconsin enacted its version of the UCC, it attempted to be clear on what it was doing.   This is a conscious attempt to assist in subsequent understanding of the statute.   There were many attempts to make this statute clear, none of them suffice.

Significantly both the official UCC Comment to sec. 1-207 and the commentary of the Commercial Code Committee of the Wisconsin Legislative Council to sec. 401.207 suggest that sec. 1-207 does not apply to a full payment check.

The official UCC Comment to sec. 1-207 reads as follows:

"1. This section provides machinery for the continuation of performance along the lines contemplated by the contract despite a pending dispute, by adopting the mercantile device of going ahead with delivery, acceptance, or payment 'without

Here the official comments to UCC 1-207 are set out. Justice Abrahamson is again careful to provide the full relevant text of what she discusses.   Without the power of computer links to other sources, you are given the full text to which the Justice refers.

prejudice,' 'under protest,' 'under reserve,' 'with reservation of all our rights,' and the like. All of these phrases completely reserve all rights within the meaning of this section. The section therefore contemplates that limited as well as general reservations and acceptance by a party may be made 'subject to satisfaction of our purchase,' 'subject to acceptance by our customers,' or the like.

"2. This section does not add any new requirement of language of reservation where not already required by law, but merely provides a specific measure on which a party can rely as he makes or concurs in any interim adjustment in the course of performance. It does not affect or impair the provisions of this Act such as those under which the buyer's remedies for defect survive acceptance without being expressly claimed if notice of the defects is given within a reasonable time. Nor does it disturb the policy of those cases which restrict the effect of a waiver of a defect to reasonable limits under ***105** the circumstances, even though no such reservation is expressed.

"The section is not addressed to the creation or loss of remedies in the ordinary course of performance but rather to a method of procedure where one party is claiming as of right something which the other feels to be unwarranted."

Various interpretations of sec. 1-207 and the official comment have been suggested. Professor Hawkland and Dean Rosenthal conclude that the official comment indicates that sec. 1-207 is not applicable to full

Having looked at the language of the statute, the UCC and the official comments of the UCC, and still unsure of how to answer her question, Justice Abrahamson now turns to legal commentary.

payment checks. Professor Hawkland reaches this conclusion by focusing on the phrase "performance along the lines contemplated by the contract" in the comment. [FN7] The official UCC Comment, according to Professor Hawkland, suggests that sec. 1-207 was intended to apply to ongoing **661 contracts, not to full payment checks that terminate the contractual arrangement. Hawkland, *The Effect of U.C.C. § 1-207 on the Doctrine of Accord and Satisfaction by Conditional Check*, 74 Comm.L.J. 329, 331 (1969).

Professors Hawkland and Rosenthal are each famous academics whose opinions on the UCC carry special power. You would find them cited frequently in cases on UCC issues, but they are only persuasive authority and can be used as the Justice wishes.

FN7. One commentator suggests that those who support the idea that sec. 1-207 overrules the common law have not offered any satisfactory explanation why payment and performance are treated separately in sec. 1- 208 but performance should be viewed as including payment in sec. 1- 207. 6 Corbin, *Contracts* sec. 1279, p. 396 (Supp.1982, pt. 2).

This footnote cites <u>Corbin</u>. The <u>Corbin</u> treatise is a venerable source. Arthur Corbin, its original author, is long dead but the set continues to be edited. On general contracts issues, <u>Corbin</u> is looked to for accepted theory. This is a fall back to the common law. The Justice picks and chosses from sources to fit her argument.

Dean Rosenthal suggests an alternative interpretation of sec. 1-207 and the official UCC Comment. He suggests that sec. 1-207 applies "only where one party's acquiescence in the other's performance or demand might, *by operation of law*, result in a waiver or other basis for prejudicing his rights.... Under this interpretation, sec. 1-207 would not apply where the challenge was *expressly* communicated, as in a check offered in satisfaction of an obligation on a clear take-it-or-leave-it basis." Rosenthal, *Discord and Dissatisfaction: *106 Section*

1-207 of the Uniform Commercial Code, 78 Colum.L.Rev. 48, 63-64 (1978).

The commentary to the Wisconsin Commercial Code Committee also suggests that sec. 401.207 was intended to apply to fact situations other than full payment checks. [FN8]

FN8. The Committee's summary of changes or clarifications of the law made by sec. 401.207 states: "*Summary of changes or clarifications*
[Sec. 401.207] provides a method of procedure whereby one party claiming a right which the other party feels to be unwarranted can make certain that the fact that he proceeds with or promises or assents to performance will not operate as a waiver of his claim to such right; there is no similar general provision in the present law, though the policy of Wis.Stat. sec. 121.49 is similar."
See sec. 401.207, West's Wis.Stat.Annot. (1964).
Sec. 121.49, Stats.1961, provided: "Acceptance does not bar action for damages. In the absence of express or implied agreement of the parties, acceptance of the goods by the buyer shall not discharge the seller from liability in damages or other legal remedy for breach of any promise or warranty in the contract to sell or the sale. But, if, after acceptance of the goods, the buyer fails to give notice to the seller of

Once again, we see the attempts of the Wisconsin legislature to explain how it was interpreting the UCC sections that it was adopting. This is not primary source material, but it is legislative history and can help you understand what the primary source means.

the breach of any promise or warranty within a reasonable time after the buyer knows, or ought to know, of such breach, the seller shall not be liable therefor."

While the official UCC Comment and the Wisconsin Commercial Code Committee's commentary indicate that sec. 401.207 should not be interpreted to apply to a full payment check, they do not conclusively settle the question. We therefore turn to the legislative history of sec. 1-207 for guidance in deciding the issue before us. The legislative history offers conflicting inferences.

One piece of legislative history suggests that sec. 1-207 should be read as not being applicable to full payment checks. When sec. 1-207 first appeared in the UCC it coexisted with another provision, sec. 3-802(3), which substantially codified the common law rule of the effect of the full payment check. Sec. 3-802(3) provided:

*107 "Where a check or similar payment instrument provides that it is in full satisfaction of an obligation the payee discharges the underlying obligation by obtaining payment of the instrument unless he establishes that the original obligor has taken unconscionable advantage in the circumstances." [FN9]

FN9. The official UCC Comment to sec. 3-802(3) reads:
"5. Checks are frequently given with a term providing that they are "in full payment of all claims," or

Here Justice Abrahamson uses a classic device of statutory interpretation. The UCC had discussed this very issue in a different section in an earlier draft. That (different) section accepted the continuance of the existence of a full payment check. Justice Abrahamson reasons that if the two sections existed at the same time in one draft, that must mean that 1-207 could not end the full payment check. The rub is, the other section was dropped. You can argue either way from this event.

similar language. The holder who obtains payment of such a check takes its benefits subject to the drawer's stipulation that he releases the original obligation. Even where the obligation is for an undisputed and liquidated debt there is no unfairness in the tender and acceptance of an accord and satisfaction; and in this respect subsection (3) changes the law in a number of states.

"The exception stated as to unconscionable advantage taken by the obligor has been recognized in a considerable number of decisions. A genuine accord and satisfaction is to be found only where the parties are dealing at arm's length and on fair terms of bargaining equality, without unfair advantage taken by either party. The following cases illustrate the application of the exception:

"a. The debtor sends the creditor a false statement of their account with a check which stipulates that it is in full payment. The creditor cashes the check in good faith reliance on the statement of account. The original obligation is not discharged.

"b. The debtor, knowing that it is the practice of the creditor's clerks to put through checks without examining accounts, sends a check for half the amount due which states that it is in full payment. The check is cashed without examining the account. The obligation is not discharged.

Justice Abrahamson is responding to arguments raised by counsel in their briefs on appeal.

"c. The debtor sends a check for less than the amount due which states that it is in full payment. The creditor insists that the amount is not correct, and finally cashes the check as the only available means of obtaining any payment. The original obligation is not discharged.

"d. An employer hands an employee a check for less than the full amount of wages due which states that it is in full payment, and threatens to fire the employee if he does not accept the amount. When the employee cashes the check the original obligation is not discharged.

"e. An employer hands an employee a check for less than the full amount of wages due which states that it is in full payment. He refuses the employee's demands for the proper amount, and the employee cashes the check in order to obtain money for subsistence. The obligation is not discharged."

**662 *108 Since sec. 3-802(3) expressly recognized that acceptance of a full payment check was effective to create an accord and satisfaction, it creates an inference that sec. 1-207 was intended to apply to a different fact situation. Sec. 3-802(3) was ultimately dropped from the UCC, but the fact that secs. 1-207 and 3-802(3) both were part of the UCC at the same time suggests that sec. 1-207 should not be read to change the common law recognizing the effectiveness of the full payment check.

On the other hand, another piece of legislative history suggests that sec. 1-207 was intended to change the common law rule. The 1961 Report of the New York Commission on Uniform State Laws, in its section-by-section annotations reflecting the relationships between the UCC and then existing New York law, viewed sec. 1-207 as changing the common law rules governing payments tendered in full settlement. The New York report stated as follows:

"[Section 1-207] permits a party involved in a Code-covered transaction to accept whatever he can get by way of payment, performance, etc. without losing his rights ... to sue for the balance of the payment, so long as he explicitly reserves his rights.... The Code rule would permit ... the acceptance of a part performance or payment tendered in full settlement without requiring the acceptor to gamble with his legal right to demand the balance of the performance or payment."

The New York report is of some significance since New York took a lead in studying the UCC and suggesting revisions during the drafting of the Code, and the report was highly influential in bringing about the adoption of the UCC in that key state. Rosenthal, *supra,* 78 Colum.L.Rev. 48, 58, 61, 62. Not surprisingly New York courts have concluded that sec. 1-207 does apply *109 to full payment checks. [FN10] The New York report has no binding effect, however, on our interpretation of the UCC as passed by the Wisconsin legislature, and there is no evidence that this state intended to follow the New York interpretation or was

The New York Commission on Uniform State Laws issued a very influential report on the early draft of the UCC. Because New York is such a commercial center, it was vital for New York to accept the UCC if it was to become a national standard. In our federal system, New York's action would not govern what Wisconsin should do, but the New York Commission's report has become a powerful, persuasive tool.

The Justice, careful craftsperson that she is, explains this in the text. Of course, we shall see that she does not follow it.

aware of it. [FN11] Because the legislative history is subject to conflicting inferences, it does not aid us in interpreting sec. 1-207.

FN10. See, *e.g., Braun v. C.E.P.C. Distribs., Inc.,* 77 App.Div.2d 358, 433 N.Y.S.2d 447 (1st Dept.1980); *Continental Information Sys. Corp. v. Mutual Life Ins. Co. of N.Y.,* 77 App.Div.2d 316, 432 N.Y.S.2d 952 (4th Dept.1980); *Ayer v. Sky Club, Inc.,* 70 App.Div.2d 863, 418 N.Y.S.2d 57 (1st Dept., 1979), *appeal dismissed,* 48 N.Y.2d 705, 422 N.Y.S.2d 68, 397 N.E.2d 758 (1979).

A bare listing of cases is called a "string cite." Each of these cases proves the point, or underpins the argument. String cites can be deceptive and are sometimes black holes of research time.

FN11. The contract provided that it was governed by the laws of Massachusetts. Massachusetts has, like Wisconsin, adopted sec. 1-207 of the UCC.   Honeywell's brief advises the court that Massachusetts has no reported decision resolving the issue presented in the instant case. Because the commentary in the Massachusetts annotation to sec. 1-207 is similar to the New York commentary, Honeywell argues that we should assume the Massachusetts court will follow the New York cases.   We are not persuaded that Massachusetts would necessarily adopt the New York courts' interpretation of sec. 1-207.   We assume Massachusetts would adopt the same reasoning this court does.

A great footnote! The Justice directly addresses the brief of counsel, which advises the Wisconsin Court to use a Massachusetts standard of interpreting the New York reading of the UCC. Massachusetts has not actually done this, the lawyers are just suggesting the way Massachusetts would use the New York view. It is a highly structured legal argument, fun to read in the brief.   The Justice pays it the honor of putting it into a footnote, but does not buy it.

Since we are not aided by the language of

the Code, the official comments, or the legislative history, we look to the rules of construction set forth in the UCC. One rule of construction set forth in the UCC itself is that the UCC is to be liberally construed and applied to promote its underlying purposes and policies.   Sec. 1-102, UCC; sec. 401.102, Stats. 1981-82.   The underlying purposes and policies of the UCC as set forth in the UCC are as follows:

"(a) To simplify, clarify and modernize the law governing commercial transactions; ****663** "(b) To permit the continued expansion of commercial practices through custom, usage and agreement of the parties;

*110 "(c) To make uniform the law among the various jurisdictions." Sec. 1-102(2), UCC; sec. 401.102(2), Stats. 1981-82.

Applying sec. 1.207 to the full payment check would not necessarily serve to "simplify," or "clarify," or "modernize the law governing commercial transactions." Nor would an application of sec. 401.207 promote the purpose and policy of the UCC of permitting "the continued expansion of commercial practice through ... agreement of the parties."   All that would be accomplished would be the elimination of the simple technique of the full payment check;   sophisticated parties might still arrange their affairs to achieve the benefits of the full payment check.   See Rosenthal, *Discord and Dissatisfaction: Section 1-207 of the Uniform Commercial Code,* 78 Colum.L.Rev. 48, 71-74 (1978).

As to the purpose of achieving uniformity

The Justice has put aside all of the possible tools that might solve her specific problem. She now recognizes that the UCC itself offered general guidance on how to interpret its language. She turns to the language of 1-102. It is not unusual for a statute to have such a general guide to its interpretation.   In situations like this one, the contextual research style discussed in the text would pay off.

among the jurisdictions adopting the UCC, we note that the state courts have not been uniform in their interpretation of sec. 401.207, and the developing trend appears to be to interpret sec. 401.207 as not changing the common law rule applicable to full payment checks.

The official UCC Comment to sec. 1-102(2) advises that "the text of each section should be read in the light of the purpose and policy of the rule or principle in question...." We should therefore consider the purposes of the common law rule of accord and satisfaction and full payment checks and the effect on commercial practices of interpreting sec. 401.207 as overriding the common law rule to determine how sec. 401.207 should be interpreted.

The common law rule that acceptance of a full payment check is an accord and satisfaction discharging the entire debt is a long-standing doctrine resting not ***111** only on principles of contract law but on principles of sound public policy, that is, interests of resolving disputes informally without litigation and of fairness. Use of the full payment check by parties bargaining at arm's length is a convenient and valuable way of resolution of dispute through agreement of the parties. The interests of fairness dictate that a creditor who cashes a check offered in full payment should be bound by the terms of the offer. The debtor's intent is known, and allowing the creditor to keep the money disregarding the debtor's conditions seems unfair and violative of the obligation of good faith

The Justice now turns to traditional common law doctrine. In the past most judicial opinions consisted largely of discussion of common law doctrine. In recent decades, discussion of statutes and administrative enactments have moved to center stage of most opinions. Here, after working through other sources, Justice Abrahamson ends with a discussion of the kind of common law doctrine that fills law school casebooks, especially in the first year.

which the UCC makes applicable to every contract or duty. Sec. 1-203, UCC; sec. 401.203, Stats. 1981- 82. The doctrine of accord and satisfaction includes safeguards designed to protect a creditor from an overreaching debtor: there must be a good faith dispute about the debt; the creditor must have reasonable notice that the check is intended to be in full satisfaction of the debt. One commentator called the rule binding the creditor upon cashing a full payment check "a short cut to complete justice." 6 Corbin,Contracts sec. 1279, p. 130 (1962). [FN12] Another commentator noted:

> FN12. In contrast, the full payment check has been described as follows: "Offering a check for less than the contract amount, but in 'full settlement' inflicts an exquisite form of commercial torture on the payee." White and Summers, *Handbook of the Law Under the Uniform Commercial Code,* sec. 13-21, p. 544 (2d ed. 1980). As we discuss later, if there is "undue advantage" in the settlement, there will be no discharge. *Kercheval v. Doty,* 31 Wis. 476, 485 (1872).

The Justice sets out each side of the argument with care, again, citing Corbin, introducing White and Summers (a very influential hornbook), and citing a case. This is the beauty of legal argument, you can line up sources on either side.

"It is unfair to the party who writes the check thinking that he will be spending his money only if the whole dispute will be over, to allow the other party, knowing of that reasonable expectation, to weasel around the deal by putting his own markings on the other person's checks. There is no reason why s. 1-207 should be interpreted as being an exception to the basic duty of good ***112** faith, when it is possible to interpret the two sections consistently. The academic writers who support this result offer no analysis, to the current knowledge of this treatise, which would justify licensing the recipient of the check to so deceive the drawer." ****664** 6 Corbin, *Contracts* sec. 1279, p. 396-97 (1982 Supplement).

[3] Inasmuch as there is no clearly expressed legislative direction in sec. 401.207, we are reluctant to impair the long-recognized settlement tool of the full payment check. Accordingly we hold that sec. 401.207 is not applicable to the full payment check.

Most cases would not take so long to get to the legal principles discussed in Headnote [3], but here is the holding. Consider that most of Justice Abrahamson's wrestling with statutory interpretation slips past the headnotes because it does not resolve a point of law. All of this discussion leads up to this conclusion of law.

III.

Since we conclude that sec. 401.207 is not applicable to the full payment check, we must decide whether there was a valid discharge by an accord and satisfaction in this case.

[4][5] An "accord and satisfaction" is an agreement to discharge an existing disputed claim; it constitutes a defense to an action to enforce the claim. 6 Corbin, *Contracts* sec. 1276, p. 114 (1962). Like other contracts, an accord and satisfaction requires an offer, an acceptance, and consideration.

The parties do not dispute that Flambeau offered the check as full payment and that Honeywell's retention of the proceeds constituted an acceptance of the terms of the offer. The sole issue in contention between the parties in this case as to whether there

Now the Justice applies the rule that she has derived to the facts of this case.

was a valid accord and satisfaction is whether there was consideration for the discharge of the claim. The requirement of consideration tends to offer protection against unfairness, but several courts have tended to move away from conceptual abstractions of consideration in commercial contexts and to consider directly the issues of duress, unconscionability, ***113** bad faith or fraud. Rosenthal, *Discord and Dissatisfaction: Section 1-207 of the Uniform Commercial Code,* 78 Colum.L.Rev. 48, 53 (1978). In any event, the parties have addressed the issue of consideration in traditional terms.

Three rules relating to consideration and accord and satisfaction come into play. [FN13]

FN13. As noted previously, the contract provided that it was governed by the law of Massachusetts. The parties took the position that the law of Massachusetts and the law of Wisconsin are the same on the question of accord and satisfaction until shown otherwise. The parties' briefs relied almost exclusively on Wisconsin cases, treating the common law of the two states the same. Following the parties' lead, we have examined Wisconsin cases, not Massachusetts cases, and we have deemed Massachusetts law to be the same as Wisconsin's since there was no showing that Massachusetts law is different.

Here the federal system is again at work. The Justice decides that Massachusetts law would be exactly like Wisconsin law on this matter, that is, in her opinion.

[6][7] First, the law in Wisconsin has long been that payment in full settlement of a claim which is disputed as to amount discharges the entire claim. Resolution of an actual controversy involving some subject of pecuniary value and interest to the parties is sufficient consideration of an accord and satisfaction. *Superior Builders, Inc. v. Large,* 52 Wis.2d 563, 566, 190 N.W.2d 901 (1971); *Kercheval v. Doty,* 31 Wis. 476, 485 (1872).

[8][9][10] A second rule, also of long-standing, is that payment of part of a debt which is not disputed as to amount does not discharge the debt altogether, even when it is expressly agreed that the partial payment is received in full satisfaction. The debtor's mere refusal to pay the full claim does not make it a disputed claim. Where the refusal is arbitrary and the debtor knows it has no just basis, the payment of less than the full amount claimed does not operate as an accord and satisfaction even though it is tendered and received as such. This ***114** rule is based on the principle that a part payment furnishes no consideration for relinquishing the balance of the debt. *Robinson v. Marachowsky,* 184 Wis. 600, 606-607, 200 N.W. 398 (1924); *Holman Mfg. Co. v. Dapin,* 181 Wis. 97, 99, 100, 193 N.W. 986 (1923), citing *Pinnel's Case,* 3 Coke's Rep. 238; *Otto v. Klauber,* 23 Wis. 471 (1868). [FN14]

> FN14. This rule has been criticized by the commentators. See, *e.g.,* Farnsworth, *Contracts* sec. 4.21-4.23 (1983). Although this

Now we are in the land of old time judicial opinion writing. Justice Abrahamson describes the law of Wisconsin on accord and satisfaction, with liberal citation to earlier cases on point. This is the doctrine of precedent at work.

The Justice is citing cases from 1923 and 1868!

court has not directly discarded the common law rule allowing the creditor to accept a check offered as payment in full and to then sue for the balance of the claim on the ground that the release was void for want of consideration, it has not viewed the rule requiring consideration with favor. *Herman v. Schlesinger,* 114 Wis. 382, 400, 401, 90 N.W. 460 (1902), quoted with approval in *Petersime Incubator Co. v. Klinke,* 248 Wis. 166, 21 N.W.2d 377 (1946).

The Justice cites a case that cites a case approvingly.

**665 [11][12] The third rule, also of long duration, is that when the amount of a debt is undisputed but an offset is claimed arising directly out of the contract of sale of goods and not out of any collateral transaction, the debt is a single claim which is disputed in amount. Payment in full settlement of less than the amount claimed operates as an accord and satisfaction. The question whether an offset renders the claim disputed depends not on whether the offset is legally valid but on whether it was asserted in good faith. *Lange v. Darling & Co.,* 233 Wis. 520, 525, 290 N.W. 188 (1940); *Robinson v. Marachowsky,* 184 Wis. 600, 606, 607, 200 N.W. 398 (1924); *Holman Mfg. Co. v. Dapin,* 181 Wis. 97, 101, 193 N.W. 986 (1923); *Thomas v. Columbia Phonograph Co.,* 144 Wis. 470, 129 N.W. 522 (1911).

The parties disagree as to whether this case falls under the second or third rule. Honeywell claims that Flambeau's payment is nothing more than a part payment of an

Battle is joined on the issue of offset. This is a tough issue, one that is a good one to work through in class. It ends up being a matter of interpretation.

undisputed debt and that this case comes within the second rule, the undisputed debt rule. On the other hand, ***115** Flambeau asserts that its good faith claim of offset rendered the entire debt disputed as to amount and that this case comes within the third rule, the "offset" rule.

[13] The circuit court made a finding that although there was no dispute about the account known to Honeywell until the check for $95,412 was tendered by Flambeau, when Honeywell received the check it was faced with an offer by Flambeau to satisfy a disputed claim. [FN15] The circuit court further found that Flambeau's claim to the $14,000 offset "had sufficient support to make it bona fide rather than dishonest or fraudulent." Because our review of the record leads us to conclude that these findings are not clearly erroneous we shall not set them aside. Sec. 805.17, Stats. 1981-82. In light of these findings, we conclude that the good faith claim of offset rendered the entire claim disputed.

Here the Justice is reviewing whether to accept the findings of the lower court about the dispute. For first year law students, the rules on the deference paid to such rulings will appear in Civil Procedure. Here, the Justice accepts them.

> FN15. Honeywell cites no authority for its assertion that a dispute must have been manifest before the settlement offer is made.

"[C]ites no authority" is a damning phrase to say about a party in a judicial opinion.

Nevertheless Honeywell asserts that Flambeau's payment of $95,412, the undisputed amount, is not sufficient consideration for a discharge of the disputed claim. Honeywell urges that where there are disputed and undisputed portions of a claim, payment of the undisputed portion by a full payment check is not consideration for settlement of the disputed portion. In other words, Honeywell is saying that there was no dispute between the parties that $95,412 was owed. The only dispute concerned what, if any, part of the sum of $14,000 in excess of the $95,412 was due. According to Honeywell, since Flambeau only paid the claim then undisputed, Flambeau has not offered a compromise and Honeywell is being asked to surrender the whole part of the disputed claim without getting anything in return. Honeywell claims that since there was no consideration for settlement of the $14,000 disputed portion of the claim, there was no discharge of this disputed portion.

*116 Honeywell relies on three cases to support its position: *Karp v. Coolview of Wisconsin, Inc.*, 25 Wis.2d 299, 130 N.W.2d 790 (1964); *O'Leary v. Hannaford*, 258 Wis. 146, 44 N.W.2d 908 (1950); *Kendall v. Sump*, 204 Wis. 514, 235 N.W. 544 (1931). We conclude that these cases are inapposite.

In *Karp v. Coolview of Wisconsin, Inc.*, *supra*, 25 Wis.2d 299, 130 N.W.2d 790, a creditor extended credit to a debtor for thirteen airline tickets. The debtor claimed it was not responsible for six of these tickets and sent the creditor a check for seven of the tickets marked "paid in full" which the creditor cashed. The creditor sued for payment for the six tickets. The debtor pleaded accord and satisfaction. The court held for the creditor. Honeywell asserts that the case stands for the rule that there was no accord and satisfaction because the debtor admitted liability for seven tickets and its payment could not be consideration ****666**

Honeywell has relied heavily on three cases to make its point. The Justice now pulls apart those cases. She shows that while they look as if they would apply here, they actually do not. This process is called "distinguishing" an opinion. In other words, she shows that while the opinions themselves are good, they do not apply. Justice Abrahamson is very good at what she does. Read these paragraphs with care. Much of the discussion in first year law school classes consists of similar exercises.

for settlement of the dispute over the remaining six. We do not read the case this way. The check specifically referred only to the seven tickets, the undisputed portion of the claim. The check made no reference to the six disputed tickets. It would be unreasonable to interpret a notation on a check as full payment of seven tickets as being full payment for thirteen tickets. This court concluded that since the debtor had not offered to settle the entire debt, the cashing of the check did not constitute an acceptance of an offer of accord.

In *O'Leary, supra,* 258 Wis. 146, 44 N.W.2d 908, unlike in this case, the amount due was liquidated and not disputed. Consequently the court held that the "amounts due the plaintiff were certain and stated ... [and] cashing a check marked 'in full' did not constitute an accord and satisfaction."

In *Kendall v. Sump, supra,* 204 Wis. 514, 517, 235 N.W. 544, a farm tenant brought an action for his share of produce. There *117 was no dispute as to his right to certain amounts for certain produce less certain credits. However, the landlord claimed an offset of $150.08 which was disputed and which left the farm tenant with an amount due of only $6.04. The landlord sent the tenant a check for the sum of $6.04 which the tenant cashed. In *Kendall,* unlike in the instant case, the check was not marked "paid in full." There was no evidence that the tenant was told that the check was intended as full settlement. As the court said, "There is no evidence that the [tenant] ever agreed to this as a final settlement."

Weidner v. Standard Life and Accident Ins. Co., 130 Wis. 10, 15, 110 N.W. 246 (1906), has been viewed by one commentator as supporting the position Honeywell is asserting. [FN16] In *Weidner*, the creditor, the insurance company, issued a check in full in the sum of $300 in settlement of a $3,000 claim by a widow under her husband's life insurance policy. *Weidner* is also distinguishable from the instant case. *Weidner* has been viewed as a case in which there were two separate and distinct claims and the acceptance of payment in full on one claim did not constitute an accord and satisfaction as to the other claim. *Sprinkmann Sons Corp. v. Bishopric Prods. Co.*, 340 F.Supp. 148, 149 (E.D.Wis.1972). See also 1 Restatement (Second), *Contracts* sec. 74, comment *c*, p. 186 (1979). Perhaps *Weidner* can best be explained by noting that a purported accord and satisfaction will not be given effect where there is overreaching by the debtor. The plaintiff offered evidence that she was suffering from nervous exhaustion at the time she signed a full payment receipt from the insurance ***118** company less than three weeks after her husband died from injuries sustained in an assault.

> FN16. 6 Corbin, *Contracts* sec. 1289, p. 163, n. 89 (1962). Corbin also cites *Schulz Co. v. Gether,* 183 Wis. 491, 198 N.W. 433 (1924), for this proposition. There is language in *Schulz* supporting the citation but it appears that the court also viewed the two claims as separate and independent. See 183 Wis. at 494,

Now the Justice faces the challenge of a 1906 Wisconsin case, home turf, that was discussed in <u>Corbin,</u> *an admittedly influential set. She does not disregard it because it is 78 years old. She takes it on and distinguishes it.*

496. See 1 Restatement (Second), *Contracts* sec. 74, comment c, p. 186 (1979).

The position Honeywell urges this court to adopt has been criticized by commentators [FN17] and courts.   The majority rule apparently is that where the total claim is disputed, payment of the amount the debtor admits to be due supports the creditor's discharge of the entire debt on the cashing of the full payment check. [FN18]

    FN17. See, *e.g.,* 6 Corbin, *Contracts* sec. 1289, pp. 163-66 (1962).

    FN18. 6 Corbin, *Contracts* sec. 1289, p. 165 (1962).   See also Calamari & Perillo, *Contracts* sec. 4-12, p. 155 (2d ed. 1977).

We find unpersuasive Honeywell's assertion that the payment of the undisputed portion of a disputed claim by a check marked "paid in full" is not consideration for the disputed portion of the claim.   Honeywell does not explain why we should treat a single contract out of which a dispute as to the performance of one party arises as if it were two divisible contracts, each of which must be negotiated separately.   Furthermore, as the Oregon Supreme Court explained, "It would be too technical **667 a use of the doctrine of consideration to release a well-counseled debtor who tenders a nominal amount beyond his admitted debt but to trap one less sophisticated who is induced to pay the undisputed amount in return for his creditor's illusory promise to forgive the rest."

The <u>Restatement of Contracts</u>, that great statement of contract law produced by the American Law Institute, makes a cameo appearance. It is a classic of doctrinal analysis. While it is not a primary source, it has great persuasive authority on common law issues. The UCC and legislation have stolen some of its thunder.

Citing an Oregon opinion, the Justice builds her point. Of course, the Oregon opinion is just secondary authority to a Wisconsin court.

Kilander v. Blickle Co., 280 Or. 425, 571 P.2d 503, 505 (1977).

Honeywell's argument raises the spectre of overreaching if the court allows a debtor to force a creditor to discharge a debt when the debtor is paying only the undisputed portion. There can, of course, be overreaching by a debtor who tenders a full payment check. But overreaching can be policed through the doctrine of good faith. See 1 Restatement (Second), *Contracts* sec. 74, comment *c*, p. 186 (1979); Hillman, *Policing Contract *119 Modification under the U.C.C.: Good Faith and the Doctrine of Economic Duress,* 64 Iowa L.Rev. 849 (1979).

Note how the Justice buttresses her argument using the <u>*Restatement*</u> *and two law review sources.*

In this case, however, the circuit court found that Flambeau asserted its offset in good faith. The parties dealt with each other at arm's length with mutual understandings as to the effect of usual commercial practices. Under these circumstances, we conclude it would be unfair to allow Honeywell to accept Flambeau's money which was offered on condition of full settlement and then to turn around and claim the right to sue Flambeau for the balance of its asserted claim.

For the reasons set forth we conclude that Honeywell's claim against Flambeau was discharged upon Honeywell's cashing the full payment check and retaining the proceeds. Accordingly we reverse the decision of the court of appeals and remand the matter to the circuit court for proceedings on Flambeau's claim against Honeywell not inconsistent with this opinion.

Justice Abrahamson concludes, sums up and sets out the ruling.

Decision of the court of appeals reversed; order for judgment of the circuit court affirmed and cause remanded.

Remanding the case sends it back down the judicial ladder for action in light of the Supreme Court's decision.

STEINMETZ, Justice (dissenting).

I disagree with the majority that the check presented and cashed in this case was an accord and satisfaction.

Here we have Justice Steinmetz's dissent. A dissent disagrees with the result of the majority opinion. Justice Steinmetz is not concerned with Justice Abrahamson's exegesis on statutory construction. He joins the issue on the common law question of accord and satisfaction. This is a terse dissent, but sometimes they can go on for many pages.

The $14,000 worth of computer programming services was an inducement to enter into the purchase of the equipment. There is nothing in this record nor the opinion to be persuasive that the services had a separate value above and in addition to the value of the equipment purchased. The programming services appear to be a "throw-in" incentive to sell the equipment. The services may have been listed as a $14,000 value to the purchaser of the equipment, Flambeau; however, there is no evidence in the record as to the cost to Honeywell to provide those services or their actual value.

*120 Flambeau did not disagree with the value of the equipment or the amount still owed on it. Its check paid for the amount due on the equipment which was not disputed minus the $14,000 for the unused programming services. It paid less than it owed on the equipment while not disputing the amount it owed on the equipment and therefore there was no accord and satisfaction.

Flambeau was not under the contract expected to pay $14,000 for programming services since it was a sales inducement only and therefore the unused services should not have been deducted from the undisputed equipment debt still owed.

I would hold that payment of part of the debt for the equipment which was not disputed did not discharge the debt altogether. The issue of $14,000 as a possible offset should have been tried to determine whether it had value independent of the equipment contract price.

WILLIAM A. BABLITCH, Justice (dissenting).

I dissent because I conclude that sec. 401.207, Stats., applies in this case. Section 401.102(2) delineates the underlying purposes and policies of the Uniform Commercial Code, including the policy of simplifying, clarifying and modernizing the law governing commercial transactions. Sec. **668 401.102(2)(a). Under sec. 401.102(1), chs. 401 to 409 must be liberally construed and applied to promote the underlying purposes and policies set forth in sec. 401.102(2).

I conclude that interpreting sec. 401.207, Stats., to allow a creditor to accept a conditional check under protest and reserve the right to obtain payment for any balance due is supported by the language of sec. 401.207. I also conclude that this interpretation promotes the policy of simplifying, clarifying and modernizing the

This second dissent is by Justice Bablitch. Note that each of the dissenting Justices feels that it is important not just to register disagreement with Justice Abrahamson, but to set out their reasons. They even write separately. This all relates to the doctrine of precedent. They wish to record the very different interpretation that they have of the case. Justice Bablitch is concerned with the issue of statutory interpretation. He draws on the White and Summers hornbook to support his argument. It is a short statement of his view. Justice Abrahamson anticipated and answered his argument in her majority opinion. This is hardly a surprise since drafts of opinions circulate among the Justices. You may read an opinion in which there is a dialogue between opinions. These are interactive creatures.

law governing commercial transactions. As White and Summers note in *Handbook of the Law Under the Uniform *121 Commercial Code,* sec. 13-21 at 544 (2d ed. 1980), "... offering a check for less than the contract amount, but 'in full settlement' inflicts an exquisite form of commercial torture on the payee." Under the common law doctrine of accord and satisfaction, the payee may have to refuse the check, even if both parties agree that the amount tendered is due, in order to reserve the right to pursue a claim for any additional amount that the payor owes. [FN1] This commercially unreasonable result can be avoided by interpreting sec. 401.207 to allow the payee to cash the check and still retain the right to sue for the balance owing if the payee has reserved his or her rights.

> FN1. This case presents a perfect example of this dilemma. In order to avoid the result that would occur under the common law doctrine of accord and satisfaction, Honeywell would be forced to return Flambeau's check for $95,412, an amount Flambeau concedes it owes Honeywell, in order to reserve the right to pursue its claim for $14,000 that it contends Flambeau still owes under the purchase contracts.

In this case, Honeywell reserved its rights under sec. 401.207, Stats., by the letter it sent to Flambeau disputing Flambeau's assertion that Flambeau had satisfied all of its obligations under the purchase contracts. Because I conclude that sec. 401.207 applies

in this case, and because Honeywell reserved

its rights under that provision, I would hold
that Honeywell reserved its right to demand
full performance of Flambeau's obligations
under the purchase contracts.

END OF DOCUMENT

Part V: *Shepard's & KeyCite*

Flambeau Products Corp. v. Honeywell Information Systems, Inc., 116 Wis. 2d 95, 341 N.W.2d 655, 1984 Wisc. LEXIS 2272, 37 U.C.C. Rep. Serv. (CBC) 1441 (Wis. 1984)

SHEPARD'S(R) Signal: Caution: Possible negative treatment
Restrictions: *Unrestricted*
FOCUS(TM) Terms: *No FOCUS terms*
Print Format: *FULL*
Citing Ref. Signal Legend:
> {Warning} -- negative treatment indicated
> {Questioned} -- validity questioned by citing refs.
> {Caution} -- possible negative treatment
> {Positive} -- positive treatment indicated
> {Analysis} -- cited and neutral analysis indicated
> {Cited} -- citation information available

SHEPARD'S SUMMARY

Shepard's FULL Summary:
No subsequent appellate history. Prior history available.
Citing References:

Cautionary Analyses:	**Distinguished (2)**
Positive Analyses:	Followed (3)
Neutral Analyses:	Dissenting Op. (1), Explained (1)
Other Sources:	Law Reviews (8), Secondary Sources (2), Statutes

(2),

	Treatises (6), American Law Rpts/Lawyers' Edition Annos (2)

PRIOR HISTORY (2 citing references)

1. *Flambeau Products v. Honeywell*, 97 Wis. 2d 759, 295 N.W.2d 834, 1980 Wisc. App. LEXIS 3737 (Wis. Ct. App. 1980)*{Warning}*

2. **Appeal after remand at:**
   Flambeau Products Corp. v. Honeywell Information Systems, Inc., 111 Wis. 2d 317, 330 N.W.2d 228, 1983 Wisc. App. LEXIS 3210, 35 U.C.C. Rep. Serv. (CBC) 1397 (Wis. Ct. App. 1983)*{Warning}*

Reversed by (CITATION YOU ENTERED):
Flambeau Products Corp. v. Honeywell Information Systems, Inc.,
116 Wis. 2d 95, 341 N.W.2d 655, 1984 Wisc. LEXIS 2272, 37
U.C.C. Rep. Serv. (CBC) 1441 (Wis. 1984){Caution}

CITING DECISIONS (60 citing decisions)

WISCONSIN SUPREME COURT

3. **Cited by:**
   Putnam v. Time Warner Cable of Southeastern Wis., Ltd. P'ship, 2002 WI
   108, 255 Wis. 2d 447, 649 N.W.2d 626, 2002 Wisc. LEXIS 507
   (2002){Caution}
       255 Wis. 2d 447 p.460
       649 N.W.2d 626 p.633

WISCONSIN COURT OF APPEALS

4. **Cited by:**
   Taylor Inv. Corp. v. PLL Marquette, LLC, 258 Wis. 2d 981, 654 N.W.2d
   94, 2002 WI App 292, 2002 Wisc. App. LEXIS 1120 (2002){Cited}
       2002 Wisc. App. LEXIS 1120

5. **Cited by:**
   Batt v. Sweeney, 254 Wis. 2d 721, 647 N.W.2d 868, 2002 WI App 119,
   2002 Wisc. App. LEXIS 431 (2002){Positive}
       254 Wis. 2d 721 p.727, Headnote: N.W.2d - 2
       647 N.W.2d 868 p.871, Headnote: N.W.2d - 2

6. **Distinguished by:**
   Kramer Bus. Serv. v. Hyperion, Inc., 242 Wis. 2d 472, 625 N.W.2d 360,
   2001 WI App 75, 2001 Wisc. App. LEXIS 160 (2001)
       2001 Wisc. App. LEXIS 160

7. **Cited by:**
   Lemke v. Arrowood, 232 Wis. 2d 558, 608 N.W.2d 438, 2000 WI App 32,
   1999 Wisc. App. LEXIS 1360 (1999)

8. **Cited by:**
   Zubek v. Edlund, 228 Wis. 2d 783, 598 N.W.2d 273, 1999 Wisc. App.
   LEXIS 728 (Wis. Ct. App. 1999){Cited}
       228 Wis. 2d 783 p.793
       598 N.W.2d 273 p.278

9. **Cited by:**
    Rowell v. Ash, 228 Wis. 2d 511, 597 N.W.2d 774, 1999 Wisc. App.
    LEXIS 554 (Wis. Ct. App. 1999)*{Cited}*

10. **Cited by:**
    Traditional Design Works v. McGourthy, 223 Wis. 2d 266, 588 N.W.2d
    927, 1998 Wisc. App. LEXIS 1325 (Wis. Ct. App. 1998)

11. **Cited by:**
    Malone v. Fons, 217 Wis. 2d 746, 580 N.W.2d 697, 1998 Wisc. App.
    LEXIS 347 (Wis. Ct. App. 1998)*{Positive}*
        217 Wis. 2d 746 p.768, Headnote: N.W.2d - 5
        580 N.W.2d 697 p.706, Headnote: N.W.2d - 5

12. **Cited by:**
    North Mem. Med. Ctr. v. Lunde, 217 Wis. 2d 291, 577 N.W.2d 388, 1998
    Wisc. App. LEXIS 118 (Wis. Ct. App. 1998)

13. **Cited by:**
    Tower Ins. Co. v. Carpenter (In re Carpenter), 205 Wis. 2d 365, 556
    N.W.2d 384, 1996 Wisc. App. LEXIS 1265 (Wis. Ct. App.
    1996)*{Positive}*
        205 Wis. 2d 365 p.371, Headnote: N.W.2d - 6
        205 Wis. 2d 365 p.371, Headnote: N.W.2d - 7
        556 N.W.2d 384 p.387, Headnote: N.W.2d - 6
        556 N.W.2d 384 p.387, Headnote: N.W.2d - 7

14. **Cited by:**
    Gundersen Clinic v. Lyden, 204 Wis. 2d 114, 552 N.W.2d 900, 1996
    Wisc. App. LEXIS 928 (Wis. Ct. App. 1996)*{Analysis}*

15. **Cited by:**
    Bier v. Wicks, 201 Wis. 2d 819, 549 N.W.2d 288, 1996 Wisc. App.
    LEXIS 485 (Wis. Ct. App. 1996)*{Positive}*

16. **Cited by:**
    Zieve v. Ness, Motley, Loadholt, Richardson & Poole, P.A., 201 Wis. 2d
    816, 549 N.W.2d 286, 1996 Wisc. App. LEXIS 459 (Wis. Ct. App.
    1996)*{Analysis}*

17. **Cited by:**
    Evers v. Fryer, 1995 Wisc. App. LEXIS 1300 (Wis. Ct. App. Oct. 24,
    1995)*{Analysis}*

18. **Cited by:**
    Nelson v. City of Mauston, 1995 Wisc. App. LEXIS 947 (Wis. Ct. App. Aug. 3, 1995)

19. **Cited by:**
    Davies v. Munz, 183 Wis. 2d 433, 516 N.W.2d 21, 1994 Wisc. App. LEXIS 322 (Wis. Ct. App. 1994)*{Analysis}*

20. **Distinguished by:**
    Cue v. Carthage College, 179 Wis. 2d 175, 507 N.W.2d 109, 1993 Wisc. App. LEXIS 1132 (Wis. Ct. App. 1993)*{Caution}*
        179 Wis. 2d 175 p.180
        507 N.W.2d 109 p.112

21. **Cited by:**
    Flintrop v. Lumbermens Mut. Casualty Co., 176 Wis. 2d 511, 502 N.W.2d 617, 1993 Wisc. App. LEXIS 424 (Wis. Ct. App. 1993)*{Cited}*

22. **Followed by, Cited in Dissenting Opinion at:**
    Myron Soik & Sons, Inc. v. Stokely USA, Inc., 175 Wis. 2d 456, 498 N.W.2d 897, 1993 Wisc. App. LEXIS 374 (Wis. Ct. App. 1993)*{Cited}*
        Followed by:
        175 Wis. 2d 456 p.463, Headnote: N.W.2d - 8
        498 N.W.2d 897 p.900, Headnote: N.W.2d - 8
        Cited in Dissenting Opinion at:
        175 Wis. 2d 456 p.467
        498 N.W.2d 897 p.902

23. **Cited by:**
    Favorite v. Glass, 173 Wis. 2d 909, 499 N.W.2d 302, 1993 Wisc. App. LEXIS 748 (Wis. Ct. App. 1992)

24. **Followed by:**
    Butler v. Kocisko, 166 Wis. 2d 212, 479 N.W.2d 208, 1991 Wisc. App. LEXIS 1610 (Wis. Ct. App. 1991)*{Cited}*
        Followed by:
        166 Wis. 2d 212 p.215, Headnote: N.W.2d - 4
        166 Wis. 2d 212 p.215, Headnote: N.W.2d - 5
        479 N.W.2d 208 p.210, Headnote: N.W.2d - 4
        479 N.W.2d 208 p.210, Headnote: N.W.2d - 5
        Cited by:
        166 Wis. 2d 212 p.217
        479 N.W.2d 208 p.211

25. **Cited by:**
   Upholstery Center v. Begg, 165 Wis. 2d 514, 478 N.W.2d 597, 1991 Wisc. App. LEXIS 1511 (Wis. Ct. App. 1991)*{Analysis}*

26. **Cited by:**
   West Side Hospital v. Labor & Industry Review Com., 145 Wis. 2d 899, 428 N.W.2d 563, 1988 Wisc. App. LEXIS 428 (Wis. Ct. App. 1988)

27. **Cited by:**
   Hengel v. Badger Corrugating, Inc., 143 Wis. 2d 901, 423 N.W.2d 882, 1988 Wisc. App. LEXIS 277 (Wis. Ct. App. 1988)

28. **Cited by:**
   Lancaster's, Inc. v. Pamida, Inc., 143 Wis. 2d 894, 422 N.W.2d 462, 1988 Wisc. App. LEXIS 65 (Wis. Ct. App. 1988)*{Cited}*

29. **Cited by:**
   Cook & Franke, S.C. v. Meilman, 136 Wis. 2d 434, 402 N.W.2d 361, 1987 Wisc. App. LEXIS 3370 (Wis. Ct. App. 1987)*{Caution}*
       136 Wis. 2d 434 p.439
       402 N.W.2d 361 p.363, Headnote: N.W.2d - 4
       402 N.W.2d 361 p.363, Headnote: N.W.2d - 5

30. **Cited by:**
   Saxby v. Saxby, 135 Wis. 2d 545, 401 N.W.2d 182, 1986 Wisc. App. LEXIS 4110 (Wis. Ct. App. 1986)

31. **Cited by:**
   FIRST AGRI SERVS. v. PRODUCTION CREDIT ASSN. OF ELKHORN, 132 Wis. 2d 473, 132 Wis. 2d 475, 392 N.W.2d 130, 1986 Wisc. App. LEXIS 3607 (Wis. Ct. App. 1986)*{Cited}*

32. **Cited by:**
   COFFEY v. LILLY, 1986 Wisc. App. LEXIS 3229 (Wis. Ct. App. Feb. 4, 1986)

33. **Cited by:**
   TALECK v. TALECK, 128 Wis. 2d 560, 384 N.W.2d 367, 1986 Wisc. App. LEXIS 3148 (Wis. Ct. App. 1986)

34. **Cited by:**
   Terrill v. Atomizer, 127 Wis. 2d 561, 378 N.W.2d 296, 1985 Wisc. App. LEXIS 3822 (Wis. Ct. App. 1985)

35. **Cited by:**
   LYCKBERG v. GRAF, 123 Wis. 2d 545, 368 N.W.2d 847, 1985 Wisc.
   App. LEXIS 3237 (Wis. Ct. App. 1985)*{Cited}*

36. **Cited by:**
   Niebler & Muren, S.C. v. Brock-White Co. of Wisconsin, Inc., 122 Wis. 2d
   445, 361 N.W.2d 732, 1984 Wisc. App. LEXIS 4572, 40 U.C.C. Rep.
   Serv. (CBC) 165 (Wis. Ct. App. 1984)*{Caution}*
   >   122 Wis. 2d 445 p.447
   >   361 N.W.2d 732 p.733, Headnote: N.W.2d - 1
   >   361 N.W.2d 732 p.733, Headnote: N.W.2d - 10
   >   361 N.W.2d 732 p.733, Headnote: N.W.2d - 4

3RD CIRCUIT - U.S. DISTRICT COURTS

37. **Cited by:**
   Occidental Chem. Corp. v. Environmental Liners, 859 F. Supp. 791, 1994
   U.S. Dist. LEXIS 10051, 26 U.C.C. Rep. Serv. 2d (CBC) 310 (E.D. Pa.
   1994)*{Positive}*
   >   859 F. Supp. 791 p.796

7TH CIRCUIT - COURT OF APPEALS

38. **Followed by:**
   Gerald R. Turner & Assocs., S.C. v. Moriarty, 25 F.3d 1356, 1993 U.S.
   App. LEXIS 27259 (7th Cir. Wis. 1993)*{Analysis}*
   >   25 F.3d 1356 p.1360, Headnote: N.W.2d - 10
   >   25 F.3d 1356 p.1360, Headnote: N.W.2d - 8
   >   25 F.3d 1356 p.1360, Headnote: N.W.2d - 9
   >   25 F.3d 1356 p.1360, Headnote: N.W.2d - 6
   >   25 F.3d 1356 p.1360, Headnote: N.W.2d - 7

39. **Cited by:**
   Porter v. Regdab, Inc., 1991 U.S. App. LEXIS 814 (7th Cir. Wis. Jan. 17,
   1991)*{Analysis}*

7TH CIRCUIT - U.S. DISTRICT COURTS

40. **Cited by:**
   United States Plastic Lumber v. Strandex Corp., 2003 U.S. Dist. LEXIS
   24624 (W.D. Wis. Feb. 7, 2003)
   >   2003 U.S. Dist. LEXIS 24624

41. **Cited by:**
     Employers Reinsurance Corp. v. Admiral Ins. Co., 822 F. Supp. 1350,
     1993 U.S. Dist. LEXIS 7931 (E.D. Wis. 1993)*{Cited}*
          822 F. Supp. 1350 p.1353, Headnote: N.W.2d - 4

42. **Explained by:**
     Lakeshore Machinery, Inc. v. Thermwood Corp., 117 F.R.D. 429, 1987
     U.S. Dist. LEXIS 10133 (E.D. Wis. 1987)
          Explained by:
          117 F.R.D. 429 p.432, Headnote: N.W.2d - 3
          117 F.R.D. 429 p.432, Headnote: N.W.2d - 6
          117 F.R.D. 429 p.432, Headnote: N.W.2d - 7
          Cited by:
          117 F.R.D. 429 p.433, Headnote: N.W.2d - 13

11TH CIRCUIT - U.S. DISTRICT COURTS

43. **Cited by:**
     Burke Co. v. Hilton Dev. Co., 802 F. Supp. 434, 1992 U.S. Dist. LEXIS
     20965, 19 U.C.C. Rep. Serv. 2d (CBC) 6 (N.D. Fla. 1992)*{Caution}*
          802 F. Supp. 434 p.437, Headnote: N.W.2d - 1

ADMINISTRATIVE AGENCY DECISIONS

44. **Cited by:**
     U.C.C. Cas. Dig. P1207
          U.C.C. Cas. Dig. P1207

45. **Cited by:**
     U.C.C. Cas. Dig. P1203.20
          U.C.C. Cas. Dig. P1203.20

46. **Cited by:**
     U.C.C. Cas. Dig. P1102.1 (1)
          U.C.C. Cas. Dig. P1102.1 (1)

47. **Cited by:**
     U.C.C. Cas. Dig. P1102.6
          U.C.C. Cas. Dig. P1102.6

COLORADO SUPREME COURT

48. **Cited by:**
     Anderson v. Rosebrook, 737 P.2d 417, 1987 Colo. LEXIS 553, 3 U.C.C.
     Rep. Serv. 2d (CBC) 1312 (Colo. 1987){*Positive*}
          737 P.2d 417 p.420

DELAWARE SUPREME COURT

49. **Cited by:**
     Acierno v. Worthy Bros. Pipeline Corp., 656 A.2d 1085, 1995 Del. LEXIS
     92, 27 U.C.C. Rep. Serv. 2d (CBC) 759 (Del. 1995){*Caution*}
          656 A.2d 1085 p.1089

GEORGIA COURT OF APPEALS

50. **Cited by:**
     Golden Peanut Co. v. Bass, 249 Ga. App. 224, 547 S.E.2d 637, 2001 Ga.
     App. LEXIS 416, 2001 Fulton County D. Rep. 1224 (2001){*Caution*}
          249 Ga. App. 224 p.230
          547 S.E.2d 637 p.643

ILLINOIS APPELLATE COURT

51. **Cited by:**
     Nelson v. Fire Ins. Exchange, 156 Ill. App. 3d 1017, 510 N.E.2d 137,
     1987 Ill. App. LEXIS 2664, 109 Ill. Dec. 516, 4 U.C.C. Rep. Serv. 2d
     (CBC) 1344 (Ill. App. Ct. 2d Dist. 1987){*Caution*}
          510 N.E.2d 137 p.140

MAINE SUPREME JUDICIAL COURT

52. **Cited by:**
     Stultz Electric Works v. Marine Hydraulic Engineering Co., 39 U.C.C.
     Rep. Serv. (CBC) 1186 (Me. 1984){*Cited*}
          39 U.C.C. Rep. Serv. (CBC) 1186 p.1186

53. **Cited by:**
     Stultz Electric Works v. Marine Hydraulic Engineering Co., 484 A.2d
     1008, 1984 Me. LEXIS 843, 39 U.C.C. Rep. Serv. (CBC) 1186 (Me.
     1984){*Positive*}
          484 A.2d 1008 p.1011

MISSOURI COURT OF APPEALS

54. **Cited by:**
     McKee Constr. Co. v. Stanley Plumbing & Heating Co., 828 S.W.2d 700,
     1992 Mo. App. LEXIS 615, 18 U.C.C. Rep. Serv. 2d (CBC) 16 (Mo. Ct.
     App. 1992)*{Caution}*
           828 S.W.2d 700 p.702
           828 S.W.2d 700 p.704

NEW YORK COURT OF APPEALS

55. **Cited by:**
     Horn Waterproofing Corp. v. Bushwick Iron & Steel Co., 66 N.Y.2d 321,
     488 N.E.2d 56, 1985 N.Y. LEXIS 17607, 497 N.Y.S.2d 310, 41 U.C.C.
     Rep. Serv. (CBC) 1591 (1985)*{Positive}*
           488 N.E.2d 56 p.56
           488 N.E.2d 56 p.58
           497 N.Y.S.2d 310 p.310
           497 N.Y.S.2d 310 p.312

OHIO SUPREME COURT

56. **Cited by:**
     AFC Interiors v. Di Cello, 46 Ohio St. 3d 1, 544 N.E.2d 869, 1989 Ohio
     LEXIS 248, 9 U.C.C. Rep. Serv. 2d (CBC) 1181 (1989)*{Warning}*
           544 N.E.2d 869 p.875

OHIO COURT OF APPEALS

57. **Cited by:**
     Klass v. Allied Coal Producers, Inc., 1988 Ohio App. LEXIS 5385 (Ohio
     Ct. App., Guernsey County Dec. 29, 1988)*{Analysis}*

TEXAS COURT OF APPEALS

58. **Cited by:**
     Robinson v. Garcia, 804 S.W.2d 238, 1991 Tex. App. LEXIS 249, 14
     U.C.C. Rep. Serv. 2d (CBC) 689 (Tex. App. Corpus Christi
     1991)*{Positive}*
           804 S.W.2d 238 p.242

59. **Cited by:**
     Pileco, Inc. v. HCI, Inc., 735 S.W.2d 561, 1987 Tex. App. LEXIS 7809, 4
     U.C.C. Rep. Serv. 2d (CBC) 1349 (Tex. App. Houston 1st Dist.
     1987)*{Questioned}*
           735 S.W.2d 561 p.562

UTAH SUPREME COURT

60. **Cited by:**
   Marton Remodeling v. Jensen, 706 P.2d 607, 1985 Utah LEXIS 893, 42
   U.C.C. Rep. Serv. (CBC) 54 (Utah 1985)*{Positive}*
   > 706 P.2d 607 p.610

VERMONT SUPREME COURT

61. **Cited by:**
   Frangiosa v. Kapoukranidis, 160 Vt. 237, 627 A.2d 351, 1993 Vt. LEXIS
   46, 21 U.C.C. Rep. Serv. 2d (CBC) 486 (1993)*{Warning}*
   > 160 Vt. 237 p.240
   > 627 A.2d 351 p.352

VIRGINIA SUPREME COURT

62. **Cited by:**
   John Grier Constr. Co. v. Jones Welding & Repair, Inc., 238 Va. 270, 383
   S.E.2d 719, 1989 Va. LEXIS 144, 6 Va. Law Rep. 385, 9 U.C.C. Rep.
   Serv. 2d (CBC) 1214 (1989)*{Positive}*
   > 383 S.E.2d 719 p.721

ANNOTATED STATUTES (2 Citing Statutes)

63. *Wis. Stat. @ 401.207*

64. *Wis. Stat. @ 402.102*

LAW REVIEWS AND PERIODICALS (8 Citing References)

65. *SYMPOSIUM: ONE HUNDRED YEARS OF UNIFORM STATE LAWS:*
   INTERPRETING CODES.,
   > 89 Mich. L. Rev. 2201 (1991)
   > > 89 Mich. L. Rev. 2201 p.2213

66. *The Evolution of Accord and Satisfaction: Common Law; U.C.C. Section*
   1-207; U.C.C. Section 3-311, 28 New Eng.L. Rev. 189 (1993)

67. *CASE COMMENT: U.C.C. Section 1-207 and the Doctrine of Accord and*
   Satisfaction: Ohio's About-Face in AFC Interiors v. DiCello, 52 Ohio St.
   L.J. 1617 (1991)

68. *SYMPOSIUM ON REVISED ARTICLE 1 AND PROPOSED REVISED ARTICLE 2 OF THE*
     UNIFORM COMMERCIAL CODE: Code Arrogance and Displacement of Common Law and Equity: A Defense of Section 1-103 of the Uniform Commercial Code, 54 SMU L. Rev. 535 (2001)
        54 SMU L. Rev. 535 p.535

69. *FAVORITE CASE SYMPOSIUM: The Ties That Do Not Bind: Flambeau v.*
     Honeywell, 74 Tex. L. Rev. 1205 (1996)
        74 Tex. L. Rev. 1205 p.1205

70. *CASENOTE: OHIO'S INTERPRETATION OF UNIFORM COMMERCIAL CODE SECTION 1-207*
        -- YOU CAN HAVE YOUR CAKE AND EAT IT TOO: AFC Interiors v. DiCello, 46 Ohio St. 3d 1, 544 N.E.2d 869 (1989), 59 U. Cin. L. Rev. 1001 (1991)

71. *ARTICLE: The Law of Negotiable Instruments, Bank Deposits, and Collections in Tennessee: A Survey of Changes in the 1990 Revisions to UCC Articles 3 and 4*, 28 U. Mem. L. Rev. 117 (1997)

72. *ARTICLE: DEFINING FINALITY AND APPEALABILITY BY COURT RULE: RIGHT*
        PROBLEM, WRONG SOLUTION., 54 U. Pitt. L. Rev. 717 (1993)

ALR ANNOTATIONS (2 Citing Annotations)

73. *Modern status of rule that acceptance of check purporting to be final settlement of disputed amount constitutes accord and satisfaction*, 42 A.L.R.4th 12, secs. 3, 6

74. *Construction and effect of UCC Art. 3, dealing with commercial paper*, 23 A.L.R.3d 932, supp sec. 21

TREATISE CITATIONS (6 Citing Sources)

75. *5-121 Banking Law @ 121.06*

76. *1-121 Checks, Drafts and Notes @ 121.06*

77. *1-1 COMMERCIAL LAW AND PRACTICE GUIDE @ 1.03*

78. *2-7 Corbin on Contracts @ 7.17*

79. *13-70 Corbin on Contracts @ 70.2*

80. *2-2 Negotiable Instruments Under the UCC @ 2.10*

SECONDARY SOURCES (2 Citing Sources)

81. Anderson, U.C.C.3d Supp. sec. 1-207
        Anderson, U.C.C.3d Supp. sec. 1-207

82. Anderson, U.C.C.3d Supp. sec. 3-408
        Anderson, U.C.C.3d Supp. sec. 3-408

❖❖❖

KeyCite

Flambeau Products Corp. v. Honeywell Information Systems, Inc., 116 Wis.2d 95, 341 N.W.2d 655, 37 UCC Rep.Serv. 1441 (Wis., Jan 04, 1984) (NO. 82-307)
History
Direct History

H   1   Flambeau Products v. Honeywell, 97 Wis.2d 759, 295 N.W.2d 834 (Wis.App. Jun 17, 1980) (TABLE, TEXT IN WESTLAW, NO. 79-1536)
Appeal After Remand

▶   2 Flambeau Products Corp. v. Honeywell Information Systems, Inc., 111 Wis.2d 317, 330 N.W.2d 228, 35 UCC Rep.Serv. 1397 (Wis.App. Jan 18, 1983) (NO. 82-307)
Decision Reversed by

=>   3 **Flambeau Products Corp. v. Honeywell Information Systems, Inc., 116 Wis.2d 95, 341 N.W.2d 655, 37 UCC Rep.Serv. 1441 (Wis. Jan 04, 1984) (NO. 82-307)**

Negative Indirect History (U.S.A.)

Disagreed With by

▶   4 Frangiosa v. Kapoukranidis, 160 Vt. 237, 627 A.2d 351, 21 UCC Rep.Serv.2d 486 (Vt. May 07, 1993) (NO. 92-345) ★ **HN: 2 (N.W.2d)**

Declined to Follow by

▶   5 Robinson v. Garcia, 804 S.W.2d 238, 14 UCC Rep.Serv.2d 689 (Tex.App.-Corpus Christi Jan 31, 1991) (NO. 13-89-140-CV) ★

Distinguished by

     6 Lancaster's, Inc. v. Pamida, Inc., 143 Wis.2d 894, 422 N.W.2d 462 (Wis.App. Feb 17, 1988) (TABLE, TEXT IN WESTLAW, NO. 87-0827) ★ ★ ★ **HN: 1,2,13 (N.W.2d)**

     7 Kramer Business Service, Inc. v. Hyperion, Inc., 242 Wis.2d 472, 625 N.W.2d 360, 2001 WI App 75 (Wis.App. Feb 22, 2001) (TABLE, TEXT IN WESTLAW, NO. 00-2358) ★ ★ ★ ★ **HN: 11,12,13 (N.W.2d)**

Citing References

Positive Cases (U.S.A.)
★★★★ Examined

8 Lemke v. Arrowood, 608 N.W.2d 438, 438+, 232 Wis.2d 558,
   558+, 2000 WI App 32, 32+ (Wis.App. Dec 16, 1999) (Table,
   text in WESTLAW, NO. 99-1490) "" **HN: 1,2,13 (N.W.2d)**

H 9 Myron Soik & Sons, Inc. v. Stokely USA, Inc., 498 N.W.2d
      897, 900+, 175 Wis.2d 456, 463+ (Wis.App. Mar 25, 1993)
      (NO. 92-0251) "" **HN: 1,2,13 (N.W.2d)**

★★★ Discussed

C 10 Zubek v. Edlund, 598 N.W.2d 273, 278+, 228 Wis.2d 783,
       793+ (Wis.App. Jun 15, 1999) (NO. 97-2197) "" **HN: 1,2,3
       (N.W.2d)**

11 Rowell v. Ash, 597 N.W.2d 774, 774+, 228 Wis.2d 511, 511+
    (Wis.App. May 25, 1999) (Table, text in WESTLAW, NO.
    98-2904-FT) "" **HN: 1,2,13 (N.W.2d)**

H 12 Matter of Carpenter, 556 N.W.2d 384, 387+, 205 Wis.2d 365,
       371+ (Wis.App. Oct 02, 1996) (NO. 95-2932) **HN: 2,7
       (N.W.2d)**

13 Gundersen Clinic v. Lyden, 552 N.W.2d 900, 900+, 204 Wis.2d
    114, 114+ (Wis.App. Jul 18, 1996) (Table, text in WESTLAW,
    NO. 96-0754-FT) **HN: 2,12,13 (N.W.2d)**

H 14 Bier v. Wicks, 549 N.W.2d 288, 288+, 201 Wis.2d 819, 819+
       (Wis.App. Apr 11, 1996) (Table, text in WESTLAW, NO.
       96-0230-FT) **HN: 1,2,13 (N.W.2d)**

15 Evers v. Fryer, 543 N.W.2d 868, 868+, 197 Wis.2d 956, 956+
    (Wis.App. Oct 24, 1995) (Table, text in WESTLAW, NO.
    95-0902) "" **HN: 1,2,13 (N.W.2d)**

C 16 Butler v. Kocisko, 479 N.W.2d 208, 210+, 166 Wis.2d 212,
       215+ (Wis.App. Dec 17, 1991) (NO. 91-1864) "" **HN: 2,9,13
       (N.W.2d)**

17 Hengel v. Badger Corrugating, Inc., 423 N.W.2d 882, 882+,
    143 Wis.2d 901, 901+ (Wis.App. Mar 24, 1988) (Table, text in
    WESTLAW, NO. 87-0750) **HN: 1,2,13 (N.W.2d)**

18 Lyckberg v. Graf, 368 N.W.2d 847, 847+, 123 Wis.2d 545,
    545+ (Wis.App. Mar 26, 1985) (Table, text in WESTLAW,
    NO. 84-1106) **HN: 1,2,11 (N.W.2d)**

H 19 Gerald R. Turner & Associates, S.C. v. Moriarty, 25 F.3d 1356,
       1360+ (7th Cir.(Wis.) Oct 14, 1993) (NO. 92-4123) **HN: 9,10
       (N.W.2d)**

▷ 20 Burke Co. v. Hilton Development Co., 802 F.Supp. 434, 437+, 19 UCC Rep.Serv.2d 6, 6+ (N.D.Fla. Sep 30, 1992) (NO. CIV A 90-50205/LAC) "" **HN: 2 (N.W.2d)**

C 21 Lakeshore Machinery, Inc. v. Thermwood Corp., 117 F.R.D. 429, 432+ (E.D.Wis. Oct 28, 1987) (NO. 85-C-528) "" **HN: 2 (N.W.2d)**

H 22 McKee Const. Co. v. Stanley Plumbing & Heating Co., 828 S.W.2d 700, 702+, 18 UCC Rep.Serv.2d 16, 16+ (Mo.App. S.D. Apr 07, 1992) (NO. 17630) "" **HN: 3 (N.W.2d)**

▷ 23 AFC Interiors v. DiCello, 544 N.E.2d 869, 875+, 46 Ohio St.3d 1, 8+, 9 UCC Rep.Serv.2d 1181, 1181+ (Ohio Oct 04, 1989) (NO. 88-1541) "" *(in dissent)* **HN: 1,2 (N.W.2d)**

★★ Cited

▷ 24 Putnam v. Time Warner Cable of Southeastern Wisconsin, Ltd. Partnership, 649 N.W.2d 626, 633, 255 Wis.2d 447, 460, 2002 WI 108, 108 (Wis. Jul 16, 2002) (NO. 99-2078) "" **HN: 2 (N.W.2d)**

25 Taylor Inv. Corp. of Wisconsin v. PLL Marquette, LLC, 654 N.W.2d 94, 94, 258 Wis.2d 981, 981, 2002 WI App 292, 292 (Wis.App. Oct 10, 2002) (Table, text in WESTLAW, NO. 01-2546) **HN: 4 (N.W.2d)**

H 26 Batt v. Sweeney, 647 N.W.2d 868, 871+, 254 Wis.2d 721, 727+, 2002 WI App 119, 119+ (Wis.App. Apr 10, 2002) (NO. 01-1717) **HN: 2,4 (N.W.2d)**

27 Traditional Design Works, Ltd. v. McGourthy, 588 N.W.2d 927, 927+, 223 Wis.2d 266, 266+ (Wis.App. Nov 18, 1998) (Table, text in WESTLAW, NO. 97-2810) "" **HN: 1,2,13 (N.W.2d)**

H 28 Malone by Bangert v. Fons, 580 N.W.2d 697, 706, 217 Wis.2d 746, 768 (Wis.App. Mar 17, 1998) (NO. 96-3326) **HN: 5 (N.W.2d)**

29 North Memorial Medical Center v. Lunde, 577 N.W.2d 388, 388+, 217 Wis.2d 291, 291+ (Wis.App. Feb 03, 1998) (Table, text in WESTLAW, NO. 97-2232-FT) **HN: 9 (N.W.2d)**

30 Asset Recovery & Management Corp. v. Plourde, 562 N.W.2d 927, 927+, 209 Wis.2d 84, 84+ (Wis.App. Feb 04, 1997) (Table, text in WESTLAW, NO. 96-1569) **HN: 4 (N.W.2d)**

31 Zieve v. Ness, Motley, Loadholt, Richardson & Poole, P.A., 549 N.W.2d 286, 286+, 201 Wis.2d 816, 816+ (Wis.App. Apr 09, 1996) (Table, text in WESTLAW, NO. 95-1930) "" **HN: 1,2,13 (N.W.2d)**

32 Nelson v. City of Mauston, 539 N.W.2d 335, 335, 196 Wis.2d 644, 644 (Wis.App. Aug 03, 1995) (Table, text in WESTLAW, NO. 94-1344)

33 Davies v. Munz, 516 N.W.2d 21, 21, 183 Wis.2d 433, 433
    (Wis.App. Mar 31, 1994) (Table, text in WESTLAW, NO.
    93-1961) **HN: 5 (N.W.2d)**

C   34 Cue v. Carthage College, 507 N.W.2d 109, 112, 179 Wis.2d
    175, 180, 86 Ed. Law Rep. 979, 979 (Wis.App. Sep 01, 1993)
    (NO. 93-0557) **HN: 13 (N.W.2d)**

35 Flintrop v. Lumbermens Mut. Cas. Co., 502 N.W.2d 617, 617,
    176 Wis.2d 511, 511 (Wis.App. Apr 14, 1993) (Table, text in
    WESTLAW, NO. 92-1230) **HN: 1,2,5 (N.W.2d)**

36 Favorite v. Glass, 499 N.W.2d 302, 302, 173 Wis.2d 909, 909
    (Wis.App. Jan 05, 1993) (Table, text in WESTLAW, NO.
    92-2336) **HN: 5 (N.W.2d)**

37 Upholstery Center v. Begg, 478 N.W.2d 597, 597+, 165 Wis.2d
    514, 514+ (Wis.App. Nov 13, 1991) (Table, text in
    WESTLAW, NO. 91-1612) **HN: 7 (N.W.2d)**

38 West Side Hosp. v. Labor and Industry Review Com'n, 428
    N.W.2d 563, 563, 145 Wis.2d 899, 899 (Wis.App. May 12,
    1988) (Table, text in WESTLAW, NO. 88-0091) **HN: 11,12
    (N.W.2d)**

H   39 Cook & Franke, S.C. v. Meilman, 402 N.W.2d 361, 363, 136
    Wis.2d 434, 439 (Wis.App. Jan 14, 1987) (NO. 85-2378) **HN:
    2,5 (N.W.2d)**

40 Saxby v. Saxby, 401 N.W.2d 182, 182, 135 Wis.2d 545, 545
    (Wis.App. Dec 22, 1986) (Table, text in WESTLAW, NO.
    85-1629) **HN: 2,5 (N.W.2d)**

41 First Agri Services, Inc. v. Production Credit Ass'n of Elkhorn,
    392 N.W.2d 129, 129+, 132 Wis.2d 473, 473+ (Wis.App. Jun
    25, 1986) (Table, text in WESTLAW, NO. 85-0161)

42 Coffey v. Lilly, 394 N.W.2d 317, 317+, 129 Wis.2d 545, 545+
    (Wis.App. Feb 04, 1986) (Table, text in WESTLAW, NO.
    84-2545) "" **HN: 7 (N.W.2d)**

43 Taleck v. Taleck, 384 N.W.2d 367, 367, 128 Wis.2d 560, 560
    (Wis.App. Jan 22, 1986) (Table, text in WESTLAW, NO.
    85-0463) **HN: 1,2 (N.W.2d)**

44 Terrill v. Atomizer, 378 N.W.2d 296, 296, 127 Wis.2d 561, 561
    (Wis.App. Oct 01, 1985) (Table, text in WESTLAW, NO.
    84-2180) "" **HN: 5 (N.W.2d)**

H   45 Niebler and Muren, S.C. v. Brock-White Co. of Wisconsin, Inc.,
    361 N.W.2d 732, 733+, 122 Wis.2d 445, 447+, 40 UCC
    Rep.Serv. 165, 165+ (Wis.App. Dec 19, 1984) (NO. 84-1382)
    HN: 1,2,13 (N.W.2d)

46 Porter v. Regdab, Inc., 923 F.2d 856, 856 (7th Cir.(Wis.) Jan
    17, 1991) (Table, text in WESTLAW, NO. 90-1283) **HN:
    1,2,13 (N.W.2d)**

H   47   U.S. Plastic Lumber, Ltd. v. Strandex Corp., 2003 WL 23144861, *8+ (W.D.Wis. Feb 07, 2003) (NO. 02-C-211-C) "" **HN: 4 (N.W.2d)**

C   48   Employers Reinsurance Corp. v. Admiral Ins. Co., 822 F.Supp. 1350, 1353 (E.D.Wis. Jun 08, 1993) (NO. CIV. A. 91-C-971) **HN: 4 (N.W.2d)**

▷   49   Anderson v. Rosebrook, 737 P.2d 417, 420+, 3 UCC Rep.Serv.2d 1312, 1312+ (Colo. May 26, 1987) (NO. 86SC166) **HN: 1,2,3 (N.W.2d)**

▷   50   Stultz Elec. Works v. Marine Hydraulic Engineering Co., 484 A.2d 1008, 1011+, 39 UCC Rep.Serv. 1186, 1186+ (Me. Dec 06, 1984) (NO. 3659, CUM-84-163) "" **HN: 3 (N.W.2d)**

▷   51   Horn Waterproofing Corp. v. Bushwick Iron & Steel Co., Inc., 497 N.Y.S.2d 310, 312+, 488 N.E.2d 56, 58+, 66 N.Y.2d 321, 324+, 54 USLW 2241, 2241+, 41 UCC Rep.Serv. 1591, 1591+ (N.Y. Oct 17, 1985) (NO. 422) **HN: 3 (N.W.2d)**

H   52   Klass v. Allied Coal Producers, Inc., 1988 WL 142302, *3+ (Ohio App. 5 Dist. Dec 29, 1988) (NO. 88-CA-13) *(in dissent)*

▷   53   Marton Remodeling v. Jensen, 706 P.2d 607, 610, 42 UCC Rep.Serv. 54, 54 (Utah Sep 17, 1985) (NO. 18400, 18401) **HN: 3 (N.W.2d)**

★ Mentioned

C   54   Occidental Chemical Corp. v. Environmental Liners, Inc., 859 F.Supp. 791, 796+, 26 UCC Rep.Serv.2d 310, 310+ (E.D.Pa. Jul 22, 1994) (NO. CIV. A. 93-5433) **HN: 4 (N.W.2d)**

H   55   Acierno v. Worthy Bros. Pipeline Corp., 656 A.2d 1085, 1089, 27 UCC Rep.Serv.2d 759, 759 (Del.Supr. Mar 08, 1995) (NO. 009, 1994)

▷   56   Golden Peanut Co. v. Bass, 547 S.E.2d 637, 643, 249 Ga.App. 224, 230, 1 FCDR 1224, 1224 (Ga.App. Mar 30, 2001) (NO. A00A2362)

▷   57   Nelson v. Fire Ins. Exchange, 510 N.E.2d 137, 140, 156 Ill.App.3d 1017, 1022, 109 Ill.Dec. 516, 519, 4 UCC Rep.Serv.2d 1344, 1344 (Ill.App. 2 Dist. Jun 26, 1987) (NO. 86-1094) **HN: 3 (N.W.2d)**

▷   58   Pileco, Inc. v. HCI, Inc., 735 S.W.2d 561, 562, 4 UCC Rep.Serv.2d 1349, 1349 (Tex.App.-Hous. (1 Dist.) Jul 16, 1987) (NO. 01-87-00030-CV) **HN: 3 (N.W.2d)**

▷   59   John Grier Const. Co. v. Jones Welding & Repair, Inc., 383 S.E.2d 719, 721, 238 Va. 270, 274, 9 UCC Rep.Serv.2d 1214, 1214 (Va. Sep 22, 1989) (NO. 880700)

Administrative Decisions (U.S.A.)

60 Appeal of Midwest Maintenance & Const. Co., Inc., 1984 WL 14141 (G.S.B.C.A.), *37, 85-1 BCA P 17,716, 17716, GSBCA No. 4743-REIN, 6225-REIN, GSBCA No. 4817-REIN, GSBCA No. 4928-REIN, GSBCA No. 4982-REIN, GSBCA No. 6225-REIN, GSBCA No. 6226-REIN, GSBCA No. 6227-REIN, GSBCA No. 6228-REIN (G.S.B.C.A. Oct 19, 1984) (NO. GS-07-DP-(P)-35141, GS-07W-65137, GS-07-DP-(P)-45096, GS-07W-00061, GS-07-DP-(P)-45097, GS-07W-00063, GS-07W-00068) ★ **HN: 3 (N.W.2d)**

61 In re: A. SAM & SONS PRODUCE CO., INC. v. SOL SALINS, INC., 50 United States Department of Agriculture Decisions 1044 (1991) ★ ★

Secondary Sources (U.S.A.)

62 Modern status of rule that acceptance of check purporting to be final settlement of disputed amount constitutes accord and satisfaction, 42 A.L.R.4th 12, §3+ (1985) **HN: 1,2,11,12,13 (N.W.2d)**

63 Construction and effect of UCC Art. 3, dealing with commercial paper, 23 A.L.R.3d 932, §21 (1969) **HN: 3 (N.W.2d)**

64 Anderson on the Uniform Commercial Code s 3-408:276, -PRE-REVISION ARTICLE 3 (2004)

65 Brady On Bank Checks: The Law Of Bank Checks P 4.12(3), REJECTION OF ATTEMPTED RESERVATION OF RIGHTS (2005) **HN: 3 (N.W.2d)**

66 21 Causes of Action 337, Cause of Action to Establish Accord and Satisfaction of Debt by "Full-Payment" Check (2004) **HN: 11,12,13 (N.W.2d)**

67 Hawkland Uniform Commercial Codes Series s 1-207:2, "FULL-SATISFACTION" CHECKS (2002) **HN: 1,3 (N.W.2d)**

68 Hawkland Uniform Commercial Codes Series REV s 1-308:2, "FULL-SATISFACTION" CHECKS (2002) **HN: 3 (N.W.2d)**

69 Law of Computer Technology s 6:51, LIMITED WARRANTIES AND REMEDIES (1998) **HN: 2 (N.W.2d)**

70 27 N.J. Prac. Series s 1-207-FORM 7, Form Letter to Accompany Check Tendered in Full Discharge of Disputed Obligation (2002)

71 2 White & Summers UCC s 16-15, Accord and Satisfaction Through Use of an Instrument (1995) **HN: 1 (N.W.2d)**

72 Williston on Contracts s 7:26, PROMISE TO PAY OR PAYMENT OF DEBTS; LIQUIDATED DEBTS (2004) **HN: 3 (N.W.2d)**

73   Williston on Contracts s 7:30, -PAYMENT OF PART OF
     DEBT WITH NEGOTIABLE INSTRUMENT (2004) **HN: 3
     (N.W.2d)**

74   Williston on Contracts s 7:34, -PAYMENT OF
     UNLIQUIDATED OR DISPUTED CLAIM (2004) **HN: 10
     (N.W.2d)**

75   Williston on Contracts s 7:35, -PAYMENT OF ADMITTED
     PART OF UNLIQUIDATED OR DISPUTED CLAIM (2004)
     HN: 1,2,13 (N.W.2d)

C   76   1 Am. Jur. 2d Accord and Satisfaction s 22, -EFFECT OF
     UNIFORM COMMERCIAL CODE (2004) **HN: 3 (N.W.2d)**

C   77   1 Am. Jur. 2d Accord and Satisfaction s 41, GENERALLY
     (2004) **HN: 12 (N.W.2d)**

C   78   CJS Accord and Satisfaction s 14, GIVING AND
     ACCEPTANCE IN SATISFACTION (2005)

C   79   CJS Accord and Satisfaction s 32, GENERALLY (2005)
C   80   CJS Accord and Satisfaction s 44, GENERALLY (2005)
C   81   CJS Accord and Satisfaction s 45, DISPUTE OR
     CONTROVERSY (2005)

C   82   CJS Accord and Satisfaction s 46, DISPUTE OR
     CONTROVERSY-NATURE AND ESSENTIALS OF
     DISPUTE (2005) **HN: 9,10 (N.W.2d)**

C   83   CJS Accord and Satisfaction s 54, GENERALLY (2005)
C   84   COMMERCIAL PAPER, BANK DEPOSITS AND
     COLLECTIONS, AND COMMERCIAL ELECTRONIC
     FUND TRANSFERS, 42 Bus. Law. 1269, 1305 (1987)

C   85   COMMERCIAL PAPER, BANK DEPOSITS AND
     COLLECTIONS, AND COMMERCIAL ELECTRONIC
     FUND TRANSFERS, 40 Bus. Law. 1147, 1175 (1985)

C   86   INTERPRETING CODES, 89 Mich. L. Rev. 2201, 2214 (1991)
C   87   THE EVOLUTION OF ACCORD AND SATISFACTION:
     COMMON LAW; U.C.C. SECTION 1-207; U.C.C. SECTION
     3-311, 28 New Eng. L. Rev. 189, 202+ (1993) **HN: 1,2,3
     (N.W.2d)**

C   88   THE 1-207 DILEMMA REVISITED, 16 N. Ky. L. Rev. 425,
     452 (1989) **HN: 3 (N.W.2d)**

C   89   AFC INTERIORS v. DICELLO: HAS THE DEATH KNELL
     TOLLED ON THE COMMON-LAW DOCTRINE OF
     ACCORD AND SATISFACTION IN OHIO?, 16 Ohio N.U. L.
     Rev. 217, 243+ (1989) **HN: 1,2,3 (N.W.2d)**

C   90   U.C.C. SECTION 1-207 AND THE DOCTRINE OF ACCORD
     AND SATISFACTION: OHIO'S ABOUT-FACE IN AFC
     INTERIORS v. DICELLO, 52 Ohio St. L.J. 1617, 1636+
     (1991) **HN: 2,3,13 (N.W.2d)**

Court Documents
Appellate Court Documents (U.S.A.)

Appellate Briefs

101 Gerald R. TURNER & ASSOCIATES, S.C., Plaintiff-Appellant, v. Michael A. MORIARTY, Moriarty & Madigan, Donna Szczesny, Hartford Casualty Insurance Company and Insurance Corporation of America, Defendants-Appellees., 1993 WL 13099077, *13099077+ (Appellate Brief) (7th Cir. Mar 15, 1993) **Brief of Defendant-appellee, Hartford Casualty ...** (NO. 92-4123) ★ ★ **HN: 2,4 (N.W.2d)**

102 Adele R. GARCIA, Plaintiff-Appellant-Cross-Respondent-Petitioner, v. MAZDA MOTOR OF AMERICA, INC., a foreign corporation, and Hall Imports, Inc., a Wisconsin corporation, Defendant-Respondents-Cross-Appellants., 2004 WL 3248580, *3248580+ (Appellate Brief) (Wis. Feb 26, 2004) **Reply Brief of ...** (NO. 02-2260) ★ ★ **HN: 1,2,5 (N.W.2d)**

103 Adele R. GARCIA, Plaintiff-Appellant-Cross-Respondent, Petitioner, v. MAZDA MOTOR OF AMERICA, INC., a foreign corporation, and Hall Imports, Inc., a Wisconsin corporation, Defendants-Respondents-Cross-Appellants., 2004 WL 3248579, *3248579+ (Appellate Brief) (Wis. Feb 16, 2004) **Response Brief of ...** (NO. 02-2260) ★ ★ **HN: 2,12,13 (N.W.2d)**

104 Adele R. GARCIA, Plaintiff-Appellant-Cross-Respondent-Petitioner, v. MAZDA MOTOR OF AMERICA, INC., a foreign corporation, and Hall Imports, Inc., a Wisconsin corporation, Defendants-Respondents-Cross-Appellants., 2004 WL 3248577, *3248577+ (Appellate Brief) (Wis. Feb 04, 2004) **Combined Briefs of ...** (NO. 02-2260) "" ★ ★ ★ **HN: 1,2,13 (N.W.2d)**

105 Ryan SCOTT, Kathy Scott, and Patrick Scott, Plaintiffs-Appellants-Petitioners, v. SAVERS PROPERTY AND CASUALTY INSURANCE COMPANY, and Stevens Point Area Public School District, Defendants-Respondents, WAUSAU UNDERWRITERS INSURANCE COMPANY, Defendant., 2003 WL 22852152, *22852152+ (Appellate Brief) (Wis. Jan 03, 2003) **Brief and Appendix of Defendants-Respondents ...** (NO. 01-2953) "" ★ ★ **HN: 1,2,5 (N.W.2d)**

106 Kerry L. PUTNAM, Carol L. Smith-Carter and Louis Boutan,
     individually and on behalf of all others similarly situated,
     Plaintiffs-Appellants-Petitioners, v. TIME WARNER CABLE
     OF SOUTHEASTERN WISCONSIN, Limited Partnership,
     Defendant-Respondent., 2001 WL 34360612, *34360612+
     (Appellate Brief) (Wis. Dec 17, 2001)
     Defendant-Respondent's Brief (NO. 99-2078) "" ★ ★ ★
     HN: 1,2,13 (N.W.2d)

107 Adele R. GARCIA, Plaintiff-Appellant-Cross-Respondent, v.
     MAZDA MOTOR OF AMERICA, INC., a foreign corporation,
     and Hall Imports, Inc., a Wisconsin corporation,
     Defendants-Respondents-Cross-Appellants., 2003 WL
     23837285, *23837285+ (Appellate Brief) (Wis.App. II Dist.
     Feb 12, 2003) **Reply Brief of Defendants-Cross-Appellants**
     (NO. 02-2260) ★ ★ **HN: 1,2,5 (N.W.2d)**

108 Adele R. GARCIA, Plaintiff-Appellant-Cross-Respondent, v.
     MAZDA MOTOR OF AMERICA, INC., a foreign corporation,
     and Hall Imports, Inc., a Wisconsin corporation,
     Defendants-Respondents-Cross-Appellants., 2003 WL
     23837284, *23837284+ (Appellate Brief) (Wis.App. II Dist. Jan
     27, 2003) **Response Brief of ...** (NO. 02-2260) ★ ★ **HN:
     2,12,13 (N.W.2d)**

109 Adele R. GARCIA, Plaintiff-Appellant-Cross-Respondent, v.
     MAZDA MOTOR OF AMERICA, INC., a foreign corporation,
     and Hall Imports, Inc., a Wisconsin corporation,
     Defendants-Respondents-Cross-Appellants., 2002 WL
     32699956, *32699956+ (Appellate Brief) (Wis.App. II Dist.
     Dec 26, 2002) **Brief of Defendants-Cross-Appellants** (NO.
     02-2260) ★ ★ ★ **HN: 1,2,13 (N.W.2d)**

110 SCHAWK, INC. d/b/a SCHAWK/LSI, DIVISION OF
     SCHAWK, INC., Plaintiff-Appellant, v. CITY BREWING
     COMPANY, LLC f/k/a CBC ACQUISITION, LLC,
     Defendant-Respondent., 2002 WL 32329786, *32329786+
     (Appellate Brief) (Wis.App. IV Dist. Sep 19, 2002) **Brief of
     Defendant-Respondent, City Brewing ...** (NO. 02-1833) ★ ★
     HN: 5 (N.W.2d)

111 Ryan SCOTT, Kathy Scott, and Patrick Scott,
     Plaintiffs-Appellants, v. SAVERS PROPERTY AND
     CASUALTY INSURANCE COMPANY, Wausau Underwriters
     Insurance Company, and Stevens Point Area Public School
     District, Defendants-Respondents., 2002 WL 32314657,
     *32314657+ (Appellate Brief) (Wis.App. IV Dist. Mar 05,
     2002) **Brief and Appendix of Defendants-Respondents ...**
     (NO. 01-2953) "" ★ ★ **HN: 1,5 (N.W.2d)**

112 TAYLOR INVESTMENT CORPORATION OF WISCONSIN,
     Plaintiff-Respondent, v. PLL MARQUETTE, LLC,
     Defendant-Appellant., 2002 WL 32311538, *32311538+
     (Appellate Brief) (Wis.App. IV Dist. Feb 12, 2002)
     Defendant-Appellant's Brief and Appendix (NO. 01-2546)
     ★ ★ **HN: 2 (N.W.2d)**

113 Luige's Pizza FACTORY, Ltd, Plaintiff-Appellant, v. Denis
     PETRI, Sr.,and Carol Petri Defendants-Respondents., 2002 WL
     32373473, *32373473+ (Appellate Brief) (Wis.App. II Dist.
     2002) **Brief and Appendix of Plaintiff-Appellant, ...** (NO.
     02-1804) ★ ★ ★

114 Luige's Pizza FACTORY, Ltd, Plaintiff-Appellant, v. Denis
     PETRI, Sr.,and Carol Petri Defendants-Respondents., 2002 WL
     32373475, *32373475+ (Appellate Brief) (Wis.App. II Dist.
     2002) **Reply Brief of Plaintiff-Appellant, Luige's Pizza ...**
     (NO. 02-1804) ★ ★ ★

115 UNIVERSAL FOODS CORPORATION,
     Plaintiff-Appellant-Cross-Respondent, v. Elizabeth A. ZANDE,
     Defendant-Respondent-Cross-Appellant; AMERICAN
     FAMILY MUTUAL INSURANCE COMPANY,
     Intervenor-Respondent-Cross-Appellant., 2001 WL 34358931,
     *34358931+ (Appellate Brief) (Wis.App. I Dist. Nov 21, 2001)
     Brief of Plaintiff-Appellant-Cross-Respondent ... (NO.
     01-0111, 01-1939) ★ ★ **HN: 5 (N.W.2d)**

116 Barbara L. BATT and Donald M. Batt,
     Plaintiffs-Co-Appellants-Cross-Respondents, v. Guineth L.
     SWEENEY and Allstate Insurance Company,
     Defendants-Respondents-Cross-Appellants, MAYLINE
     COMPANY, INC., Subrogated Defendant-Appellant, BLUE
     CROSS & BLUE SHIELD UNITED OF WISCONSIN,
     Subrogated Defendant., 2001 WL 34356825, *34356825+
     (Appellate Brief) (Wis.App. II Dist. Oct 31, 2001) **Reply Brief
     of Subrogated ...** (NO. 01-1717) ★ ★ **HN: 2,13 (N.W.2d)**

117 Barbara L. BATT and Donald M. Batt, Sr.,
     Plaintiffs-Co-Appellants-Cross-Respondents, v. Guineth L.
     SWEENEY and Allstate Insurance Company,
     Defendants-Respondents-Cross-Appellants, MAYLINE
     COMPANY, INC., Subrogated
     Defendant-Appellant-Cross-Respondent, BLUE CROSS &
     BLUE SHIELD UNITED OF WISCONSIN, Subrogated
     Defendant., 2001 WL 34356823, *34356823+ (Appellate Brief)
     (Wis.App. II Dist. Oct 01, 2001)
     Defendants'-Respondents'-Cross-Appellants' ... (NO.
     01-1717) "" ★ ★ **HN: 1,2,10 (N.W.2d)**

118 Barbara L. BATT and Donald M. Batt,
     Plaintiffs-Co-Appellants-Cross-Respondents, v. Guineth L.
     SWEENEY and Allstate Insurance Company,
     Defendants-Respondents-Cross-Appellants, MAYLINE
     COMPANY, INC., Subrogated
     Defendant-Appellant-Cross-Respondent, BLUE CROSS &
     BLUE SHIELD UNITED OF WISCONSIN, Subrogated
     Defendant., 2001 WL 34356863, *34356863+ (Appellate Brief)
     (Wis.App. II Dist. Aug 29, 2001) **Brief and Appendix of
     Subrogated ...** (NO. 01-1717) "" ★ ★ ★ **HN: 13 (N.W.2d)**

119 Jane A. BENTZ, D.D.S., S.C.,
     Plaintiff-Respondent-Cross-Appellant, v. Michael MOSLING,
     D.D.S., Defendant-Appellant-Cross-Respondent., 2001 WL
     34359363, *34359363+ (Appellate Brief) (Wis.App. IV Dist.
     Jul 27, 2001) **Cross Appellant's Brief and Appendix** (NO.
     01-1250) ★ ★ **HN: 5 (N.W.2d)**

120 Lynn WONKA and Jerome Wonka, Plaintiffs-Appellants, v.
     Samuel CARI, Special Administrator of the Estate of Edward E.
     Bierbrauer, and Donna Bierbrauer, Defendants-Respondents.,
     2001 WL 34357993, *34357993 (Appellate Brief) (Wis.App.
     III Dist May 23, 2001) **Plaintiffs-Appellants' Reply Brief**
     (NO. 01-0184) ★ ★

121 Susan SHOEMAKER, Plaintiff-Appellant, v. THE HEARST
     CORPORATION, A Delaware Corporation,
     Defendant-Respondent., 2001 WL 34359511, *34359511+
     (Appellate Brief) (Wis.App. IV Dist. Mar 26, 2001)
     Plaintiff-Appellant's Brief (NO. 01-0283) ★ ★ **HN: 9,12,13
     (N.W.2d)**

122 In re the Marriage of: Myra LEVINE (HEILPRIN),
     Petitioner/Respondent, Richard HEILPRIN,
     Respondent-Appellant., 2000 WL 34218500, *34218500+
     (Appellate Brief) (Wis.App. IV Dist. Dec 27, 2000)
     Appellant/Respondent's Response Brief (NO. 00-1181) ★ ★
     HN: 4 (N.W.2d)

123 KRAMER BUSINESS SERVICE, INC. d/b/a Kramer Printing,
     Plaintiff-Appellant, v. HYPERION, INC.,
     Defendant-Respondent., 2000 WL 34220269, *34220269+
     (Appellate Brief) (Wis.App. IV Dist. Dec 20, 2000) **Reply
     Brief of Plaintiff - Appellant** (NO. 00-2358) ★ ★ ★ **HN:
     2,11,13 (N.W.2d)**

124 KRAMER BUSINESS SERVICE, INC. d/b/a Kramer Printing, Plaintiff-Appellant, v. HYPERION, INC., Defendant-Respondent., 2000 WL 34220358, *34220358+ (Appellate Brief) (Wis.App. IV Dist. Dec 20, 2000) **Reply Brief of Plaintiff - Appellant** (NO. 00-2358) ★ ★ ★ **HN: 2,11,13 (N.W.2d)**

125 KRAMER BUSINESS SERVICE, INC. d/b/a Kramer Printing, Plaintiff - Appellant, v. HYPERION, INC., Defendant - Respondent., 2000 WL 34220268, *34220268+ (Appellate Brief) (Wis.App. IV Dist. Dec 06, 2000) **Defendant - Respondent's Brief and Appendix** (NO. 00-2358) ★ ★ ★ **HN: 11,12 (N.W.2d)**

126 KRAMER BUSINESS SERVICE, INC. d/b/a Kramer Printing, Plaintiff - Appellant, v. HYPERION, INC., Defendant - Respondent., 2000 WL 34220357, *34220357+ (Appellate Brief) (Wis.App. IV Dist. Dec 06, 2000) **Defendant - Respondent's Brief and Appendix** (NO. 00-2358) ★ ★ ★ **HN: 11,12 (N.W.2d)**

127 In re the Marriage of: Myra LEVINE (HEILPRIN), Respondent, v. Richard HEILPRIN, Appellant., 2000 WL 34218499, *34218499+ (Appellate Brief) (Wis.App. IV Dist. Nov 22, 2000) **Respondent's Response Brief** (NO. 00-1181) ★ ★ ★ **HN: 1,2,3 (N.W.2d)**

128 KRAMER BUSINESS SERVICE, INC. d/b/a Kramer Printing, Plaintiff-Appellant, v. HYPERION, INC., Defendant-Respondent., 2000 WL 34220267, *34220267+ (Appellate Brief) (Wis.App. IV Dist. Nov 06, 2000) **Brief and Appendix of Plaintiff - Appellant** (NO. 00-2358) "" ★ ★ ★ **HN: 2,11,12 (N.W.2d)**

129 KRAMER BUSINESS SERVICE, INC. d/b/a Kramer Printing, Plaintiff-Appellant, v. HYPERION, INC., Defendant-Respondent., 2000 WL 34220356, *34220356+ (Appellate Brief) (Wis.App. IV Dist. Nov 06, 2000) **Brief and Appendix of Plaintiff - Appellant** (NO. 00-2358) "" ★ ★ ★ **HN: 2,11,12 (N.W.2d)**

130 In re the Marriage of: Myra LEVINE (HEILPRIN), Petitioner/Respondent, Richard HEILPRIN, Respondent-Appellant., 2000 WL 34218498, *34218498+ (Appellate Brief) (Wis.App. IV Dist. Oct 26, 2000) **Respondent's/Appellant's Brief** (NO. 00-1181) ★ ★ **HN: 8 (N.W.2d)**

Appendix B

STATE LEGAL RESEARCH GUIDES AND BIBLIOGRAPHIES

While state legal research generally follows the patterns discussed in this book, the legal system and bibliographic resources of a particular state may cause specialized problems or may offer shortcuts not available elsewhere. A general treatise such as this cannot fully treat the many special characteristics of legal research in each state. There are, however, an increasing number of guides and manuals available for particular states. Some of these are major, detailed treatments, while many are brief pamphlets prepared for American Association of Law Libraries (AALL) meetings. In addition to the following separately published works, articles in bar journals and law reviews sometimes provide valuable information on research strategies in particular jurisdictions.

Alabama	Hazel L. Johnson, *Guide to Alabama State Documents and Selected Law Related Materials* (AALL 1993). Gary Orlando Lewis, *How to Find and Understand the Law in Alabama* (Gary Orlando Lewis 2001).
Alaska	Alaska State Legislature, Legislative Reference Library, *Guide to Alaska Legislative History Materials* (Legislative Reference Library 2002). Aimee Ruzicka, *Alaska Legal and Law-Related Publications: A Guide for Law Librarians* (AALL 1984).
Arizona	Kathy Shimpock-Vieweg & Marianne Sidorski Alcorn, *Arizona Legal Research Guide* (Hein 1992). Richard Teenstra et al., *Survey of Arizona State Legal and Law Related Documents* (AALL 1984).
Arkansas	Lynn Foster, *Arkansas Legal Bibliography: Documents and Selected Commercial Titles* (AALL 1988).
California	Karla Castetter, *Locating the Law: A Handbook for Non-Law Librarians With an Emphasis on California Law* (4th rev. ed. Southern California Association of Law Libraries 1995). Larry D. Dershem, *California Legal Research Handbook* (Rothman 1997). John K. Hanft, *Legal Research in California* (3rd ed. West 1999).

Veronica Maclay & Laura Peritore, *Government Publications and Legal Resources* (AALL 1991).

Daniel Martin, *Henke's California Law Guide* (6th ed. LexisNexis 2002).

Colorado   Robert C. Richards & Barbara Bintliff, *Colorado Legal Resources: An Annotated Bibliography* (AALL 2004).

Connecticut   Judith Anspach et al., *State Legal Documents: A Selective Bibliography* (AALL 1985).

Lawrence Cheeseman & Arlene Bielefield, *The Connecticut Legal Research Handbook* (Conn. Law Book Co. 1992).

Legal Research Handbook (Commission on Official Legal Publications, Judicial Branch, State of Connecticut 1997-).

District of Columbia   Carolyn P. Ahearn et al., *Selected Information Sources the District of Columbia* (2nd ed. AALL 1985).

Leah F. Chanin et al., *Legal Research in the District of Columbia, Maryland and Virginia* (Hein 2000).

Florida   Barbara J. Busharis & Suzanne E. Rowe, *Florida Legal Research: Sources, Process, and Analysis* (2nd ed. Carolina Academic Press 2002).

Betsy L. Stupski, *Guide to Florida Legal Research* (6th ed. Florida Bar, Continuing Legal Education 2001).

*Guide to Florida Legislative Publications &
Information Resources* (Edward J. Tribble & Connie J.
Beane, eds., 3rd ed. Capitol 1990).

Georgia   Leah F. Chanin & Suzanne Cassidy, *Guide to Georgia
Legal Research and Legal History* (Harrison 1990).
Updated with 1997 pocket part.

Nancy Johnson & Nancy A. Deel, *Researching
Georgia Law*, 14 Ga. St. L. Rev. 545 (1998).

Paul T. Hardy, *How to Find and Access Georgia Law*
(Carl Vinson Institute of Government, University of
Georgia 1993).

Rebecca Simmons Stillwagon, *Georgia Legal
Documents: An Annotated Bibliography* (AALL
1991).

Hawaii   Richard F. Kahle, Jr., *How to Research Constitutional,
Legislative and Statutory History in Hawaii* (rev. ed.
Hawaii Legislative Reference Bureau 1997).

Idaho   Michael J. Greenlee, *State Documents: A
Bibliography of Legal Publications and Related
Materials* (AALL 2003).

Leinaala R. Seeger, *Idaho Practice Materials: A
Selective Annotated Bibliography* (Law Library
Journal 1996).

Illinois   Cheryl R. Nyberg, Joyce Olin & Peter Young, *Illinois
State Documents: A Selective Annotated Bibliography
for Law Librarians* (AALL 1986).

Laurel Wendt, *Illinois Legal Research Guide* (2nd ed.
Hein 2004).

	Mark E. Wojcik, *Illinois Legal Research* (Carolina Academic Press 2003).
Indiana	Linda K. Fariss & Keith A. Buckley, *An Introduction to Indiana State Publications for the Law Librarian* (AALL 1982).
Iowa	John Edwards, *Iowa Legal Research Guide* (Hein 2003).
	Angela K. Secrest, *Iowa Legal Documents Bibliography* (AALL 1990).
Kansas	Joseph A. Custer et al., *Kansas Legal Research and Reference Guide* (3rd ed. Kansas Bar Association 2003).
	Martin E. Wisnecki, *Kansas State Documents for Law Libraries: Publications Related to Law and State Government* (AALL 1984).
Kentucky	Paul J. Cammarata, *Kentucky State Publications: A Guide for Law Librarians* (AALL 1990).
	Kurt X. Metzmeier et al., *Kentucky Legal Research Manual* (University of Kentucky College of Law, Office of Continuing Legal Education 2002).
Louisiana	Charlene Cain & Madeline Hebert, *Legal Documents and Related Publications* (3rd ed. AALL 2001).
	Win-Shin S. Chiang, *Louisiana Legal Research* (2d ed. Butterworth 1990).

Maine	Christine E. Hepler & Maureen P. Quinlan, *State Documents: A Bibliography of Legal Publications and Law-Related Materials* (AALL 2003).
Maryland	Leah F. Chanin et al., *Legal Research in the District of Columbia, Maryland and Virginia* (Hein 2000).
	Robert J. Colborn & Dennis C. Schnepfe, *Research Guide for Maryland Regulations* (Office of the Secretary of State, Division of State Documents 1992).
	William L. Taylor, *State Publications in Law and Related Fields: A Selective Bibliography with Annotations* (AALL 1996).
Massachusetts	Margaret Botsford et al., *Handbook of Legal Research in Massachusetts* (Mary Ann Neary & Ruth G. Matz eds., rev. ed. Massachusetts Continuing Legal Education 2002).
	Leo McAuliffe & Susan Z. Steinway, *Massachusetts State Documents Bibliography* (AALL 1985).
	Viginia Wise et al., *How to Do Massachusetts Legal Research: Maximizing Efficiency in the Print and Online Environment* (Massachusetts Continuing Legal Education 1998).
Michigan	Richard L. Beer, *Michigan Legal Literature* (2nd ed. Hein 1991).
	Guide to the Michigan Administrative Code and the Michigan Register (Michigan Legislative Service Bureau, Legal Editing and Law Publications Division 1994).

Stuart D. Yoak & Margaret A. Heinen, *Michigan Legal Documents: An Annotated Bibliography* (AALL 1982).

Minnesota   Marsha L. Baum & Mary Ann Nelson, *Guide to Minnesota State Documents and Selected Law-Related Materials* (AALL 1985).

John Tessner et al., *Minnesota Legal Research Guide* (2nd ed. Hein 2002).

Mississippi   Ben Cole, *Mississippi Legal Documents and Related Publications: A Selected Annotated Bibliography* (AALL 1987).

Missouri   Mary Ann Nelson, *Guide to Missouri State Documents and Selected Law-Related Materials* (AALL 1991).

Montana   Margaret Ann Chansler, *State Documents: A Bibliography of Legal and Law-Related Material* (AALL 2004)

Stephen R. Jordan & Meredith Hoffman, *A Guide to Montana Legal Research* (State Law Library of Montana 2002).

Nebraska   Kay L. Andrus, *Research Guide to Nebraska Law* (LexisNexis 2003).

Mitchell J. Fontenot et al., *Nebraska State Documents Bibliography* (AALL 1988).

Nevada   Ann S. Jarrell & G. LeGrande Fletcher, *Nevada State Documents Bibliography: Legal Publications and Related Material* (2nd ed. AALL 2000).

New Jersey	Paul Axel-Lute, *New Jersey Legal Research Handbook* (4th ed. New Jersey Institute for Continuing Legal Education 1998).
	Robert L. Bland & Marjorie Garwig, *New Jersey Legislative Histories* (New Jersey State Library 1990). Christina M. Senezak, *New Jersey State Publications: A Guide for Law Librarians* (AALL 1984).
New Mexico	Patricia D. Wagner & Mary Woodward, *Guide to New Mexico State Publications* (2nd ed. AALL 1991).
New York	Robert Allan Carter, *Legislative Intent in New York State: Materials, Cases and Annotated Bibliography* (2nd ed. New York State Library 2001).
	Susan L. Dow & Karen L. Spencer, *New York Legal Documents: A Selective Annotated Bibliography* (AALL 1985).
	Ellen M. Gibson, *Gibson's New York Legal Research Guide* (3rd ed. Hein 2004).
North Carolina	Mary Louise Corbett, *Guide to North Carolina Legal and Law-Related Materials* (2nd ed. AALL 1996).
	Jean Sinclair McKnight, *North Carolina Legal Research Guide* (Rothman 1994).
North Dakota	*For All Intents and Purposes: Essentials in Researching Legislative Histories* (North Dakota Legislative Council 1981).
Ohio	Christine A. Corcos, *Ohio State Legal Documents and Related Publications: A Selected, Annotated Bibliography* (AALL 1986).

Mike Franczak et al., *A Guide to Legislative History in Ohio* (Legislative Service Commission 1998).

Ohio Legal Resources: An Annotated Bibliography and Guide (4th ed. Ohio Regional Association of Law Libraries and Ohio Library Association 1996).

Melanie K. Putnam & Susan M. Schaefgen, *Ohio Legal Research Guide* (Hein 1997).

Oklahoma Marilyn K. Nicely, *Legal and Law-Related Documents and Publications: A Selected Bibliography* (2nd ed. AALL 1995).

Oregon Lesley A. Buhman et al., *Bibliography of Law Related Oregon Documents* (AALL 1986).

Suzanne E. Rowe, *Oregon Legal Research* (Carolina Academic Press 2003).

Pennsylvania Joel Fishman, *State Documents: A Bibliography of Legal and Law-Related Material* (AALL 2002).

Joel Fishman, *Pennsylvania Legal Research Handbook* (American Lawyer Media 2001).

Rhode Island Gail I. Winson, *State of Rhode Island and Providence Plantations: Survey of State Documents and Law-Related Materials* (AALL 2004).

South Carolina Paula Gail Benson & Deborah Ann Davis, *A Guide to South Carolina Legal Research and Citation* (South Carolina Bar, Continuing Legal Education Division 1991).

South Dakota	Delores A. Jorgensen, *South Dakota Legal Research Guide* (2nd ed. Hein 1999).
	Delores A. Jorgensen, *South Dakota Legal Documents: A Selective Bibliography* (AALL 1988).
Tennessee	D. Cheryn Picquet & Reba A. Best, *Law and Government Publications of the State of Tennessee: A Bibliographic Guide* (AALL 1988).
Texas	Malinda Allison & Kay Schlueter, *Texas State Documents for Law Libraries* (AALL 1983).
	Lydia M. Brandt et al., *Texas Legal Research: An Essential Lawyering Skill* (Texas Lawyer Press 1995).
	Brandon D. Quarles & Matthew C. Condon, *Legal Research for the Texas Practitioner* (Hein 2003).
	Pamela R. Tepper & Peggy N. Kerley, *Texas Legal Research* (Delmar Publishers 1997).
Vermont	Virginia Wise, *A Bibliographical Guide to the Vermont Legal System* (2nd ed. AALL 1991).
Virginia	Leah F. Chanin et al., *Legal Research in the District of Columbia, Maryland and Virginia* (Hein 2000).
	A Guide to Legal Research in Virginia (J.D. Eure & Gail F. Zwerner eds., 4th ed. Virginia CLE Publications 2002).
	Jacqueline Lichtman & Judy Stinson, *A Law Librarian's Introduction to Virginia State Publications* (rev. ed. AALL 1988)

Washington   Penny A. Hazelton et al., *Washington Legal Researchers Deskbook, 3d* (Marian Gould Gallagher Law Library 2002).

Peggy Roebuck Jarrett & Cheryl Rae Nyberg, *Washington State Documents: A Bibliography of Legal and Law-Related Material* (AALL 1997).

West Virginia   Sandra Stemple et al., *West Virginia Legal Bibliography* (AALL 1990).

Wisconsin   *Introduction to Legal Materials*: A Manual for Non-Law Librarians in Wisconsin (Law Librarians Association of Wisconsin, Inc. 2003)

Janet Oberla, *An Introduction to Wisconsin State Documents and Law Related Materials* (AALL 1987).

Wyoming   Nancy S. Greene, *Wyoming State Legal Documents: An Annotated Bibliography With Commentary* (AALL 1985).